Blacks in Eden

The African American Novel's First Century

J. Lee Greene

Blacks in Eden

The African American Novel's First Century

University Press of Virginia   *Charlottesville and London*

The University Press of Virginia
© 1996 by the Rector and Visitors of the University of Virginia

First published 1996

∞ The paper used in this publication meets the minimum requirements of the
American National Standard for Information Sciences—Permanence of Paper
for Printed Library Materials, ANSI Z39.48-1984.

Library of Congress Cataloging-in-Publication Data

Greene, J. Lee, 1944–
    Blacks in Eden : the African American novel's first century / J. Lee Greene.
        p.   cm.
    Includes bibliographical references and index.
    ISBN 0-8139-1670-4 (cloth : alk. paper). — ISBN 0-8139-1671-2 (paper : alk.
paper)
    1. American fiction—Afro-American authors—History and criticism.
2. American fiction—19th century—History and criticism.   3. American
fiction—20th century—History and criticism.   4. Afro-Americans in
literature.   5. Eden in literature.   I. Title.
PS374.N4G74   1996
813.009′372—dc20
                                                                            96-4581
                                                                            CIP
Printed in the United States of America

For my parents, Buleaner Alexander Greene
and the late Raymond Greene, Sr.

Contents

Preface   vii

Introduction   1

1. Genesis   12
   White Tillers   12
   Black Harvesters   17
   Gardens South, Gardens North   41

2. Belles and Beaux   47
   Black Female Subjectivity and the Social Skin   47
   Rituals for Aggregation   49
   White Male Subjectivity and the Cult of Chivalry   60
   A Renaissance of Chivalry: The House Behind the Cedars   65

3. Beauties and Beasts   75
   A Peculiar Sensation, This Double-Consciousness   75
   Black Man, New Man: Chesnutt's John (Walden) Warwick   80
   The Beast-Bridegroom: Johnson's Ex-Coloured Man   89
   The Machine-Made New Negro: Schuyler's Matthew Fisher   96

4. New Slaves and Lynching Bees   104
   The Deformation of Black Subjectivity   104
   A Strange Fruit in the New Garden   115
   A New South, a New Religion   119
   Subjects, Societies, and Tropes: The Marrow of Tradition   124

5. The Wars for Eden   134

    Hell: War and Racism   *134*

    France: (In)versions of Paradise   *143*

    Harlem: Black Garden, White Snake   *148*

    Southern Edens and the "Spoils" of War   *153*

6. Black Adams   168

    Subjectivity and the Adamic Paradigm   *168*

    The Cosmography of Native Son's *Fictive World*   *176*

    Configurations of Desire in The Street   *188*

7. Totems and Taboos   201

    Configurations of a Southern Fictive World   *201*

    Totemic Character and Biracial Liminals   *213*

    Totemism and White Male Subject Formation   *216*

    Historiographic Counterdiscourse: The Rootless   *222*

8. The Textualization of Blackness: *Invisible Man*   235

    The Trope: "Here in This Eden"   *235*

    The Subject: "Who Was I, How Had I Come to Be?"   *239*

    The Society: "The Patterns of Men's Lives"   *251*

Conclusion   271

Notes   277

Bibliography   285

Index   299

Preface

I have written *Blacks in Eden* for an audience that includes but is broader than seasoned specialists in African American literature or in the African American novel. Specialists are familiar with the overall contours of the sociocultural, sociopolitical, historical, and literary contexts that helped configure the genre's norms between the 1850s and the 1960s. The background information I provide is intended to assist students, beginning scholars in African American literature, and general readers in understanding the conditions and contexts that helped shape formalist and thematic conventions and traditions in the African American novel.

Unlike several book-length studies that generally are considered histories of the African American novel,[1] *Blacks in Eden* is not a history of the genre. Its focus on the genre's formalist and thematic anchors in the Eden trope precludes a general and chronological survey of novelists and novels under the rubric of "periods," trends, and movements one finds in histories of the African American novel. My discussion of how the tropic process configured and reconfigured subjectivity, emplotment, structure, and other formalist features during the genre's first century cuts across standardized (though arbitrarily defined) periods in African American literary history. The discussion of an individual novel, therefore, is not confined to one chapter or to one section of a chapter. Because my emphasis in each chapter (or section of a chapter) is on a particular fictional device, I do not provide an overview (or plot summary) of each novel I include in the discussion.

In this study, I consider the nineteenth century the genre's apprentice period, when its craft was not yet honed. My discussions of nineteenth-

and twentieth-century African American novels are situated within the Eden trope; they neither rely upon nor take issue with standard interpretations of these novels. I have, therefore, kept to a minimum citations for critical studies of individual novels. Computerized bibliographic tools (such as the one the Modern Language Association produces) now make this information readily accessible and up to date.

The question of genre is still debated about a few of the novels I consider in this study, such as Jean Toomer's *Cane* and John M. Paynter's *Fugitives of the Pearl*. I agree with those who consider these works novels. My comments throughout this book about the text of James Weldon Johnson's *The Autobiography of an Ex-Coloured Man* are based on the novel's 1927 edition, which (unlike the 1912 edition) uses the British spelling *coloured* in its title and text. The vast majority of critics who have written about Johnson's novel since the late 1920s have based their comments on the 1927 edition. In his textual note to the 1990 reprint (Penguin Books) of the 1912 edition, William Andrews correctly states that the 1927 edition is the standard one.

My work on this book was facilitated by a fellowship year at the Center for Advanced Study in the Behavioral Sciences, Stanford, California, a fellowship year funded in part by the Andrew W. Mellon Foundation. I am grateful to the center and to the Mellon Foundation for their support. James Coleman, Mary Kemp Davis, and Louis Rubin read portions of this study in manuscript form and gave me valuable advice. I am deeply appreciative of them, and I extend a special gratitude to Louis Rubin.

Blacks in Eden

The African American Novel's First Century

Introduction

Remember, *Christians, Negroes*, black as *Cain*,
May be refin'd, and join th' angelic train.

THE LINES QUOTED above are from one of Phillis Wheatley's best-known poems, "On Being Brought From Africa to America." These lines, the poem's title, its content, and Wheatley as an African American embody ideas and issues pertinent to this book's focus on the seminal place of the Eden myth in the African American novel's formalist and thematic configurations from the 1850s through the 1950s. In the poem Wheatley uses biblical allusions to treat tropologically and dialogically African Americans' marginal status in American society. This literary rubric also is a defining characteristic of salient formalist and thematic features in the African American novel.

Eden as a controlling metaphor for the New World was in use long before the first European immigrants established settlements in North America. Well before the colonies were formed into an autonomous nation, the colonists began to designate themselves Americans. In the example of Wheatley's contemporary, St. John de Crèvecoeur, they defined "the American" as "either an European, or the descendant of an European" (*Letters*, 54). Building upon the image of America as a New Eden, Anglo-Americans from the colonial period onward appropriated, transformed, and conflated passages from the Judeo-Christian Bible to justify their exclusion of Africans and descendants of Africans from the American family. The biblical stories of the Garden of Eden and of Man's Fall provided the nucleus around which they formulated tropological images of American society and subjects—what I call the Eden trope. As social theorists and literary artists in America have (re)inscribed and employed it over the centuries, the Eden trope is not confined to the biblical narratives of the Creation and of the Fall. The trope revises, incorporates, and conflates passages from other sections of Genesis, from other books in the Old Testament, and from sections of the New Testament. It also appropriates nonbiblical and nonreligious discourses and signifying practices.

The Eden trope has been germane to both the production and the reception of African American literary texts. In critically assessing Wheatley's poetry, one of her contemporaries, Thomas Jefferson, wrote in *Notes on the State of Virginia* (1787): "Religion, indeed, has produced a Phyllis Whately; but it could not produce a poet. The compositions published under her name are below the dignity of criticism" (135). This and other comments about African American subjectivity and the African American creative imagination anticipate the predominant thematic concerns of the African American novel and prefigure the academy's critical reception of works in the genre, particularly those critical of the nation's treatment of the black population.

Interestingly, Jefferson's disparaging comments about blacks and race relations forecast the course the African American novel has followed since the mid–nineteenth century. The tradition has been preoccupied with the generic experience of being black in a society that denigrates blackness and valorizes whiteness.

Apropos of Jefferson, from the eighteenth century until the present much African American literary discourse has been shaped by the writers' "ten thousand recollections . . . of injuries [blacks have] sustained" (*Notes*, 135) in the New World. As the past recedes and history advances, the memory of what that past means remains vibrant in the collective mind of black America and at the discursive core of its literature. This is especially true for the African American novel: the genre is largely characterized by the novelists' and their characters' "recollections" of physical and psychic wounds whites inflicted on the race in the past and by their reactions to "new provocations" that periodically inflame these wounds.

Through aspects of its form (especially referentiality, intertextuality, and subjectivity) and its general theme about blacks' plight in the United States, the African American novel from the 1850s through the 1950s challenges Jefferson's views about blacks. The integral place Jefferson occupies in African American novelistic discourse is evident from the numerous specific references to the man and his writings and from the equally numerous instances in which the novels constitute a "hidden polemic" against Jeffersonian ideology. In addition, several post-1960 novels also respond directly and indirectly to Jefferson, using his views about blacks as a touchstone to treat race relations.

History is a key consideration in a critical discussion of the African American novel. To repeat a statement by Robert C. Davis and Ronald Schleifer and to place it in a slightly different context, one goal of literary criticism "is to grasp a literary work as it reflects the historical forces that shaped it initially, to understand how an historical moment produced a particular work of literary art. This projects the historical process itself as a kind of ultimate author, both the origin and composer of any work."[1] This statement aptly describes a major part of my approach to tracing the influence of the Eden trope on the genre's development. To examine the development of the African American novel against the backdrop of the nation's history, I define American history broadly to include its social, political, legal, sexual, racial, and literary branches, and I focus on the Eden myth's primacy in shaping this general history and its branches.

As the nation's history has evolved, so have the figurations of Eden in the African American novel. Since the genre's beginning in the mid–nineteenth century, African American novels in one way or another have drawn upon African Americans' shared historical experience: antebellum novels about black life under the "peculiar institution"; novels published between the end of the Civil War and the end of World War I about black life under the new forms of slavery in the New South; Harlem Renaissance novels about the northern environment's debilitating effects on black city-dwellers; depression-era novels about the southern black folk community's spiritual sustenance; and protest novels published between the 1940s and the 1960s about the physical and psychological violence whites perpetrated against blacks. Since the 1970s, blacks' rememory of slavery and their reactions to its legacy have given vitality to important works in the genre, such as Ernest J. Gaines's *The Autobiography of Miss Jane Pittman*

(1971), Gayl Jones's *Corregidora* (1973), Ishmael Reed's *Flight to Canada* (1976), Octavia Butler's *Kindred* (1979), Sherley Anne Williams's *Dessa Rose* (1986), Toni Morrison's *Beloved* (1987), and Charles Johnson's *Middle Passage* (1990), among others. The Eden myth is a trope that governs the novelists' figurations of these historical periods.

A survey of the African American novel from the beginning to those published recently reveals the genre's grounding in the nation's mythic (Edenic) and actual history. William Wells Brown's *Clotel; or, The President's Daughter* (1853), the first African American novel, prefigures the seminal place history will have in the genre's development. A century after *Clotel*, James Baldwin published *Go Tell It on the Mountain* (1953), which emphasizes the integral place of Judeo-Christian religion in African American life and history. As a link to novels that preceded it, *Mountain* also exemplifies how pervasive the Eden trope has been in blacks' historical experience and how inclusive the trope is of biblical sources. During the century of fictive discourse that connected Brown and Baldwin, the African American novel combined politics and religion (both broadly defined here) into a perspective on America's history that revised, mainly through refutation, Anglo-Americans' official record of the nation's history. I argue, therefore, that dialogism and intertextuality as narrative strategies are integral to the genre's development.

I use the term *intertextuality* to refer to a relationship (often thematic) between and among texts, and I use the term *text* in two senses. In the first instance, the term refers to an individual work, such as a literary or historical one, whether written or visual. In the second instance, it refers to subject matter. African American novels typically assume an oppositional, revisionist stance toward Anglo-American historical and literary texts that promulgate the nation's mythic history. This intertextual revision is at times direct and at other times indirect. For example, through character portrayal, authorial commentary, allusions, incidents, and other techniques Sutton Griggs's *The Hindered Hand* (1905) and Charles Waddell Chesnutt's *The Marrow of Tradition* (1901) revise (i.e., refute and correct) Thomas Dixon's portrayal of blacks, of whites, and of race relations in his *The Leopard's Spots* (1902) and *The Clansman* (1905). This intertextual relationship is direct, for it involves specific authors and specific texts. Frequently, African American novels revise the ideas and subject matter of numerous Anglo-American texts without specifying the authors or the titles. In such instances, the discourse is a hidden polemic.

4

It is more than mere rhetorical posturing when a nineteenth-century African American novel (such as Frank J. Webb's *The Garies and Their Friends* [1857] or James H. W. Howard's *Bond and Free* [1886]) announces in its prefatory matter that the narrative contains only a slight thread of fiction. This rhetorical strategy is less common in the twentieth century. As the genre developed, its fictional devices became more sophisticated and more profuse, but it remained firmly anchored in an African American perspective on historical reality. History embellishes the autobiographical mode in novels such as James Weldon Johnson's *The Autobiography of an Ex-Coloured Man* (1912) and *The Autobiography of Miss Jane Pittman*. History informs the autobiographical acts that shape Jean Toomer's *Cane* (1923), Nella Larsen's *Quicksand* (1928), Richard Wright's *Black Boy* (1945), and *Go Tell It on the Mountain*. A specific historical incident often provides the architectonics for a particular novel, such as *The Hindered Hand*, *The Marrow of Tradition*, *Native Son*, and *Beloved*. In some instances a novel is saturated with places, people, and events associated with a specific historical act, as in John M. Paynter's *Fugitives of the Pearl* (1930), Arna Bontemps's *Black Thunder* (1936), and Barbara Chase-Riboud's *Sally Hemings* (1979); in other instances a novel explores a historical period, as in Raymond Andrews's trilogy *Appalachee Red* (1978), *Rosiebelle Lee Wildcat Tennessee* (1980), and *Baby Sweet's* (1983). Historical formations that recall a historical moment (the Great Black Migration in Walter White's *Flight* [1926]), explore the continuity of the generic black experience (Ralph Ellison's *Invisible Man* [1952]), explore the historical continuity of a specific black masculinist experience (John A. Williams's *Captain Blackman* [1972]), or explore the historical continuity of a black feminist experience (Alice Walker's *The Third Life of Grange Copeland* [1970]) are among the numerous ways the African American novel uses history. As the genre developed through different social and literary periods in the United States, the writers used history (in its broad definition) to modify the contours of conventional Western fictional techniques such as characterization, plot, story line, imagery, and symbolism.

African Americans' formulation of a black discourse in the novel was in large part a direct response to Anglo-Americans' use of the Eden trope as a blueprint for American society. Several historians and literary critics have offered perspectives on American history and literature that speak directly to how fully the Bible's Eden myth has shaped the nation's historical experience and much of its literature (particularly Anglo-American literature). Three standard works that conjoin history and literature and foreground an Anglo-American experience are Henry Nash Smith's *Virgin Land: The American West as Myth and Symbol* (1950), R. W. B. Lewis's *The American Adam: Innocence, Tragedy, and Tradition in the Nineteenth Century* (1955), and Lewis P. Simpson's *The Dispossessed Garden: Pastoral and History in Southern Literature* (1975). Both black and white writers have drawn upon the nation's general history and mythic undergirding, but black writers, particularly novelists, have proffered a view of American history that on the whole inverts the pervasive paradigm of Anglo-American literature.

This study will show that during each of five successive periods in the history of the nation (with emphasis on the South), the Eden trope among Anglo-Americans assumed a slightly different permutation. These images of the country are generally as follows: America as an earthly paradise (prevalent during the period of discovery, exploration, and development, the 1490s to the 1770s), America as a civil utopia (the era of the American new man during the revolutionary and early national periods), the South as a plantation idyll (the early 1800s to the end of the Civil War), the South's age of modern chivalry (the period between Reconstruction and World War I), and the nation's age of the American Dream (World War I to the 1950s and beyond). Each permutation served to (re)construct, to sanction, and to maintain a social order that marginalized blacks. African American novelists treated their race's liminal status and reacted to the sociopolitical and literary manifestations of Anglo-America's Eden trope in ways that significantly shaped the novel's techniques during its first hundred years.

To support the study's central points, I discuss most African American novels published before 1900 and a representative number of those published from 1900 through the 1950s. During this period, of course, several novels did not adapt the Eden trope, and others incorporated the trope in ways not directly related to my approach. I have omitted these novels from my discussion. And, given space limitations, I have not included all pre-1960 African American novels that exemplify this study's basic premises. However, the Eden trope is prevalent in the configuration of so many African American novels before and after the 1950s that it can be considered one of the genre's salient characteristics.

During its first century the African American novel was essentially a southern novel. Not only were most of the novelists Southerners, but the genre's standard themes, emplotments, subject formations, structures, settings, and other aspects of form were anchored in a southern black experience. The earliest African American novels established the genre's generic norms. From post-Reconstruction through the 1950s many of these norms underwent modification, primarily to refute Anglo-American literary, social, scientific, and pseudoscientific texts that denigrated blacks and to incorporate contemporary historical events, prominent persons, and social conditions that directly affected black life.

Following a summary of the Eden myth's historical and tropological place in American life, chapter 1, "Genesis," discusses selected discursive formations that are standard in nineteenth-century novels. These formations are predicated on the tropic process southern whites (primarily) employed to enfigure the New World as Eden—as a topological paradise during the colonial period and as a sociopolitical utopia during the revolutionary period—and they are integral in the genre's discursive praxis until the turn of this century. The genre's nineteenth-century conventions are reference points from which I develop the study's subsequent chapters.

Chapter 2, "Belles and Beaux," and chapter 3, "Beauties and Beasts," concentrate on selected pre–World War I conventions in the genre. Both chapters draw attention to the black body's tropological functions, to the alignment of subject formation with plots, settings, patterns of imagery, and other formalist and thematic features, and to the genre's discursive interfacing of biblical lore with fairy lore. In its discussion of society and black female subjectivity, chapter 2 foregrounds the fairy tale "Cinderella." The chapter illustrates how symbolic spaces associated with the colonial period, origin myths associated with the revolutionary period, belles and beaux from the antebellum and postbellum periods, white mulatto women as centered subjects, and other conventions that developed in the nineteenth-century novel reached an apex and congealed in the contexture of Chesnutt's *The House Behind the Cedars*.

Chapter 3 uses the fairy tale "Beauty and the Beast" tropologically to frame a discussion of nineteenth-century novels in which white mulatto men are centered subjects in subplots and parallel plots and of novels from 1900 to the 1930s in which these men are protagonists. The African American novelistic use of this fairy tale is largely a response to Anglo-America's incorporation of this specific story into its Eden trope and its use of it analogically to decry miscegenetic unions. The chapter draws attention to how the centering of white mulatto males further modifies some conventions in the genre. With a focus on the Eden trope, the chapter traces these conventions and their modifications to their culmination in George S. Schuyler's *Black No More* (1931). The architectonics of Schuyler's novel innovatively updates the genre's incorporation of the Eden trope to include changes that occurred in American society after World War I.

Thematic and formalist conventions in African American novels focused on white and bright mulatto protagonists derive in large part from the novelists' dialogic responses to the third (the antebellum plantation idyll) and fourth (the postbellum cult of modern chivalry) principal manifestations of the Eden myth in southern white life and literature. In both of these permutations, southern society and southern subjects are cloaked in trappings from medieval lore. White-authored texts of and about the periods minimize the level of racial violence (psychological and physical) inherent in both social orders. African American novels foreground it.

When African American novels early in this century moved the mulatto male to the novel's center, they also began to treat issues germane to the black masses. Chapter 4, "New Slaves and Lynching Bees," traces changes and continuities as the genre develops into the twentieth century. Within the context of the Eden trope, this chapter discusses the relation between racist violence and the white South's self-image; the religious underpinnings of lynching as a social ritual; the continuity between the chivalric tradition and the ritual violence whites used to maintain their turn-of-the-century Eden; and the changes in structure, plot, subject formation, and theme in the genre as a response to and reflection of changes in the society at large.

While during the aftermath of the Civil War the white South was energetically engaged in creating its myth of the past, elsewhere in the nation the seeds of industrialization were being planted to stir the growth of the American Dream, the nation's latest image of itself as Eden. By the turn of the century, the South was beginning to follow the path of the rest of the country. As the southern age of modern chivalry declined, a new era emerged in the American South, with industrialization and the sharecropping system as two of its strongest cornerposts, supporting the region's own version of the American Dream and thus engendering its fifth principal image of the region as Eden.

Historical, political, and imaginative texts of and about the period ap-

propriately characterize it as the New South, an appellation that emphasizes the origin myth overarching the region and the era. With its distinctly
southern flavor and with clear vestiges of the four principal images that
preceded it, the New South's concept of the American Dream remained
preeminent through the first half of this century. African American novels
through the middle of this century most readily respond to the southern
white version of the American Dream.

Chapter 5, "The Wars for Eden," uses the American Dream as rubric
and World War I as historical context to discuss continuities in the African American novel's development between the 1850s and the 1910s and to
monitor certain changes in its fictive norms between the two world wars.
The Eden trope and war as a trope interlace and constitute the discursive
girders for a group of novels concerned primarily with psychosexual tensions between black and white males during the interwar era. Yet certain
conventions that developed in the genre are not exclusive to novels that
treat World War I or that center black veterans of the war.

Between the wars the Eden trope embellished and interrelated theme,
setting, and subjectivity. For example, when setting in the prewar novel
became more inclusive of areas outside the South, a typical protagonist's
physical journey away from and back to the South signified his or her
spiritual quest for Eden. After the early 1920s, a tripartite structure reflecting this journey-quest became standard in the genre, a consequence of its
foregrounding the Great Black Migration and incorporating social and
racial conditions associated with World War I. With men occupying center stage in the genre after about 1920, interracial sex (in its broad definition) is a prevalent theme, and the lynching bee is a seminal symbolic act
in a novel's narrative structure. These factors combine with others to shift
the genre's overarching construct from the more general Eden myth to the
more specific Adamic myth. Chapter 6 highlights the effects of this shift
on the genre's conventions.

Chapter 6, "Black Adams," begins with a discussion of two nineteenth-
century works, Frederick Douglass's poem "What Am I to You" and
Charles Chesnutt's tale "The Fall of Adam." The two pieces demonstrate
how African American writers began early to appropriate the story of
Adam's Fall in the Garden of Eden as an analogy for black males' plight in
American society. Richard Wright's short story "Big Boy Leaves Home,"
which uses the Adamic story as a discursive paradigm for the entire work,

anticipates its use as a major construct in African American novels of the 1940s. During this decade, the following characteristics of the genre appeared: the representative protagonist usually is male and is considerably darker in color than his mulatto predecessors; the representative white male character is the chief antagonist in a plot structure that foregrounds a psychosexual and psychosocial war between him and the black male protagonist; the symbolic white woman assumes the role of the archetypal Eve; and novels favor the urban North as setting.

Using the concept of triangular desire as its scaffolding, this chapter focuses on Wright's *Native Son* and Ann Petry's *The Street* (1946), two novels that exemplify the wide variety of ways in which novelists adapted the biblical narrative of Adam's Fall. Launching the protest era in African American fiction, *Native Son* directed the genre's reshaping of conventions in form, content, and meaning and made the Adamic paradigm axial in a masculinist discourse that would dominate the genre for at least a generation. Through repetition and inversion, Petry's *The Street* revises this masculinist discourse and adapts the Adamic paradigm to her fictive vision by using a black woman as the centered subject.

Chapter 7, "Totems and Taboos," synthesizes issues covered in the previous chapters, underscores continuity in the genre's development, and highlights specific traditions in the African American novel that emanate from its installation of the Eden trope. Concentrating on the fictive world that the genre formulated during its first century, the chapter explores that world's cosmology. In the nineteenth century, African American novels began to refute whites' assertion that blacks were subhuman. With the turn of the twentieth century, the dialogic and intertextual contours of this refutation drew heavily from contemporary discourse in anthropology and psychology. Through its cosmology, the genre's fictive world reflexed onto whites the assertion that they, not blacks, had not fully evolved socially. African American novels from 1900 forward portrayed the southern white social order as a totemic society. Chapter 7 concentrates on Turpin's *The Rootless*, which incorporates many of these issues, contains several novelistic traditions that had developed by the 1950s, and exhibits nascent forms of features that became traditions after the 1950s.

Chapter 8, "The Textualizaton of Blackness," is devoted to Ellison's *Invisible Man*, one of the most eclectic and well-wrought novels in the period being discussed. Its textual complexity and richness exemplify how an individual novel synthesizes several traditions the genre had established by midcentury. In identifying literary influences on his novel, Ellison privileged his "literary ancestors" (European and Anglo-American writers) over his "literary relatives" (African American writers). This chapter, however, reads *Invisible Man* through the lens of the African American novelistic tradition.

Genesis

White Tillers

THE IMAGE OF America as the new Eden preceded the discovery, exploration, and settlement of the New World. Well before the end of the fifteenth century, the belief in a mythic earthly paradise—whether Eden, Atlantis, Arcadia, the Golden Age, or some other utopian society—was an established part of the European imagination.[1] Columbus's belief that on his third voyage he had found the original Garden of Eden apparently helped turn legend into fact for many sixteenth-century Europeans.[2] Following Columbus's reports, Europeans rejuvenated several legends about an earthly paradise. The one about Eden rose to the fore in the 1500s, and there was a widespread belief "that the New World had been populated, or discovered, or settled, by a second Adam and Eve and their descendants."[3] This legend seemed especially attractive to the English, for biblical imagery strongly shaped their early concepts of the New World.

The Garden of Eden thus became a controlling metaphor in many of the descriptive and narrative accounts by those Europeans who explored and settled in the New World, especially in the region that became the

American South. As Leo Marx points out, "The image of America as a garden was no mere rhetorical commonplace" among "Elizabethan voyagers"; the image embodied the concept of an idealized world.[4] For the early settlers of the South, the garden metaphor embodied economic, social, political, religious, and other considerations about the New World as a social organization, as is evident from the metaphor's pervasiveness in southern writings from the early colonial period until well into the twentieth century. These works paint an idealized portrait of the region's social organization.

Though the image of America as a new Eden has predominated since the earliest English contact, there were also two major counterimages, that of the colonial New Englanders and that of the New World Africans. Not only did the first English settlers in America bring with them a pastoral image of America based metaphorically on the Garden of Eden, but they also brought with them an image of the New World as a vast wilderness that in large part they had imbibed from Judeo-Christian thought.[5] New Englanders, especially the Puritans, and some early European explorers of that region often viewed and described the region's topography as an "insalubrious desert" inhabited by Indians who were "inferior degenerates" or "Satan's children."[6] The Puritans' predominant image of their region was that of a primeval forest where evil lurked, not that of a lush, abundant landscape reminiscent of Eden.[7] This concept of the wilderness shaped their view of the New World and is apparent in New England texts from early histories through the imaginative writings of the first half of the nineteenth century.

In describing the reaction of the *Mayflower* immigrants on first arriving in Massachusetts, William Bradford comments, "What could they see but a hideous and desolate wilderness, full of wild beasts and wild men—and what multitudes there might be of them they knew not" (*Of Plymouth Plantation*, 62). Indeed, Bradford, Cotton Mather, St. John de Crèvecoeur, Nathaniel Hawthorne, and many other writers over this two-century period saw the New England landscape factually and symbolically as ominous and foreboding. Eventually, however, New Englanders followed Southerners' lead. By the mid–nineteenth century, the Eden myth had become a dominant trope in New Englanders' social and imaginative texts about contemporary life in the region.

The second and most enduring counterimage emanated from New

World Africans. The glaring paradox introduced into the American Eden in 1619 with the arrival in Virginia of twenty African slaves (though they were not called slaves at the time) persisted as a rebuttal to (i.e., a continual revision of) the nation's idealistic image of itself.[8] Seventeenth-century colonists attempted to explain, justify, and therefore reconcile this contradiction within the context of biblical doctrine. To do so, of course, they were required to distort the Scriptures, or at best to work from a very loose interpretation (or revision) of the Bible. While several explanations were advanced, Puritans in the Northeast essentially explained the existence of slavery in their society in a manner consistent with their Calvinistic principles and with their mission in the New World.

The Puritans' belief in the doctrine of the elect in some ways provided a convenient justification for their exclusion of New World Africans from the society of man. Given that the Puritans' mission was to effect a New Eden in this wilderness, African slaves (and Native Americans) were, in time, to be Christianized and brought into the religious fold. Until then, blacks generally were to be considered a separate society. Cotton Mather even wrote a guide for this separate society, "Rules for the Society of Negroes" (1693), and revised the Ten Commandments to fit blacks' status as pariahs in Puritan New England.[9]

Christianization of the African slave also was an objective in the southern region, but for entirely different reasons. Many whites thought that a Christianized slave would be more pliable and would less readily object to his position in society, thus constituting less of a threat to undermine the southern replica of Eden. The underlying motivation was economic. Well before the end of the colonial period, material prosperity had become a central ingredient in the southern vision of Eden, and wealth could not be sustained by indentured servitude alone. Attempts to use the Native American population as a slave labor force had been unsuccessful, so from an economic perspective, this manifestation of the New Eden as Southerners envisioned it could not have been effected without black slave labor.[10]

Southern whites gleaned from the Bible justification for the slavocracy's attitude toward and treatment of blacks. The assertion that blacks were not descendants of the original parents and that their presence in the biblical Garden of Eden stemmed from the intruding evil (the snake) had popular support during and well past the colonial period. Southern whites concluded that because blacks were excluded from the original Eden, they did not merit a place in the South's Eden that compared to that of whites (supposedly the true descendants of Adam and Eve). In both the North and the South, the majority of American colonists dismissed the contradiction that slavery presented to the concept of a new Eden.[11] The New World African, however, was not as readily blinded to the paradox, as slave revolts and other forms of active resistance (as well as legal petitions by slaves and free blacks) evidenced in both the southern and northern colonies.[12]

The mode in which the American colonists wrote about the New World experience is what I call Anglo-American discourse on the American Edenic ideal (to which African American discourse on the same ideal is in binary opposition). This discourse is defined in large part by the rhetorical strategies in a given text. It emanates from a mind-set produced by the writer's image of self in contradistinction to his (and typically the writer is male) image of the Other with whom he shares physical space in the Americas. This space is either the metaphorical "garden" of the colonial South or the "wilderness" of the colonial Northeast. The self, of course, is the Anglo-American, and, depending on the text, the Other is the Native American, the New World African, or both. Seldom is the Other a white indentured servant or a white social pariah (such as a criminal banished from Europe to the colonies).

When one uses modern definitions of discipline and genre to classify these colonial texts, they vary according to subject and form. The better-known ones include histories, biographies, personal narratives (autobiographies, journals, diaries), and religious and social tracts.[13] Even by modern-day definitions of form, such designations, when applied to these texts, are not definitive distinctions of genre. And even by the text-specific standards of the time, these colonial works share several affinities in form and many more in content.

In both content and aspects of form these texts echo the Judeo-Christian Bible. They usually include descriptions of the New World's landscape and animal life as well as statements about the manners and mores of Natives and the colonial settlers. The southern texts usually idealize Native Americans, while the northern ones typically denigrate them as evil savages. On the whole, texts from both regions ignore the New World Africans' plight, or they cite biblical doctrine to sanction their status as slaves, whether for religious reasons (as in New England) or for socioeconomic ones (as in the South). While at times criticizing Anglo-American social behavior, the texts nevertheless venerate colonial whites and champion their utopian mission in the New World.

The southern colonial text that best exemplifies this discourse is Robert Beverley's *The History and Present State of Virginia* (1705), one of the most important colonial descriptions of America to fully employ the Eden myth as an extended trope. When Beverley speaks metaphorically of Virginia as Eden, he is referring to all of England's holdings in the country as well as specifically to that region that later became the state. For his image of early America, Beverley builds upon writings by previous explorers and settlers, including Captain Arthur Barlowe, Sir Walter Raleigh, and Captain John Smith. To construct his portrait of the region's present state, Beverley installs Barlowe's description of the region's topography and ecology as a paradise. His depiction of contemporary Native Americans, however, is much less flattering than those of his predecessors. His inclusion of the black presence is marked by an indifference to the slaves' plight. He does not acknowledge how antithetical the colonists' treatment of Native Americans and their enslavement of Africans are to an image of Virginia as Eden.

Beverley's *History*, what he calls his "Discourse" (5), joins other early Anglo-American texts in narrating America's cosmogonic (or creation) myth. There are noticeable similarities in form and rhetorical strategies between the *History* and the King James Version of the Bible (1611). Beverley speaks of the "Discovery" of America in much the same way that the King James Bible speaks of the creation of the world. His *History*'s organization strongly resembles the King James Bible's division into books, chapters, and verses. In general, the rhetorical devices that distinguish the King James Bible from translations or versions that preceded it are much like the devices that distinguish Beverley's *History* from its predecessors.

As Beverley points out in his preface, the *History* begins with "a Chronological History, of the most remarkable Things that have happen'd in *Virginia*, ever since it was first seated by the *English*" (10). Occupying a significant place "in the development of American ideas" as "one of the earliest literary works that is self-consciously American" (xxi), Beverley's narrative of the American cosmogony begins not with Columbus but with Sir Walter Raleigh, not with the discovery proper but with the first English attempts to establish a permanent settlement in North America. To be sure, the distinction between America's actual and its mythic history perhaps never has been clear, because the record of the discovery and settling of the continent and of the founding and building of the nation has been couched in myth, especially for the South. Overall, the America-as-Eden trope has been much stronger and has persisted much longer among Southerners than among Northerners.

The generative relationship among the five permutations of the Eden myth discussed in the introduction closely resembles the relationship Mircea Eliade identifies between the world's cosmogony and subsequent origin myths: "From the structural point of view, origin myths can be homologized with the cosmogonic myth." [14] In the mythic history of America, the cosmogony is the "discovery" of the New World. Structurally, therefore, the "history" of each of the subsequent four chronological periods is recorded as an origin myth. According to Eliade, "Every origin myth narrates and justifies a 'new situation'—new in the sense that it did not exist *from the beginning of the world.* Origin myths continue and complete the cosmogonic myth; they tell how the world was changed, made richer or poorer" (21). Each of the four historical periods in the American South following the one of discovery certainly represents a "new situation"; as a structural extension of the American cosmogony, each continues and completes the American cosmogonic myth.

Black Harvesters

As a blueprint for society and subjectivity, the third permutation of the South's Eden trope (the plantation idyll) almost had run its course by the advent of the African American novel in the 1850s. However, by appropriating the trope to refute the Anglo-American image of the New World as an all-white Eden, African American social, religious, and literary writers, particularly the slave narrators, already had harvested the Eden myth's first three permutations and thus produced a discursive model from which the nineteenth-century African American novel constructed several of the genre's generic norms.

Though there are very few extant accounts by seventeenth-century New World Africans of their impressions of the American Eden, one can conclude from the colonial period's historical record that the vast majority did not see America as an earthly paradise. By the later colonial period, several New World Africans had produced written texts that conveyed their impressions of America. The first significant group of African American literary texts belongs to the eighteenth century (though a few social and political texts, such as petitions, appeared in the seventeenth century).[15] In most instances, these texts' revisions of the trope are indirect rather than direct.

The poetry of Phillis Wheatley is illustrative. Wheatley's "To the University of Cambridge in New England" depicts the New World as an earthly paradise and New World whites as a "human race divine." Her poem "On Being Brought From Africa to America," however, utilizes the trope to argue implicitly that blacks, too, can and should be included among Americans as a "race" of chosen people (the New World Adams).

In the colonial period, those African American texts that most fully refute the Anglo-American Edenic ideal are the personal prose narratives, among the earliest of them one by Job ben Solomon (the Anglicized name for Ayuba Suleiman Diallo). "A devout Muslim merchant, literate in Arabic," and son of an African king, Diallo was enslaved in Africa and brought to America.[16] His narrative, *Some Memoirs of the Life of Job . . . Who Was a Slave about Two Years in Maryland* (1734), includes only a few details about his relatively brief enslavement in Maryland. According to his narrative, once he is freed (after several attempts to escape), he travels to England and later returns to Africa. The contrast between his sojourn as a slave in Maryland and his privileged life in England and in Africa produces an image of America as Eden after the Fall. For Diallo, Africa is Eden before the Fall. Subsequent slave narratives are more detailed in refuting the Edenic image of America.

One of the most significant and fullest early accounts of how the New World African viewed the American Eden comes from the late eighteenth century—Olaudah Equiano's *The Interesting Narrative of the Life of Olaudah Equiano, or Gustavus Vassa, the African. Written by Himself* (1789). Equiano begins his *Narrative* with an account of life in his native country, Guinea. The description he provides of his homeland's natural environment and culture is cast in the same tropological (Edenic) mode several European explorers used to describe America. But from this New World African's vantage, Africa is Eden, and Virginia, if an Eden at all, is Eden after the Fall.

Equiano's inversion of the Eden trope repeats and affirms Diallo's as well as revises and inverts Wheatley's contrasting portrayals of Africa and America.

Having endured the Middle Passage from Africa to the West Indies, Equiano is transported to the mainland of colonial America. As a New World African, his description of his first contact with America, like that of the *Mayflower* immigrants, draws attention to the horrors in this strange new world:

> We were landed up a river a good way from the sea, about Virginia county, where we saw few or none of our native Africans, and *not one soul who could talk to me.* I was a few weeks weeding grass and gathering stones in a plantation; and at last all my companions were distributed different ways, and only myself was left. I was now exceedingly miserable, and thought myself worse off than any of the rest of my companions, for *they could talk to each other, but I had no person to speak to that I could understand.* In this state, I was constantly grieving and pining, and wishing for death rather than anything else. While I was in this plantation, the gentleman, to whom I suppose the estate belonged, being unwell, I was one day sent for to his dwelling-house to fan him; when I came into the room where he was I was very much affrighted at some things I saw, and the more so as I had seen a black woman slave as I came through the house, who was cooking the dinner, and the poor creature was cruelly loaded with various kinds of iron machines; she had one particularly on her head, which locked her mouth so fast that she could scarcely speak; and could not eat nor drink. (34, emphasis added)

Language and the significations of silence are important in this passage. Upon entering the New World Eden, European immigrants could and did speak and write about their experiences. William Bradford (*Of Plymouth Plantation*) and other early New England settlers wrote about the horrors they encountered on entering the American wilderness, and explorers and settlers in the southern region wrote panegyrics to the Garden of the South. But the colonists, particularly the Southerners, propagated a mythic vision of the New World in their lives and writings that engendered a social machinery that in effect "locked" the New World Africans' mouths and prevented them from speaking/writing their ordeal in this New Eden.

As his narrative shows, Equiano's despair when he finds himself unable to talk to other native Africans or even to whites and his description of the shackled black slave woman constitute a potent image of the silence forced upon the New World African, an image that itself bespeaks the counterimage of America as an earthly paradise. It is significant that only after leaving this New Eden was Equiano "allowed" to voice his impression of the New World. His situation is representative, for only after slaves were outside the Southern or American Eden were they relatively free to voice their impressions of the New World. When given the opportunity to "speak," Equiano and his ex-slave compeers told a chilling tale of the horrors of life in the New Eden.

One prominent feature of southern colonialist discourse that propagated the Anglo-American Edenic ideal is the description of America as a vast, natural garden in which fruits, fish, and fowl are bountiful for man's nourishment and pleasure. Book 2 ("The Natural Productions and Conveniences of the Country, Suited to Trade and Improvement") of Beverley's *History* exemplifies how he tills the garden trope his predecessors planted. *Variety* and *Plenty* are among the terms Beverley uses repeatedly to inform his readers of the abundant food the landscape yields "for the Benefit or Pleasure of Mankind" (123). Book 4 discusses the present state of Virginia, in which the natural garden continues to afford its inhabitants (i.e., the "gentry") "great Plenty and Variety of Provisions for their Table" (291). The "Graziers, Seedsmen, Gardiners, Brewers, Bakers, Butchers, and Cooks" (291), many of whom are slaves and thus are not included in the category of "mankind" Beverley references, are tillers in this natural garden. The white gentry lays claim of ownership to both the garden and its black tillers.

Equiano's *Narrative* is representative of African American discourse that through revision highlights the paradox of this Edenic image. The slave narrative genre (and subsequently the African American novel) emphasizes the slave's ever-present hunger in a land in which food, to use Beverley's description, is in "great Abundance" (129). Moreover, the slave as the tiller of the garden functions as a human machine to assure the continued supply of this "great Plenty." But the Edenic society's social "machinery" denies the slave access to the fruits of his own labor. Equiano's description of the black slave woman forcefully refutes Beverley's representative description of life in colonial America's Southern Garden. The iron machines that prevent the woman from eating and drinking signify the social machinery that prevents her from telling her version of life in the New Eden.

Equiano's *Narrative* and Frederick Douglass's 1845 *Narrative* are two of the classics in the genre. In chapter 3 of his *Narrative*, Douglass uses the garden trope to refute an Anglo-American idyllic perspective on the New World's Garden. Douglass published three versions of his autobiography (the original in 1845, *My Bondage and My Freedom* in 1855, and *Life and Times of Frederick Douglass* in 1881), substantially expanding it each time. He published the final version of *Life and Times* in 1892, three years before he died. The garden trope's revised and expanded version in *Life and Times* is even more effective as refutation than in the *Narrative* because it adapts the mode of Anglo-American colonialist discourse to subvert the trope. Beverley's *History* is a useful text for comparison.

Douglass's description of Colonel Lloyd's "cultivated garden" (*Narrative*, ch. 3) repeats Beverley's description of Virginia as a natural garden. Colonel Lloyd's garden "abounds in fruits of almost every description." "Fish, flesh, and fowl were here in profusion. Chickens of all breeds, ducks of all kinds, wild and tame, the common and the huge muscovite, guinea fowls, turkeys, geese, and peafowls," and other animals and plants in "all their strange varieties" were in "bounteous profusion" in Colonel Lloyd's garden (*Life and Times*, ch. 7). The same terms characterize Beverley's description of the natural Virginia Garden. The essential difference between Douglass and Beverley (and thus between an African American and an Anglo-American perspective) can be discerned from the vista from which one views the American Garden. In essence, Beverley views the slave's laborious life (271–74) from the plantation owners' "Table" (291), and he asserts that the slave's labor does not exceed that of whites (plantation owners excepted) on the plantation (272). Douglass in effect presents a dialogic refutation of this view.

When Douglass writes, "Viewed from Col. Lloyd's table, who could have said that his slaves were not well clad and well cared for," he underscores the significance of perspective. To see Lloyd's plantation and garden as replicas of Eden, they must be "viewed from his table, and *not* from his field" (*Life and Times*). From the vantage of the slave on Lloyd's plantation, the Southern Garden offers "course cornmeal and tainted meat"; the slave does not dress in fine clothes, but in "crashy tow-linen" (*Life and Times*). To the affluent whites, the beautiful climate provides opportunity to enjoy a life of leisure; from the slave's vista, the climate exacerbates unrelenting "toil through the field in all weather, with wind and rain beating through his tattered garments" (*Life and Times*). But "Alas," writes Douglass, "this immense wealth, this gilded splendor, this profusion of luxury, this exemption from toil, this life of ease, this sea of plenty, were not the pearly gates they seemed to a world of happiness and sweet content to be." "Lurking behind the rich and tempting viands were invisible spirits of evil" (*Life and Times*).

Slaveholders are the "spirits of evil," the snakes, in the New World Garden. The metaphor inverts the images of blacks as intrusive evil and whites as the embodiment of good. Douglass skillfully employs the inverted trope in his account of Colonel Lloyd's "stratagems to keep his slaves out of the garden. The last and most successful one was that of tarring his fence all around; after which, if a slave was caught with any tar upon his person, it was deemed sufficient proof that he had either been into the garden, or had tried to get in. In either case, he was severely whipped by the chief gardener. This plan worked well; the slaves became as fearful of tar as of the lash. They seemed to realize the impossibility of touching *tar* without being defiled" (*Narrative*). This passage lends itself to several interpretations, one of which is a comprehensive statement about New World whites' machinations to exclude blacks from the American Garden, a statement that is repeated in numerous African American novels and is, therefore, at the core of the genre's paradigmatic use of the Eden trope.

In this chapter Douglass repeats not only Equiano's image of the black cook who was prevented from eating but also his signification of the slave's forced silence. The scene that illustrates the latter is one in which Colonel Lloyd, without identifying himself, asks one of his slaves a series of questions about his life. The man responds with an unflattering portrait of his master and of slavery. Colonel Lloyd's response is to sell the man "to a Georgia trader. . . . This was the penalty of telling the simple truth in answer to a series of plain questions" (*Life and Times*). Douglass concludes that slaves "would suppress the truth rather than take the consequences of telling it, and in so doing they prove themselves a part of the human family" (*Life and Times*).

In the accounts Equiano, Douglass, and other slave narrators provide of their lives in the New World, alienation, oppression, cruelty, and exclusion from the "human family" are preeminent themes. These themes have been central to an African American perspective on the New World from the colonial period to the present, in both African American life and literature. Very few African American novels, however, include in their settings a period that precedes 1800. They include the period when settlers in the New World considered America a topographical paradise (with the various ramifications that the image involved) primarily as a passing historical reference or as a general context in which the authors and narrators react specifically to the other permutations of Edenic America that directly affected African Americans.

William Wells Brown's *Clotel; or, The President's Daughter* (1853) illustrates this phenomenon. Brown refers to the colonial period primarily to establish a historical context for his criticism of American hypocrisy during the early national period, thus establishing a thematic link between the past and the novel's present. The author-narrator introduces chapter 21 ("The Christian's Death") with a vision in which he manipulates historical facts to emphasize the image and counterimage of America as Paradise and, more specifically, to show how the nation's traffic in human flesh has undermined its moral and religious principles (the chapter's central concern). In effect, by inverting the two images (the southern paradise and the northern wilderness) Brown revises several Anglo-American and African American works that preceded his novel. More specifically, he indirectly revises Beverley and Bradford as well as Equiano and Douglass.

The narrator's vision includes three ships, each of which has a seminal place in the country's history. The first ship is the "mother" ship in which Columbus is sailing to the New World and charting a path for two ships that follow. Each of the sister ships is bringing passengers who will determine the New World's character. The first is the "tempest-tost," "weather-beaten," but stately *Mayflower*. En route to New England, it is transporting "the seed-wheat of states and empire." Its passengers "are great and good men," "constitution-making . . . with the high commission sealed by a Spirit divine, to establish religious and political liberty for all" (147). On its way to the South is "a low rakish ship" with "the first cargo of slaves on their way to" the American Eden: "She is freighted with the elements of unmixed evil." The vision ends with the sister ships anchored in America, the first at Plymouth Rock and the second at Jamestown. Brown not only appropriates and perpetuates formations from America's mythic history to construct this vision, he also produces an origin myth about the simultaneous introduction of good and evil into the New Eden. The narrator concludes that "these ships are the representation of good and evil in the New World, even to our day" (148).

Brown installs formations that contrast the North and the South in other sections of his novel. This thesis-antithesis generally prevailed in African American life, literature, and thought prior to the middle of the twentieth century. In part, the contrast derived from the fact (or at least the perception) that life for blacks in the North after the colonial period was less harsh than in the South. Other Americans also have viewed the North as more fully exercising the country's principles of democracy than the South, despite the fact that the leading Founding Fathers more often were Southerners than Northerners.

One of the most useful sources for determining how blacks viewed the North and the South in relation to the Eden trope is the African American slave narrative. This genre provides a fuller survey of daily life among antebellum blacks than any other primary written source. Slave narratives, along with African American slave songs, certify that the North in African American thought (which before the Civil War included Canada as well as territory north of the Mason-Dixon line) assumed mythic proportions in the vernacular culture of antebellum blacks. From these early years until well into the twentieth century, African Americans associated the North with life, liberty, and the pursuit of happiness. It was their Promised Land, their New World Eden. In practically all of the early African American novels, the North retains this symbolic stature, which accounts for Brown's North-South dichotomy to express an African American perspective on life in the New World.

Brown himself wrote a slave narrative, and as an active abolitionist he was quite familiar with the form and function of the extended slave autobiography. It is not surprising, then, that even as a novel written mainly in the third person, *Clotel*'s form and content derive in large part from conventions of that narrative genre. The same is true for most other African American novels written before the late nineteenth century. Like the slave narrative, one of the early African American novel's primary functions was as an instrument in the struggle for black liberation. By the 1850s, such narratives were well established as one of the most effective weapons in the abolitionists' cause as well as a useful tool in the petition for better treatment of free blacks and ex-slaves living in the North. Given the genre's popularity during this period, its rather easy adaptability to a fictional mode, and the effectiveness of its chief purpose, it was the most familiar, easily accessible, and logical source to which the early African American novelists could turn for a prose narrative model.

America's image as a civil utopia has a much more prominent place in the African American novel than the image of a topographical paradise. Novels published between the 1850s and the 1950s often incorporate specific references to times, places, events, persons, texts, and ideas associated with the revolutionary period. Brown uses the era as a backdrop for the setting in *Clotel*. Lorenzo Dow Blackson weaves trappings from the Revolutionary War into the allegorical form of his novel, *The Rise and Progress of the Kingdoms of Light and Darkness* (1867). In *Imperium in Imperio* (1899), Sutton Griggs draws upon the era's politics of nation formation. These works represent the wide variety of ways that the genre incorporates America's Age of Revolution and foregrounds the period's most historically prominent figure, Thomas Jefferson. Before examining Brown's and Griggs's parodic installations of the revolutionary period's permutation of the Eden trope (which establish discursive norms for twentieth-century novels), I will highlight aspects of the period's mythic trappings and sociopolitical policy upon which the African American novel drew through the 1950s.

In *The Machine in the Garden*, Leo Marx demonstrates that by the last quarter of the eighteenth century the myth of America had turned from "an essentially literary device to ideological or (using the word in its extended sense) political uses."[17] He cites the appearance of Jefferson's *Notes on the State of Virginia* (1785) as a watershed, indicating persuasively that "the pastoral ideal had been 'removed' from the literary mode to which it traditionally had belonged and applied to reality"; in essence, it served "as a guide to social policy" (73). To be sure, Jefferson's *Notes*, the Declaration of Independence, the Constitution, and various other texts that espoused the American Edenic ideal chronicled the evolution of the image of America from an earthly paradise to a civil utopia. Moreover, during this period the American cosmogonic myth generated the nation's first major origin myth, that of the American new man.

In Judeo-Christianity, the myth of the creation of the world (the Primal Event) was written down long after the event itself had occurred. The Bible, of course, was the principal text that recorded this myth. Subsequent translations and versions of the biblical text repeated, reaffirmed, and revised the creation myth. This process repeated itself in the generation and propagation of the American cosmogonic myth, with the "Discovery" as the Primal Event. Notwithstanding the precolonial and colonial reports, histories, and descriptions of the discovery, the earliest definitive texts of the American cosmogony were produced during the revolutionary period. The Constitution and the Declaration of Independence, probably the best known of these texts, record the myth of America's virgin birth as a political entity. In effect, this is a revision of the discovery myth. Succinctly stated, virgin America is born from a consummate union between "male heaven" and "female earth," as Garry Wills notes.[18] It "is a miraculous conception. . . . The nation is conceived by a mental act, in the spirit of liberty, and *dedicated* (as Jesus was in the temple) to a proposition" (xv–xvi). This proposition, the bedrock of American democracy and therefore of the American Edenic ideal, is stated in the Declaration of Independence: all men are created equal and are endowed by their Creator with certain inalienable rights.

As a structural extension of the American cosmogonic myth, the origin myth that recounts the birth of the American new man also emerged during the revolutionary period and was recorded in the texts of Jefferson, William Wirt, Crèvecoeur, and several other prominent political and social figures of the era. This origin myth uses the same basic construct that recounts the nation's birth, and among its several versions is one that suggests that the American new man was born fully grown from the head (i.e., intellect) of his creator, recalling the Greek myth of the birth of Athena, who sprang fully grown (and fully armed) from the head of her father, Zeus. She was the protectress of the city-state Athens, and the newly born American nation was modeled in part on Athenian democracy. According to the myth, the American new man (a collective entity of white males from a specific social class) is of virgin birth. He is the progeny of an intercourse between the intellect of the Founding Fathers and the virgin land. Not only is this fully grown child of the American Edenic ideal white and male, but he occupies a privileged position in the new nation's social hierarchy. Thus, while the mythic new man is a male construct, all males in America are not his equal.

Exactly what the Declaration of Independence and other Anglo-American texts of the period meant by *men* and *equal* has sparked many discussions and has generated numerous texts that define and redefine the concepts. Pre-1960 African American writers—religious, political, social, and imaginative—react to the basic proposition about the equality of man in their repetitions, refutations, and affirmations of specific texts in Anglo-American discourse on the Edenic ideal. Black America's first major prose narrative form, the slave narrative, revises this ideal and consequently establishes a pattern that many subsequent African American texts follow. The slave narrative is inherently an autobiographical chronicle that in large part records the subject's desires and attempts to be treated as a human equal to others in the New World. As part of its indirect revision of Anglo-American colonial texts—which in effect do not place blacks in a category with other humans but in a category at best on par with the fauna and flora—the slave narrative constitutes an extended speech act that monitors the centered subject's transformation from subhuman (slavery) to human (freedom). In this sense, the genre generates its own origin myth, and in so doing it counters the Anglo-American new-man (white) myth.

This process of self-creation and self-definition, of writing the self, against the background of the American cosmogonic myth and the nation's first major origin myth helps define the form and function of African American prose narratives in the autobiographical mode from the colonial slave narrative through the twentieth-century novel. Prominent examples include the religious conversions (transformations) recounted in slave narratives and in other eighteenth- and nineteenth-century African American texts as well as the concept of the New Negro in African American novels and other subsequent works. In these texts the subjects (usually men) who reinvent themselves do so to enjoy certain inalienable rights that the society is supposed to guarantee to all people.

The Declaration of Independence is the principal text that recounts the nation's mythological birth. The Constitution is the principal text that gives sanction to the nation's formation as a political entity and to its mythological origins as recorded in the Declaration of Independence. Equiano published his *Narrative* in the same year that the Constitution was ratified, 1789. Though I do not claim that Equiano had this text in mind when he wrote his *Narrative*, his work, which Arna Bontemps deems the "first truly notable book in the genre,"[19] is implicitly an intertextual revision of the Constitution. In their nonfiction texts, as in their lives, African Americans for nearly two centuries have invoked the Constitution as the principal legal justification for claims to social equality. In their fictive texts, they overwhelmingly have cited and revised (affirmed) the Declaration of Independence.

As stated in the Declaration, the attempt "to establish a more perfect Union" suggests that revolutionary patriots envisioned a society in which man lived in harmony with his human and natural environments, according to "the Laws of Nature and of Nature's God." The Declaration succinctly states the vision of a political and civil Eden in America: "We hold these truths to be self-evident, that all men are created equal, that they are endowed by their Creator with certain unalienable Rights, that among these are Life, Liberty and the pursuit of Happiness." Despite such declarations in this and other Anglo-American texts, blacks' status in the South during the revolutionary and national periods remained that of chattel; in other regions of the country they were pariahs. Since the American Revolution, African American social and political critics and literary artists alike have not failed to exploit the irony of the situation. Many pre–Civil War black texts that support an active resistance to slavery often repeat Patrick Henry's statement regarding America's first major war for freedom ("Give me liberty or give me death") to help sanction revolutionary methods. These writings sharply focus the contradictions between the Framers' concepts of liberty and some of their active participation in the institution of slavery.

Jefferson's image of America, as articulated in *Notes,* the Declaration, and some of his other texts, long has been a source to which opponents and proponents of the mythic ideal of America have turned to justify their stances. The man and many of his writings embody the basic ambivalence of the two primary and opposing images of America evident from the country's beginning. Since the early nineteenth century, African American social critics have used Jefferson and his works more frequently than any other historical personage, event, or text to underscore the contradiction embedded in the myth of America as a civil utopia. David Walker's *Appeal to the Coloured Citizens of the World* (1829) is the earliest major social text to use Jefferson extensively in this manner. Prior to the emergence of the novel, Walker's *Appeal* probably was the most direct African American intertextual response to the Declaration.

African American novels that reference the period typically point out that two of the nation's most revered Founding Fathers, Washington and

Jefferson, owned slaves. While Jefferson certainly is on record as opposing slavery, African American (and other) critics and writers have observed that during his life he manumitted very few of his slaves and freed only seven additional ones in his will.[20] In pre-1960 African American novels Jefferson is prototypical for his period: while framers of the new nation debated the disposition of the slave population, they kept chattel slavery basically intact. Moreover, during the ensuing years, slavery expanded in the South. Indeed, the civil utopia the Founding Fathers sought to effect included a black presence, but only as property and pariahs.

It seems quite appropriate, then, that in the first African American novel, *Clotel*, Brown uses Jefferson to represent the antinomy of the Anglo-American Edenic ideal. Several subsequent African American novelists followed suit, including Barbara Chase-Riboud more than a century later. Like *Clotel*, Chase-Riboud's *Sally Hemings* (1979) and *The President's Daughter* (1994) utilize contradictions between the public and, as legend has it, the personal life of Jefferson and emphasize psychosexual currents in refuting America's self-image.

In incorporating the revolutionary period's permutation of the Eden myth into *Clotel*'s tropological framework, Brown emphasizes the personalities over the politics associated with the era. Periodically (usually using a subjective, authorial voice) Brown unabashedly criticizes Jefferson, Washington, Thomas Paine, and others who helped conceive and form a nation in which they debated but finally ignored the "inalienable rights" of blacks. Regarding the revolutionary period, the novel's focus more on subjectivity than on society (politics) is consistent with its foregrounding of black subject formation against the backdrop of a slaveholding society. (See ch. 2 for a fuller discussion of subjectivity in Brown's novel.)

Of the revolutionary era's most prominent subjects, Brown, of course, chooses Jefferson as his exemplar. He makes Jefferson a character in the novel, and aspects of Jefferson's personal life as they directly affected black subjectivity provide the background for the plot, as indicated in its subtitle (*The President's Daughter*). He asserts that this most revered of the Founding Fathers not only was a racist but also was guilty of sexually exploiting at least one young black slave woman. By pairing subjectivity and society, Brown chastises the real-life Jefferson and thus the nation on moral grounds. For the purposes of this discussion, it is not paramount whether the story about Jefferson's sexual exploitation of Sally Hemings is true.

What is significant is that repetition of the story since Jefferson's day has been an effective indictment of America's failure to live up to its professed principles. When blacks (or whites) repeat the story, even to the present day, they almost assuredly exacerbate the sensitivities even of those whites considered most progressive and liberal. In attacking Jefferson, they knowingly attack one of Anglo-America's most sacred human icons and, consequently, the society's racial politics.

As a character, Jefferson does not participate in the action of *Clotel*. However, at strategic places in the novel, through narrative exposition, dialogue, or characterization, Brown invokes the spirit of Jefferson. In this regard, one of the primary functions of several of his minor characters (black and white) is to refute the myth of America by demythologizing Jefferson. One such character, Georgiana Carlton, is exemplary. The description of Georgiana states that she "had viewed the right to enjoy perfect liberty as one of those inherent and inalienable rights which pertain to the whole human race, and of which they can never be divested, except by an act of gross injustice" (93). Georgiana is the moral exemplar for Brown's portraiture of the "good" white, and Jefferson is her antithesis.

Throughout the novel Brown includes direct quotations and close paraphrases from sections of the Declaration of Independence, revising this text to develop and support his overall theme. In addition, he incorporates scenes and incidents that derive from the historical reality of the revolutionary and early national periods. Thematically, Brown uses specific historical references to colonial America to connect the Age of Revolution and nationhood to its Columbiad beginnings. He places the backdrop of the novel firmly within the framework of the Eden trope by conjoining America's cosmogonic myth and its first principal origin myth.

Griggs's fictive vision in *Imperium in Imperio* is concerned primarily with nation formation and secondarily with black subject formation. It is the nineteenth-century African American novel that most fully harvests the revolutionary period's permutation of the Eden myth. Griggs appropriates this variation as a blueprint for establishing a black civil utopia in the New World, utilizing the revolutionary era's political texts more than its political personalities. He aptly chooses Virginia as the novel's dominant setting, and he creates two protagonists who, as Virginians, embody that revolutionary spirit usually accorded Jefferson and other framers of the

American democracy. The novel opens in 1867 and focuses on post–Civil War black life. The two protagonists emerge immediately as rival and contrasting characters: one, Belton Piedmont, is descended from field slaves; the other, Bernard Belgrave, is the son of a privileged and wealthy mulatto mother and a wealthy and influential U.S. senator. Through their respective color and class, the two exhibit a contrast in black subjectivity that was codified during the revolutionary period and is sustained in the novel's postbellum society.

Using a theme popular in nineteenth-century African American novels, Griggs concentrates *Imperium's* early chapters on the importance of education for improving the freed slaves' quality of life. By dramatizing that both protagonists have a high native intelligence, discourse in this section of the novel is a hidden polemic against those (Jefferson and others) who asserted that blacks are innately less intelligent than whites and that intelligent blacks are mulattoes who owe their intellectual capacities to the white part of their ancestry.[21] By the end of twelve years of schooling, each protagonist has achieved "an academic education that could not be surpassed anywhere in the land" (29). Each presents a valedictory that reveals how thoroughly he has immersed himself in the history of the American Revolution.

The next several chapters in the novel are designed to show that the protagonists as representatives of the race are more complementary than competing characters. The narrative follows them through their college education—Bernard at Harvard and Belton at Stowe University (a fictional black college in Nashville, Tennessee, named in honor of Harriet Beecher Stowe). Griggs characterizes Stowe's overall setting in the same ironic and metonymic manner that he characterizes the assembly hall in which Belton gives the valedictory for his college class—as having "the appearance of the Garden of Eden" (73). Griggs repeats Douglass's trope on the Anglo-American garden trope. The novel's emplotment reveals a distinction between appearance and reality, for behind the college's idyllic facade racism thrives.

As a united front, the black student body at Stowe launches a protest against the discrimination to which Stowe's white faculty and administration subject the college's one black faculty member and its black students. Inspired by their motto, "Equality or Death"—Griggs's obvious allusion to Patrick Henry's famous statement—and under Belton's leadership, the students' successful revolt inspires student bodies at other black colleges to follow Stowe's lead, with similar results. The young student rebels represent "a new Negro, self-respecting, fearless, and determined in the assertion of his rights" (62), an appellation that, given the context in which Griggs develops this section of the novel, recalls the concept of the new man that presided over the revolutionary period. Indeed, Griggs is appropriating and revising Anglo-America's new-man myth. He depicts these student rebellions metaphorically as a microcosm of the colonists' rebellion against England: "These men who engineered and participated in these rebellions were the future leaders of their race" (62), just as those who effected the American Revolution became the future leaders of the nation.

The first third of the novel, then, uses the spirit of the Revolution to take the two protagonists from childhood through college. In the middle of the novel, Griggs manipulates his protagonists' private and public lives to include issues germane to the general black population during and after Reconstruction. Overall, he constructs parallels between the social and political issues that affect his central characters' lives and the social and political issues that formed an integral part of Anglo-American life during the early years of nationhood. In the novel's last third, Griggs uses the Age of Revolution (but now more straightforwardly) as a backdrop for the novel's rather exclusive concentration on its central political concerns, adopting the rhetorical strategies of political discourse. To be sure, this section's tractarian mode signifies on Anglo-American political discourse and constitutes a rather direct and literal revision of several political and historical texts produced during the revolutionary era, with particular emphasis on Jefferson's *Notes*.

Set in Texas, once the western border of the slavocracy, the novel's last third explores the political implications of its title and major theme. Denied freedom during the American Revolution and having failed to gain equality in fact following the Civil War, the nation's black citizens now organize to effect for themselves the same quality of life the Constitution guarantees white males. The numerous secret black societies organized before the war to resist slavery now merge and form a nation within a nation, an *imperium in imperio*. This organization's texts and leaders' speeches indicate that the Imperium is dedicated to correcting the "flaw or defect in the

Constitution of the United States" (181) that defines a black as property and as only 3/5 of a person.[22]

The Imperium is formed around the core of an antebellum secret society that a group of free blacks organized and operated "according to the teachings of Thomas Jefferson" (191), strongly resembling an organization called the Knights of Liberty.[23] A brilliant black scientist, a free man of color, served as the guiding force behind the society. Given the details Griggs provides about this scientist, the character appears to be a fictional representation of Benjamin Banneker, a black contemporary of Jefferson whose career and several of whose thoughts ran parallel to those of his friend Benjamin Franklin.[24] Banneker accused Jefferson of failing to adhere to his own stated principles about the rights of man.[25] An accomplished mathematician and astronomer, Banneker wrote an almanac and sent Jefferson a copy of it to disprove Jefferson's hypothesis about blacks' innate inferiority. Jefferson's responses to Banneker's letters were polite and on occasion flattering, yet elsewhere he wrote that Banneker's life did not disprove the hypothesis, suggested that Banneker's display of intelligence was actually the work of whites, and that whatever intellectual capacity Banneker possessed derived from his white ancestry. Jefferson continued to maintain that he had used "scientific" methodology to arrive at his "objective" conclusions about differences between the intellect of blacks and whites.[26]

Grigg's Imperium appears to be a composite of several historical African American persons, organizations, events, and policies, although Moses Dickson and the Knights of Liberty seem to be the most direct historical sources.[27] The novel also strongly echoes Martin R. Delany's ideas and ideologies, especially as articulated in *The Condition, Elevation, Emigration, and Destiny of the Colored People of the United States, Politically Considered* (1852). In an appendix to this work, Delany speaks of African Americans as constituting "a nation within a nation"—an *imperium in imperio*. Like Banneker, Delany was a scientist (he attended Harvard's medical school).

In the novel, the philosophical, political, and financial legacies of the antebellum black scientist who initiated the revolutionary movement among blacks engender the coalition or, as the novel terms it, the "combination." From this seed the Imperium is formed. Its capitol "is known as Jefferson College" (196) and its government is a virtual structural replica of that of the United States (195). Located in Texas, the threshold of the American West in the second half of the nineteenth century, the Imperium's citizenry in effect attempts to establish its own political Eden in America.

Griggs uses the ironies and paradoxes of the revolutionary period to structure and develop the novel's third section and to tie it thematically to its preceding two sections, both of which are developed as a narrative of sequential actions. References to Columbus and Washington, to the Constitution and the Declaration of Independence, to thematically pertinent events, persons, places, and ideas in American and world history, particularly to the revolutionary age and Thomas Jefferson, abound in this part of the novel. The extended monologues in the novel's final section are rhetorical strategies that invoke and revise through repetition and inversion several Anglo-American and African American texts. In its form and function, the novel's last third is primarily an intertextual revision of standard documents in American political discourse. Says Belton, "Americans fought for a theory and abstract principle" (231); the Imperium, which has a population of over seven million and a standing army, will go to war to see that those principles are concretized for black citizens. Herein lies the plot's resolution.

Bernard, president of the Imperium, has the support of its congress when he proposes that (in the example of the thirteen colonies) the Imperium "strike a blow for freedom" (221) by declaring war against the United States to enable blacks to gain political and civil equality with whites or to establish a separate black empire on lands now belonging to the United States. The Imperium expects to receive international support and sanction for the war and subsequently to receive recognition as a sovereign nation. Belton disagrees with this military solution, is declared a traitor to the Imperium, and is executed. Berl Trout, secretary of state in the Imperium and the narrative voice Griggs uses to achieve authorial distance from the story, betrays the Imperium's existence and its plans (ostensibly to the U.S. government) and thus brings about its destruction.

Through the lives of its protagonists, the novel demonstrates that in the course of human events it does indeed become necessary for a group of people to shake off the oppression of a parent nation and to establish a nation of its own. By prefacing the novel with Berl Trout's self-deprecating deathbed confession, Griggs affirms the intents for which the Imperium was founded and at the same time implicitly casts Trout in the historical role of Aaron Burr. Giving the student rebellion a central place, Griggs implicitly makes the relationship between the rebellion and the Imperium's plans for war against the United States similar to the relationship between the Boston Tea Party and the American Revolution.

Other aspects of the novel also align with the revolutionary period. As part of the first generation of black freedmen, Belton and Bernard and most of their cohorts are legally Americans. Within the context of the novel's historical backdrop and controlling analogy, they are "new men," as are the more than 7.5 million other blacks who make up the Imperium's citizenry. As citizens of the Imperium in *Imperio*, their identity as "new Negroes" is nationalistic, a subjectivity that primarily grows out of the Imperium's relation to the U.S. government. This process of self-definition, a result of contrasts and tensions between a parent country and its offspring, certainly recalls the "mental act" that generated the American new man of the revolutionary era. For instance, in the opening paragraphs of Letter 3 ("What is an American?") in his *Letters from an American Farmer* (1782), Crèvecoeur (like William Wirt and others) uses the political and social relations between England and the colonists to formulate his definition of an American as "this new man" (54). This new man, of course, was a New Adam in a new world, and herein lie vestiges of the Eden trope.

Imperium is a prime example of a nineteenth-century African American novel whose paradigmatic use of the Eden trope centers the revolutionary period's civil and political tenets. In the twentieth century, African American novels incorporate the Revolution variously and to different degrees as part of the genre's paradigmatic scheme. Jessie Fauset uses the historical period rather straightforwardly in *There Is Confusion* (1924), and Arna Bontemps uses it rather subtly in *Black Thunder* (1936), just two of numerous instances in the genre.

Bontemps's *Black Thunder*, a fictionalized account of the Gabriel Prosser slave conspiracy of 1800, puts in sharp relief the South's third principal image of itself as Eden, the plantation idyll. Practically every African American novel that references or incorporates the slave South refutes the era's idyllic self-image. *Black Thunder* is one of very few African American novels between 1900 and 1960 to focus exclusively on slavery. In the first book of the novel's five, Bontemps incorporates specific references to the

American, French, and Haitian Revolutions, and he casts his protagonist, Gabriel, in the historical mold of Haiti's Toussaint L'Ouverture. The novel's references to Anglo-American texts produced during the era of the American Revolution and specifically to *Notes* and other writings by Jefferson form the core of its direct intertextual revisions. With the revolutionary spirit forming a contextual backdrop, *Black Thunder* directs its attack against the slavocracy, repudiating notions that masters were kind, slaves were contented, and the social organization was beneficent.

Black Thunder does not employ specific trappings from the Eden trope in a manner typical for African American novels. Nevertheless, its emplotment and its antebellum plantation setting implicitly challenge the plantation idyll's social ideology. In debunking the myth and justifying the slaves' revolt against the system, the narrator writes summarily that "a slave's life was bad enough when he belonged to quality white folks; it must have been torment on that Prosser plantation" (33). The statement contradicts the portrait of southern society extolled in much antebellum literature, as does the entire novel. Thus, while the novel's historical setting and intertextual revisions link the South's second (civil utopia) and third (plantation idyll) permutations of Eden, its dialogism centers the latter.

There was a rather natural evolution from the political manifestation of the Eden trope as associated with the Founding Fathers to the literary manifestation of the myth, which flourished between the 1830s and the 1860s. William Wirt's political and literary careers readily illustrate the transition between the two periods. Wirt associated with and revered the architects of the new nation, but he never attained the historical stature accorded the leading revolutionary patriots. If he has a secure place in American political and legal history, it is for his role as defense attorney for Harman Blennerhassett in Aaron Burr's 1807 treason trial. A romanticist, Wirt considered Blennerhassett, Burr's co-conspirator, a romantic hero and characterized him "as an innocent, a sort of natural aristocrat, duped and misled by the scheming and insidiously persuasive Burr." [28] To Wirt, America was the New Eden, particularly during the early national period, and Blennerhassett was a new Adam: "Such was the state of Eden when the serpent [Burr] entered its bowers." [29]

As "one of the South's most energetic mythmakers," Wirt "possessed a rhetorical flair for the sentimental and the nostalgic," for which American readers—especially Southerners and more particularly Virginians—

hungered.[30] His discourse on the American Edenic ideal—in *The Letters of the British Spy*, a collection of essays first issued in 1803; *Sketches of the Life and Character of Patrick Henry* (1817); and other texts—praises an entire society (principally the South) and depicts it as a utopia of the past.[31] In *Discourse on the Lives and Characters of Thomas Jefferson and John Adams* (1826), Wirt states that Jefferson (and by implication other American patriots of his era) "was the product of an aristocratic and chivalric Virginia, America's Athens, over which the 'spirit of Raleigh' had presided since its founding."[32]

Wirt's romantic characterization of Jefferson exemplifies the various myths, realities, literary legends, and political ideologies that converged in the southern white mind by the 1830s. This portrait reveals how aristocratic and chivalric images merged in a concept of the New World, and it connects an essentially literary tradition (chivalry) to political ideology (Athenian democracy) using historical myth and legend (the "spirit of Raleigh") as a nucleus. It also foreshadows the plantation idyll's social policy. By the time Wirt was writing, the myth of the South as Eden certainly had become firmly entrenched; however, the use of terms such as *Eden* and *Paradise* to describe the society was subsiding in favor of other terms. Emphasis now centered on cotton and rice plantations as representative of the region's topography rather than on the gardenlike topography of the first principal image. Despite these outward changes, the Edenic image of the South, with a decidedly southern flavor, continued to embed itself in the southern imagination and to be expressed in phrases such as the "Old South," the "Old Dominion," and the "Plantation South."

The plantation idyll did not generate as full blown an origin myth as did the revolutionary period's civil utopia. But the idyll's structural extension from the American cosmogony is apparent. Its major texts are literary and principally of the South, yet the image also appears in the writings of James Fenimore Cooper and other Northerners.[33] In this period's literary texts (as well as in several twentieth-century ones) the "Old South," the "Old Dominion," and the "Plantation South" connote an aristocratic southern white society economically sustained by slaves' labor, and the terms express slight differences in the versions of the South as Eden that followed the revolutionary and national periods. Wirt's portrait of the South as Eden provided a bridge between the earlier versions and that of the plantation idyll: the American new man Wirt envisioned, quintessentially a Southerner, was both patriotic and chivalric.

According to William R. Taylor, the romanticized, patriotic revolutionary hero was a progenitor of the planter aristocrat who populated plantation literature in the 1830s.[34] The lords and knights of European chivalric literature also were his ancestors. Still open to debate are the extent to which the literature reflected or influenced life and the extent to which life in the antebellum South influenced or was reflected in the period's literature.

The most widely recognized progenitor of the literary component of the myth of the plantation South is John Pendleton Kennedy, whose *Swallow Barn* (1832) offered contemporary and subsequent Southerners a blueprint from which they could construct their own particular version of the South's Eden. *Swallow Barn* is dedicated to Wirt, and plantation idyll discourse in this vein proffers a close nexus between society and subjectivity in the slave South. Antebellum Southerners typically considered the structure of their society to be a replica of medieval Europe. Feudalism provided an analogy for the plantation South that many writers in the plantation tradition readily adapted. Their usage, however, omitted the southern white yeomanry and concentrated on the planter aristocrats, the slaves, and the poor whites as the primary constituents of the society's class structure.[35] Discourse in this idyllic vein draws from medieval legend and lore to inscribe a southern social structure in which the planter class occupies the roles of lords, knights, and ladies, and slaves occupy the roles of serfs.

From Kennedy's purview, contented slaves are a rather natural if inconspicuous feature of the era's literary and social landscapes. His idyll of the South certainly is Edenic, with a place for every person and every person in his place. In the decade preceding the Civil War, Kennedy revised and reissued *Swallow Barn*, intending it as "an antidote to the abolition mischief" (xl). His most "carefully revised and somewhat enlarged" (xl) section of the novel is the chapter entitled "The Quarter," in which his portrayal of slaves generalizes to the black presence in the South. They are a genial, happy "tribe," fortunate to have "beneficent guardianship" while in a transitional stage from "barbarism to civilization" (452–53).

There is, however, an interesting flaw in Kennedy's plantation idyll tapestry—his portraiture in the novel's penultimate chapter (entitled "A Negro Mother") of a heroic slave named Abraham (Abe). Abe does not exhibit the typical slave's contentment, his siblings' acquiescence to the system, or his father's fidelity to the owner. Abe covets freedom and displays the spirit of a revolutionary hero who resents another person's authority over him.

As the vignette about Abe develops, it appears as though Kennedy will invoke the slavocracy's reigning ideology to construct this subject as an ungrateful slave spoiled by too many advantages from his parents' privileged status at Swallow Barn. But very early in the vignette, Kennedy changes his tone and method dramatically. He abruptly abandons the animal imagery, racist epithets, and condescending tone that characterize his early descriptions of Abe and his caricatured portraits of other slaves. By the time he completes the vignette, Kennedy has made Abe perhaps the most admirable character in the book.

In the novel's final chapter Kennedy writes what in effect is a panegyric to the heroes and mythmakers of the Southern Eden, including Captain John Smith, William Stith, Sir Walter Raleigh, and that generic Virginian, the "courteous cavalier who is so pre-eminently entitled to be styled the True Knight of the Old Dominion" (500). The chapter appears in part to be an attempt to diminish by comparison the portrait of Abe he has created; if so, this attempt is unsuccessful. This vignette is indeed a curious deviation from the rest of the novel and from the plantation idyll's literary conventions. The novel is ambiguous about Abe's fate: he either dies a heroic death at sea or finally succeeds in his attempts to escape from slavery.

The African American novel dialogically refutes the numerous offshoots of *Swallow Barn*. Though southern whites used biblical lore to justify the antebellum social order, they used medieval lore to structure and describe it. Thus, when treating the white South's image of itself as a feudal order, African American novels through the 1950s appropriately install the biblical Eden myth as a governing trope.

Particularly through its formation of subjects, the African American novel negates those plantation idyll texts that portray the South as a well ordered, harmonious society. It combines theme (miscegenation) with character and incident to reveal that white men more often are unethical and prone to abuse blacks physically and sexually than ethically and morally pure; that black women much more often are victims of sexual, physical, and psychological abuse than lascivious temptresses; and that white women more often are jealous, vindictive vixens than refined "ladies."

Through setting, incident, and structure, the genre dispels the myth of kind masters and contented slaves, and it reveals a social order so thoroughly diseased and inhumane that slaves risk life and limb to escape it. In these and other ways, the earliest African American novels (and later ones that treat the antebellum South) repeat social formations that are standard in antebellum slave narratives. Both the novels and slave narratives revise the image of the Old South by giving a fuller picture of what life was actually like. These features are part of the norms the genre established in the 1850s and 1860s to constitute the skeletal form of a novelistic paradigm based on the Bible's Eden myth. It speaks thematically to the question of blacks' marginal place in the American Eden.

In the Bible's narrative of Eden there is harmonious interaction among the different forms of life, with Adam and Eve having ascendancy over the animals. According to antebellum racial theories, Adam and Eve were the original parents of whites. Negrophobes advanced three major propositions to account for the origin of blacks: blacks were not descendants of the original parents but were intrusions (manifestations of the Devil) into Eden; blacks were direct descendants of Adam and Eve but later were cursed and consequently ejected from the human family; blacks originally were in Eden but belonged to the category of animals (subhumans) rather than to the family of man. Whatever the specific details of the assertion, the common denominator was that blacks did not merit a place equal to whites in any version of the New World Eden. After all, the Constitution had defined blacks as subhuman. Early African American novelists use these propositions as a foundation for their treatment of African Americans' historical experience in the antebellum South. The systematic manner in which they do so constitutes what I call the genre's Edenic paradigm.

The paradigm thematically foregrounds miscegenation and frequently ties the theme to subject formation. Novelists' construction of planter-class subjects within the paradigm draws upon the plantation idyll's images of the southern gallant as both a knight and Adam and the belle as both a romantic damsel and Eve (before the Fall). It negates the images of these subjects (particularly white men) as exemplars of moral and sexual purity. In its reconstruction, the paradigm merges the feudal model and the Bible's Eden story as part of its exposé of antebellum life.

The biblical Eden myth narrates man's fall from grace and his ejection from Paradise as a result of moral (i.e., sexual) transgression. Those who propagated the plantation idyll typically considered sexual transgression a formidable threat to the New World Paradise's perpetuation. In this purview, black slaves were the ever-present symbol of this transgression, and any sanction of miscegenation (or of sexual transgression among the belles) would destroy the entire system. To be sure, for many antebellum whites miscegenation was the most potent threat to the survival of the dominant social order.[36] But southern white literary texts published between 1830 and 1860 basically ignored the widespread evidence of miscegenation and asserted that manumission and emancipation were the greatest threats to the Southern Way of Life.

Like the slave narratives, early African American novels' survey of the antebellum South includes characters and incidents that expose the slaveholding world as one in which human beings, if they are black, are stripped of their human rights and used as commodities. The narratives and novels depict a society that is not the metaphorical Garden of Eden where humans live in harmony with nature and with other humans but a society in which both nature and humanity (especially blacks) are abused, exploited, and even destroyed by those who have designated themselves as keepers of the Garden.

Gardens South, Gardens North

The slave narrative prefigures aspects of structure, setting, and emplotment in the earliest African American novels. The novels' episodic structure allows the authors to include numerous instances of corporeal and psychological sufferings among the slaves in the Southern Garden. In both genres the centered subjects' (and other blacks') dysphoria in the Southern Eden and their desire for freedom materialize in their attempts to escape from this dystopia and to reach the symbolic Promised Land of the North. In *Clotel* and in most other African American novels published before 1900 and set in part or entirely in the slavery period, the narrator's critical survey of American society (South and North) is closely linked with the escape-to-freedom motif. The plight of *Clotel*'s central characters unfolds as part of their forced migration farther and farther South, which directly and indirectly intensifies their desire to escape to freedom, in the North, in Europe, or, in some cases, through death.

Like several novelists who succeeded him, Brown explores a symbolic relation between geographical space and social place. *Clotel*'s opening chapter is set in Richmond, Virginia, the city that was to become the capital of the Confederacy and the state that once was the symbol of Edenic society in the South and in America. In Virginia, Currer and her daughters live as close to an ideal state as slaves can. When in the second chapter Brown shifts the novel's setting to Natchez, Mississippi (historically a showplace of the grandeur of plantation society), he draws a contrast between the best and worst conditions under which a slave could live in the South.

By alternating through much of the novel between the two settings, Brown also contrasts the Anglo-American and African American versions of the South as Eden. From the viewpoint of those whom the slavocracy benefited most, Natchez and the prosperous centers of Virginia in many respects were models of utopian life in the New World. Brown inverts the trope. In large measure, both Natchez and the affluent centers of Virginia were built and maintained on the exploitation and degradation of a slave population. From this perspective, Brown's use of Jefferson as an integral figure in the novel's portrait of the American South assumes a large part of its significance. After all, Jefferson's status as a shining example of how rewarding life in the New World could be for whites was effected through the labor of black slaves, as John C. Miller points out.[37]

Once his political career begins to ascend, the novel's Jefferson sells his slave mistress and her children, whom he fathered. Clotel eventually becomes the property of a slaveowner in Vicksburg, Mississippi, from which she escapes to the North. She disguises herself as a young white man of delicate constitution, a symbolic transformation in subjectivity that signifies the prerequisite for freedom in the Southern Eden. With the aid of a fellow slave named William, Clotel effects a plan that allows both of them to escape to the North. Brown bases the details of this segment of the novel on William and Ellen Craft's machinations to flee from slavery in Georgia in 1849. Brown was acquainted with the Crafts and their story, and he probably was the first to put it in print.[38]

The intertextual relationship between *Clotel* and the slave narrative texts (including Brown's own *Narrative*) is primarily one of affirmation through repetition. Like other nineteenth-century African American novels, *Clotel* corroborates these slave texts' refutation of proslavery discourse that promoted and was cast in the mold of the plantation idyll. These novels corroborate the northern Anglo-American ideal with qualifications. For example, Brown's allegory of the ships in *Clotel* (chapter 21) negates the southern New World ideal and affirms the northern one. His installation of the Crafts' narrative as an intertext tempers his affirmation by exposing racism against blacks in the North as "another form of slavery" (138).

Nevertheless, Clotel's desire to be reunited with her daughter, Mary, rather than her scorn for racial repression in the North, causes her to leave Cincinnati and return to Virginia. Her migration from the North to the South provides for the dramatic and tragic conclusion to her story. Brown uses features of the Eden trope to record her death scene. He infuses the scene (175–79) with a combination of religious and political allusions that would become characteristic of subsequent African American novelists (as late as James Baldwin's depiction of Rufus Scott's death scene in *Another Country*).

By utilizing the escape-to-freedom motif as a structuring device, by providing a critical survey of northern and southern life, and by employing various other conventions from the slave narrative genre, Brown formulated a schema in *Clotel* that African American novelists followed closely until the late nineteenth century: African American novelists typically wrote in the third person and therefore did not replicate the slave narrative's first-person voice as a key narrative strategy. (The African American novel in the guise of autobiography is a twentieth-century rather than nineteenth-century practice.) But their appropriation of other norms from the slave narrative directly related to its autobiographical form influenced the shape of the first group of nineteenth-century African American novels.

Covering basically the same thematic concerns as *Clotel,* and with similar tragic consequences, the second African American novel, Frank J. Webb's *The Garies and Their Friends* (1857), uses South Carolina and Pennsylvania as symbolic settings to draw comparisons and contrasts between the South and the North. In effect, *The Garies* revises Anglo-American texts of both regions. Aristocratic whites in colonial South Carolina enjoyed an affluent lifestyle that was sustained in large part by the labor of the state's black majority, a condition that survived until the Civil War. But even for those black slaves whose lives were relatively comfortable and prosperous, such as this novel's heroine, Emily Garie, life in South Carolina was far from Edenic. The racism to which blacks (including the title characters) in *The*

Garies are subjected in Pennsylvania is nearly as harsh as that in South Carolina. Webb's choice of Pennsylvania as setting is an ironic comment on the fact that the state was home to one of the most active and influential abolitionist groups, the Quakers. Through its central characters' experiences, the novel certifies that a black cannot live an Edenic existence in any region of the United States.

The third African American novel published, Harriet Wilson's *Our Nig; or, Sketches from the Life of a Free Black* (1859), set in New England, again convincingly demonstrates that whether in the South or in the North, under the worst or best conditions for one of the black race, America is not a New Eden. Wilson adopts the form of slave narrative discourse to revise the northern ideal. *Our Nig*, therefore, straddles the line that separates the slave narrative from the early novel. Even though the principal subject in *Our Nig* is an indentured servant, the novel makes it clear that based on the conditions under which blacks live, the difference between indentured servitude (North) and slavery (South) is semantic rather than substantive. In *Blake; or, The Huts of America* (1861−62), Martin Delany supports the position of other early novelists, attacking almost every facet of the American slavocracy.[39]

The North-South contrast has an integral place in the African American novel's fictive design. Generally, the contrast signifies (with some qualifications) a distinction between a utopian (northern) and dystopian (southern) existence for blacks in the United States. Interwoven with the novel's Eden trope, the contrast frequently shapes theme, emplotment, and structure (the quest for Eden); setting and symbolism (i.e., the function of geographical space); and subject formation (the general distinction between positive and negative characters). The earliest works in the genre establish this contrast as a norm that undergoes only slight modifications before the mid-twentieth century.

More emphatically than the slave narratives, the early novels demonstrate that for blacks in the New World, the symbolic nexus between space (geographical region) and place (social status and quality of life) is relative. Through emplotment, setting, and characterization, the early novels reveal that the harshness of life for blacks is greater in the lower South than in the upper South, greater in the South than in the North, and greater in the United States than in Canada. Only when contrasted with the South does the North become a metaphorical Eden or Promised Land.

With regard to race relations, the North-freedom synonymy is a mainstay in African American literary (and vernacular) expressions before the 1960s. Prior to the twentieth century, African American literary discourse (unlike the nonliterary discourse) generally based its image of the North more on myth than reality. It is understandable that in the antebellum period those fugitive slaves (and ex-slaves) who found temporary or permanent sanctuary in the North tempered their written criticism of that region's failure to adhere to the principles of the American ideal. Then, too, a sharp contrast between the two regions (with the North depicted as the better) was a convenient rhetorical device for the slave narrators and pre–Civil War novelists to refute the southern plantation idyll. To be sure, both the slave narrative and the African American novel were instruments for social change—specifically, the abolition of slavery.

Chattel slavery was a decade away from abolition in the South when the first novel by an African American was published. But the emancipation of blacks in 1863 did not bring them freedom, and for more than a century they used whatever weapon was available to them, including literature, to petition for their rightful place in the American Eden. Accompanying the Emancipation Proclamation were literary and political texts that reaffirmed the Anglo-American Edenic ideal and in many ways revitalized old myths that had helped shape American society since Columbus first landed on America's shores. Abraham Lincoln was the most prominent of the nation's new mythmakers. His Gettysburg Address (though it is only ten sentences) is the principal national text of its period to reaffirm the myth of America as the New Eden, as is evident in the address's opening sentence: "Four score and seven years ago our fathers brought forth on this continent, a new nation, conceived in Liberty, and dedicated to the proposition that all men are created equal." The address is a structural extension of and therefore repeats the American cosmogonic myth. Its ending states the conception of a new origin myth for the nation: "that this nation, under God, shall have a new birth of freedom." This new origin myth implicitly includes African Americans as members of the New Eden's Adamic family.

Post–Civil War white Southerners, however, did not embrace the nation's new origin myth. Instead, they wrote political, social, and literary texts that narrativized the New South and thus produced the region's own origin myth. The New South they constructed in literature was as old (perhaps more so) as it was new, for the formulators drew heavily from the images of the old ideal, with particular emphasis on the chivalric tradition and the feudal idyll. These texts (known collectively as Plantation School literature) dominated southern white literature from the end of the Civil War to World War I. They helped generate the New South's cult of modern chivalry, and in large part they shaped southern society and subjectivity during this half-century.

As the following three chapters will argue, novelists gradually but steadily developed a textual system of form and meaning that by the end of the century became readily identifiable as the Edenic paradigm. This model is most evident as a pervasive rhetorical strategy in the literary texts of Charles Waddell Chesnutt, the major turn-of-the-century African American novelist.

Belles and Beaux

Black Female Subjectivity and the Social Skin

IN AFRICAN AMERICAN novels published before World War I, black women are typically the protagonists. With few exceptions, the novels thematically foreground miscegenation, which in large part is the novelists' response to white society's obsessive fear that unions between blacks and whites (specifically black men and white women) portend the destruction of white civilization. Most often setting is in the South, and plot structures argue for mainstreaming bright and white mulattoes and tacitly for including the black race more fully in the region's social structure.

Pre–World War I African American novels dialogically oppose Negrophobic texts of the period. A plethora of white southern (and nonsouthern) literary, sociological, and historical texts published during the decades that followed the Civil War launch vitriolic attacks on blacks by portraying them as a defiled race of subhumans while concomitantly depicting whites as godlike. To emphasize the contrast, this Negrophobic discourse usually highlights interracial sexual relations as a pretext and context for constructing and installing white women (belles) and black men (brutes) as binary inner texts to assert the diametric opposition of the two races. Typically, the discourse draws pointed attention to and exaggerates white women's and black men's physiological features, projects the white woman as a symbol of a white society it considers sacred, and portrays the black man as an ever-present threat to the white woman and thus to the society she symbolizes. This Negrophobic discourse uses these two corporeal forms as principal agents to communicate messages from and about the South's Edenic society.

In their direct challenge to the South's social ideology and its mythopoeic writings, the novelists of this period do not create white female characters whose portraiture directly castigates the southern belle icon and the white South's Eden trope. Instead, these authors appropriate the character prototype and inscribe it as black female subjectivity, emphasizing physiological, sociological, psychological, and intellectual similarities between the novels' black heroines and southern white belles. It is a strategy designed to nullify Negrophobes' assertion that innate differences between blacks and whites justify blacks' continued marginal status in the society. While Negrophobic texts of the period typically argue against miscegenation by portraying black men as obsessed with raping white women, African American novels foreground a romantic relationship between a black woman and a white man and generally couch the relationship within the cult of southern chivalry.

With bright mulatto and white mulatto women as centered subjects, the novelists present these women's plight as indicative of the social class and color caste to which they belong as well as representative of their race. The surface of these women's bodies functions as a discursive center, and the novels' general themes, structures, emplotments, principal characterizations, and other formalist features are aligned with these subjects' portraiture. These features overwhelmingly constitute the genre's norms from the 1850s through World War I.

William Wells Brown's *Clotel; or, The President's Daughter*, the first published African American novel, establishes the genre's generic norms for those novels (the majority) that use the black woman's body as a text to critique race relations in the American Eden. Integral to the tropology-society-subjectivity nexus is Brown's dialogic response to racial ideology articulated by or associated with Thomas Jefferson and Brown's appropriation of white character prototypes (particularly the southern belle) from the white South's chivalric literature. Though standard aspects of black female subject formation and attendant issues are discernible in practically all pre-1900 African American novels, the centered female subjects in *Clotel*, Frank J. Webb's *The Garies and Their Friends*, Frances E. W. Harper's *Iola Leroy; or, Shadows Uplifted*, and Sutton E. Griggs's *Imperium in Imperio* illustrate the extent to which the novelists adapt and vary this character type.

Catherine Burroughs, Jeffrey Ehrenreich, Ted Polhemus, and Mary Douglas are among the contemporary scholars who have studied the human body as discourse, as a social text, and as a conveyor of sociopolitical and sociocultural messages.[1] While contemporary scholarship that theorizes the human body as a social text informs this chapter's discussion, the novels themselves, following the example of *Clotel*, draw directly from Thomas Jefferson's reading and writing of (theorizing) white bodies and black bodies. In *Notes on the State of Virginia* Jefferson summarizes in query 14 his ostensible attempts to determine through "scientific" reasoning whether or not to "incorporate the blacks into the State" (132). He uses his "scientific" method to justify blacks' exclusion from the American Eden. Reading the surface of the body as a social text, he points to physiological features such as color, hair, and physique as evidence of blacks' physiological inferiority, and he identifies the "suffusions of color," the "flowing hair," and the "elegant symmetry of form" as proof positive of whites' "superior beauty" (133). After a rather thorough denigration of blacks as a race, near the end of query 14 he states, with a modicum of hesitation, that he advances "as a suspicion only, that the blacks . . . are inferior to the whites in the endowments both of body and mind" (138). Contending a nexus between black subjectivity and white society, Jefferson voices his fear that miscegenation will escalate following the emancipation of slaves, thereby threatening the social structure more seriously. He proposes, therefore, that "when freed, [the slave] is to be removed beyond the reach of mixture" (139).

Rituals for Aggregation

The core of these novels' emplotments is the women protagonists' attempts to be included in the white mainstream—in essence, to be considered and treated as fully human. Liminality is a useful construct for examining how emplotment in these novels emanates from the surface of the centered subjects' bodies.[2] As social selves, the subjects are "necessarily ambiguous, since [liminality] and these persons elude or slip through the network of classifications [i.e., neither black nor white] that normally locate states and positions in cultural space." They are "liminal entities [who] are neither here nor there; they are betwixt and between the positions assigned and arrayed by law, custom, convention, and ceremonial."[3]

The novels' rather formulaic emplotments, then, involve a series of rites of passage—that is, rituals that "accompany every change of place, state, social position and age" and therefore constitute the "liminal phase" of a person's movement in society.[4] All rites of passage have three phases: separation, margin (or limen), and aggregation. These three phases largely define action, incident, and subjectivity in these novels' "drama of socialization."[5]

When a novel's mulatto protagonist represents the race in general, the first phase signals the separation of blacks from the human family and reflects how the Constitution and other texts of the American Edenic ideal defined American personhood. In antebellum America, it was primarily (but not only) slave status that separated one from the human family. After the war, the condition of being black defined a person as subhuman. When a novel's mulatto protagonist represents mulattoes as a distinct group, the first phase, then, refers to the separation of mulattoes not only from the human family (i.e., from whites) but also from the black race, relegating them to a liminal state.

Within this same construct, the third phase, (re)aggregation or (re)incorporation, is, simply put, that of being white in the sociocultural sense of the term.[6] When a novel's centered subject is a mulatto who represents both the race and the mulatto subgroup (which is often the case), the character's aggregation (acceptance as a white person) should signify the acceptance of blacks into the human family, which would give them access to the privileges of American democracy on par with whites. The novels, however, stop short of this logical extension. Seldom in these novels does a mulatto heroine "pass" with the intent to transform herself into a white person. In those instances when she allows herself to be considered white in order to be treated as human, whites accept her as a white person, not as someone who passes. As the novels present the situation, whites can accept the individual while still refusing to acknowledge the subgroup (mulattoes) and the race as human.

The second phase of the construct, liminality, speaks to the heart of these novels' plot structures. Liminality constitutes a state of instability, and the condition of the mulatto is neither black nor white. Terence Turner observes, "The surface of the body, as the common frontier of society, the social self, and the psychobiological individual, becomes the symbolic stage upon which the drama of socialization is enacted" (15). Physical attributes, intellectual capacity, moral stature, and marital status are the major rites of passage in these novels' dramas of socialization.

The subjects' social status as the Other—their race (black), their gender, their color (bright and white mulattoes), other of their physiological attributes (exceedingly beautiful and exceptionally well formed), and their intellect—automatically places them in the separation phase, where they exist in a sociocultural "state" "that has few or none of the attributes of the past"—i.e., slavery.[7] The slaveholding mind-set, in the example of Jefferson, asserted that blacks were physically malformed and intellectually deficient, which these women obviously are not. Yet regardless of evidence to the contrary, those whites who most ardently espoused a belief in black inferiority could (and did) in their own minds transform any black, including mulattoes, to fit the prescribed Negrophobic mold. From the perspective of liminality, then, the novels' plot structures take their heroines through a series of rites of passage in preparation for their anticipated movement into mainstream society (aggregation).

When these nineteenth-century novels are considered collectively, the first rite of passage in the subjects' drama of socialization concerns physiology and has two major components: the women's biological or genetic heritage (they must be physically indistinguishable from a white person) and their physical attributes (they must meet white standards of beauty). Quite often this rite has been completed before a novel's action begins. The biological or genetic factor concerns the circumstances of these women's birth; in some instances it further distinguishes the bright from the white mulattoes as the liminal or ritual subjects. When establishing the parentage of the protagonists, the novels create another origin myth about mulattoes in which these ritual subjects are the progeny of a nonhuman mother (a bright or white mulatto slave) and a human father (a member of the slaveholding class). Brown's *Clotel* establishes and exemplifies the literary manifestation of this origin myth through the characteristics of its title character. Clotel, like her sister, Althesa, is the daughter of a bright mulatto slave, Currer, and a prominent aristocrat, Thomas Jefferson. Marie Leroy (*Iola Leroy*) and her daughters, Iola and Gracie, and Fairfax Belgrave (*Imperium in Imperio*) have similar parentage.

Birth, the initial component in the first rite of passage, separates these women from the subgroups mulatto and bright mulatto as preparation for their entry into the mainstream. Certainly, one prerequisite for aggregation is that these women physically look the part. Thus, the physiological manifestation of their African heritage is perceptible (if at all) only to the most acute observer. Even though Emily Garie is described as having a "light-brown complexion [with] the faintest tinge of carmine" (2), when she migrates to the North some observers think she is white.

In addition to their color (or lack thereof), these women also must possess exceptional beauty. Brown's Clotel and Althesa qualify as ritual subjects because physiologically they appear to be white, and Brown constructs them as almost perfect in their physical beauty. The point is relevant to Brown's drama of socialization, for he constructs black female subjectivity in this novel as a generational nexus. The extraordinary beauty that inheres in Mary (Clotel's daughter) and in Ellen and Jane (Althesa's daughters) can be traced back to their grandmother, Currer. Several other novels repeat the pattern. Emily Garie and her daughter by the same name; Marie Leroy and her daughters, Iola and Gracie; and Fairfax Belgrave are likewise extraordinarily beautiful. This phenomenon recalls Jefferson's comments in *Notes* that whites' "elegant symmetry of form" is evidence of their "superior beauty" (133). The novelists construct these subjects' physical attractiveness to equal and generally to exceed that of the elite group of white heroines who populated southern white chivalric fiction in the nineteenth and early twentieth centuries.[8]

The second rite of passage also involves an innate characteristic, intellectual capacity. A nexus between body and mind is consequent with the mythic (Edenic) origin of man and woman. As Burroughs and Ehrenreich state, "From the beginning—the dominant myth of Western culture informs us—knowledge has been intimately linked to reading the social body" (1). Jefferson makes the same intimate link in query 14 when asserting qualitative differences between blacks and whites "in the endowments both of body and mind" (138). Reading the black body in binary opposition to the white body, Jefferson privileges the social skin as the principal indicator of a person's degree of humanness. In *Notes* he considers the assertion that the "improvement of the blacks in body and mind" is a result "of their mixture with whites" but decides that any such mental "improvement" is minimal. He concludes that miscegenation "proves [only] that their inferiority is not the effect merely of their condition of life" (136). He identifies not only an unadulterated African, Phillis Wheatley, but also the British mulatto Ignatius Sancho as examples of blacks who are noted for their intelligence but who remain inferior to whites. (In other writings Jefferson includes the American mulatto Benjamin Banneker among his examples.) The lack of interest the historical Jefferson showed in the education of blacks could be a result of his stated opinions about the race's mental incapacity.[9] The fictional Jefferson in *Clotel* is certainly unlike the other beaux in these novels in that he is unconcerned with the education of his mulatto mistress and their children.

Brown's choice of the historical Thomas Jefferson as the source for his fictional character by the same name is apt. Perhaps in direct response to the historical Jefferson, Brown makes each of the ritual subjects in *Clotel* highly educated for women of their time and place, suggesting that their educational development is a barometer for their high native intelligence. Though the fictional Jefferson is inattentive to the development of Currer's mind, the other women's white beaux in these novels become their ritual guides for this rite of passage. Althesa's husband provides her a private tutor who teaches her what is "necessary for one's taking a position in society" (86). Through tutorials, Clarence Garie, Emily Garie's master and eventual husband, educates her to the point that she is at least the intellectual peer (often the superior) of educated white women in the area of South Carolina where they live.[10]

Typically in antebellum black novels, a respective subject's education is confined to knowledge that will enhance her ornamental function—her socially liminal status as a (black) southern belle—approximating her white model as created by men before the war. Postbellum black novels stress the heroine's intellectual growth; thus, their subjects resemble the southern belle some white women writers created in their postbellum novels.[11] Centered mulatto subjects in both antebellum and postbellum novels possess intellectual capacities and educational training that equal or exceed those of white belles in nineteenth-century life and literature. These aspects of black female subjectivity in the novels derived primarily from black society's emphasis on the importance of education in moving into the mainstream, a significance it retained among blacks until the mid–twentieth century.

However, none of the women in *Clotel* attains the superior level of education accorded the women in the other novels. Eugene Leroy sends his prospective wife, Marie, and later their daughter, Iola, to school in the North, where each receives a superior formal education. In her treatment of education in *Iola Leroy*, Harper focuses as much on gender as on race. In this regard, she differs significantly from most African American male novelists of the nineteenth century. Her formation of the principal mulatto women in *Iola Leroy* argues that women have intellectual capacities at least on par with men. Her stance in this instance echoes arguments found in nonfiction works by and about black women as well as in white women's fictional treatments of the southern white belle. Moreover, the situation as Harper depicts it is drawn from life, for it was not uncommon in the South for white fathers who were emotionally attached to their mulatto children to send these children to school in the North.

Like Clarence Garie Sr., the unnamed senator in *Imperium in Imperio* undertakes the tutorial education of his slave and future wife, Fairfax Belgrave. As time passes Fairfax improves her intellect and refines her education. "Mrs. Belgrave," the narrator says, "was a woman with very superior education. The range of her reading was truly remarkable. She possessed the finest library ever seen in the northern section of Virginia, and all the best of the latest books were constantly arriving at her home. Magazines and newspapers arrived by every mail. Thus she was thoroughly abreast with the times" (84). The narrator's comment appears to be a reference to Jefferson, whose private library was one of the best in America during his era (it became the nucleus of the Library of Congress), and he has been considered one of the most learned Americans of his time.[12] Thus, deviating significantly from the chivalric mode of white female subjectivity on which he in part bases Fairfax's character, Griggs makes her intellectual capacities superior to both white women and white men.

The authors use a plethora of hyperbolic terms to sketch the portraits of these mulatto women. The degree of their superior intelligence and formal education gradually increases as the novels developed chronologically, culminating in Griggs's characterization of Fairfax Belgrave. The progression appears justified, for blacks' quest for literacy in the antebellum period grew into their passion for formal education after the war. In fact, the historical counterpart for these women's mental capacity can readily be found among the post-1865 "black aristocracy."[13] Even so, the southern black aristocracy was more inclined to sustain its liminal place in the overall social structure than to merge socially with the white mainstream or with the black masses. Nevertheless, in arguing for the inclusion of blacks in the mainstream, African American novelists' formation of their centered female subjects reflects the novelists' desire to create characters representative of the race. Yet in their attempt to portray the race in a favorable light, these novelists in effect offer exceptional, not representative, black women.

The third rite of passage tests and affirms these women's sexual morality. The formulaic plot of these novels requires that the ritual subject be sexually "pure" for aggregation to occur. To create a state of purity without totally violating the historical reality in which they situate these subjects, the novelists contrive "marriages" for most of the women. This manipulation of plot speaks in part to the novelists' desire to defend black women (and thus the race) against the age-old claim that blacks were by nature licentious. To defend black women's character and at the same time to portray the gender's perilous situation as a victim of white men's random sexual abuse is a problem that the novelists attempt to resolve by situating their novels more firmly in the mode of social romance than in social realism.

Again, the women in *Clotel* exhibit the literary norm and its standard deviations for the pre–World War I African American novel. Consistent with a chivalric code, it would have been imprudent for the novelists to include detailed accounts of sexual indiscretions involving these women. Brown's comments on the topic are, in the main, indirect, and at times his authorial comments contradict narrative situations in the novel. He points out, for instance, that in "all the cities and towns of the slave states, the real negro, or clear black, does not amount to more than one in every four of the slave population" (36). The statement is fairly accurate and points to the pervasiveness of miscegenation.[14] Elsewhere in the novel he states, "Every married woman in the far South looks upon her husband as unfaithful, and regards every quadroon servant as a rival" (114).[15] He holds slave women partially accountable for what he calls this "league with crime" (82) when he states, disapprovingly, that "most of the slave women have no higher aspiration than that of becoming the finely-dressed mistress of some white man" (40). Comments such as these in *Clotel* hint at the sexual liberties white males took with enslaved black females. Brown, however, generally makes his women's situations exceptions to the rules.

He sanctions the union between Horatio and Clotel as a marriage in heart and heaven before he includes any mention of sexual relations (the birth of their daughter) between the couple. With this manipulation of plot, Brown is able to affirm Clotel's sexual morality as a representative black woman. The contrivance allows him to present a historical situation without completely violating its accuracy. Once Horatio legally marries a white woman, he proposes that Clotel remain his mistress. Clotel, however, true to her portraiture as a chivalric heroine, finds the suggestion repugnant. She will not be an adulterer; therefore, she remains celibate after her separation from Horatio, despite her many trials through various areas and conditions of the slavocracy. The narrator concludes that she rejects Horatio's proposition because "she had the heart of a true woman" and "her spirit was too pure to form a selfish league with crime" (82).

Brown repeats, with slight variations, this discursive formation to validate the virtue of the novel's other ritual subjects. The extraordinary beauty of all five of these women is simultaneously their greatest liability and their greatest asset (for their owners and for themselves). Their beauty is their greatest liability in that it leads directly to their commodification and thus to their exchange value, a situation grounded in historical reality. But in the novel's plot, their beauty also is their greatest protection against total objectification and commodification, a situation that is not as realistic.

All of these women are sold in a lower South slave market, where their potential to produce sexual pleasure for white males rather than their potential to produce other commodities (including slave children) determines their exchange value. The lower South historically has been depicted in history and in literature as a region in which a slave's humanity was more viciously assaulted than in the upper South. New Orleans, where the focal women in *Clotel* are sold, was infamous as an important regional slave-labor market that catered to white "gentlemen" who wanted to purchase "fancy girls" (particularly bright and white mulattoes).[16] But with virtue as their armor, the women in *Clotel* use their captivating beauty and charm and their intelligence to prevent assaults on their virtue. Brown contrives the plot so that the men who purchase these women to satisfy their sexual appetites end up purchasing wives rather than mistresses. The notable exceptions are Ellen and Jane: Ellen commits suicide and Jane dies of a broken heart, yet each dies with her chastity intact.

Later nineteenth-century novelists use basically the same discursive formation to affirm their heroines' virtue. Webb makes Emily Garie the mistress of her owner, Clarence Garie Sr., but portrays the relationship as thoroughly virtuous. Garie buys Emily specifically to exploit her sexually, but her charm and refinement cause him to abandon his original design and he forsakes "the connection that might have been productive of many evils" (2). Before they consummate the relationship, the two marry in heart (and later in fact).

Harper casts Iola Leroy in a similar idealized mold. Circumstances following the death of her father-master reduce Iola to the status of other slaves, and she is left at the mercy of a lustful new master. In effect, Harper inverts this rite of passage. Prior to her father's death, Iola lived as and believed that she was a white person. With the changes that her father-master's death precipitates, Iola does not move from separation through transition to incorporation into the dominant society. Rather, she is ejected from the incorporation phase and placed in the separation phase. She is denied the liminal status of a mulatto with privileges greater than those accorded to typical slaves. Consequently, Iola should be prime prey for white men's sexual abuse. But Harper glosses over Iola's vulnerability and instead emphasizes her stoicism in resisting the expected consequences of her enslaved state. After the Emancipation Proclamation, Iola is, of course, a bastion of virtue and rejects any situation that might compromise or defame her honorable state of chastity.

Griggs continues the rather stock situation of exalting the black heroine's virtue. Fairfax Belgrave grows into strikingly attractive womanhood in the household of a prominent southern gentleman, the senator, who falls "madly in love with her" but restrains himself from even propositioning her until both admit their mutual affection. Fairfax, however, finds the propositions repugnant. She easily persuades the senator to forgo any illicit intentions and marry her, though the marriage is performed in Canada and kept secret (89). Even though Fairfax lives alone in a house with her master and would-be lover, she has little trouble staving off any intentions he might have of violating her virtue. Griggs presents the situation rather matter-of-factly, as if it were typical. In these novels, contrary to the general historical setting, the slave woman is given a choice. As the novelists inscribe the formation, the woman's slightest objection deters any unwanted advances.

Marriage is the principal mechanism for affirming sexual purity. Moreover, when the novelists construct a bright or white mulatto woman as a liminal character, her marriage to a white man functions as the final transitional rite of her passage, signifying her incorporation into the white race and thus into the American Eden and her (re)incorporation into the Adamic (human) family. As an individual rite, the subject's marriage to a white man is essentially a rite of union with another person, and thus the marriage argues that mulattoes merit inclusion in the human family. When a novelist uses the woman to represent the black race, her marriage to a white man argues for the inclusion of all blacks in the human family. As Arnold van Gennep states, "Some rites [of incorporation] are both individual and collective": they "have a collective significance, either in joining one or the other of the individuals to new groups or in uniting two or more groups" (132). In addition, van Gennep posits that the marriage rite also has the power to bestow a "soul" upon the person as part of his or her incorporation rite (133). These ideas certainly are implicit in the function of interracial marriages in the pre–World War I novel. When the novelist argues for the race generally, the interracial marriage rite is a symbolic action calling for the joining not only of the liminal mulatto subgroup to a new group (whites) but also of the black race to the human race. In asserting that blacks were subhuman, whites contended blacks lacked souls. Thus, the interracial marriage certifies that blacks do indeed possess souls.

However, an interracial marriage is not often the resolution to the plight of the principal white mulatto subjects in African American novels before World War I: this type of closure is usually reserved for secondary characters or for the pre–Civil War setting. Rejecting this type of resolution not only allows the novelists to keep their emplotments within the broad confines of social realism but also permits them to help justify their use of bright and white mulattoes to represent the black race. In most instances, the resolution to the mulatto character's plight is her marriage to a black man or her death, either of which signifies her relegation to a permanently liminal state.

In *Clotel*, there is neither a quasi-legal nor mock ceremonial marriage between Currer and Jefferson, and Jefferson does not intend or desire to marry her. The other interracial unions in *Clotel* and most of those in the other novels under consideration in this chapter are sanctioned by some type of marriage ceremony, though not always a legal one. Yet one should not conclude that the novelists who use interracial marriages as symbolic rituals of (re)aggregation are condoning or encouraging interracial marriages per se. In spite of Brown's idealization of character and situation, he does not stray in *Clotel* from his purpose of exposing the ills of slavery. The content of *Clotel* and of other African American novels of the century indicates that these writers consider marriage as the minimum prerequisite for a sexual union between a white man and a black woman. Brown opens *Clotel* with an extended discussion of marriage as a sacred institution, and he considers the denial of this institution to slaves one of the slavocracy's most inhumane and destructive acts: "The marriage relation, the oldest and most sacred institution given to man by his Creator, is unknown and unrecognized in the slave laws of the United States" (37). The denial of marriage to slaves degrades them morally and shows the degradation of the slaveholding class and "undermines the entire social condition of man" (39). Brown asserts that marriage is "the first and most important institution of human existence—the foundation of all civilisation and culture" (38). The author's stance on marriage is key to his "narrative of slave life" (39); it defines his major thematic concerns and controls the manner in which he handles plot structure and subject formation. African American novelists through World War I adapted Brown's pattern.

Clotel's marriage to Horatio Green occurs without a public ceremony; therefore, it neither bestows a soul upon Clotel nor gains her entry into the human race and thus into the white mainstream. Mary (Clotel's daughter) legally marries a white man in a public ceremony in France; thus, it constitutes a rite of passage that incorporates Mary into the white race but not into the American Eden. The marriages of Althesa, Emily Garie, and Marie Leroy to white men are legally and socially sanctioned only for as long as their racial identity remains concealed from the public. In each case the ceremony effects only a temporary passage for the subject into the American Eden. The slavocracy's power structure nullifies each marriage and reassigns the woman to a liminal state, and the subsequent and premature death of each of these women relegates her to a state of permanent liminality. After the death of Eugene Leroy, the ruling elite nullifies his marriage to Marie, redefines her as subhuman, and thus reassigns her to a state of separation reserved for slaves as property. Fairfax Belgrave's legal marriage to a white man remains intact, but because it is secret, the ceremonial rite never enables her passage out of the liminal condition for mulattoes. Thus, bright and white mulatto women in the African American novel before World War I almost never successfully complete the final rite of passage into the American mainstream.

White Male Subjectivity and the Cult of Chivalry

Subject formation for the white male in these novels who is involved romantically with a black woman closely resembles that of the young cavalier in southern white literature and life of the nineteenth century.[17] African American novels typically portray this character as a gentleman of honor from the middle class or the aristocracy. When associated with the antebellum plantation, he is an owner rather than an overseer. When not a plantation owner, he usually is a professional who is ambitious, successful, and often wealthy. Fairfax Belgrave's husband in *Imperium in Imperio* is a prominent U.S. senator, and Jefferson and Green in *Clotel* are statesmen. In *Clotel*, Althesa's husband, Henry Morton, is a successful and prominent physician, as is Iola Leroy's suitor, Dr. Gresham. Mary's first husband is a wealthy Frenchman, and Clarence Garie and Eugene Leroy both are wealthy planter aristocrats.

In each case the man's social position and thus his honor among whites remain intact as long as he does not violate the informal code that stipulates that he not marry the woman or treat her in public as if they were. An interracial marriage would be a symbolic action conferring personhood upon the black woman, a condition the ruling society found objectionable. This same white male–dominated society at different junctures during the nineteenth century outlawed interracial marriage, yet on several occasions refused to outlaw concubinage of white men and black women.[18] In this instance, discursive formations that align society and subjectivity reinscribe historical reality; in other instances, the formations stray markedly from historical reality.

All of the beaux in the novels foregrounded in this chapter are kind and compassionate, and in some cases they initially are drawn to these women out of pity for their degraded state. Cast in the mold of a chivalrous knight, the men therefore believe it their duty to act as champions and protectors of the black woman's virtue, despite their knowledge of her racial ancestry and despite the fact that the southern code of honor among white men did not apply to their relations with black women.[19] Each of them (except Jefferson) is a romantic hero in some way or another who immediately falls in love, usually at first sight, with his prospective "wife."

The men are attracted to a black woman whose body surface (her physiology) signifies whiteness rather than blackness. The signification is compounded in that all the women (except Currer) are exceptionally refined and exhibit only a bare minimum of psychological, intellectual, and social characteristics (other than their legal status) usually associated with an enslaved condition. The novelists, therefore, forgo the opportunity to explore the complex psychology of the southern white male within the context of miscegenation.

As oppositional discourse, these novels are designed to revise texts of the plantation idyll and the chivalric tradition by emphasizing the historical reality of black-white relations; as instruments for social change, they argue for blacks' incorporation into the mainstream. But the novelists' construction of white male characters as chivalrous knights seriously undermines these purposes, especially when these male characters are native Southerners (as most of them are). Story (in this instance, a plot ostensibly intended to replicate historical and social reality) conflicts with discourse (the manner in which the story is told) to such an extent that a novel's textual components contradict one another. More specifically, white male subject formation and story are at odds. It is quite credible that in many instances liaisons between white men and black women in the nineteenth-century South conformed to the century's chivalric code of behavior, given the cult of chivalry's hold on southern society at large. So in these novels, this aspect of story is not a problem within itself, for there were certainly many more instances of this situation than these novels present. It also is quite credible that numerous white men refrained from raping black women to whom they were sexually attracted and who rebuffed their sexual advances, as is the situation in several of these novels.

The assertion is not, therefore, that these white male characters' chivalrous treatment of black women is without a historical base. Indeed, one finds such a historical formation in Harriet Jacobs's slave narrative, *Incidents in the Life of a Slave Girl* (1861). Through her portraiture of Dr. Flint, Jacobs conveys the psychological complexity of a southern white man who sexually exploits several of his female slaves but whose sense of honor conflicts with and restrains his sexual passions for Jacobs, whom he ostensibly loves.

White male subjectivity in nineteenth-century African American novels is so at variance with some of the novels' other components that it challenges their textual logic and pushes them dangerously close to becoming self-deconstructive texts. The novels' rhetorical stance argues that blacks are just as human as whites and thus should be treated accordingly. Though their centered subjects are white mulattoes, the novels sustain the argument through the subjects' representational roles. However, the argument's force is diminished when these women's white beaux assume representational functions. The novelists align the centered women's subjectivity so closely with the idealized white woman prototype that they in effect erase the women's blackness—their difference. They use white beaux whose characterizations argue for discounting racial difference, yet they do not allow these men to confront (except in the abstract) the difference. They use these men's characterizations representationally to decry white males' sexual abuse of black women, but these men do not sexually abuse the women with whom they are involved. The novelists rarely dramatize the white male's objectification of the black woman through minor white male characters.

Clotel exemplifies the norm in pre-1900 novels. Brown decries the New Orleans slave market (which favored Virginia slaves, especially mulattoes) for pandering to white men's sexual proclivities for bright and white mulattoes. But narrative situations in *Clotel* do not dramatize—in fact, they belie—the novel's rhetorical stance toward this historical situation. In practically all instances, white male characters in *Clotel* are so chivalrous that they refrain from forcing extramarital sexual relations with black women whom they purchase primarily for this purpose. Though *Clotel* and other novels proffer plot devices intended to minimize the text's self-deconstruction—such as making the interracial marriage short-lived by having one of the partners die prematurely—such devices are not sufficient to restore completely the respective novel's textual logic.

In the generation following the Civil War, the chivalric tradition assumed two primary forms in southern life, the pastoral and the Negrophobic, both of them mechanisms for excluding blacks from the mainstream.

(Chapter 4 explores the Negrophobic form in detail.) Built upon a romantic image of the Old South's social structure that antebellum mythmakers had constructed largely from the pages of medieval and contemporary romances, this pastoral form of the chivalric tradition significantly defined society and subjectivity in southern whites' literature and in their lives.

Before the Civil War, Americans in general were attracted to the romantic novels of Sir Walter Scott and other writers of chivalric literature. For many white Southerners, however, the line between fact and fiction was narrowly drawn; at times, it was obliterated. It was not unusual to find upper-class antebellum Southerners acting out the rituals of chivalric literature, both in staged events, such as tournaments, and in the rituals of their daily lives.[20] These aristocrats as well as the chivalric literature they read and wrote provided the social models for many Southerners following the Civil War. According to Jay Martin, "Young Southerners after the War began to call themselves 'disinherited knights' and gathered together to hold what they styled 'tournaments,' modeled after the jousts in *Ivanhoe*."[21] To be sure, after the war as before there was a reciprocal relationship between southern white literature and life.

The pastoral form of the chivalric tradition in postbellum southern white literature has been identified with a group of writers known as the Plantation School. Among them, Thomas Nelson Page was foremost in re-creating in fiction the myth of an Edenic plantation South. Literary critics long have considered Page's short story "Marse Chan" to be the quintessence of this mythopoeic discourse. This school of writers nostalgically viewed the Old South as a utopian society. To a large extent, their fictive version of antebellum life was predicated on what they viewed as harmonious relations between blacks and whites during the slavocracy. As they saw it, the Civil War destroyed the harmony of these relations and the ordered society that revolved around them. By analogy, then, the Civil War destroyed the South's Eden.

Some southern white imaginative writers outside the Plantation School were even more explicit in their use of the Eden trope. For instance, Sidney Lanier in his long poem "Psalm of the West" envisions America as the New World Eden. Though in this poem he includes the South as part of this American Eden, he does not concentrate on the region as a separate or distinct garden. In his other writings, particularly those in which he contrasts the Old South with the New South, Lanier is more specific. For example, in *Shakespeare and His Forerunners* (1902), a collection of lectures that Lanier gave in the late 1870s, he exhorts his audience to read the Elizabethan poets, who elevated the woman to "adorable heights of worship" and gave "to all earnest men and strong lovers . . . a dear ritual and litany of chivalric devotion." The poets "enlightened us with . . . celestial revelation of the possible Eden which the modern Adam and Eve may win back for themselves by faithful and generous affection."[22] Lanier wrote several books about the chivalric age, many of them for boys—budding white southern beaux who were to rebuild the Southern Paradise that had been lost.

Racist propagandists between the Civil War and World War I also utilized the Eden trope in nonliterary discourse. For instance, in 1900 Professor Charles Carroll published *"The Negro a Beast," or, "In the Image of God,"* a book in which he asserts that an "ape-like" black man, not a "snake," actually tempted Eve (215–23). In 1902 he published *The Tempter of Eve*, in which he asserts "that the beast of the field which tempted Eve was a negress" (402). Drawing a parallel between the Fall of Man and the fall of the Old South, Carroll also maintains that miscegenation was the Old South's great sin, and that God destroyed the slavocracy because of this transgression (*"The Negro a Beast,"* ch. 9, esp. 290–91).

Most white Southerners of the time probably would not have agreed totally with this statement because to have done so would have been tantamount to defaming the generic antebellum white man. Whites' concept of honor was pervasive and was closely aligned with their principles of sexual morality. To suggest that southern upper- and middle-class white men were responsible for the large number of mulattoes among the black population was to affront the concept of honor. So those who regarded plantation idyll literature as an accurate reflection of antebellum society must have concluded (to paraphrase Mary Boykin Chesnut) that mulattoes just dropped from the clouds (diary, 21–22).

By using white belles and beaux as models for their novels' centered subjects and their major white male characters, nineteenth-century African American novelists tacitly corroborate the white South's cult of chivalry as a social ideology, for their appropriation of these character types is not primarily to burlesque or to satirize the chivalric tradition. Among this group, the novelist who most fully appropriates, repeats, and affirms the pastoral form of the chivalric tradition is J. McHenry Jones in his *Hearts of Gold* (1896), a novel in which aristocratic blacks' social rituals duplicate those of their southern white counterparts. But Jones does not model his heroine (whose portrait he draws primarily from the period's black aristocracy) and his major white male characters on the belle and beau prototypes, and thus he prevents *Hearts of Gold* from becoming a self-deconstructive text.

A Renaissance of Chivalry: The House Behind the Cedars

In Charles Waddell Chesnutt's *The House Behind the Cedars* (1900) the components of nineteenth-century African American novels first cohere in a manner that produces an artistically sophisticated novel. Chesnutt is no less concerned with the advance of blacks than were his predecessors, but he is more dutifully and successfully attentive to fictional craft than they were. *Cedars*'s themes, settings, subject formations, allusions, language, and other textual features coalesce harmoniously under the Eden myth as trope. Chesnutt uses the permutations the myth had assumed in the South from the colonial period through post-Reconstruction to embellish the novel's fictional techniques. But he directs *Cedars*'s dialogic and intertextual thrusts primarily to the South's "renaissance of chivalry" (47), the permutation of the Eden myth in effect during the novel's setting and its publication year.

In a broad sense, *Cedars* is about race relations in the post–Civil War South. It incorporates the region's social, psychological, political, and literary histories as they affected black-white relations and defined southern subjects up to the time of the novel's setting. *Cedars* centers the experiences of the Walden family—Rena, her brother, John, and her mother, Molly. In their representational functions, these three characters' lives recapitulate in several ways the dilemmas many blacks faced after the Civil War when they tried to move closer to the social structure's center. More particularly, their lives as mulatto liminals typify various social structures aligned with the Eden trope as it was applied to race relations. Part black and part white, Rena and John are the mediation between polar racial opposites. On one level the novel's plot structure therefore concerns the attempt to reconcile these oppositions. The reconciliation would be these characters' transition in the social structure from liminality to incorporation by successfully passing for white, which John achieves but which Rena does not (a fuller discussion of John follows in chapter 3).

The novel's primary story line builds to the tragic consequences of Rena

Walden's aborted rites of passage into the white mainstream. She is the illegitimate daughter of a prominent white gentleman and his free black mistress. Born free during the slavery era, Rena is relegated to a liminal status in the antebellum South's social structure. As a white mulatto, she grew up socially separated from both the slave class and the slaveholding class. Emancipation, declared when Rena was a young adult, was supposed to incorporate both slaves and free blacks into the mainstream of southern life. It did not. For bright mulattoes such as Molly Walden, emancipation even diminished the advantages their liminal status afforded them during the antebellum period. For white mulattoes such as Rena and John, emancipation accented their status as liminals. Thus, while Rena and John enjoy a more privileged lifestyle than do most dark-complexioned blacks in their community, they nevertheless remain social and racial pariahs. Like his nineteenth-century predecessors, Chesnutt uses these white mulatto subjects to represent alternately the black race and its mulatto subgroup.

By analogy, Rena Walden's story is the dilemma ex-slaves faced immediately after slavery. Emancipation did not remove the stigmas and repercussions attached to being black in the South. The survival of Old South ways and thoughts among whites proved too formidable a barrier for most first-generation freedmen seeking entry into the South's mainstream. Rena also represents those mulatto liminals who straddled the color line. Thus, Chesnutt appropriately sets the novel "a few years after the Civil War" (1), the transitional period between the Old South and the New South when racial, social, political, and other oppositional forces were supposed to be reconciled and when blacks would enjoy their millennium in the New World Eden.

The novel opens with a heavily symbolic setting that establishes the Eden myth as a framing construct. The Waldens (including John until he was a young adult) live in a house bordered by a hedge of dwarf cedar trees. The cedar hedge, which symbolically isolates the House of Walden from the outside world, in effect signifies the mulatto family's liminal condition (Eden after the Fall) in Patesville, North Carolina, where they live. For the novel's heroine, Rena, the cedar hedge also signifies a condition metaphorically equivalent to Eden before the Fall, for it symbolically shields her from the outside world's negative influences. Chesnutt uses the house's garden as a focal point to frame Rena's introduction into the novel. The imagistic patterns that help establish this garden setting's ecology associate her with Eve in the biblical Garden as well as with the prototypical white belle in the Southern Garden. Through the novel's imagery, language, and incident, Chesnutt fuses the Garden of Eden and the Southern Garden to constitute a single trope and to foreshadow the tragic events that later occur. Thus, theme, setting, and imagistic patterns are mutually supportive as they relate to Rena's story.

The garden setting that opens the novel foreshadows the cosmogonic sin Rena will commit in the Southern Garden by attempting to pass for white. Her transgression against the white South's social code will precipitate her metaphorical fall from grace (for which punishment is death). In this garden setting she meets the archetypal tempter, her brother, John. The two sets of twin trees (magnolias and elms) (11) in the Waldens' garden not only suggest the twin trees in the Garden of Eden (the Tree of Knowledge of Good and Evil and the Tree of Life) but also are symbolically relevant to the mythic history of the South in particular and of America in general. The magnolia trees associate Rena with the southern white belle mystique, which connotes innocence, goodness, and a lack of knowledge (including sexual experience) about evil. As a symbol, the magnolia trees prefigure the identity Rena later will seek as a member of the southern white aristocracy.

In the social history from which this novel draws, to be white is to be free. Chesnutt incorporates America's pre–Civil War manifestations of the Eden myth to emphasize that for Rena (as for John) passing for white is a means for attaining freedom. The elm trees in the Waldens' garden link Rena to the concept of liberty associated with the American Revolution. The Liberty Tree, which originated as an elm tree, was a symbol of the colonists' struggle for life, liberty, and the pursuit of happiness. Depending on the geographical region, the Liberty Tree sometimes was an oak, a pine, or a cedar tree rather than an elm; the symbolism occasionally was embodied in a mere pole. But regardless of the kind of tree the colonists used, the symbolic significance was the same as that of the original Liberty Tree (an elm) in Boston. In America's mythic history as it extended from the revolutionary period, the Liberty Tree took on cosmic and religious significance and political and sexual connotations.[23]

With the setting established, the novel's action begins when a stranger from South Carolina enters Rena's "cedar-bordered garden" (14) world of innocence. This stranger is her estranged brother, John, who at this point in the novel's chronology is actually a white man. But Rena doesn't "know [John] from Adam" (18). Metaphorically, he is a serpent in her garden world, the devil in disguise. John tempts her to violate one of the mainstream society's taboos—to pass for white. In succumbing to his seductive urgings, she replicates her mother's precipitous fall in that a white man (John, in this instance) is the agent for her transgression (as the social structure would define it). She moves with him to South Carolina, and the contrast between South Carolina and North Carolina appropriately supports the novel's plot structure within the context of the Eden trope. The differences in their lives in the two settings in many ways mirror the historical contrast between Old World culture in Europe and New World culture in colonial and antebellum America. Chesnutt incorporates the colonial permutations of America's Eden myth principally through setting and plot.

Virginia and South Carolina constituted the epitome of New World culture, especially in colonial America. In North Carolina the Waldens live essentially in an Old World setting where social stratification is the order of the day. Further, their roots in this setting are exemplified in part by the books that comprise their library as well as by the vestiges of Old South culture that define and limit them. Like the original English settlers, Rena and John also migrate to a locale in which, they believe, their visions of an utopian life can be concretized. Within this context, South Carolina represents this New World order. Indeed, Clarence, South Carolina, in comparison to Patesville, North Carolina, suggests the status Charleston held during the colonial period. Like Williamsburg of the Old Dominion, Charleston was a showplace for the colonial development and prominence of New World aristocracy with its ties to Old World culture.

The biblical myth of Eden and the American colonial, revolutionary, and antebellum appropriations and transformations of it function in the novel's opening chapters as a tropological framework to establish its principal themes and to identify Rena as its centered subject. After the opening chapters, Chesnutt uses the postbellum white South's transformation and application of the Eden myth, its chivalric tradition, to undergird the novel's thematic and structural symmetry, to advance its plot, and to embellish the construction of its principal subjects.

When Chesnutt first introduces the reader to Clarence society, he presents it in the context of the age of chivalry, complete with tournament, the queen of love and beauty, and other direct references to the chivalric tradition. When the elite of Clarence's white society selects Rena as the queen of love and beauty at a local tournament, the selection certifies that Rena's masquerade as a white woman has been successful. Rena's coronation also sets in motion the events that will define the rest of the novel's plot, lead to Rena's demise, and seriously threaten John's ability to continue to live as a member of white society.

Chesnutt in part attributes the South's modern-day chivalry to the influence of chivalric literature. During the tournament season in this area of South Carolina, the narrator points out, the "local bookseller" quickly sells all of his copies of *Ivanhoe* and takes orders for more: "The tournament scene in this popular novel furnished the model after which these bloodless imitations of the ancient passages-at-arms were conducted, with such variations as were required to adapt them to a different age and civilization" (45–46). The white aristocracy and "poorer whites" as well as "colored folks" attend the tournament, indicating that each level of the social structure is involved to some degree in this major social ritual, which itself affirms the social hierarchy. It is a ritual of aggregation that distinguishes the elite class from the rest of society and reinforces the social myth.

But the influences of the chivalric tradition on the lives of people in this area of South Carolina (and by extension on the South of this era) go far beyond frequent reenactments of the tournament. The tradition pervades lives and shapes interpersonal relations. At the tournament Rena meets George Tryon and begins what whites (if they knew her racial identity) would consider a deadly threat to the Southern Way of Life—miscegenation. Through several of the novel's white characters Chesnutt reveals how thoroughly the cult of chivalry shapes whites' perspectives on reality. For instance, one character at the tournament speaks of Tryon's attraction to Rena as a "romantic situation" out of the age of chivalry: "If George were but masked and you were veiled," she says to Rena, "we should have a romantic situation—you the mysterious damsel in distress, he the unknown champion" (52). This sort of dialogue not only emphasizes the theme of chivalry but also connects that theme to the racial issue in the novel through the thematic and imagistic uses of masks and veils, thereby embellishing characterization. Developing the romance between Rena and Tryon against the background of the chivalric tradition, Chesnutt gives an ironic twist to Tryon's knightly character by unmasking him and thus peeling away the chivalrous veneer of the class of southern gentlemen and beaux that Tryon represents. As did his predecessors, Chesnutt models the novel's leading white male character on the prototypical southern white beau. But unlike his predecessors, Chesnutt uses this characterization as a vehicle for exposing the pernicious effects of the South's cult of chivalry (even its milder form) on black life.

In addition to incidents, aspects of setting, and direct authorial-narrative commentary, Chesnutt includes other trappings of the chivalric tradition to develop the novel. Rena's new name is a signification of her change in racial identity, a reconstruction of self from chivalric texts. As a new social self she is Rowena Warwick (her first name from Scott's *Ivanhoe* and her surname from Edward Bulwer Lytton's *The Last of the Barons* [1843]). As Rowena Warwick, she is a modern-day replica of a chivalric heroine. Her racial-ethnic duality also recalls the combined roles of Rowena and the Jewish Rebecca in *Ivanhoe*. In addition, the name of Rena's beau, George Tryon (whom she meets in Clarence, South Carolina), recalls George of Clarence, a character in *The Last of the Barons.*

In (re)constructing their social selves, the Walden siblings conjoin biblical and literary myths. Like many southern whites of the time, John in essence derives his subjectivity from chivalric literature and uses biblical mythology to validate his claim as one of society's "chosen" people. Rena reluctantly follows suit. Eventually, after her attempts to gain entrance into the Edenic society are shattered, she determines not to try again. She vows that she will remain in the permanently liminal position blacks have been assigned in society, and by doing so she will be following God's will (180–81).

Chesnutt merges elements of the chivalric tradition with trappings of the biblical Eden myth to develop a perspective on miscegenation, which he uses as the sine qua non of black-white relations. As Chesnutt uses them, the chivalric tradition and the Bible's Eden myth suggest the continuity between the past and the present. More specifically, they suggest that in southern society the sins of the fathers and the mothers account for much of the suffering in their children's lives. As in the biblical myth, the sin exacts greater penance from the woman than from the man—more from Rena than from John and more from Miss Molly than from her lover. In *Cedars*, the unpardonable sin is indeed miscegenation, and the Waldens are human symbols of the South's transgression. As did several of his predecessors, Chesnutt focuses his theme on a mother-daughter nexus: the daughter's position in the social structure must follow her mother's condition.

Considering the mores of the antebellum South, the novel's narrative voice questions whether Molly Walden committed a sin (either against biblical law or the South's social law) by being involved in a sexual affair with a white man. The narrator concludes, "If she had sinned, she had been more sinned against than sinning" (28). Indeed, her status as a mulatto mistress gave her a fixed place in the structure of southern antebellum society. Her marginal status (because she was a free black, a mulatto, and a prominent white man's mistress) placed her "betwixt and between" the slave class and the slaveholding class. Her white beau protected and shielded her as a knight would protect and shield his lady from the harsher realities of life. Under the circumstances, Molly's life was about as paradisical as a black's could be during the slavocracy, but the emancipation and her lover's death destroyed her Edenic existence. After the slavocracy had been destroyed, neither her status as mulatto nor that as former mistress entitled her to a privileged position in the post–Civil War Eden.

Having once lived on the outer edge of the antebellum white Eden, Molly Walden now is ejected completely from the Eden of the New South. The days of the plantation idyll and chivalry when her liminal place in society was assured are irrevocably lost. Because "she was not white [and] was shut out from this seeming paradise . . . she did not sympathize greatly with the new era opened up for the emancipated slaves, . . . and she sighed for the old days, because to her they had been the good days. Now, not only was her king dead, but the shield of his memory protected her no longer." With emancipation came "new standards of life and character," and Miss Molly as well as others in the society see her transgression in a different light (159–60). It is a sin for which she now must do penance.

Molly Walden is the matriarch (by analogy, the Eve) whose original sin is visited upon her children. Chesnutt uses direct references to the biblical Eden myth to examine critically her sexual union with one of the South's fair young sons, the coupling that produced John and Rena. Several times, the narrator and Miss Molly characterize her transgression as a sin. And indeed, many Negrophobes considered miscegenation a sin, even when it involved white men and black women, though those who held this opinion (including Miss Molly's lover) were in the minority.[24] As a result of her sin, Molly Walden is isolated in her house behind the cedars, a house for which shrubs, flowers, trees, and other plants create a garden setting but also furnish "additional shade and seclusion." In this condition, "the aspect of this garden must have been extremely sombre and depressing, and it might well have seemed a fit place to hide some guilty or disgraceful secret" (11).

There is a symbolic relationship between the space and the place the Waldens occupy in Patesville's social structure. Miss Molly having violated the laws of the South's Eden, is situated in a setting analogous to Eden after the Fall. Her physical isolation is a metaphor for her exclusion from mainstream society. Miss Molly's "disgraceful secret" is that "she had eaten of the fruit of the Tree of Knowledge" (143), and she now pays the penalty. With this reference, Chesnutt directly links miscegenation to the Bible's narrative of Eden. In addition, he uses the biblical myth tropologically to focus attention on the consequences of transgression for the woman rather than for the man.

Through various characters, actions, and narrative commentary, Chesnutt debates the miscegenation issue by using as reference points the biblical, sexual, and social myths that defined the South. He focuses, of course, on the narrative of Rena Walden's efforts to become a member of the dominant social order: her initial exclusion from the South's Eden, her entrance into it, and her final expulsion from it. This tripartite pattern aligns itself with the tropology-society-subjectivity nexus evident in African American novels that preceded *Cedars*

When Chesnutt first introduces Rena in the novel, it is clear that her biological heritage and her physiological attributes make her a viable ritual subject. She is in the separation phase, for she is without the educational training, the material or economic prosperity, the social status, and the (legal) racial identity that mainstream society demands for inclusion in its circle. In essence, she is not a southern belle as the plantation idyll or the post–Civil War chivalric South defined the type.[25] Once her brother and mother convince her that she can and must pass for white and, therefore, that she deserves to share in the fruits of the society, all three make preparations for her passage into the socially elite class of Clarence and thus into the white race. This constitutes the second stage (the liminal phase) of this tripartite pattern in the novel. First, she changes her name, an act designed to confer a new identity. Then she acquires the educational, economic, social, and racial status that the society requires to be a member of the white upper crust.

A member of the "chosen" society, John (at this point a white man) functions as her ritual guide as she undergoes the transitional process designed to effect her incorporation into the human family. He sends her to boarding school to become refined rather than to become educated, in essence, to fit her for her ornamental role as a southern white belle in this society. In treating Rena's intellect, Chesnutt deviates significantly from his predecessors, who exalted their heroines' mental capacities. Rena shares in John's material and economic wealth, which gives her access to the socially elite circles of Clarence. Finally, as the penultimate rite of passage in this liminal phase, she is accorded that society's highest honors when she is crowned the Queen of Love and Beauty at a tournament and thus declared the epitome of southern white womanhood by a young present-day white knight, George Tryon. These events pave the way for the ultimate rite of aggregation, her betrothal and pending marriage to Tryon, which would make her a legal member of the society.

But Tryon discovers Rena's racial ancestry before the marriage takes place, and this knowledge produces a drastic alteration in his mind and character. To convey this alteration, Chesnutt blends fairy lore, medieval romance, southern chivalry, and motifs from the biblical narrative of Eden. He also draws attention to Rena's body as a text that Tryon reinscribes to fit a Negrophobic mold. Foregrounding (typically through inversion) several motifs (dreams, magic, transformation, and so forth) from fairy-tale discourse, Chesnutt presents Tryon's epiphany through a dream in which the young knight witnesses Rena's transformation from Beauty to Beast: "In all her fair young beauty she stood before him, and then by some hellish magic she was slowly transformed into a hideous black hag. With agonized eyes he watched her beautiful tresses become wisps of coarse wool, wrapped round with dingy cotton strings; he saw her clear eyes grow bloodshot, her ivory teeth turn to unwholesome fangs. With a shudder he awoke, to find the cold gray dawn of a rainy day stealing through the window" (146–47). Though in his mind Tryon has transformed Rena from a beautiful southern belle to a "hideous black hag," he nevertheless views her now as an object of sexual desire, another discursive formation from the nineteenth-century African American novel that Chesnutt modifies in *Cedars* and that is consistent with social reality. Tryon choosing a black woman as his wife would violate the southern code of honor; choosing one as his mistress would not.

Tryon's discovery of Rena's race is the transitional device that moves the novel to the third stage of its tripartite structural pattern. In this stage her final transitional rite (marriage) is aborted and she is expelled from the South's Eden (literally from Edenic South Carolina). She returns to North Carolina, Eden after the Fall, and resumes her liminal position. In her metaphorical fallen state Rena assumes a role typical of mulatto heroines in previous African American novels—she becomes a teacher, which emphasizes her practical rather than her ornamental function in society. But her contented state in Patesville is short lived, because having committed the ultimate transgression (consistent with the biblical myth of Eden), she must pay the ultimate penalty—death, through which she is assigned to permanent liminality.

The ominous forest that provides the setting for Rena's demise functions as the closure for an imagistic pattern that Chesnutt uses to frame her story line. The imagistic pattern begins the novel with a setting reminiscent of Eden before the Fall (a topographical paradise) and ends with one reminiscent of Eden after the Fall (an ominous wilderness). Rena's plight literally concludes in a setting reminiscent of the wilderness image of America prominent among those colonial New Englanders who believed that the forest was a haven for the children of Satan and a setting that nurtured evil. Chesnutt similarly depicts this wilderness setting in *Cedars*. In Rena's mind, and given the descriptions of the setting Chesnutt provides, the forest is a haven for a depraved child of Satan, Jeff Wain, who lurks there "with evil passions" (271) and intends to violate Rena's virtue. Wain does not effect his design, but the ordeal to which he subjects her leads directly to her death.

In telling Rena's story, Chesnutt departs in several instances from the formula African American novelists used and the formula southern white plantation romanticists used in novels about mulatto heroines. Indeed, just when it appears that he is merely echoing stock sentiments, using stock devices, and creating well-worn characterizations, Chesnutt moves in entirely different directions and gives freshness and innovation to familiar situations and character types. The result is a well-wrought novel predicated on the Eden trope. *Cedars* brings to an apex the genre's first phase of development.

THREE

Beauties and Beasts

A Peculiar Sensation, This Double-Consciousness

IN MUCH OF white America's discourse on race, the Bible's Eden myth as trope is aligned with, incorporates, and interfaces other tropes, discourses, and signifying practices. The African American novel's fusion of the biblical story of Eden and the fairy tale "Beauty and the Beast" reflects and responds dialogically to how white society historically has interfaced these two "stories" as part of its discourse on race. Preceding Thomas Jefferson in the late 1700s and following Charles Carroll in the early twentieth century, Negrophobic discourse has read and written white bodies and black bodies as inscriptions of Beauty and Beast, respectively. Not only does Carroll explicitly read the black body as beast in *"The Negro a Beast,"* he also situates this reading specifically within the story of Eden as a framework and within the social construct (the chivalric tradition) that prevailed in the South at the beginning of this century. Carroll's text is a watershed in that it incorporates many of the published "scientific and biblical" studies on the discourse on race that helped constitute the Eden trope.

Fairy-tale discourse as it developed in Europe between the sixteenth and eighteenth centuries and as it underwent changes in Europe and the United States in the succeeding two centuries maintained its primary ideological function as an "institutionalized symbolic discourse on the civilizing process." [1] Discourse on race (particularly Negrophobic discourse) in America from the colonial period forward has addressed the socialization process—how, to what extent, or whether to incorporate blacks into the state. These two processes merge in the African American novel's discursive praxis. Among the common thematic links between the civilizing process and the socialization process are sexuality and transformation. In male-centered story lines and emplotments about passing, African American novelists make their subjects' minds and bodies focal, and they use the bodies as texts through which they write (and read) the men's individuated and representational selves as well as the larger society.

The African American novel usually appropriates Madame Jeanne-Marie Leprince de Beaumont's English version of "Beauty and the Beast" (1756). The novels differ significantly in how they tropologically adapt this tale. In general, though, the following morphological features of the tale as trope are common among pre-1940 novels: Beauty is a white woman, usually from the affluent class; Beast usually is a white mulatto man; a sexual union between the two (typically marriage or a prospective marriage) is the vehicle that completes (or should complete) the transformation of Beast (i.e., a black man) into a handsome prince (i.e., a white man). The pre-1940 novel occasionally inverts features of the generic tale, but after 1940, when seldom is the black male subject a white mulatto, such inversions are standard.

The convergence of tropology, society, and subjectivity under this form of miscegenation as rubric and the significance of this convergence in the genre's evolution can be exemplified through an examination of the male subject's formation in four novels: Frank J. Webb's *The Garies and Their Friends*, which introduces the formation's principal thematic and formalist features into the genre as a secondary plot line; Charles Chesnutt's *The House Behind the Cedars*, which draws heavily upon the Eden trope to expand the formation into a parallel plot; James Weldon Johnson's *The Autobiography of an Ex-Coloured Man* (1912), which centers the subject and explores more fully than any previous novel the subject's psychobiological duality; and George S. Schuyler's *Black No More* (1931), which builds upon the paradigm his predecessors constructed and innovatively updates it to include salient features of the early-twentieth-century's modifications of the Eden trope.

As a narrative of socialization, *The Garies* dramatizes several of the laws and customs—northern and southern—that regulated sexual unions between blacks and whites during the colonial and antebellum periods. For three-quarters of the novel, the author sympathetically treats the interracial union of Clarence Garie Sr. and his slave mistress, Emily Wilson. Intense social opposition to their marriage eventually precipitates the couple's death. At this point the novel focuses more sharply on the lives of the two children born of this union. By tracing the tragic fate of Clarence Garie Jr. Webb establishes the beauty-and-the-beast trope as a paradigm that subsequent African American novelists employ.

Webb's construction of Clarence Jr.'s psychobiological self argues in favor of the strong influence of environment on shaping racial attitudes and concepts of self. He contrasts the formation of Clarence's subjectivity with that of his younger sister, Emily, by having them grow up under quite different psychosocial circumstances following the deaths of their parents. The children grow up in different foster families (Emily in a black one and Clarence in a white one), which by some definitions could be considered abnormal family units. However, Webb's distinction between normal and abnormal as it relates to families and to individuals is not predicated on the individual's membership in the small family unit (whether biracial or foster) but primarily on his or her membership in the larger family unit (community or nation).

Consistent with Frantz Fanon's premises, Webb's construction of black subjectivity in this instance argues that the individual's normal or abnormal development is determined by whether or not the individual's racial identity coincides with the racial identity ("psychological sphere," to use Fanon's term) of her or his community/family.[2] By all social and legal definitions, both Emily and Clarence are black. Her psychological sphere, which includes her community/family, is black, and thus she develops into a normal adult. Clarence is a black who passes for white. His psychological sphere is white, and thus he develops into an abnormal adult.

The white environments in which Clarence lives never allow him to forget or escape the stigmas attached to being black. During his formative years his physical separation from blacks is accompanied by a psychological distancing from his African American heritage. Further, he imbibes his social environment's general disdain for blacks. By young adulthood, he has developed staunchly racist attitudes toward blacks in general and has come to hate himself because he is black. At this stage in his social maturation, he exists in a psychologically liminal state and is plagued by an identity crisis.

Clarence's dilemma, his abnormality, as a young adult stems primarily from the war within him in which the binary oppositions are black versus white, Beast versus Beauty, self versus Other. Webb creates a liminal character of psychological complexity and thus avoids a one-dimensional treatment of the psychic tensions endemic to this form of black male subjectivity (biraciality). In his formation of Clarence, Webb dramatizes what nearly half a century later W. E. B. Du Bois characterizes more generally as the African American's double-consciousness: "an American, a Negro; two souls, two thoughts, two unreconciled strivings; two warring ideals in one dark body, whose dogged strength alone keeps it from being torn asunder" (*Souls*, 3).

While living as a white man in New York, Clarence becomes engaged to a young white woman, Anne "Birdie" Bates. The episode dramatizes the tragic consequences of this subject's psychobiological duality. As a black, his betrothal to a white woman, a major incorporation rite for a mulatto liminal, prefigures what should be his final rite of passage (the marriage ceremonial) into the Anglo-American mainstream.[3] Webb provides dramatic tension for this segment of the story line by establishing the Bates family as affirmed racists before he has them learn of Clarence's racial identity. They regard all blacks as "if they were brutes," and Clarence occasionally joins them "in their heartless jests" about the race (325). His behavior in this instance and similar ones exhibits a classic symptom of the form of neurosis from which he suffers. With full knowledge that he is black, the neurotic subject nevertheless identifies with whites and, in Fanon's words, "subjectively adopts a white man's attitude."[4] In such a psychological state, the subject earnestly views whites as civilized and blacks as savages. Paranoia, irrationalism, and other psychological aberrations dictate his contradictory thoughts and actions. For example, Clarence believes that the marriage will be a rite of transformation that will eradicate the beast within him. One moment he is determined to bring his marriage plans to fruition; the next moment he has misgivings about using it for aggregation. Such fears and phobias, such vacillations in emotions and actions, are common for persons whose neurosis is racially induced.

Physiologically, Clarence is white. In this novel's social world, Clarence's blackness, his beasthood, is a matter of perception, a condition in which the powers of the white mind can transform (or negate) material reality. Proffering Birdie as an exemplar, Webb demonstrates that the concept of race is so strong in the white psyche that it has the power to supersede all other emotions. In treating Clarence and Birdie's relationship, Webb negates and inverts various "romantic" notions. He argues that in the American social structure love does not conquer all: it does not conquer the beast in the skull, it does not override the concept of race, and it does not conquer fear and hate.

To reflect the general history of the nation's race relations in his treatment of Clarence and Birdie, Webb inscribes and reads these subjects' bodies from the purview of the beauty-and-the-beast trope, and he situates the prospective miscegenetic marriage metonymically within the biblical Eden myth.

He installs the core of this corporeal writing/reading as Birdie's dream-vision, a premonition of her later discovery that Clarence is black. In the dream the two of them are walking in an Edenic setting of "flowers and fruit, and lovely cottages" when "a rough ugly man" overtakes them and demands that Clarence release his attachment to her (329). When Clarence refuses, the ugly creature gives him a "diabolical look" that causes "loathsome black spots" to break out on Clarence's face (329). Because the dream is Birdie's, she in effect mentally transforms the surface of the black body to fit the prescribed Negrophobic text. The dream-vision blends two metaphors: the Eden metaphor of the snake in the Garden and the fairy-tale motif of the beauty and the beast. In addition, the passage is an allegorical portrayal of how white men have transformed black men from humans to beasts, from men to myths. The interpolated scene also speaks to Clarence's duality, for in it he is both the handsome prince and the "rough ugly man," both Beauty and the Beast.

The inverted fairy tale structures the conclusion to the story line about Clarence and Birdie. Webb resolutely demonstrates through the novel's emplotment that miscegenetic unions in the United States do not have fairy-tale endings, that there is little if any chance for an interracial couple to live happily ever after in American society of the time, in the South or in the North. Like other African American novelists of his century, he aborts the mulatto liminal's final rite of passage.

The beauty-and-the-beast trope (though not necessarily drawn from the fairy tale) often controlled descriptions of actual and alleged sexual unions between black men and white women in the society long before Webb published *The Garies and Their Friends*.[5] After the Civil War the trope gained even more widespread use among whites and perhaps was the most frequent analogy they used until well past World War I to describe this form of a miscegenetic union. In addition, the number of marriages between black men and white women sharply increased in the South following the Civil War, a period during which the image of the black male as sexual fiend rose to the fore in the Negrophobic mind. The war had drained the South of much of its white male population, leaving many white women not only economically destitute but also without the prospect of marriage to a white man. Consequently, an unprecedented number of these women married blacks, no doubt for both economic and conjugal reasons.[6]

Given southern whites' attitudes toward blacks after the Civil War, it seems reasonable to conclude that this relatively large number of interracial marriages exacerbated the antipathy toward miscegenation. These unions provided conclusive evidence for those who had argued and believed that emancipation would lead to large-scale miscegenation and thus to the destruction of the white race and the civilization it had built in the United States. Yet despite the social situation immediately following the Civil War, African American novelists between 1860 and 1900 seldom foregrounded miscegenetic unions between black men and white women. The beauty-and-the-beast trope, therefore, remained prominent in white life and literature but lay dormant in the African American novel from *The Garies* until near the turn of the century. Around 1900 it began to emerge as a prominent contextual feature of the novelists' use of the lynching bee as a symbol of strained tensions between the races.

Black Man, New Man: Chesnutt's John (Walden) Warwick

During the century that followed *The Garies*'s publication, subject formations (with attendant story lines and emplotments) in African American passing novels that centered white mulatto males were cut from *The Garies*'s pattern. Principal discursive formations in the pattern include the following: an abnormal or dysfunctional family unit; a childhood incident (often in a school setting) that precipitates an identity crisis; a mirror scene that induces a traumatic self-recognition; a psychological and cultural estrangement from blacks; a change in geographical space (migration) as a mechanism for changing one's social place; a self-willed racial transformation; and an engagement or marriage to a white woman.

Each novelist who adopts this pattern modifies it to interface with narrative modes his or her novel foregrounds. Chesnutt's *Cedars* and Willard Savoy's *Alien Land* (1949) utilize conventions from fictive and nonfictive discourse on the Anglo-American Edenic ideal to emphasize that their male subjects are sons of Adam. Johnson's *Ex-Coloured Man* and Will Thomas's *God Is for White Folks* (1947) foreground conventions of the slave narrative genre. All four novels use rites of passage to structure the male subject's story line, a feature they have in common with other passing novels that center men as well as those that foreground female subjects.

These male subjects reject their black parentage, hate themselves, and often develop and exhibit racist attitudes toward other blacks. Portrayed as psychologically complex characters, their problems intensify with their attempts to pass for white. While they physically can remove themselves from a black environment and refrain from direct contact with blacks, most of them cannot successfully break the emotional and psychological ties to their heritage (which the authors manifest in a parent or another close relative and often in some cultural component of black life). As a result, these characters vacillate between being psychologically black and psychologically white, two contradictory emotional states that precipitate an internal conflict, self-hate.

The novelists typically portray this conflict as one between the self and the Other, between two oppositional, competing forces housed in the same mind and body. For example, when in the psychological state of being white (the self), the character feels disdain for blacks (the Other). But unable to escape the knowledge that he, too, is black, his hate for blacks as the Other concretizes as self-hatred. When joining whites in expressing antiblack sentiments (as he occasionally does), the character cannot prevent that sentiment from being internalized to include the black component of his subjectivity. When his disdain for blacks heightens to the point that, ironically, it evolves into an empathetic identification with them, his black psyche assumes dominance as the self and his white psyche becomes the Other. The character then resents whites for their antiblack sentiments and thus resents the white side of himself. Consequently, the vacillation in his racial identity precipitates his psychological transformation from being a black to being a white (or vice versa), and thus it dictates the symmetry of the novel's thematic structure.

In *Cedars* Chesnutt does not dramatize a sexual union (marriage) between a black man and a white woman; instead, he treats the topic suggestively and briefly. Given the novel's sociohistorical context and the manner in which he develops John (Walden) Warwick's character, one could argue that John's marriage to a white woman is actually not an instance of an interracial marriage. After all, by the time the marriage occurs in the novel Chesnutt has delineated John as physiologically, sociologically, psychologically, and legally a white man. Nevertheless, as the son of a bright mulatto mother and a white father he is a mulatto; therefore, his marriage is interracial.

Chesnutt's creation of John exemplifies how he innovatively embellishes the themes of passing for white and interracial marriage with which his predecessors worked. He does not create John as a clone of previous fictional black males who pass for white, and he does not create him as an exact copy of the southern white gentlemen who populated nineteenth-century African American novels. Nor does he use the most obvious trappings (physical appearance and sexual ramifications) of the beauty-and-the-beast trope as an overriding frame for his treatment of John's interracial marriage. Rather, Chesnutt's application of the beauty-and-the-beast tale to John's story line focuses attention on other features of the generic tale. In fact, he uses "Cinderella" to construct this novel's beauty-and-the-beast trope. In addition to motifs about manners, morals, social class, and wealth, transformation is a motif central to subjectivity in both "Cinderella" and "Beauty and the Beast." All of these motifs have parallels in the social and literary manifestations of the Eden trope.

Among male-centered story lines and emplotments about passing, Chesnutt's construction of John best exemplifies how African American novels appropriate the revolutionary period's permutation of the Eden myth to inscribe the centered subject. In large part, Chesnutt constructs John's character and his story by revising the Judeo-Christian Eden myth and interfacing his revision with two American sociopolitical myths, an American cosmogonic myth that narrates the creation of the American nation as an autonomous political entity and an origin myth that narrates the birth of the sociocultural being who would populate this new nation. (The "New Adam," the "American Adam," the "New World Adam," the "natural aristocrat," and "the new man" are the standard appellations.) Both sociopolitical myths are structural and analogical outgrowths of the biblical myth of Eden.

In casting John from the historical mold of the Anglo-American new man, Chesnutt draws directly from the definition of this American new man as recorded in the texts of Thomas Jefferson, Benjamin Franklin, St. John de Crèvecoeur, William Wirt, Thomas Paine, and others of the revolutionary era. Several of these mythopoeic writings endow this socio-cultural being with an identity that replicates that of their authors, who in effect reinvented themselves. In those sections of *Cedars* that focus on John, Chesnutt engages in an intertextual dialogue with earlier mythopoeic texts, affirming and negating them and using his representational portraiture of John to argue for the equitable inclusion of blacks in the Adamic family and therefore in the American Edenic ideal. Part of the affirmation is that in the example of these revolutionary patriots, John Walden reinvents himself. He becomes a self-made man, rather literally, for he is both father and son, both the subject and the object of his own creation.

In narrativizing John's self-creation, Chesnutt employs the concept of liminality. John resembles other white mulatto heroes and heroines in that he undergoes a series of rites of passage in preparation for his transition into the white mainstream. John Walden is born and spends his childhood in Patesville, North Carolina, the novel's principal setting. In Patesville's racially stratified social structure, the Walden family, members of a small "society" of mulattoes, belong to a group that in many instances is considered neither black nor white but is affixed between these bipolar opposites. The social history of racial isolates such as this group dates back to the colonial period. By the early revolutionary era, the power structure rather sharply distinguished Negroes from mulattoes and mulattoes from whites—racially, socially, and legally. In postbellum Patesville, as elsewhere in the South, this society of mulattoes created a condition of communitas—that is, a situation in which its members share an isolated psychosocial space within the larger social landscape. The thematic and tropological scaffolding for the novel's plot structure, then, chronicles the attempts of John and Rena Walden, two racial liminals, to secure for themselves the rights and privileges reserved for whites in the Southern Eden.

In inscribing John's subjectivity, Chesnutt systematically advances his argument that blacks (specifically white mulattoes but perhaps also bright mulattoes) are entitled to nothing less than those rights and privileges the nation's founding documents guaranteed the American citizenry. Extra-textual support for Chesnutt's stance in this instance can be found in his 1889 essay entitled "What Is a White Man?" in which he castigates "the white leaders of the South" for legally marginalizing what he terms "a very large class of the population who certainly are not Negroes in an ethno-logical sense." The monomaniacal "zeal" with which these "white leaders" espouse the one-drop rule causes them to violate their own principles to an extent "that they contemplate the practical overthrow of the Constitu-tion and laws of the United States to secure" a society that privileges only those who are defined as legally white. The power structure's use of the one-drop rule to define "free citizenship," Chesnutt argues, liminalizes "white" mulattoes to such an extent that they do not "know what race they belong to." Drawing upon his knowledge of jurisprudence, Chesnutt offers examples of additional contradictions and complications that arise from the statutes enacted in many states to sustain this legalized liminality. The essay contains several of the principles, situations, and conditions that he dramatizes in *Cedars*.

Chesnutt endows John at birth with characteristics ("race" and gender) prerequisite to beget, to become, and to be an American new man. The core of John's story line, therefore, concerns his acquisition of the other criteria necessary to assume his "divinely sanctioned" place as an American new man—that is, to become legally a white man and thus to assume his rightful place among the New World's chosen people. The cultural scaf-folding for this concept comes from another biblical origin myth as re-corded in the story of Abraham, Isaac, and Ishmael, the story of the origin of God's chosen people and the consequent exclusion of the first-born, illegitimate son (Ishmael) from his father's (Abraham's) house and thus from the privileges attendant to the House of Abraham.

The slavocracy, its defenders, and its detractors frequently used the Abrahamic paradigm as a structural model to explain analogically the po-sition of the mulatto (and of blacks in general) in southern society. Published in the same year as Chesnutt's *Cedars*, Carroll's *"The Negro a Beast"* reinscribes this antebellum discourse on race in his portrait of postbellum society and subjectivity. Carroll's construction exemplifies how expansive the Eden trope became at times in its inclusion of biblical sources. Carroll does not confine his construction to what he calls the "Narrative of Creation" and the "Narrative of the Fall" (98). He includes stories from Genesis that center Cain and his brother, Noah and his sons, and Abraham and his progeny. In addition, Carroll incorporates and conflates passages from other books of the Old Testament as well as from books of the New Testament, which he then offers as corroboration for his overarching thesis that blacks are not part of the Adamic family.

The expansive paradigm certainly fits John's situation. The axis of the novel's plot that concerns John, a New World Ishmael who metamorphoses into a New World Adam, turns on how he reverses his excluded and liminal status through the process of a self-effected racial transformation. He acts out the myth of the American new man, textual variants of which can be found in such diverse forms as Benjamin Franklin's *Autobiography* and Horatio Alger's novels.

In the context of America's new-man myth, John's first rite of transition out of this liminal status is to acquire the intellect necessary to give birth to oneself. Chesnutt adapts the Eden myth's Tree of Knowledge metaphor (quite differently than he does for Molly and Rena Walden) to help develop the intellectual component of John's subjectivity. Through his characterization of John, Chesnutt concurs that racists who believed that the fruits of society should be reserved exclusively for whites labored to deprive blacks of a formal education because it would provide one means for them to move into the mainstream. John is a victim of this denial. He and his sister, Rena, as well as other blacks in the area where the Waldens live (as throughout the South), receive at best an education intended to be inferior to that of whites, a topic that Chesnutt emphasizes in the novel. By reading voraciously in the library that his biological white father bequeathed to him, John develops to the point that he is the intellectual equal of any white man in the area.

In addition to parodically incorporating into the narrator's narration specific and generic texts from the American Edenic ideal, Chesnutt shows how John appropriates white-authored texts to reinvent himself, proffering a direct connection between John's self-creation and white-authored texts.

The narrator remarks that when John "had read all the books [in the Waldens' library],—indeed, long before he had read them all,—he too had tasted of the fruit of the Tree of Knowledge" (163). Among the books in the Waldens' library are ones directly related to the different motifs Chesnutt associates with John's subjectivity: the works of Henry Fielding, Daniel Defoe, and Samuel Richardson; the Bible and John Bunyan's *Pilgrim's Progress;* Tobias Smollett's *Roderick Random,* Cervantes's *Don Quixote,* and Le Sage's *Gil Blas;* Thomas Paine's *Age of Reason* and a history of the French Revolution. Fortified with the combined knowledge he gleans from these literary, social, religious, chivalric, political, and other books, John Walden becomes discontented with his status and identity as a black and initiates a strategy to acquire "the object of [his] desire"—a legally and divinely sanctioned white maleness (163).

In several passing novels the centered male's object of desire is a white female (either literal or symbolical). John's object of desire is white maleness. In John's case, the ultimate rite of passage to achieve (re)aggregation is to attain legal status as a white man rather than to marry a white woman. In treating this idea, Chesnutt combines the concept of liminality with the concept of the American new man and thus places John's plight squarely within the context of American mythic history. John reinvents himself at age fifteen. In a conversation with Judge Straight, he proclaims himself a white male and cites "divine foreordination" as his justification. Having successfully completed two of the primary rites of passage, the biological and the intellectual, John now intends to use legal history to sanction his self-creation. To construct the scene between John and Judge Straight, Chesnutt draws specifically from juridical definitions of race and identity that were in effect by the revolutionary period as well as from laws in effect in North Carolina and other southern states at the time of the novel's setting.[7] In one instance, Judge Straight's comments about legal definitions of race (171–72) closely paraphrase the text of a decision that Judge William Harper rendered in South Carolina in May 1835 (with the concurrence of two other judges), in a case (*State v. Vinson J. Cantey*) to decide racial identity.[8]

Chesnutt situates Warwick in a social landscape predicated on the chivalric tradition and endows his subjectivity with basic characteristics from two major conceptions of the Anglo-American male—Jefferson's natural aristocrat (revolutionary period) and Wirt's new man (national period). The two conceptions are competing (almost diametrically opposed) constructs that Chesnutt harmonizes in his formation of John. Jefferson hoped his New World men would constitute the dominant class in post-revolutionary America. This new man's aristocratic stature did not derive from inherited wealth, status, and Old World definitions; instead, his superior virtue and talents gave rise to his stature as a natural aristocrat.[9] "Wirt's natural aristocrat was not the carefully selected and highly trained scholar-statesman whom Jefferson had in mind when he spoke of a natural aristocracy. Rather he was a man steeped in American nature, guided by the elemental forces which direct it and sharing their capacity for moral grandeur."[10]

Speaking to George Tryon, who proposes to marry Rena, John uses the new man concept to explain his family background and to define his and Rena's subjectivity: "We are *new people*" (83; emphasis added). John ostensibly refers to the white mulatto class of liminals to which he and Rena belong, but the term also alludes to the historical rise of new men and new families that Wirt's life and writings typified. Wirt's concept of "new men" is a formidable part of his romantic vision of the Edenic South. His writings strongly foreshadow the plantation idyll in southern literature of the 1830s and the chivalric image of the Edenic South immediately following the Civil War, the period in which *The House Behind the Cedars* is set. Indeed, in its dialogic response to southern literary and nonliterary texts and in its inscription of culture and character formation, *Cedars* mirrors this periodized evolution.

After their racial identity has been exposed, John's proposal to Rena that they "go to the North or West . . . far away from the South and the Southern people, and start life over again" (183) underscores the racial duality of his identity within the framework of America's Eden trope. The symbolic migration he proposes to the North (the Promised Land) evokes the mythic history of his African American heritage; the symbolic migration he proposes to the West (the ever-new New Eden) evokes the mythic history of his Anglo-American heritage.

John indeed embodies two historical and racial American experiences, a black one and a white one, and thus his dilemma is in many ways representative. He certainly exemplifies the plight of many white mulattoes in the post–Civil War South, a group of racial liminals to which Chesnutt himself belonged. In fact, there are several similarities between Chesnutt and John. For instance, John's physiological characteristics replicate Chesnutt's, and in large part Chesnutt was a self-educated man. He acquired postsecondary education as a lawyer, much like John, through the sheer power of his own intellect and ambition. Despite these and other similarities between the author and his character, Chesnutt's construction of John is not an autobiographical act.

In writing his subject, Chesnutt is, however, (re)writing biography, specifically Jefferson's. For instance, a significant portion of John's influence and power derives from his acquisition of wealth as a landowner (he is "rich in his wife's right" [22]); he is a type of "natural aristocrat" who has come into his own. John, as did Jefferson, aggrandizes his economic status and prosperity by inheriting property from his late wife, wealth that had been accumulated from the trafficking in human flesh. Indeed, there are several parallels between John's life and Jefferson's: each inherited a select library from his father; each read deeply in history, philosophy, and the classics; each became largely a self-taught lawyer; as a widower, each brought his younger sister into his household and made her mistress of the house. These and several other parallels seem more than coincidental, for certainly in his critique of the contradictions between the principles and practices of America Chesnutt has in mind Jefferson, an exemplar of the New World's new man.

Cedars's closure is indicative of a gendered difference in the African American passing novel. Rena and John become "new people" in a "new world" (193). But while Rena eventually is ejected permanently from this metonymic New World Eden in which she lived "for a brief time," the novel's closure leaves John as a member of the mainstream's chosen people. As part of their socialization process, both John and Rena metaphorically try on the glass slipper, but it fits only John. Rena is a Cinderella-heroine and John is a Cinderella-hero.[11] During the height of her racial masquerade Rena fears that she is "Cinderella before the clock has struck" (62) and that her "prince would never try on the glass slipper" (71). Her fears are realized and her story does not have the classic fairy-tale ending. John, however, fairs much better as the Cinderella-hero. Rising from a life of "poverty, open and unabashed" (8) to assume his "inalienable birthright"

(22) as a natural aristocrat, as a white man, John is metaphorically transformed from Beast (black) to Beauty (white).

The Beast-Bridegroom: Johnson's Ex-Coloured Man

Johnson's *Ex-Coloured Man* is one of the best examples of how a novelist constructs this subject largely through a foregrounding of fairy-tale motifs. *Ex-Coloured Man*'s discursive figuration conflates the fairy tale, the picaresque novel, the slave narrative, and other narrative forms. The picaro's narrative and the fairy-tale hero's narrative have several morphological features in common, and both share affinities in form with the slave narrative.

A transformation, or metamorphosis, is a prevalent trope in nineteenth-century African American prose narratives, particularly in the religious conversion narrative/spiritual autobiography (such as Jarena Lee's or Rebecca Jackson's), and the slave narrative (such as Solomon Northrop's or Frederick Douglass's).[12] In the slave narrative (Douglass's, for instance) the trope typically monitors the subject's transformation from beast (subhuman) to beauty (human), and the inverse of this transformation is secondary in the narrative's design. In a few instances, though, as in Northrop's narrative, the focal transformation is from beauty (person) to beast (property). Whether authors present their respective subject's/self's transformation as one from sinner to saint, from slavery to freedom, from beast to human, or from black to white, this tropological device is a defining characteristic. *Ex-Coloured Man* is a prime example.

Through a recollection (at points hazy) of parentage and birthplace, *Ex-Coloured Man*'s narrator-protagonist begins his story with the slave narrative's formulaic "I was born."[13] He attempts as best he can to establish an identity and to situate himself in the world. The opening pages of the novel follow the discursive pattern of Douglass's opening chapter in the *Narrative*. The protagonist "was born in a little town of Georgia a few years after the close of the Civil War" (3), the illegitimate child of a southern aristocratic white father and a bright mulatto mother. Though born free, he in effect enters the world in the status of an animal: the one-drop rule for racial classification designates him black and therefore subhuman. Nevertheless, he lives through his childhood in Connecticut believing that he is white, unaware that his dysfunctional family situation is primarily a consequence of miscegenation. His "transition from one world into another" (20)—in this instance, from white to black—occurs at a point in his childhood when he is made painfully aware that he is black, not white. This childhood trauma induces the protagonist's adult neurosis, which Johnson conveys through discursive formations infused with fairy lore.

In his discussion of fairy tales as portrait of man, Max Lüthi identifies several characteristics of the generic fairy-tale hero: he often is an only child; he is estranged from the larger social environment because of the circumstances of his birth (it is not unusual for the hero to be born in animal form); appearance versus reality is a theme that helps structure the narrative of his experiences; problems originating from his familial situation cause him to leave home to wander in the world, never to return permanently to his point of origin; out in the world he is rather helpless, but several persons (helpmates) whom he encounters during his journey assist him.[14] These and other characteristics that Lüthi identifies also aptly describe the male-centered subject in African American passing novels, particularly the unnamed protagonist in *Ex-Coloured Man*.

After *Ex-Coloured Man*'s publication, psychoanalysts such as Jacques Lacan (the mirror stage) and Frantz Fanon (Negro psychopathology) provided descriptions of clinical situations and of subjects that are aligned with portraiture in African American novels.[15] From fairy-tale discourse Johnson appropriates a stock device, the mirror and its reflection. He introduces the formation near the end of the novel's opening chapter in the scene in which ex-coloured man first learns of his racial identity. The lesson, couched in a school setting, precipitates the protagonist's first instance of a critical self-examination.

Constructed as an inverted formation, the scene equates blackness with Beast and whiteness with Beauty and reveals that as a child the protagonist has imbibed these analogies as part of society's civilizing process. Utilizing the mirror as a reflection of truth, Johnson has his protagonist seek the truth of his racial identity in a mirror in an attempt to refute the lesson he has learned at school. Standing before his "looking-glass" to read his body surface, the character is afraid to look lest the mirror reveal that he is the beast (a black) rather than the "pretty boy" (a white) many have claimed he is: "I was accustomed to hear remarks about my beauty; but now, for the first time, I became conscious of it and recognized it. I noticed the ivory whiteness of my skin, the beauty of my mouth, the size and liquid darkness of my eyes, and how the long, black lashes that fringed and shaded them produced an effect that was strangely fascinating even to me. I noticed the softness and glossiness of my dark hair that fell in waves over my temples, making my forehead appear whiter than it really was" (17).

The discursive formation recalls a motif from "Snow White" and other fairy tales. Such a feminized image recalls fictive portraits of southern belles, white and black—Beauty incarnate. Unconvinced by the message in the mirror, the protagonist seeks verification from his mother that he is not a "nigger" and thus does not possess the same "defects" she has as a black person (17); he seeks verification beyond the mirror that he is Beauty, not Beast.

What ex-coloured man and his literary compeers seek in the mirror is their ego-ideal—a white male. John Warwick finds his in the mirror (*Cedars*, 160–61); ex-coloured man does not. What each finds in the mirror is directly related to the success of the subject's racial transformation and to the stability of his psychological state.

Following the novel's mirror scene, Johnson begins to trace methodically the development of the neurotic protagonist's dual racial psychology. His neurosis deepens as he matures—or it becomes more and more evident to the reader as his narrative unfolds. After he in effect is orphaned, the protagonist begins his picaresque journey out into the world. His body surface signifies that he is white, but in reality he is black, and this tension between appearance and reality structures his exterior (geographical) and his interior (psychological) journeys. The protagonist's journey into the world allows Johnson to survey critically American society North and South, a feature standard in the slave narrative. His journey into self allows Johnson to probe the subject's neurosis and in the process to underscore the protagonist's representational role as part of the author's treatment of racism's function in the civilizing process.

Through a series of narrative formations thematically focused on miscegenation, Johnson underscores the racial dichotomy in the subject's personality by exteriorizing his war within. One instance is a tractarian section in the novel, in which the protagonist witnesses a Northerner and a Texan debate the race question. One of the focal topics in this debate between two white men is the black man as a sexual competitor. By shifting his sentiments between the Northerner and the Texan, the protagonist reveals the extent to which transference is symptomatic of his neurosis.

In another formation Johnson foregrounds the beauty-and-the-beast trope and dramatizes more fully the protagonist's contradictory attitude toward miscegenation. The scene is set in a black club in New York that interracial couples frequent. In narrating the scene, the protagonist admits that he "never exactly enjoyed the sight" (109) of white women with black men, and he is particularly jealous of a black man with whom he is a potential rival for the affections of a wealthy white widow. The ambiguity here is whether his jealousy emanates primarily from his black or from his white psyche. His contrasting descriptions of the couple within the beauty-and-the-beast trope suggest that at this point in his racial vacillation his white psyche is dominant. He reads the woman's body surface as a personification of Beauty (108). Concurrently, his description of the man is controlled by Negrophobic images of the black male as a "surly," "ugly" beast. By the end of the club episode the narrator has completed a Negrophobic portrait of the man by dramatically revealing that the man is the murderer of a white woman (123–24).

In yet another formation Johnson flirts with the incest motif, also a morphological feature of the beauty and the beast tale, specifically the relationship between the incest taboo and the theme of family stability, as Bruno Bettelheim has observed.[16] The ex-coloured man describes the woman in this scene, to whom he is attracted, as "the most dazzlingly white thing [he] had ever seen" (198). In an ironic twist, however, he immediately discovers that she is his half-sister. Johnson forgoes the opportunity to probe more deeply into the neurotic subject's psyche by exploring the theme of incestuous miscegenation.

An interracial marriage as a symbolic action—or more specifically, a white woman as a symbolic character—is one narrative device in the passing novel that shows the form's conflation of the slave narrative and the male-centered fairy tale. For the fugitive or ex-slave, the North was the symbol of freedom. In the passing novel a white woman is a symbol of the male subject's freedom, and she thus performs essentially the same function in the male subject's racial transformation that a beautiful maiden performs in fairy tales. Most passing novels, like *Ex-Coloured Man*, reveal this slave narrative–fairy tale nexus through their use of the beauty-and-the-beast trope and by portraying the male subject as a type of beast-bridegroom.

Foregrounding his protagonist's biracial psychology and inverting the standard beauty-and-the-beast formation, Johnson shows that his protagonist reflexes onto himself the black-beast and white-beauty analogies, as is especially clear in the protagonist's involvement with white women—from his teenage infatuation with a young white girl, to his flirtation with a wealthy white widow, to his marriage to a white woman. In confessing his love for his wife-to-be, ex-coloured man feels that he also must reveal his racial heritage to her. Her reaction to his confession causes him to envision the prospective marriage as a union between the beauty and the beast. To convey this, Johnson repeats a formation from Webb's *The Garies* and Chesnutt's *Cedars* that emphasizes the transformative power of the white gaze. She reacts to his confession "with a wild, fixed stare as though [he] was some object she had never seen. Under the strange light in her eyes [he] felt that [he] was growing black and thick-featured and crimp-haired" (204). Even after their marriage he lives "in constant fear" that she will detect a savage beneath the exterior, that she will attribute some aspect of his behavior to his "blood" rather than to his "human nature" (210).

In the major African American novels published before World War I, ex-coloured man is the only white mulatto to marry a white woman from the better class of white society who is fully aware of his racial ancestry before she marries him. After he informs her of his heritage, her final response to his beauty/beast, civilized/savage, white/black duality replicates a formation in fairy-tale discourse about animal bridegrooms. She accepts his proposal and marries him as an expression of her unqualified love, which serves as the magic potion that turns the beast to beauty, the savage to civilized, the black to white.

Sociologically defined as a white mulatto, ex-coloured man embodies what Maria Tatar in her study of fairy tales calls "the dual nature of fairy-tale beasts (civilized/savage)," for the adjective *white* designates him civilized while the noun *mulatto* designates him savage, two oppositional states within the same being.[17] As several passing novels suggest, the subject is either a white man imprisoned in a black body or a black man trapped in a white body. The marriage ceremony releases whatever self is trapped in the body of the Other and gives the subject his object of desire.

In pre–World War I passing novels, however, rarely is the liberation of the white self and the consequent destruction of the black Other a completed process, and thus rarely is the subject allowed to retain his object of desire. As is the case with John Warwick, ex-coloured man's direct object of desire (in its abstract form) is white maleness. To metamorphose into his ego-ideal would gain him rights, privileges, and opportunities he would be denied as a black man. According to the dominant society's formal and informal social codes (its written and unwritten laws), only a white man can marry a white woman. Thus, for ex-coloured man and for many of his literary peers, a white wife is an indirect object of desire, or the mediation for his primary desire. Given the social codes, his marriage to a white woman will, if only symbolically, define him as a white man. Yet the definition is exterior, not interior, for the mediation between the desiring subject and his object of desire is ephemeral.

So Johnson, like practically all of his African American predecessors who treated the topic, rejects a fairy-tale ending to the interracial union. The couple do not live happily ever after, the marriage dissolves as a result of the wife's death, and the centered subject's racial transformation is in effect reversed. Ex-coloured man's wife dies a few years after they are married, as does John Warwick's wife. The desire to protect his children from the stigma and subsequent experiences of being classified as black supersedes his concern for providing them a mother's care. So he vows, as does Warwick, never to marry again. In part his resolve is mere rationalization for continuing his racial masquerade. If he were to marry again, given the racial orientation of his psyche, he probably would marry another white woman and thus run the risk of and endure the psychological stress associated with his racial identity being discovered. Though he claims concern about the welfare of his children to justify his actions, his situation is more complex than his rationalization indicates. Now that he no longer is married to a white woman, he is an ex-white man. Having begun his ordeal as a white child trapped in a black (mulatto) child's body, he now is a black man trapped in a white man's body. For him to contract another miscegenetic union would be to risk the beast within at some point revealing itself. Both Chesnutt and Johnson use confirmed widowerhood as a closure to their stories about white mulatto liminals who marry white women. Such a closure is a gentle touch to defuse a potentially volatile issue and perhaps to minimize any racial tension that their works might precipitate. Later novelists, such as Thomas and Savoy, reject such closure.

Ex-Coloured Man's confessional mode, then, is a narrative strategy that allows Johnson to foreground the conflicting internal impulses that his protagonist's racial duality produces. Despite the material, social, and other advantages ex-coloured man enjoys as a white man, he suffers from "a vague feeling of unsatisfaction, of regret, of almost remorse," from which he seeks release by confessing his "practical joke on society." In fact, his psychological instability as a would-be white man is evident in the opening and closing paragraphs of his confessional narrative. A moral coward who is unable to follow the dictates of his conscience, he in essence wants the reader to act for him, to be a helpmate, and to return him to the black race. Indeed, his motivation for confessing his racial masquerade is "the same impulse which forces the un-found-out criminal to take somebody into his confidence, although he knows that the act is likely, even almost certain, to lead to his undoing" (3).

The criminal-hero motif is another way Johnson blends the slave narrative mode with fairy lore and the picaresque as part of his dialogic response to contemporary Negrophobic discourse. In the slave narrative, a slave who escapes to freedom is, according to the slavocracy's "legal" codes, guilty of stealing himself, and theft is a crime. In "hero-centric" fairy tales, the male figure's bestial impulses make him "a creature capable of violent mutilation and murder,"[18] and in picaresque fiction the picaro often is a borderline criminal. In Negrophobic discourse applicable to this novel's setting, a black man who masquerades as a white man or, even worse, who has any form of sexual contact with a white woman is summarily judged a criminal (a beast, a potential rapist and murderer). Both the dominant society (through its institutionalized racism) and the subject (through his careful control of his behavior) are programmed to keep the beast contained. Given his biracial psyche, ex-coloured man therefore has a double duty, which brings to the novel's foreground the neurosis from which he suffers. This situation also represents an instance of his white self desiring to expose the fraud his black Other is perpetrating.

In conjoining fairy-tale discourse and the slave narrative mode and in responding dialogically and intertextually to Negrophobic discourse and discourse on the American Edenic ideal, Ex-Coloured Man develops the white mulatto liminal as a character type to its fullest form in the pre-1960 African American novel. Though African American novelists use several biblical stories to inscribe their literary version of the Eden trope, Johnson appears to be unique in appropriating and ingeniously applying the narrative of Jacob and Esau, twin sons of Isaac. He culls several motifs from the biblical story—twins, incest, birthright, mistaken identity, confidence game, among others—revises them and weaves them neatly into his construction of the novel's centered subject. The novel's last line—"I have sold my birthright for a mess of pottage"—indicates Johnson's conscious use of this biblical source as a tropological frame for the entire narrative.

After *Ex-Coloured Man*, little is added to develop the form of the male-centered passing novel. African American novelists did, however, embellish this character type's story line to adapt it to different times, places, and circumstances, to adapt it to different modes of fictive discourse, and to speak directly to modifications in the American Dream that affected black life after World War I.

The Machine-Made New Negro: Schuyler's Matthew Fisher

In *Our Nig; or, Sketches from the Life of a Free Black* (1859) Harriet E. Wilson introduces into the genre a narrative formation that centers an interracial marriage between a dark-complexioned, self-deprecating black man (Jim) and a white woman (Mag) in New England during the 1820s. She inserts the formation primarily to help establish the personal history of the novel's biracial protagonist (Frado). During the genre's first century several novels repeat this formation (a conjugal union inside or outside wedlock) and make few alterations to its basic elements or to its function within the respective novel. Before Ann Petry's *The Narrows* (1953) seldom does a novel use a miscegenetic union of this type as the principal element in a plot structure that centers a male protagonist.

J. McHenry Jones's *Hearts of Gold* (1896), Jessie Fauset's *There Is Confusion* (1924), and Nella Larsen's *Quicksand* (1928) are among those novels that closely replicate the formation that Wilson introduced into the genre. These and other pre-1940 novels (such as Claude McKay's *Home to Harlem* [1928]) that incorporate a sexual relationship between a dark-complexioned man and a white woman rarely give the union extended treatment or use the beauty-and-the-beast trope explicitly to characterize it. They do, however, make the union thematically relevant to the centered subject's quest for Eden, whether for the subject Eden is a physical place (as in *There Is Confusion*) or a psychological space (as in *Quicksand*). In novels that do install the formation, the protagonist usually is not a partner in a union of this type but the progeny of one. Under the Eden trope as rubric, the first important work in the genre in which this formation is a full-blown paradigm is George S. Schuyler's *Black No More* (1931).

Schuyler thematically centers miscegenation in *Black No More* and in general adheres to a standard practice in the genre: he approaches a contemporary topic germane to the race's experiences by surveying the topic's history in America and by installing and building upon its literary representations in the genre. Yet he does not merely duplicate the thematic and formalist conventions his predecessors used to treat miscegenation; he innovatively modifies several of them and cloaks his novel in the mode of satire. The novel's content does not differ substantively from previous novels that treat miscegenation; however, several of the formalist configurations in which Schuyler casts the novel's content are radically new, as are some of the perspectives that emanate from these innovations.

Set primarily in New York and Atlanta, *Black No More* traces the experiences and exploits of Max Disher, a "coffee-brown" (1) black who avails himself of a state-of-the-art technological invention by Dr. Junius Crookman—a machine that physically transforms a black person into a white person. After undergoing this metamorphosis and thus acquiring a new racial identity and a new name, Matthew Fisher, Fisher pursues and eventually marries the daughter of the head of the country's leading white supremacist organization, is instrumental in helping blacks undermine the system of white supremacy, and through various maneuverings and confidence games successfully acquires the material aspects of the American Dream's promise of life, liberty, and happiness.

Privileging science fiction as the predominant discursive frame and situating within this frame formations from a variety of other discursive modes, particularly historical narrative and fairy lore, Schuyler dramatizes his fictive vision by reformatting African American (and to some extent, Anglo-American) subjectivity. The narrative's thematic axis is racial transformation as a rite of passage into the white aggregate. Schuyler is particularly innovative in constructing the white mulatto as a centered subject to interface with this theme. He uses an interplay of biological, social, cultural, historical, legal, and technological determiners of race to inscribe the protagonist's (and other characters') subjectivity and to motivate the novel's sequential actions. By thematizing, dramatizing, and satirizing subject formation, the author scathingly attacks the nation's ideological conception and social construction of race and thus the societal institutions that are predicated on race.

To formulate Fisher's "twoness," Schuyler parodically installs, revises, and fuses salient aspects of two novelistic prototypes, Webb's Clarence

Garie Jr. and Wilson's Jim. During the course of the novel the protagonist is physiologically both a dark-complexioned black and a white mulatto. Yet he does not exhibit the classic neurotic symptoms of either of his prototypical predecessors. Even after his physiological metamorphosis from black to white, Fisher rarely wavers in his psychological and cultural identification as a black. As Max Disher, he wants to be physiologically white so that he can enjoy the privileges that the society extends only to whites. He shares this desire and motivation with the novel's other blacks, most of whom undergo the racial transformation process. Though a technological version of a psychobiological white mulatto, Fisher is ideologically a fuller and more convincing representative of the black race than are white mulatto subjects in other novels.

The racial transformation machine effects the preliminary rites of passage (biological, social, economic) requisite for Fisher's final rite of transition into the white aggregate, the marriage ceremonial, which, ostensibly, he completes by marrying Helen Givens. Though Schuyler installs these and other generic norms from previous male-centered passing novels, he revises them to fit his narrative's ideological stance. How he constructs the central character's subjectivity is illustrative of the revisions he makes. Born physiologically and psychologically "black" and situated as an adult in the cultural milieu of the Harlem Renaissance, Max Disher does not metamorphose into a culturally constructed new man, like many of his white mulatto predecessors, but into a biotechnological, machine-made New Negro. It is not by consummating a marriage to a white woman that he becomes legally a white man. Rather, it is being reconceived by and reborn from a biotechnological mother that gives him the legal status of white.

In addition, Max is not an idolater devoted to white womanhood. He is an iconoclast. He initially establishes a conjugal relationship with Helen Givens, daughter of the Grand Wizard of the Knights of Nordica, as a means for gaining revenge against an oppressive white male power structure. Using retribution as motivation for subject formation and emplotment, Schuyler constructs Helen's subjectivity principally from various social and literary types and stereotypes of white women from different historical permutations of the South as Eden. He makes her the epitome of the white woman as icon. However, by having Max fall madly in love with Helen, Schuyler creates a narrative fracture in the novel's textual logic. He attempts to repair this fracture by reinscribing Helen's racial subjectivity. He endows her with the mighty one drop, which she inherits from her father (Henry Givens). What initially is a marriage between a white mulatto male and a white woman turns out to be a marriage between two white mulattoes. With this ironic twist, Schuyler's use of marriage (the Fishers' and the Givens') as closure for the plot structure (an anti–fairy tale ending) remains consistent with novels that preceded his.

Schuyler's formation and subsequent reformation of Helen and her father's subjectivity helps reconcile key elements in the novel's emplotment and supports key issues in its ideology. Yet it weakens the attack he levels against the nation's obsession with skin as a signifier of one's essence. The novel argues that Americans (white and black) embrace a theory of being that is reductionist. In American society, being is epidermalized, exteriorized, essentialized, reduced to the subject's social skin. As a would-be democracy, the nation is hamstrung because its subjects politicize the body.

The racial transformation machine is Schuyler's literal and figural device for exploring the society-subjectivity nexus under the Eden trope as rubric. Blacks' physiological transformation en masse signals a transformation in the character of American society. As part of the novel's textual system, science interrelates the North's and the South's historically propagated images of America. Schuyler intertextually and tropologically plays upon the counterposition of these two images. One aspect of the novel's intertextuality is first made apparent in its complete title: *Black No More: Being an Account of the Strange and Wonderful Workings of Science in the Land of the Free*, A.D. *1933–1940*. The subtitle's phrasing reminds one of titles in American colonial discourse, such as Edward Johnson's *The Wonder-Working Providence of Scion's Saviour in New England* (1653) or Robert Calef's *More Wonders of the Invisible World* (1700). The subtitle is a parodic comment on early Euro-American narrative accounts of life in the New Eden. From the perspective of the novel's blacks, the image of America as a New Eden parallels the wilderness image colonists in the Northeast reflected in their accounts of life in the New World and therefore counters the image southern whites generated of the New World as a topographical paradise.

Since this country's early years of nationhood, Anglo-Americans certainly have debated the impact of science (broadly defined) on American society. Some of the debate centered on the introduction of scientific technology into the American social and ecological landscapes and the debilitating effects of this technology on the American pastoral (or agrarian) ideal—the "machine in the garden" debate.[19] Several Southerners who participated in the debate during the latter part of the nineteenth century and the first half of the twentieth century assessed the region's industrialization from the purview of race relations (and vice versa). Within this group, opponents of technological advancement often argued that industrialization would destroy the feudalistic system that sustained the southern agrarian ideal and thus would diminish racial stratification. Among opponents in the forefront of the debate's literary wing were Thomas Dixon (in *The Leopard's Spots*, for example) and Walter Hines Page (e.g., *The Southerner*). Both cite continuity with the Old South as a point of departure and take differing perspectives on the impact of technology on the New South's social structure.

In the Old South, the cotton gin was a predominant symbol of industrialization. In the New South, the gin was the region's economic anchor. In some areas of the New South a political economy based on the textile industry supported the ruling elite in its efforts to replicate the social structure (based on race and class) of the mythic Old South. Schuyler's portrait of life in a southern mill town (Paradise, South Carolina) draws upon and emphasizes this point.

The author makes it clear that he intends Paradise to be a microcosm of the South and of industrialized America (138). The town's history replicates the South's history. It was founded and developed into a commercial paradise by and for a group of rather recent European immigrants. Anchored ideologically in the antebellum past, the town is a social organization in which the construction of race dictates the inhabitants' emotions and behavior and controls all of the town's institutions. To their economic benefit, those who own the mill and thus the town instigate and perpetuate racial tensions between the underclass of whites and blacks. In effect, those at the top of the hierarchical social structure commodify racism.

The narrator's statement about life in Paradise summarizes what the entire episode dramatizes: "The deep concern of the Southern Caucasians with chivalry, the protection of white womanhood, the exaggerated development of race pride and the studied arrogance of even the poorest half-starved white peon, were all due to the presence of the black man. Booted and starved by their industrial and agricultural feudal lords, the white masses derived their only consolation and happiness from the fact that they were the same color as their oppressors and consequently better than the mudsill blacks" (141–42). Fisher and the machine-made-New-Negro phenomenon that invade Paradise destroy the town's social fabric by creating a condition in which whites must make the impossible choice between satisfying their racist emotions and behaviors and securing their economic welfare.

Before *Black No More* a few African American novels treated southern race relations within the context of the region's industrialization—for instance, Chesnutt's *The Colonel's Dream* (1905) and W. E. B. Du Bois's *The Quest of the Silver Fleece* (1911). *Black No More* explores more expansively than earlier novels the positive effects of technology on the American Eden's social landscape. It asserts that technology can improve American race relations in a way that politics, education, economics, and other institutional remedies cannot. The novel's exploration of the theme proffers the "machine" as anything (person, object, or idea) that threatens the perpetuation of the so-called American Eden. Metaphorically, then, Dr. Crookman, his machine, and the black men who pass as white are new versions of the beast in the American Garden in that they threaten the Garden's most sacred icon, the white woman.

More specifically, whites consider Dr. Crookman an incarnation of the snake in the American Garden, for his invention effects "chromatic emancipation" for blacks by giving them the means—the physicality of whiteness—to become full participants in the American Dream. Their physiological transformation threatens to alter permanently the social, political, and economic configurations of American society. Dr. Crookman becomes an agent for social change more powerful than any other person in American history, including Abraham Lincoln.

Though he uses the machine-in-the-garden trope from the perspective of science fiction, Schuyler's purposes nevertheless are identical to those of his predecessors who use forms of historiographic fiction to explore race relations within the context of the myth of America as Eden. Drawing upon the history of southern industrialization and its relation to the Eden trope, Schuyler's plot structure suggests agreement between those social critics who argued that miscegenation would destroy the Southern Way of Life and those who believed that industrialization was the threat. To be sure, the machine creates an entire "race" of white mulatto males. It is responsible for a rapid acceleration in miscegenation, technologically and biologically, and thus portends the destruction of white civilization in the United States.

The machine makes manifest Negrophobes' greatest fear: the Negro male loose (in most senses of the term). It frees black men from the prison-house of their social skin. Once they are set free, they run rampant and infiltrate every institution and organization in white society. With their black minds and bodies housed in a new, protective skin, they begin the process of repopulating the country by violating with impunity the great national taboo—miscegenation. As sex machines turned loose in the American Garden, particularly in the Southern Paradise, they reconfigure the national power base by reconfiguring American subjectivity, and their potential to reformat American civilization and culture beyond recognition is greater than that of the printing press, gunpowder, the cotton gin, the steam engine, the airplane, or any other technological invention or scientific development in this novel's setting.

Schuyler's construction of Max as a dual racial self embodies the nation's race problem and the potential solution to it. Reformists in the past failed to solve the race problem, the author maintains, because they sought to reform American institutions rather than to reconstruct American subjects. What the novel proposes and envisions, then, at least on its narrative surface, is a dramatic alteration in the exteriority rather than the interiority of African American subjectivity. Simply put, blacks must be liberated from the prison-house of their social skin to join the democratic fold.

As the narrative progresses, it emphasizes that during past centuries legislative decrees, presidential proclamations, a variety of social movements, a plethora of social programs, and even full-scale wars have not been able to effect blacks' movement into the national aggregate. The racial transformation machine does so relatively quickly. Yet in the novel's concluding chapters it becomes clear that the machine is not a panacea for the nation's race problem. The effects of the machine on the centered subject's dual racial selves indicate its different impacts on blacks and whites.

In an ironic twist, the racial transformation machine makes blacks whiter than whites, endowing them with a pigmentation that backfires because in the novel's chronology the whitest persons become the objects of discrimination. The excessive whiteness signifies blackness. Instead of creating a democracy, the machine creates a technocracy, a social organization in which those who have access to the most advanced technology rise to the top of the social hierarchy. It also worsens humanistic values by reinforcing the form of age-old tensions between classes, colors, regions, and genders. The machine fails to move Americans beyond the perception and construction of race, of skin, as a signifier of being. The novel discursively concludes that because discrimination is endemic to American subjectivity, it is entrenched in American society.

Black No More is much more imaginatively conceived than it is skillfully executed. Nevertheless, the fundamental issues it foregrounds about American subjectivity and American society through its formation of the centered subject are conventional in the African American novel. Schuyler constructs Matthew Fisher (alias Max Disher) from prototypes that appeared early in the genre. In several ways this protagonist becomes a prototype for black male subjects in several novels from the 1940s to the present.

FOUR

New Slaves and Lynching Bees

The Deformation of Black Subjectivity

BY 1900 IT was clear that the African American novel was gradually shifting emphases in its content and in aspects of its form to incorporate the era of new slaves and lynching bees into the genre's paradigmatic use of the biblical Eden myth. The novel's portrait of a paternalistic white South dominated by great white fathers began to change gradually to a portrait of a Negrophobic white South dominated by those who advocated a violent repression of black aspirations. Between 1900 and 1930 changes in theme, story line, plot, characterization, and other formalist features produced a fictive discourse in the genre in which the portrait of a Negrophobic white South predominated. Consequently, the theme of white-on-black violence shifted from psychological to physical as novels dramatized issues germane to the lives of the dark-complexioned southern black masses. Though after the turn of the century dark-skinned blacks began to occupy key roles in the novels, they continued to use bright mulattoes (but less often white mulattoes) as protagonists, and the genre increasingly foregrounded mulatto males rather than females as representative of the race's plight.

Focusing on the black male experience, the novelists also continued to use transformation as a major trope and as a major structuring device, but they adapted the trope to the shifting emphasis in racial themes and to changes in aspects of form. For instance, when a novelist centered a bright or white mulatto as subject, the trope usually bespoke the intent of the Emancipation Proclamation to transform a black person from a thing (property) to an American new man. Charles Chesnutt's *The House Behind the Cedars*, James Weldon Johnson's *The Autobiography of an Ex-Coloured Man*, and Walter White's *The Fire in the Flint* (1924) are among the examples. When a novelist foregrounded issues central to the lives of the black masses, the trope signified the attempts of the post-Reconstruction white power structure to transform the freedman into a new slave. The trope is evident in Chesnutt's *The Marrow of Tradition* (1901), Paul Laurence Dunbar's *The Sport of the Gods* (1902), Sutton Griggs's *The Hindered Hand* (1905), and other novels set in the South and published during the early twentieth century.

After 1900, a dramatic change in the novels' formation of representative white subjects accompanied the genre's increasing emphasis on the ritual violence of race relations. In treating the white power structure's attempts to deform the freedman into a new slave, the novels' portraiture of the representative white male changed overwhelmingly from a soft image of him as a great white father to a harsh image of him as a destroyer (lyncher) of black men's bodies and souls. In nineteenth-century African American novels, white women characters seldom had key roles in a novel's plot. After 1900, the novelists explored more fully and differently than their predecessors the symbolic function of white women in southern race relations. As the twentieth century advanced, the symbolic white woman became an integral character in the novels, though her characterization was more abstract than concrete. By the early years of the Harlem Renaissance, the genre's changes in thematic emphasis and in character portraiture (among other changes not related directly to its use of the Eden trope) had become standard.

Basic differences between Chesnutt's first two novels, *The House Behind the Cedars* and *The Marrow of Tradition*, exemplify the changes that occurred in the genre during the first third of this century. Though both novels use the Bible's Eden myth tropologically as a framing device to inscribe a society immersed in the chivalric tradition, each highlights different aspects of this modern-day chivalry. *Cedars* depicts the tradition as a basically innocent form of social intercourse among the elite white society of Clarence, South Carolina, and it uses ritual activities associated with the Clarence Social Club to critique society's attraction to the tradition. Emphasizing the tradition's quaintness, Chesnutt constructs most of the novel's characters— major and minor, black and white—largely from the materials of chivalric romance. He chooses white mulattoes as the centered subjects, and he foregrounds psychological rather than physical violence to demonstrate their aborted rites of passage into the white aggregate. Chesnutt does little in this novel to explore the plight of the era's black masses and the physical racist violence that pervaded their lives or to expose the group of whites who perpetrated the violence.

Marrow focuses on the experiences of the Millers, relatively affluent bright mulattoes, yet it includes significant thematic materials and narrative actions about other classes and hues of blacks. The plot revolves around the ritualistic physical violence whites use to keep blacks on the margins of southern society. In this novel, Chesnutt's perspective on the era's chivalric tradition is lodged in his portrayal of white male characters intimately associated with the Clarendon Club, a "social" organization some of whose members are dedicated to maintaining white supremacy by any means necessary. In particular, his characterization of the "Big Three" (Captain McBane, Major Carteret, and General Belmont) underscores the chivalric tradition's baneful state at the turn of the century and its seminal role in the violent oppression of blacks.

Cedars and *Marrow* clearly charted two principal and different courses in the genre that twentieth-century novelists followed, with *Marrow* the more influential of the two. For example, in *The Autobiography of an Ex-Coloured Man* Johnson continued in the tradition of *Cedars* and its nineteenth-century forerunners. W. E. B. Du Bois aligned *The Quest of the Silver Fleece* (1911) with the themes and techniques of *Marrow* and its nineteenth-century cousins (such as Sutton Griggs's *Imperium in Imperio* [1899]). But whether aligned with *Cedars* or with *Marrow*, many African American novels published between 1900 and 1930 showed that New South whites' immersion in modern chivalry was integral to their attempt to replicate the mythic Old South, and the novels underscored the debilitating effects of whites' obsessive nostalgia on blacks. The principal difference between novels in these two groups can be discerned from each group's perspective on the chivalric tradition—one foregrounded the tradition's paternalism and the other highlighted the tradition's Negrophobia. This difference in perspective dictated how the authors handled theme, characterization, and other aspects of form.

Using the South's modern-day chivalry either as backdrop or as foreground, several novelists formed subjects, inscribed social landscapes, and constructed emplotments that betrayed whites' "social" clubs as white supremacist organizations that used terrorist tactics against blacks to activate their myth of the Old South. Within a few years after the Civil War, perhaps hundreds of white supremacist organizations sprang up throughout the South.[1] The Ku Klux Klan (also known as the Invisible Empire) was and has remained the most widely known of these groups since Reconstruction. Organized in Pulaski, Tennessee, in 1865, the KKK was foremost among these groups in using the trappings of the medieval age of chivalry to define its hierarchical structure and its organization's purposes.[2] When viewed from the psychosocial and psychosexual tensions of the time and place, the Klan and its sister organizations' principal mission was to protect southern white womanhood from what they considered the beastlike sexual passions of the "brutish Negro" male.

As the novels reveal, the white female body and the black male body became texts on which were inscribed and from which were read the New South's social and racial ideologies. Abstracted into a symbol, the generic white woman came to represent the holiness of whites' efforts to reinstate the mythic Eden of the Old South. Negrophobes read—and through the lynching bee's torture and mutilations they wrote—the black male body as a manifestation of the devil, an evil force that threatened the purity of the entire white South by being an ever-present threat to the sanctity of its chief symbol, the white woman.

J. McHenry Jones's *Hearts of Gold* and Dunbar's *The Sport of the Gods* exemplify major trends during this period in the genre's use of tropes, its construction of a fictive world, and its subject formations as part of its assertion that whites' creation of a New South slave was key to their replicating an antebellum social structure. In both novels setting is a key indicator of how the political, social, economic, and legal components of post–Civil War southern society mutually conspired in an attempt to reduce blacks to basically the same place they occupied in the antebellum social structure.

Setting *Hearts of Gold* initially in the North, Jones blends chivalric discourse and fairy-tale discourse to create a social milieu in which he situates the novel's principal black characters, and he asserts close cultural affinities between this group and those affluent whites who possess "the bluest blood in the land" (66). Choosing practically all of his northern black characters from what he and others of this period called the black aristocracy (the middle and upper classes), his portrayal of these black subjects is such that their speech, interests, social behavior, and appearances are almost indistinguishable from those of the white belles and beaux who populate much southern white fiction of the period. In fact, Jones refers to the black men and women he portrays as the "beau and belle" who "at heart" are aristocrats (5, 66).

Jones argues that refined character, not color, binds this group of blacks in communitas, and he contends that "writers like W. D. Howells and others" have overlooked this observation (67). As part of his dialogic refutation of whites' texts, particularly southern white romances, he points out, "This is evidently not the class from which the usual American writer draws his characters, when moralizing upon the peculiarities of the Afro-American" (66). However, when the novel's setting changes to a southern landscape, Jones casts practically all of his southern black characters within those same stereotypical character molds he disavows when justifying his choice of principal black characters.

The novel's protagonist is a white mulatto woman and its main story line concerns the problems those who straddle the color line encounter. Jones's secondary story line about the plight of a black male (Lotus Stone) draws the South's neoslavery into focus. Jones also uses the Eden trope as rubric and highlights the more pernicious form it assumed as part of the post–Civil War South's chivalric tradition.

To contextualize Stone's story, Jones constructs a series of interrelated narrative situations based on the legal, juridical, and penal systems of the post-Reconstruction South. Collectively, these formations (in conjunction with others) show that the New South's social codes reflect its attempts to activate the mythic Old South by replicating a political economy characteristic of the old regime. Before dramatizing this thesis, Jones argues the similarities and differences between race problems in the North and in the South, and he emphasizes the extent to which the southern present is a mirror of its past. The discourse is heavily tractarian. Nevertheless, the characters' positions on the issues are integral to Jones's formation of those characters as subjects and to the novel's emplotment.

Immediately following the Civil War, southern states began to institute Black Codes that were intended to regulate practically every aspect of a black's life. In some respects the Black Codes, which varied from state to state, accorded the freedmen rights as citizens comparable to rights that whites enjoyed. But in most respects the codes not only were racist and discriminatory but were tantamount to a reactivation of the slave codes.[3] The harshest features of the Black Codes were those relating to vagrancy, apprenticeship, labor, and land.[4] The Civil Rights Act of 1866 and pressure from liberal Northerners encouraged some southern states to temper their codes and others eventually to rescind them. Nevertheless, the harshest features of the Black Codes operated de facto in the South for several decades. Jones's juxtaposition of the slave codes and the Black Codes through the characters' dialogue and through dramatic action reveals continuity between the South's antebellum and postbellum social structures.

Having established this overview of the South through the dialogue of its characters in a northern setting, *Hearts of Gold*'s plot structure requires that its central black characters move geographically from the North to the South and thus experience firsthand the effects of the new form of slavery. The novel's thematic structure also is designed to refute those who defended the South's legal and quasi-legal practices on the ground that the North also discriminated against blacks and to refute those who maintained that in the North blacks enjoyed rights equal to whites. Jones draws from social reality when he maintains that blacks were the victims of unequal enforcement of civil laws in the North almost as much as they were in the South.[5] After all, one of the major motivations for the black characters' migration to the South is their disillusionment with northern racism.

Stone's spatial journey (North to South) is in effect also a temporal journey (present to past), and Jones uses a conjunction and conflation of spatial and temporal realities to narrativize Stone's southern experience and make it emblematic of blacks for the time and place. Stone is self-confident, highly educated, aristocratic, assertive, and a Northerner. In addition, his social idealism, optimism, and extreme naïveté put him in immediate peril of becoming a victim of the Southern Way of Life. Dr. Leighton, a northern white of southern origin and Stone's rival for the affections of the novel's heroine, returns to the South and hastens Stone's entrapment by the southern system.

Stone's southern ordeal emphasizes the tropological link Jones establishes between white society and black subjectivity. Through Leighton's machinations, Stone is sued for medical malpractice and brought before the bar of southern justice. The judge instructs the jury to return a guilty verdict. He seizes Stone's assets, levies a $250 fine against him, and sentences him to three years in the convict mines. The novel remains close to historical reality in showing that the penal system is a major component in the New South's systematic dehumanization of blacks, closely aligned with the peonage, sharecropping, and convict-leasing systems and carefully co-ordinated with the region's economic and legal institutions. The penal system is one of the power structure's most direct means for turning the freedman into a New South slave, and Stone's sentence is intended to effect his transformation. As the novel reveals, by 1900 the South's legal system (particularly Jim Crow laws) had helped create and had sanctioned a society that in substance differed little from the slavocracy.[6]

The allegory Jones uses to trace the history of the convict camp to which Stone is sent evokes the mythic history of America as the image of the country changed from that of a topographical paradise (early colonial period) to that of a civil utopia (revolutionary period). His patterns of imagery in the chapter entitled "Convict Mines" support his thesis that the forced labor of blacks undergirds the political economy of the New South and thus support his analogy between chattel slavery and the chain gang as affinal significations.

According to the narrator, before the convict camp was built, the landscape was reminiscent of the Garden of Eden. "Into this natural paradise, like the serpent into Eden, came man" (235). The man, of course, was white, and with him he brought black men in chains. Violating these men's humanity and forcing their labor, he profaned the sanctity of this paradise by transforming it into an agricultural and industrial moneymaking venture, all for his personal financial gain. Jones's overall description of the origin of this convict mine is a generative parallel to the origin of the American Eden and the black presence therein.

The metaphor is explicit, for instance, in the narrator's description of the cell house, where the prisoners—men, women, boys, and girls—are forced to live under conditions "utterly regardless of the laws of morality."

They are scantily clothed, poorly fed, tortured and tormented by "cruel and vindictive" guards, and forced to work fifteen or more hours each day, regardless of severe weather conditions (237). The guards whip, maim, and brutalize the convicts much in the same manner that white overseers brutalized slaves. If a convict manages to escape, the guards hunt the fugitive using the same tactics "nigger catchers" used to hunt fugitive slaves. Certainly the penal system (the legal umbrella for convict-leasing and the chain gangs) and the peonage system in the New South had many of the trappings of chattel slavery. Under these conditions, this once "delectable garden of the gods" (238) has been transformed into a living hell for blacks.

Jones betrays the region's self-projection as a new Eden and dramatically reveals its new form of slavery partially through a series of abbreviated personal narratives about the lives of those incarcerated in the convict camp. For example, one representative narrative is about an inmate who is serving fifteen years for stealing a collard plant from an abandoned field; his wife is serving ten years for being his accomplice. Jones's inscription of the inmates' collective "stories" in effect constitutes a narrative history of black life in an emerging New South society. These narratives of alleged crimes and punishments do not exaggerate historical reality.

In the vast majority of instances, as this novel certifies, once a black was caught in the clutches of this Southern Way of Life, the only reprieve was death or escape from the mines (and thus from the South). Yet successful attempts to escape from the mines were very rare. The resolution to Stone's situation, therefore, is exceptional, for a black friend (not a great white father) rescues him from the convict camp, and the governor of the state eventually pardons him. This particular convict camp is destroyed and Stone leaves the South, but the region's systematized new slavery remains intact for the foreseeable future.

In the fictive world of *Hearts of Gold*, Jones juxtaposes historical formations of the Old South with those of the New South to develop his thesis about new slavery and its perpetuation. By the beginning of the twentieth century, "human slavery, with its most revolting features, was openly practiced" in the South and sustained by a "conspiracy between the officers of the law—justices and constables, mostly white men of the baser sort—and heartless employers, all white men."[7] This legally sanctioned new slavery remained operative until the middle of this century, and it engendered psychological, sociological, and physical landscapes reminiscent of the Old South.

Dunbar uses these landscapes to configure setting, plot, characterization, and theme in *The Sport of the Gods*. Whereas the Eden myth's tropological function is explicit in *Hearts of Gold*, it is implicit in *Sport*, whose fictive world Dunbar constructs from basically the same social reality Jones inscribes. Dunbar focuses his novel's action on the lives of the son, daughter, and wife of Berry Hamilton, and he adopts the period's literary naturalism to chronicle their rise and fall. The novel demonstrates that circumstances beyond the family's control force all but the father to migrate from the rural South to the urban North. In the North their lives slowly degenerate, and only the mother, Fanny, is spared complete destruction. The circumstances that force their migration stem from legal problems New South aristocrats create for the family patriarch, whose story frames the novel.

The Hamiltons live in a small cottage situated "some hundred paces" from the rear of their employer's "great house" (17, 18). The spatial relations between the two families' living quarters are "somewhat in the manner of the old cabin in the quarters, with which usage as well as tradition had made both master and servant familiar" (17). The survival of spatial fixity indicates and is congruent with the survival of psychological, social, economic, and other formations from the slavocracy, which becomes clear as the novel's plot unfolds. Thus, setting in *Sport* functions in part to reveal affinities between the Old South and the New South (and thus between old slavery and new slavery).

The Civil War crumbled the structure of antebellum society in the South, in essence displacing both Berry and Maurice Oakley, his current employer. Following the war, their lives take directions that in large measure lead to a replication of the antebellum social structure, as is evident from the novel's opening chapter and subsequent incidents. About the time Maurice is beginning to recover the way of life he had lost, he hires Berry as his butler, and Berry hopes his own fortunes will rise with those of his employer. In effect, Maurice assumes the role of Berry's great white father in this New South social setting.

As Oakley's fortunes increase, his social circle of Old South aristocrats, his "house, his reputation, his satisfaction, [are] all evidences" that he is "able quickly to recover much of the ground lost during the war" and that he succeeds in creating a New South Eden for himself (22). With Berry and his family living in "the little servant's cottage in the yard" (18) behind the Oakley's "mansion," Maurice's New South idyll is complete; it lasts for twenty years.

The Hamiltons' material prosperity and psychosocial contentment are in relative harmony with those of the Oakleys. For twenty years they live contentedly in their little cottage flanked by a vegetable garden and bordered in front and back by flowers. The complete setting is a "bower of peace and comfort" (19) in which the black family measures their happiness principally by their close proximity (spatial and psychological) to their employers. The narrator's portrayal of these New South serfs and their "great house" landlords is a central feature of the social landscape.

The narrator's description of the setting as a southern idyll is Dunbar's parodic installation of Plantation School texts in which the black freedman is a contented New South serf. The author's intents are clear when shortly after the novel opens the narrator shatters this blissful image and its accompanying idyll. The general situation Dunbar depicts in the first two chapters actually ridicules the idealized master-servant relationship that many late-nineteenth-century white writers perpetrated as part of their nostalgic view of the Old South. In fact, in the novel's opening paragraph the narrator engages in an intertextual dialogue with the period's social romances because they fail to provide a realistic treatment of antebellum and postbellum race relations.

The destruction of the southern idyll begins when Frank Oakley, Maurice' half-brother, rather inadvertently allows Berry to be accused of stealing money that Frank himself misappropriated. Since Berry has money (which he has accumulated through initiative and sacrifice), he immediately is suspected of the alleged theft, for New South society has been designed to assure that blacks do not achieve economic prosperity or independence. Reflecting social reality, the novel shows that in the New South of this era, for a black to be accused of a crime is for him to be pronounced guilty. Thus, the social, political, and legal institutions of the society conspire to indict, convict, and punish Berry. The court sentences him to ten years of hard labor, of which he serves five.

The novel's use of animal imagery supports its thesis that hard labor transforms Berry from a man to a beast of burden, which is what the system of chattel slavery did to blacks. As in *Hearts of Gold*, the prison is the social space in which the black body as text is reinscribed as a New South slave. Released from prison, Berry's "lips drooped pathetically, and hard treatment had given his eyes a lowering look. . . . He had lived like an ox, working without inspiration or reward, and he came forth like an ox from his stall" (180). Dunbar's use of imagery and metaphor (the slavery-to-freedom analogy) and Berry's body as text substitute for a detailed account of Berry's physical and psychological transformation as a victim of the penal system.

In other ways the analogy between Old South slavery and New South slavery is integral to the novel's emplotment. For instance, it takes the Yankee reporter Skaggs (another great white father) to effect Berry's ostensible emancipation from this new form of slavery. As was the case during the slavocracy, the Yankee in the South disrupts the Edenic social order. The resolution to Berry's story is also the novel's end. While the ending lends itself to different interpretations, Dunbar certainly suggests that slavery never actually ended in the South; rather, it assumed a new form and began a new cycle. Though Berry Hamilton is freed from prison (his second emancipation), he gains little if any control over the forces that dictate his life in the society. His experiences after the war teach him that the freedman in the South is never free and that whiteness (the white-controlled power structure) is omnipotent. At the novel's end Berry and his wife return to their former employers, the Oakleys, resettle in the cottage, continue their lives, and thus with resignation reassume the space and place New South blacks are supposed to occupy on this social landscape.

The transformation trope is integral to subject formation in *The Sport of the Gods,* and Dunbar applies it to major and minor characters, blacks and whites. In the formation of Maurice Oakley's subjectivity, Dunbar not only dramatizes Oakley's psychological and physiological metamorphosis from a paternalist to a Negrophobe (he mentally and physically deteriorates) but also uses Oakley's body as an ideological text to betray the diseased nature of culture formation in the New South. In this novel and others of the period, character and culture are interlocked in a diabolic cause-effect relationship.

With concentrated attention on white male characters, several African American novels from the late nineteenth century through the middle of this century incorporate discursive formations to show that the South's new slavery assumed two different yet interrelated manifestations, both of them hinged on the deformation and the recommodification of the freedman. In presenting the first instance, the novels foreground the psychological and social landscapes of the post-Reconstruction South. On these landscapes the paternalistic great white father dominates, and there is a psychosocial exchange nexus between the postemancipation master and his servant. The medium of exchange is the servant's subjectivity. In return for being (or at least assuming the guise of) a self-deprecating "good nigger," a human deformity, he or she receives the protection and support of a great white father. In return, this great white father receives psychological massaging for his self-image as a superior human, and he is allowed the fantasy of living more completely the myth of the feudal Old South. Most southern white Plantation School writers corroborate this milder form of the new slavery and most African American novelists refute it.

In the harsher manifestation of the new slavery, a black person's value is determined by his ability to produce commodities whose exchange value allows the white power structure to sustain itself in a manner reminiscent of the mythic Old South's plantation aristocracy. In exchange for his productivity, the black person is allowed to remain alive. A black who accepts this role without complaint is considered a "good nigger." One who rejects this assigned role is considered, of course, a "bad nigger." The more blacks assert their humanity, the less productive they are and therefore the less valuable they are as human commodities. The less productive they are, the less "good" they are, and, consequently, the less valuable are their lives. When and if they fully assert their humanity, their lives no longer have exchange value in the system. At this point they typically fall victim to the lynching bee or in some other way are erased from the social landscape.

To incorporate the harsher manifestation of the new slavery, the novels typically focus on the historical reality of the South's political economy. Several of them speak specifically to how effectively the South used its political institution to safeguard the peonage, sharecropping, and convict-leasing systems that in effect reduced many freedmen to New South slaves. Others weave this information into their plot structures by having a central character, usually intended as representative, become a victim of these interrelated systems of economic exploitation.

A Strange Fruit in the New Garden

The deformation of black subjects, particularly males, was not limited to Negrophobic discourse in the New South. At least for blacks, the New South's emergence as a historical era evokes images of black men's physical destruction, among other violent atrocities perpetrated against the black population. In popular and vernacular culture, the term *strange fruit* has come to signify a lynched black man. African American novelists have drawn upon the same signification and have produced a novelistic discourse that situates the metaphor within the sociocultural context that produced it.

By 1890 the sight of a lynched black man in the South usually meant that he had been judged guilty of sexually violating a white woman. Most African American novels published during the last quarter of the century include at least a passing reference to the region's prohibition against sexual contact between black men and white women, and a few of them incorporate a lynching scene (as allusion, anecdote, or interpolation). Yet they seldom thematically or structurally link these two discursive facts. In the 1890s the novels begin gradually to use characterization, structure, and other formalist features to connect the theme of the new slavery with the themes of miscegenation and ritual violence. Within less than a decade this interfacing of themes produces the lynching bee as a major symbolic action in the genre to show how entrenched the new slavery had become in the post-Reconstruction era.

A survey of the genre for the 1890s reveals that the various reasons the novels attribute to the lynching of a black man are consistent with the reasons historians and social critics have identified in their studies of the practice.[8] Though a popular notion in the early twentieth century was that the majority of black males who were lynched were guilty of sexual crimes against white women, most published studies of lynching contradict this notion. Nevertheless, the idea was powerful. Under the code of the new slavery, whites considered a black's rape of a white woman or murder of a white person the most heinous crimes. In either instance whites often treated mere allegation as proof positive. A frequent assertion was that if the homicide victim was a white female, whether woman or child, the black also had raped her.

The definitions of rape and murder from racial perspectives were so broad that in the Negrophobic mind a black who sought "social equality" was guilty (or soon would be) of rape or murder, and his lynching was merely an instance in which the punishment preceded the crime. A black man or even a black woman who violated the code of the white South's social structure easily could become the victim of a lynching bee. Though it is rare that a novel of this (or any) period portrays the lynching of a black woman, black women often were lynched—at least seventy-six of them between 1882 and 1927.[9]

Novels published after the turn of the century utilize the Eden trope to connect the lynching of a black to the psychosocial and psychosexual mind-set of the white power structure. The process through which the genre creates this formation is discernible from a group of novels beginning with Sanda's (Walter H. Stowers and W. H. Anderson's) *Appointed* (1894) and ending with Chesnutt's *The Marrow of Tradition* (1901).

In *Appointed*, Sanda endows John Saunders, the co-protagonist, with essentially the same character traits Jones assigns to Lotus Stone in *Hearts of Gold*. Like Jones, Sanda creates narrative situations that highlight tensions between white society and black (male) subjectivity. But Saunders violates the sanctity of white personhood, for which the penalty is death. His violations include accidentally bumping into, "talking back" to, and—in a defensive gesture—accidentally striking a white man. Whites consider all of these incidents serious crimes against the social codes that regulate racial contact. To allow the crimes to go unpunished would be to admit Saunders to social equality, which in turn would be tantamount to sanctioning a sexual relationship between him and a white woman. After three thwarted attempts to lynch Saunders, a member of the last mob shoots him.

In *Hearts of Gold*, published two years after *Appointed*, Jones interpolates a lynching scene in which he verifies Sanda's reasons for the lynching of a black man as well as includes basic components that help distinguish the lynching scene from the lynching bee. Like Sanda, Jones demonstrates how relatively minor violations of the Southern Way of Life can lead to a black man's death. Jones adds the ritualistic mutilation of the victim's body to the lynching scene. His description of the lynching is particularly graphic, and these physical mutilations assume symbolic significance in later novels in which the lynching bee is a central symbolic action, integral to plot structure and directly related to the lives of the protagonists. Among the varieties of atrocities in *Hearts of Gold*, the men beat the victim (Harvey Meeks) mercilessly, cut off his fingers as "mementoes of the occasion" (226), and finally decapitate the dead body and display its head in town.

Meeks's social crimes are "defending a helpless child" (221) and operating an economically more successful business than whites (especially a rival white grocer) think a black man should. His civil "sin" is striking a white man. In this interpolated story, Jones concentrates on the religious dimensions of the lynching as ritual. For the whites, the lynching constitutes Meeks's atonement ritual to expiate his sin as well as a purification ceremony for whites to decontaminate their society.

The ritualistic trappings, carnival-like atmosphere, and sadistic brutality of the lynching bee in *Hearts of Gold* indicate the state to which the lynching of a black man had evolved in southern society and consequently in the African American novel's fictive version of that society. For the first twenty years after the Civil War, the practice was confined mainly to hanging and shooting the victim. In the 1880s lynching became a sadistic ritual of mutilation and torture, and the savagery of the ritual steadily increased during the next three or four decades.[10] Lynching of a black was a means for the defeated southern whites to vent their anger at the North on a readily accessible scapegoat, the freedman. It did not take long, however, for the practice to assume much larger significance. According to Wilbur J. Cash, by 1900 lynching was considered "an act of racial and patriotic expression, an act of chivalry, an act, indeed, having a definitely ritualistic value in respect to the entire Southern sentiment." Not only lower-class whites considered the sadistic act an expression of southern patriotism. Lynchings, with accompanying torture and mutilation, had the approval "and often the participation of the noblest and wisest of that revered generation of men which was now bending to the grave"; far from considering the practice wrong, these men considered it "the living bone and flesh of right."[11] Its chivalric and religious overtones had become trenchant by the turn of the century.

In the last year of the nineteenth century, Sutton Griggs's *Imperium in Imperio* installs another major component of the lynching scene that situates the formation within the Eden trope, further distinguishes the lynching scene from the lynching bee, and thus anticipates the perspective of twentieth-century African American novels when treating the act as a social ritual of religious dimensions. *Imperium* includes a direct connection between the lynching of a black man and whites' phobia regarding social (i.e., sexual) relations between black men and white women. By violating Jim Crow laws, one of the novel's two protagonists, Belton Piedmont, commits several social crimes. For these transgressions his punishment includes verbal abuse, an arrest, a citation for vagrancy, and a five-dollar fine.

Some time later, though, Belton violates the South's strictest prohibition by inadvertently touching a white woman. He commits a civil sin. In large part, Griggs provides motivation for this segment of the plot by creating three interrelated discursive formations that reveal the following: that southern white social conventions are predicated on the medieval age of chivalry; that the chivalric tradition in the New South has produced "social clubs" dedicated to the ideology of white supremacy; and that the concept of white personhood is a sustaining force in the purposes and activities of these terrorist social clubs. As part of the novel's emplotment, Belton is hanged and shot, but he does not die from either.

Chronologically, then, novels of the late nineteenth century gradually embellish the lynching scene to the point that in twentieth-century novels these embellishments crystallize as the lynching bee. With its political, social, sexual, religious, and ritualistic undergirdings, the lynching bee became the dominant symbol of volatile race relations in the South. As a symbolic action, the lynching bee thematically merges the organized and institutionalized violence directed against the black population. After 1900, it interfaces emplotment, characterization, and other features of form into a paradigm of form and meaning in several African American novels.

A New South, a New Religion

After 1900, the lynching bee is central to the genre's portrait of the psychodynamics of a white-dominated society in which racism is so entrenched and pervasive that it has the status of a religion. In twentieth-century novels, religious ramifications encase the political, social, sexual, and ritualistic components of the lynching bee and therefore further configure the genre's Eden trope. The continuing configuration is concurrent with the increasing sophistication of craft in the genre. The white power structure controls all of society's institutions and denies blacks equal access to them. In this context, all things white—institutions and persons—are sacred, and the entire social order is ruled over by a god of whiteness. In African American novels published before 1960, whiteness is a concept that the authors project and their characters perceive as a force of cosmic proportions.

Dunbar refers to this cosmic force at the end of *The Sport of the Gods* when the narrator points out that Berry Hamilton and his wife "were powerless against some Will infinitely stronger than their own" (189). This will's agents are principally white men (Negrophobes and paternalists) whose arbitrary power to take or to save a black's life is like the power of the Judeo-Christian God. Dunbar suggests that not only is whites' power basically omnipotent and arbitrary, but the violence it engenders is essentially a sport for them.

Implicit in the title and in the content of Dunbar's novel are the religious underpinnings of the white South's social structure. Appropriating Judeo-Christian biblical tropes, weaving them into a generic portrait of southern society, and inscribing the black body as a text, African American novels published during the early years of this century formulate a novelistic cosmology in which the lynching bee is a key figuration. It is the portrait of a white South immersed in ritual murder.

With the publication of a seminal article entitled "Civil Religion in America," sociologist Robert Bellah initiated this generation's scholarly discussion of American civil religion. Scholars who participate in this discussion basically agree that civil religion has its own beliefs, symbols, rituals, saints, sancta, liturgical calendar, sacred scriptures, and other features that differ from those of church religion. Nevertheless, civil religion draws heavily from the features of church religion in that, as Bellah points out, the "political realm" assumes a "religious dimension." [12] Historically, politics and church religion in the white South have differed significantly from politics and church religion in other areas of the country. Consequently, the civil religion that developed among white Southerners differs markedly from civil religion among other American groups.

The pre-1960 African American novel uses the Eden trope to explore the entrenched religious dimensions of the white South's civil society, and it shows that racism plays a significant role in southern white civil religion. Certainly by the beginning of this century racialism had welded the social, political, economic, educational, religious (church), and other societal institutions in the white South into "an organic structure of ideas, values, and beliefs" [13] as well as symbols and rituals that aptly can be called southern white civil religion (or the Southern Way of Life). Racialism is the key for distinguishing southern white civil religion as pre-1960 African American novels inscribe it from what scholars call American civil religion.

Typically, an African American novel's fictive world aligns closely with the actual world from which this fictive world is derived. Thus, given church religion—or Christianity—as a construct, the godhead of southern white civil religion is the generic white man. The tremendous power a white man (and gender is significant here) has over the life of a black person in the South of this period and in the novels' depiction of the South in effect makes him like the Judeo-Christian God. African American novelists (Chesnutt, Wright, Ellison, and several others) speak specifically of the all-powerful white man as God. The sacred persons and rituals of southern white civil religion are focal in the genre's appropriation and transformation of the Bible's Eden myth. For at least a century following the Civil War, the most sacred person in the white South's civil religion was actually a collective, abstract entity—the southern white woman. During this period, one of the most sacred rituals of this civil religion was the lynching bee. From post-Reconstruction through the 1930s, civil religion superseded church religion in its sacredness, as illustrated in such nineteenth-century novels as *Appointed* and *Imperium in Imperio* and in most twentieth-century novels that treat organized, ritualistic racist violence.

During the last quarter of the nineteenth century, racist violence in a variety of forms—spontaneous and random white-on-black violence, organized vigilante violence, and violence endemic to the South's sharecropping and penal institutions—begins to rival miscegenation for thematic preeminence in the African American novel. By 1900 these two themes have conjoined in several novels and have produced fresh novelistic perspectives on the white South's Eden trope. Compared to the nineteenth-century, settings, symbols, symbolic actions, and imagistic patterns are more fully integrated with thematics. The genre expands its delineation of characters—major and minor, black and white—and draws attention to key characters' psychosocial makeup. These changes reflect how the chivalric tradition helps shape group psychology in the region. Overall, the novels demythologize the white paternalist and (to a lesser extent) the ever-faithful black servant, and they begin to demystify the white belle. The steady progression of changes in subject formation and other fictional techniques as part of the African American novel's use of the Eden trope is particularly evident in Chesnutt's *The Marrow of Tradition* and its intertextual relationship to texts of the southern white ideal. By the turn of the century one of the central features in the genre's textual design has shifted from a catalogue of social evils (i.e., Brown's *Clotel* or Webb's *Garies*) to a dialogue between the novel and (often contemporary) Anglo-American texts.

Between post-Reconstruction and World War I, the texts of southern writers, black and white, literary and nonliterary, are frequently engaged in a dialogue over the nature of the New South. At times these texts speak directly to each other; at other times the dialogue is implicit, indirect. Novels "talk" to other novels as well as to sociological, legal, historical, and anthropological texts. Southern texts by blacks and by whites of this period are not always in dialogic conflict; indeed, at times these texts corroborate one another. But in most instances, African American novels engage in a dialogic refutation of those texts that espouse an ideology of white supremacy.

Texts by Griggs and Chesnutt, the two most prolific southern black fiction writers of the period, are among the most assertive in refuting southern white texts predicated on the New South ideal. In general, the period's black novels respond vociferously to the position on race promulgated in white texts of social criticism such as *Race Problems of the South*, a publication of the proceedings of a conference held in Montgomery, Alabama, in May 1900; in pseudoscientific texts such as those by Charles Carroll, whose *"The Negro a Beast"* and *The Tempter of Eve* (1902) claim biblical and scientific sanction for the thesis that blacks are subhuman; and in fictional texts such as those by the Reverend Thomas Dixon Jr., principally *The Leopard's Spots* and *The Clansman*, which portray blacks as sexual fiends. A common thesis among Negrophobic texts of the period is that on the chain of being blacks at best occupy a position between the lower animals and man—and of course these texts define "man" as white.

From the genre's portrait of southern white society comes an operational definition of southern white civil religion that finds corroboration in studies such as Charles Reagan Wilson's *Baptized in Blood: The Religion of the Lost Cause* (1980). From the African American novel's purview, southern white civil religion is a cosmological construct in which race is a key factor. The godhead of this civil religion is white and male. Those created in his image (whites) are what Chesnutt characterizes in *The Marrow of Tradition* as "the heaven-crowned Anglo-Saxon" race (185). Those not created in his image (blacks), to borrow a characterization from Charles Carroll and his fellow Negrophobes, are humanoids who (at best) belong to the beasts of the fields.

The saints of this civil religion are persons, living and dead, whose vehement espousal of the tenets of the Southern Way of Life has earned them a revered status in the social history of the South; in some instances they are revered as secondary gods. John C. Calhoun is such a saint, as the reference in Chesnutt's *Marrow* makes clear (38). In other African American novels, Thomas Jefferson, Robert E. Lee, Jefferson Davis, Thomas Dixon, and others are depicted as saints or secondary gods in this civil religion and appear frequently through references and allusions. The memorials erected to these southern saints are part of the sancta in this civil religion. The most important sancta, however, include such sacred places associated with the South's holy war as Appomattox, to which Chesnutt alludes in *Marrow* (1), Richmond, Fort Sumter, and even the hallowed ground on which stands a memorial to the Confederate soldier in the town square of many southern communities.

The sacred scriptures of this civil religion are formed from a compendia of legal, historical, political, sociological, anthropological, pseudoscientific, and literary texts that espouse the premises of white supremacy, and the African American novel of the period most often responds dialogically to these texts. Those who preached these premises—either orally or in writing—are the priests of the New South's civil religion; among them Carroll, Thomas Nelson Page, and Thomas Dixon, along with nineteenth-century Negrophobic exhorters such as Thornton Stringfellow, Edmund Ruffin, Hinton R. Helper, William G. Brownlow, Henry Watterson, and Josiah C. Nott. Indeed, in his comments about the purposes of *The Marrow of Tradition* Chesnutt singles out Dixon and other contemporaries as examples of the priests and the texts to which *Marrow* is in part a dialogic response.[14] In some instances, as in the novels of Sutton Griggs, direct references to Dixon and his novels or romances appear within the text. For example, in the first two editions of *The Hindered Hand* Griggs provides "a review of Mr. Dixon's 'Leopard's Spots' . . . in the form of a conversation between two characters of the book." In the novel's third edition, Griggs appends to the last chapter a section entitled "A Hindering Hand: A Review of the Anti-Negro Crusade of Mr. Thomas Dixon, Jr." (298–99, 301–33). Dixon was an impressive pulpit preacher in the Baptist church, but was much more influential when preaching the white South's civil religion. Kelly Miller acknowledges this influence in an open letter to Dixon: "Through the wide-spread influence of your writings you have become the chief priest of those who worship at the shrine of race hatred and wrath" (3).

The essence of southern white civil religion as it is portrayed in

The Marrow of Tradition, The Hindered Hand, and several other African American—and southern white—novels of this and later periods is embodied in the religion's principal icon (the white woman) and in its primary social ritual. While tournaments and jousts are forms of social group behavior linked to this civil religion, its principal and therefore most sacred ritual is the lynching bee, an orgiastic ritual that functions as a nuclear structuring device in several African American novels.

Subjects, Societies, and Tropes: The Marrow of Tradition

With the publication of *The Marrow of Tradition* in 1901 Chesnutt took the first major twentieth-century step toward making the lynching bee an integral part of form and meaning in the African American novel. He sets the novel near the turn of the century, bases it on an actual race riot that occurred in Wilmington, North Carolina, in 1898, and uses the Eden trope to overarch his conjunction and critique of society and subjectivity in the New South.[15] The lynching bee episode (though without an actual lynching) is at the novel's thematic and structural center. Chesnutt uses it to reveal the white South's civil religion, which he proffers as a defining criterion for society and subjectivity in the turn-of-the-century South.

The lynching bee segment in the novel formally begins when the white community learns that a prominent, elderly white woman (Mrs. Polly Ochiltree) has been robbed and murdered. Because whites do not immediately know who the murderer is, they conclude that he must be a black and, consequently, that rape assuredly accompanied the other crimes. The white community's reactions to the alleged crimes are immediate, predictable, and in concert; they target Sandy Campbell.

Shortly before Campbell is to be lynched, he is exonerated. John Delamere (Sandy's employer, his great white father, and former slave master) intercedes, provides Sandy an alibi, and reveals that his grandson, Tom Delamere, is the culprit. Though Campbell is released from custody and the lynching bee is aborted, the racists will not be deterred from their intent to use violence to subjugate the black population and to create a social structure based on that of the slave past. In developing the novel's plot, Chesnutt makes the lynching bee crucial to the novel's structural design and to its central themes.

Chesnutt locates the lynching segment (nine of the novel's thirty-seven chapters) in an axial position in the novel's overall binary structure. Situated at the beginning of the novel's second half, the incident provides both structural and thematic transition between the novel's first-half emphasis on psychological violence and its second-half emphasis on physical violence. The lynching bee also links the novel's two primary story lines, both of which revolve around the white South's view of miscegenation as a sin. The first story line involves tensions between two families, the white Carterets and the black Millers, and it establishes the thread of psychological violence that runs through the novel. The uncanny physical resemblance between Olivia Carteret and Janet Miller makes their body surfaces texts that signify the sins of the southern past and the survival of those sins into the present. Samuel Merkell (their father) committed the original sin by legally marrying his black housekeeper (Janet's mother). Atonement for Merkell's "unpardonable social sin" (266) is exacted from his black progeny through the second generation, which ostensibly expiates the original sin.

Central to the novel's second story line are the physical violence associated with southern race relations and the religious dimensions accorded it. In the white psyche, Sandy Campbell's civil crimes (the alleged robbery and murder) are secondary to his unpardonable, cosmic sin (the alleged rape). The narrator echoes the white community's sentiment when he points out that the proposed ritual death would be "the swift and terrible punishment which would fall, like the judgment of God, upon any one [black] who laid sacrilegious hands upon white womanhood" (186).

In portraying the entrenchment of the mind-set that would precipitate a lynching bee, the novel presents a pessimistic outlook on southern race relations by portraying how "the present is woven with the past, how certainly the future will be but the outcome of the present" (112). The novel's title, therefore, is apt. The novel explores the white South's traditional obsessive belief in the inviolability of its social structure and of white people. As Chesnutt and other novelists present it, the tradition is predicated on the New South's mythic image of the Old South and the "holy war" that gave form and substance to this mythic image in the New South. The marrow of this tradition is southern white civil religion. The social construct, therefore, is the South's version of a civil theocracy in which the white woman is the principal icon, and around her revolves a system of taboos, prohibitions, and phobias that defines the value system and regulates race relations.

Using the intended lynching bee as a center for several thematic and structural radii, Chesnutt builds the novel on a series of oppositions and thus provides an analysis of the three principal levels of the region's social structure: the overall social organization, the black community, and the white community. He accomplishes his critique largely through his construction of the two racial groups.

In the author's analysis of the aggregate social order, the mulatto occupies the mediating position between the polar opposites of black and white. Biologically, socially, economically, and in other ways, the mulatto class is closely related to the white community. Nevertheless, the novel demonstrates that entrenched racism keeps this class outside the boundaries of the power base. The mulatto class (represented by Dr. Miller) does not prevent the lynching bee. During the riot the white power structure renders the mulatto class powerless and forces several of its members to leave town. Through these two episodes and through other narrative formations Chesnutt unequivocally suggests that mulattoism is not a viable means for improving southern race relations. In the novel, the failure of fusion politics signifies the failure of mulattoism. Chesnutt's stance on mulattoism (i.e., miscegenation) is a dialogic refutation of texts that emanated from a small but vocal school of thought near the turn of the century.[16]

The ineffective mediating position of the mulatto class in Chesnutt's structural model of the South as a whole matches its role in his model of the black community. He emphasizes a causal relationship between society and subjectivity. At the model's opposing ends are what can be termed the class of "ole time darkies" (or the retainer group) and the class of "New Negroes." Sandy Campbell is one of the characters through whom Chesnutt inscribes the retainer group's subjectivity. Devoted to his former slave master, Mr. Delamere, Sandy in several ways represents continuity between the past and the present. He belongs to that group of "old family retainers, brought up in the feudal atmosphere now so rapidly passing away" (43), that in large part derives its sense of self-worth and identity from its association with and fidelity to the former slaveholding class.

There is a psychological and material nexus between the retainer class and the former slaveholding class. These New South aristocrats extend protective kindness and a modicum of material support to the retainer class. Yet they do not allow the retainers to prosper materially to the extent that they elevate their status in the social structure. These whites benefit materially, though not extensively, from the labor of their retainers, but their psychological benefit is much greater. In this exchange nexus the retainer class defers to the former slaveholding class in a manner that allows the latter to replicate, at least psychologically, the feudal antebellum past. If a member of the retainer class prospers materially or ceases to genuflect, he forfeits the paternalism and renders the exchange nexus null and void. This system of social exchange value exists between John Delamere and Sandy Campbell, the most benign form of the system that Chesnutt includes in this novel.

In the system's most pernicious form, blacks in the retainer class become willing commodities (materially and psychologically) without any exchange value. Mammy Jane Letlow and her grandson, Jerry Letlow, are the representative types in *Marrow*. As self-commodified blacks— "darkies"—the Letlows satisfy the former slaveowners' psychological need to be close to but quite separate from blacks. In return for being the "darky" they receive neither protective kindness nor material reward from the ruling class. The various ways that Chesnutt uses masks, mistaken identity, and appearance versus reality in the novel make it quite clear that the Letlows are not wearing masks and therefore their posture is not in the trickster mode. Chesnutt's utter disgust for the "darky" class is clear from the fate he assigns to Mammy Jane and Jerry Letlow during the riot. Both participate in the erasure of their humanness and thus are conspirators in their deformations. Both die with pleas and statements of fidelity to the Carterets on their lips (296, 307), and thus both are themselves erased.

At the other end of the black community model are the New Negroes, who actively resist being turned into a commodity, with or without an exchange value. The chief representative of this group is Josh Green, a rebellious young black "general" intent on defining, asserting, and defending his racial identity. Chesnutt constructs Green as the direct opposite of Jerry Letlow (whom whites define as a "good nigger"). From the purview of the racist powermongers, Josh Green is a "bad nigger." With "the instinct of a born commander" (301), Green will fight for the rights of blacks. Brave and assertive, he fears little for his own life and does not reject violence as a defensive mechanism for correcting the society's ills. Josh not only resents a wrong but also will defend a right (112). In Chesnutt's formation, Josh Green embodies the best qualities of the New Negro. What faint glimmer of optimism Chesnutt injects into the novel he invests in the New Negroes as potentially effective mediators of the South's race relations. But this class's ability to improve the race's condition lies far in the future.

Though Chesnutt does not completely discredit the class that forms the middle tier between the "ole time darky" and the New Negroes, he places little if any faith in this class as an effective mediator. Its members possess "neither the picturesqueness of the slave," which survives in the modern-day ole time darky, "nor the unconscious dignity" of the New Negroes (42). As the lynching mania spreads, whites basically erase whatever distinctions they previously have made between this group (mainly mulattoes and professionals) and the black masses.

Chesnutt's analysis of the structure of the white social order, the novel's third model, resembles the one he provides for blacks and is predicated on whites' psychosocial relation to the black community. At one extreme of the white continuum is the surviving Old South aristocracy, whose chief representatives are John and Tom Delamere, respectively the best and the worst of this class. John Delamere believes that he has arrested time: in his relationship with Sandy Campbell he has defined present race relations in terms of past race relations. To him, the "best" blacks are those who, like Sandy Campbell, are childlike, dependent on, and faithful to the system of white paternalism (as Chesnutt's use of parent-child imagery in various sections of the novel indicates). The concept of honor that Delamere imbibed during the feudal antebellum past maintains a strong hold on his character and guides his emotions and actions. His honor prompts him to rescue Sandy from the lynch mob and to expose his grandson as the criminal. The elder Delamere's code of honor dictates his "devotion" to Sandy, but he does not extend his paternalism to blacks in general.

By having John Delamere die before the novel's end, Chesnutt in effect rules out white paternalism as an effective mediation in the New South's social structure. Delamere's death also is Chesnutt's way of signifying that time is not static, that the old order must pass. Tom Delamere, initially self-exiled because of his crimes, returns to the community, implying that the sham aristocracy will continue to wield power in a manner that will negatively affect the welfare of the black population. Eventually, Chesnutt posits, this power structure, too, shall pass.

At the other extreme of this structural model of white society are the Negrophobes, whom Chesnutt uses to penetrate the marrow of race problems in the New South. His construction of the Negrophobe as part of a discussion of the psychosocial forces that give rise to lynchings and other forms of racist violence in the South is an addition to his predecessors' treatment of the lynching bee. The proposed lynching bee, not the riot, is therefore the focal event in the novel that reveals subjectivity. Chesnutt delineates fully (but does not develop) several of the novel's Negrophobes to coincide with his analysis of the psychodynamics that produces certain character types on this New South landscape.

Because subjectivity is Chesnutt's benchmark for integrating the novel's themes of race and sex and for reflecting historical reality, he forms some of the principal white characters from historical sources. His construction of the "Big Three" is an example. The specificity of the ideological bonds and the professional and personal friendships and tensions that exist among them recall the triad of William Brownlow, Henry Watterson, and Thomas Nelson Page. The fine lines that distinguish the racist ideology among the members of the triad and biographical details about each man strongly suggest that Chesnutt uses Brownlow, Watterson, and Page as models respectively for Captain McBane, Major Carteret, and General Belmont.[17] On this continuum of Negrophobia, Belmont occupies the middle ground between the unadulterated racism of McBane and the tempered racism of Carteret. Chesnutt indicates this gradation in part by the manner in which each pronounces (or mispronounces) and uses the word *Negro* (36).

McBane (whose name connotes deadly harm) once belonged to the Ku Klux Klan, which in the novel's present is basically defunct. Chesnutt's formation of this subject foreshadows the resurgence of the KKK, which occurred within two decades after the novel takes place. In this character Chesnutt embodies the most pernicious principles and practices of New South whites as they affected the political, social, economic, and legal aspects of race relations after the Civil War.

McBane represents those New South whites who attempted to effect their mythic Eden by establishing the most dehumanizing form of the new slavery. The son of an antebellum white overseer, McBane inherits the characteristics of the class from which he is descended. He is given "a contract with the State for its convict labor, from which in a few years he had realized a fortune" (34). When his fortune and thus his political and social aspirations falter, he blames his misfortune on blacks' new status as freedmen.

Captain McBane is Major Carteret's complement. He raises to the level of action the racist ideology Carteret articulates as abstract concept. He, therefore, is Chesnutt's focal subject for treating physical violence between the races. By the time the novel's action has progressed to the proposed lynching, it is clear that the alleged rape is merely an excuse by whites for their oppression and brutalization of freedmen who have moved into the margins of the societal mainstream. Once the proposed lynching bee is aborted, it becomes even clearer that whites would have used it as a symbolic action to disenfranchise blacks, to remove black officeholders, to deter blacks' educational and economic advancement, and in general to negate the socialization process Reconstruction had set in motion. McBane is the leader of the pack.

The Big Three invoke the tenets of southern white civil religion in proclaiming that "the provisions of the Federal Constitution . . . must yield to the 'higher law,' and if the Constitution could neither be altered nor bent to this end, means must be found to circumvent it" (240). This "higher law" emanates from the concept of cosmogonic whiteness that undergirds the white South's civil religion and supports its "sacred principle" of white supremacy (235). The means, of course, are various forms of racist violence used to make the civil law subservient to white supremacist ideology. Captain McBane, Major Carteret, and Colonel Belmont are, therefore, self-ordained priests of the white South's civil religion. For them, the ritualized murder would be an appropriate sacrifice not only to the godhead but also to one of the chief saints or secondary gods of southern white civil religion, "no less a person than the great John C. Calhoun himself" (38).

The dialogue of the novel's extreme white racists on the topics of lynching and white womanhood reiterates sentiments that a large number of Negrophobes voiced during the period. More specifically, the dialogue reveals the close intertextual relationship between *The Marrow of Tradition* and popular white racist texts of the time. One specific text is the published proceedings of the Montgomery conference on race, held in 1900. A comparison between Alex C. King's address to the conference and these characters' dialogue shows how fully Chesnutt installs this publication as an intertext.[18]

In this structural model of southern white society the "liberal" whites are the mediating force. Lee Ellis best represents this position in the novel. He is descended from the nonslaveholding modified Quakers of the South. A product of his "ancestral traditions" (95), Ellis shares southern whites' basic prejudices against blacks, but "his prejudices had been tempered by the peaceful tenets of his father's sect" (217). He believes in fair play (which for him is not synonymous with racial equality) and thus he rhetorically condemns lynch-law justice. However, he prefers to deceive himself that such hostility is temporary and in time will subside. In a time of crisis between the races, racial loyalties rather than his own stated principles of right and wrong guide his thoughts and actions. He can prove Sandy's innocence, but to do so would mean exposing Tom Delamere. Ellis represents a class (that in the novel includes Jews) whose actions or lack of actions and whose alignment with the white power structure render its mediating position ineffectual in southern race relations.

Through a structural analysis of the different racial and social tiers of this southern community, Chesnutt reveals the unwillingness of most whites and the inability of most blacks to reconcile the problems of race relations. In the fictional Wellington, North Carolina, the novel's setting, the belief that the South is a white man's Eden is entrenched in the minds of those who control the power structure. Dialogue, narrative commentary, symbolic actions, and other aspects of the novel's discourse situate it firmly within the Eden trope. Notwithstanding whites' use of the lynching bee to deter freedmen from seeking access to the Southern Eden, the New Negroes' resistance to being reduced to slaves poses the greatest threat to the maintenance of a society predicated tropologically on the Bible's Eden myth. Myth exists as concept, while ritual exists as action. Thus, from the 1880s through the 1930s, the lynching bee was a ritualized dramatization of the Eden trope's hold on the white South's self-concept. The trope provided the bedrock for this form of racist violence to emerge as a "religious" rite in consonance with the white South's civil religion.

Within this civil religion all whites are deified, as Chesnutt dramatizes in the novel's riot scene. When in a defensive posture one of the black men kills a white man, the mob becomes enraged. Chesnutt explains the meaning of this symbolic action within the purview of southern white civil religion: "A negro had killed a white man,—the unpardonable sin, admitting neither excuse, justification, nor extenuation. From time immemorial it had been bred in the southern white consciousness, and in the negro consciousness also, for that matter, that the person of a white man was sacred from the touch of a negro, no matter what the provocation" (303).

By using the white South's civil religion to overarch his treatment of the violence of race relations, by exploring a cause-effect relationship between the concept of white womanhood and the lynchings of black men, and by using the Bible's Eden myth as a controlling trope in his literary approach to southern race relations, Chesnutt in *The Marrow of Tradition* forecasts definite changes in the content, and consequently in the form, of a large group of subsequent African American novels. The manner in which he treats miscegenation in *The House Behind the Cedars* and racist violence in *The Marrow of Tradition* makes Chesnutt and these two novels pivotal in the African American novel's development of the Eden trope as a paradigm in the genre.

African Americans published fewer than thirty novels between *The Marrow of Tradition* in 1901 and Jean Toomer's *Cane* in 1923. In these novels as a group, miscegenation remained a predominant theme. Novelists also continued to use the lynching bee as a standard feature during this period to discuss or to dramatize whites' violence against blacks. Most of the novels thematically included the white South's obsession with white womanhood, and many of them foregrounded trappings from the biblical Eden myth as part of their fictional techniques. However, few novelists during this period interrelated the topic of miscegenation between black men and white women with the lynching mania of the South in the way Chesnutt did in *The Marrow of Tradition.*

In 1905 Griggs published *The Hindered Hand,* in which he surveyed different forms of racism in the South. Though Griggs included in this novel one of the most graphically brutal lynching scenes ever to appear in the genre, he did not make the lynching bee seminal to the novel's structural and thematic design, and he did not utilize the Bible's Eden myth paradigmatically. In 1912 Johnson used a lynching scene in *The Autobiography of an Ex-Coloured Man* symbolically to monitor the protagonist' experiential and psychological development and to underscore his representational function in the novel. But Johnson did not connect the lynching to explicit motifs from the Bible's Eden story.

During and immediately following World War I, most African American novelists included the lynching of a black male soldier as part of their treatment of the war years, but they seldom made the lynching bee more than a stock device. In fact, after *The Marrow of Tradition*, not until the Harlem Renaissance did the lynching bee resume a central place in the African American novel as part of a paradigmatic approach to race relations predicated on the biblical Eden myth. On the whole, then, the Bible's narrative of Eden as a paradigm in the African American novel lay dormant between 1901 and the mid-1920s. When novelists made the lynching bee a salient feature of the post-1920 novel, they did so as part of their exploration of the totemic nature of southern white civil religion. (See chapter 7 for a discussion of southern white totemism.) Consequently, the Eden trope resumed its prominence as a fictional construct in the genre, and novelists modified the construct to coincide with the genre's centering of black males as representational protagonists and with other changes in the genre's form and content.

The Wars for Eden

Hell: War and Racism

THE AMERICAN DREAM as a variant of the image of America as Eden moved to the forefront during the first two decades of the twentieth century, and there it has remained. The political, social, economic, religious, and racial dimensions of the dream conjoined with its military dimension in 1917, when the nation entered the war in Europe. As the war effort invigorated American patriotism, the white South's self-image and that of the nation became more closely aligned. Like the Revolutionary War, World War I helped unite the North and the South ideologically around a common cause, the defense of the American ideal, and helped to narrow the ideological gulf between the two regions, which had widened with the Civil War.[1]

Responding to social forces that emanated from the American Dream concept and from World War I, African American novelists gradually altered the genre's configuration during the generation that followed the war's end. Those novelists who incorporated the world war (directly or indirectly) through theme or some aspect of form gave more concentrated attention than did their predecessors to the Civil War as a historical event, and they incorporated more fully ideological premises associated with the nation's other major wars, particularly the Revolution.

In 1915 F. Grant Gilmore published *"The Problem": A Military Novel*, which is devoted to the Spanish-American War. Before the 1960s, however, few African Americans produced what can be classified as war novels. In fact, from the mid-1910s to the mid-1920s, novelists in general did not foreground black soldiers' World War I military experience or the war's direct effects on African American civilian life. Rather, they juxtaposed historical formations relevant to the black population that repeated themselves during the nation's major wars of the eighteenth, nineteenth, and twentieth centuries to emphasize the ongoing civil war between blacks and whites. This tropological use of war became even more prevalent in novels published after the mid-1920s and helped define discourse in the genre until well after the 1950s.

Between World War I and the 1940s, modifications to the genre's thematic and formalist conventions derived directly from changes in American society at large and thus indirectly from the World War I military campaign. One modification was that representative protagonists in the genre after 1917 more often than not were male, and until the 1960s many of them were veterans of World War I. Setting in the novel after 1917 became more inclusive of locales outside the South. Postwar novelists' alterations to the genre's conventional settings and subject formations engendered a tripartite structure that remained standard for decades after the 1920s. Novelists conjoined the civil war trope with the Eden trope to embellish subjectivity, setting, and structure in novels that thematized World War I. Walter White's *The Fire in the Flint* (1924), Claude McKay's *Home to Harlem* (1928), Victor Daly's *Not Only War: A Story of Two Great Conflicts* (1932), and George Washington Lee's *River George* (1937) incorporate the direct and indirect influence of World War I on the nation's race relations and consequently exemplify the era's impact on the African American novel's formalist and thematic contours.

In his foreword to *Not Only War*, Daly revises Sherman's famous Civil War metaphor by equating hell and war and the racist oppression under which African Americans live: "William Tecumseh Sherman branded War for all time when he called it Hell. There is yet another gaping, abysmal Hell into which some of us are actually born or unconsciously sucked. The Hell that Sherman knew was a physical one—of rapine, destruction and death. This other, is a purgatory for the mind, for the spirit, for the soul of men. Not only War is Hell" (7). Through its setting, formation of key characters, narrative structure, and inscription of historically based incidents, *Not Only War* makes this analogy dramatically specific. One of Daly's principal discursive strategies is the parallel between the historical progression of America's great wars for freedom (Revolution, Civil War, World War I) and the historical continuity in the racist oppression of African Americans. He uses the Civil War and its aftermath thematically to embellish the novel's setting in the World War I era.

Not Only War foregrounds racism as the ideological nexus between the American Civil War and World War I. Daly draws upon various features of the Eden trope to specify his analogy between race relations in the Old South (the Civil War era) and those in the New South (the World War I era). He demonstrates that the Civil War did not effect a sharp demarcation between the two Souths: the New South in many ways replicates the Old South. Daly's dramatization of this point is situated on the novel's principal American setting, South Carolina, a social landscape dominated by whites whose devotion to Jim Crow bespeaks in part their grounding in Old South social ideology. The end of the Civil War as a military campaign between two factions of whites signaled the escalation of a non-militarized civil war between southern whites and blacks, which continues into the novel's present. Daly uses this war trope to narrativize present-day southern and American society against the backdrop of World War I.

When the United States entered the war in 1917, its call for national unity, under President Woodrow Wilson's slogan "to make the world safe for democracy," put into sharp relief the ironic status of the nation's black citizenry in relation to the nation's democratic ideals. The federal government tacitly admitted that blacks had not been extended the civil liberties that the Constitution guaranteed. In fact, when courting the African American vote in 1912, Wilson promised that if he became president blacks could count on him to "assist in advancing the interests of their race in the United States." He vowed to work to effect "not mere grudging justice, but justice executed with liberality and cordial good feeling."[2]

Wilson served as president during the entire war. His administration's promises to the black population constitute a narrative formation in most novels that treat the war. Black characters debate the federal government's sincerity, with the centered subject usually espousing a progovernment stance. The formation introduces World War I as theme into a novel, constitutes the initial narrative scaffolding for the author's construction of the centered subject as exceptionally naive, and serves as a key element in a novel's emplotment. The formation also helps establish the centered subject as a representative of the race, for the government's promises seduced many blacks into supporting the war in the belief that the nation would reward the race's support by more fully extending the privileges of American citizenship.[3] The government reneged on its promises. African American novelists draw upon this general situation to configure plot and subjectivity in novels that cover the war years.

Not Only War demonstrates in its first half that the federal government tightened rather than loosened the reigns of racial discrimination during the early years of the war. Daly's novel provides one of the fullest treatments among pre-1960 African American novels of the racism to which black recruits were subjected while preparing to defend the nation's democratic ideals. Southern whites in the novel, while supporting the nation's war efforts, adamantly oppose the training of northern-influenced black recruits in the South. It is a repetition of the age-old belief among whites that blacks exposed to life outside the South will resist and undermine the Southern Way of Life. To southern whites, maintaining the traditional structure of power relations between the races is more germane than training black soldiers to defend the American ideal.

From this mind-set, in literature and in life, the southern white power structure defines a black (particularly a male) as colonized, noncolonized, or decolonized. A colonized black (usually a native Southerner) remains in the place and space to which his race has been assigned. A noncolonized black typically is a Northerner unschooled in the Southern Way of Life; occasionally, he is a native Southerner who continually refuses to conform to Jim Crow laws and customs. A decolonized black is a native Southerner who has lived outside the South and who rejects southern laws and customs regarding race. Through either direct agitation or example he encourages local blacks to challenge the white power structure. Centered subjects in novels that treat the war and its aftermath most often are decolonized blacks, and this status is integral to the novels' standard emplotment.

Daly relies on historical reality when he chooses Spartanburg, South Carolina, as the setting in which to explore the white southern perspective on black colonization, to construct the novel's centered subject, and to structure much of the action in the novel's first half. Montgomery Jason, the novel's protagonist, is a southern black who for some years has lived in the North. When he returns to his native Spartanburg as a recruit to be trained as an officer, local whites consider his violation of Jim Crow laws typical of a black whose exposure to life in the North has "spoiled" him and who in turn threatens southern white society. Many if not most of the blacks in the camp are native Northerners whose mere presence in the South whites consider an affront to the Southern Way of Life. Daly draws upon whites' historical image of blacks as diseased animals, a view that was reactivated during Wilson's first presidential term. Such an image in part undergirded Jim Crow laws and their intensification during World War I. Daly weaves this idea into other sections of the novel and shows that part of southern whites' irrational fear is their belief that "blackness" is an infectious disease (of which outsiders are the primary carriers) that threatens "whiteness."

In the historical situation on which Daly bases this segment of the novel, Spartanburg's mayor and Chamber of Commerce as well as the state's governor petitioned the War Department to keep northern black recruits out of South Carolina on the ground that these soldiers' refusal to adhere to Jim Crow laws would create trouble.[4] According to Mayor J. F. Floyd, "With their northern ideas about race equality, [these blacks] will probably expect to be treated like white men." But, he maintained, "We shall treat them exactly as we treat our resident negroes."[5]

True to the Negrophobes' predictions—in historical reality and in the novel—the noncolonized and decolonized outsiders challenge the social order by violating the city's Jim Crow laws. Racial tension between local whites and "New York's National Guard regiment of colored soldiers" (the novel's name for the actual Fifteenth New York Regiment) erupts when several black soldiers use public facilities designated for whites only. To the resident whites, this assertion of social equality inevitably will lead to widespread miscegenation and an undermining of the entire social order. In both the historical and the fictive reality, northern white soldiers support the black recruits' stand against Jim Crow laws, further challenging the southern white power structure and compounding the interracial conflict with an interregional one.

In the novel's plot structure, the "numerous petty clashes" (59) that ensue between the soldiers (both black and white) and the white citizenry of Spartanburg are miniature wars that prefigure the larger war for which the soldiers are preparing. The union of black and white soldiers does not permanently change the social structure in ways that benefit blacks. In the novel's presentation of the larger war, black and white soldiers again unite to challenge what they perceive as a common enemy—the Germans. The novel's emplotment and subject formations reveal, however, that the combined effort against the Germans does not unify the races. Instead, the military campaign overseas perpetuates rather than eradicates racist policies and practices designed to keep blacks marginalized in America's Eden.

The novel's two principal settings—South Carolina and France—coincide with its bipartite division. Under the Eden trope as rubric and in an inverted form, these two social landscapes intimate a binary opposition between paradise (France) and hell (a white-dominated American social structure, both stateside and abroad). Daly's formation of the novel's centered subject and of key secondary and minor characters derives from the history of the social landscapes on which he locates these characters, and character portraiture maintains continuity with conventional portraiture in the genre, particularly for the novel's southern setting and characters. The psychosexual war between the novel's protagonist and antagonist mirrors the root cause of the ongoing conflict between American blacks and whites.

Daly makes the novel's white antagonist, Lieutenant Robert Lee Casper, a reincarnation of the prototypical Old South gentleman, complete with military title, social prominence, and racist paternalism. Moreover, Casper, like many of his real-life counterparts, considers World War I a holy war whose principles are identical to those of the South's Lost Cause. In fact, for him and his historical peers World War I vindicates the white South's Civil War ideological stance (which is embedded in this character's first and middle names).[6] Casper's perspective on the world war diametrically opposes Jason's and helps fuel their personal war.

Installing a conventional story about an (ostensible) interracial love triangle as the novel's narrative nucleus, Daly makes dramatically specific the conflict between protagonist and antagonist. He uses this discursive formation to reveal and to monitor the persistence of Old South ideologies and to bolster the novel's tropological nexus between war and race relations. Jason's erroneous belief that Casper is sexually exploiting a black woman, Miriam Pinckney, to whom Jason is romantically attached, occasions the initial conflict between the two men. The miscegenetic triangle forms a thematic nucleus from which extend other forms of racial conflict in the novel; it generates tiers of analogies in the novel's story line. On one tier, the analogy is between antebellum race relations and postbellum race relations, as revealed through the psychosocial and psychosexual conflicts between white and black men in the novel's present. On another tier, the sexual rivalry between Jason and Casper is analogous to the ongoing power struggle between American blacks and whites. On yet another level, this nuclear situation highlights friction between the North and South over the proper place of blacks in the American social structure. When the analogy is at its most expanded form in the novel, the conflict between Jason and Casper mirrors the conflict between nations during World War I. The centrifugal narrative movement is from the personal to the racial to the regional to the international. On each tier the warring males fight over a woman (either specific or generic), and Daly's expanding war trope recalls what from a literary perspective might be considered the Western world's most famous literary war, the Trojan War.

War functions tropologically in the novel's first half primarily to reveal that life for blacks in the South repeats a historical situation the race encountered during the country's great wars of the eighteenth and nineteenth centuries. The Revolutionary War and the Civil War were struggles between two factions of whites for dominance, and both wars essentially left blacks as the dominated. With the onset of World War I, there are few concrete signs that the power struggle between American and European whites will result in a better life for African Americans. On this point Daly's narrator disagrees with the protagonist. Jason believes that World War I will change the substantive character of southern (and American) race relations for the better. His naïveté is a fatal character flaw.

To convey the idea of historical continuity in America's great wars for freedom, the effects of these wars on African American life, and the ongoing psychological warfare between America's blacks and whites, Daly demonstrates that in the white mind miscegenation is a more serious issue than world war. His assertion undergirds plot structure in the novel's second half, set in France.

Daly's construction of discursive formations that underscore symbolic relations between space and place is integral to this novel's thematic and formalist figurations and to the Eden trope's functions in these figurations. The symbolic space-place nexus in *Not Only War* draws upon historical reality to convey the conjunction between civilian and military life indicative of American society. In Europe the army invokes racist policies and practices from America's civil society to regulate black soldiers' interactions with American and European whites in and outside the military. One historical fact upon which Daly draws to emplot the novel's second half is an army proclamation that prohibited black soldiers from speaking to French white women.[7]

When the white commander of Jason's company deviates from military rules and orders Jason and two other black officers to stay in a French home rather than in the haylofts where black soldiers usually stay, he inadvertently puts Jason and his cohorts in the position of profaning the sacredness of space as the white American power structure defines it. Jason also establishes a warm friendship with the two white women, the Aubertins, in whose home he stays. The army, with Lieutenant Casper as its representative, considers this situation an egregious transgression against the American Way of Life. Daly uses this incident to install the Eden trope as a framing construct for the novel's second half.

Typically in twentieth-century African American novels, black soldiers' optimism about the meaning the war will have for the race at home equates with their quest for Eden. It also is characteristic of these novels to invert Anglo-America's Eden trope as part of their depiction of these soldiers' experiences among European, especially French, civilians. The inversion hinges on the authors' and their characters' contrast between the Old World and the New World. For the novelists and their black characters, France is a land offering personal opportunity and freedom to the African American.

As a consequence of their travels abroad, these soldiers discover a metaphorical New Eden. The standard situation is that as a result of white Europeans' humane treatment of them, the soldiers more readily affirm their rightful place as members of the human family and refute white America's claim that they are naturally depraved and subhuman. In essence, the novelists portray them as black Adams seeking to gain (or to regain) Paradise.

Because white American racism has conditioned the way Jason sees his social environment, he initially is skeptical about the seeming lack of racism he experiences in his relations with the French. He soon discovers, however, that their hospitality and friendship are genuine. By contrast to America's social landscape, France is a social utopia, and Jason feels that when in France he indeed is in "a Garden of Eden" (74).

By inverting the Eden trope in the novel's second half, Daly portrays Jason as a black Adam who loses the paradise he believes he has gained. The miscegenation theme is central to this portrayal, and Jason's fall results from Casper's allegation that he is consorting sexually with a white woman. In the novel's first half, the author creates a situation in which the antagonism between Casper and Jason, as a metaphor for antagonism between whites and blacks, emanates from the rivalry between white men and black men for the affections of a woman. In this southern setting, the woman is black. Casper is the historical (rather than the mythic) New World white Adam whose power to control relations in the Southern Garden is manifested in his power, as Jason perceives it, to control black men by sexually exploiting the black woman, an exploitation that betokens his power to exclude all blacks from the South's Eden.

When in the novel's second half the setting changes to France and the French include rather than exclude Jason from what he considers an Edenic society, Daly's inversion of the miscegenetic situation bespeaks his inversion of the Eden trope. The white Casper is now the snake in the black Adam's garden. Daly makes protagonist and antagonist representative characters. Casper considers blacks as outside the Adamic family, and he considers French white women the American white man's sociogenic sisters, symbols of the sacredness of the world's all-white Eden. Thus he is infuriated when he learns that the French accept Jason as part of the human family. His fury turns to blind rage when he discovers that Jason has established a friendship with the white Blanche Aubertin. Casper erroneously concludes that it is a romantic liaison, and considering it an unpardonable sin, Casper initiates Jason's court-martial, the final battle in the psychosexual war between the two.

In Casper's mind, Jason is a traitor to America, a more potent enemy than the Germans: instead of fighting to preserve what Casper deems the American Way of Life, Jason is undermining it by being "over here socializing with white women" (90). As Daly and others depict the situation, American soldiers, black and white, had two enemies in France—each other and the Germans. As the snake in Jason's garden, Casper's revenge creates circumstances that lead directly to Jason's death on the front lines. Casper's actions also are self-destructive.

Jason's death is the novel's closure and lends itself to different interpretations, among them Daly's tacit call to the black populace to unite in the war against American racism. The novel's content and its dedication to "THE ARMY OF THE DISILLUSIONED" (5) do not confine its meaning and message to black military personnel but extend them to the black citizenry at large. Juxtaposing civilian and military life, tropologically using Eden, war, and disease, and endowing the soldier-subject with an extreme case of naïveté are among the novelistic features *Not Only War* shares with other African American novels that incorporate World War I as historical context.

France: (In)versions of Paradise

During the first half of this century, African American artists, political activists, and others who emigrated to France found a society far less hostile to blacks than was the United States. Following World War I, Langston Hughes, Countee Cullen, Claude McKay, Richard Wright, and other African American writers who traveled or lived in France wrote of it in nonfiction prose as the African American New Eden in the Old World.[8] But in the United States the rather widespread image of France as a social utopia for blacks derived in large part from African American soldiers' reports of their cordial interaction with French whites during the war years. African American novels that inscribe these soldiers' wartime experiences usually install the Eden trope as a narrative frame and war as a trope to critique race relations in the United States. Typically, the novels affirm—but occasionally ˈthey refute—this image of France. Daly's *Not Only War*, White's *The Fire in the Flint*, and McKay's *Home to Harlem* exemplify the different ways in which novels inscribe this critique.

These and other novels set during the World War I era portray black soldiers as subjects who encounter in France two diametrically opposed social worlds (French civilian and American military) and who confront two formidable enemies (white American military personnel and the Germans). By inscribing the U.S. Army as a social structure that duplicates (or extends) American civilian society, the novels directly reflect the period's social reality. For instance, in an attempt to avert the anticipated consequences of French whites treating American blacks as human, on 7 August, 1918, the army issued an official document entitled "Secret Information Concerning Black American Troops." The document succinctly states the prevailing attitude with which white civilians in the United States and white military personnel at home and abroad regarded the presence of African American troops in France. In addition, the work iterates racist views that prevailed among white Americans and from which the genre by the 1920s already had established thematic and formalist conventions—such as the black (male) body as text, whites' miscegenation phobia, and the view of blacks as diseased interlopers who threatened the survival of white American civilization.

Addressed primarily to French officers under whom black American troops would serve, the document purports to give these officers and the French people in general "an exact idea" of the inferior social place blacks have been assigned in the American social structure. It encourages the French to help maintain white Americans' racial attitudes toward and treatment of African Americans. Failure to do so, the document argues, would create a menacing situation for whites in the United States. According to the document, if blacks were exposed to humane treatment from European whites, they would become less willing to submit to American racial stratifications and thus would create a direct threat to the white power structure.

Characterizing African Americans as intellectually inferior and morally degenerate, the document points out that though the army has selected from among the males "the choicest with respect to physique and morals," these soldiers still fall far below white standards of morality. The statement asserts that even the "choicest" of them are not quite human. "For instance, black American troops in France have, by themselves, given rise to as many complaints for attempted rape as all the rest of the army." Given the white American mind-set, rape was the clearest indicator that black men indeed were savage beasts. (Official investigators for the War Department, however, proved that the allegation of large-scale attempted rapes and similar atrocities black soldiers allegedly committed were false.)[9] The document concludes by reemphasizing the white American taboo against black men associating with white women, warning, "White Americans become greatly incensed at any public expression of intimacy between white women and black men." On the whole, the French ignored this racist propaganda, but the French ministry collected and burned as many copies of this secret document as possible.[10]

The document provides a gloss for various narrative formations and characterizations in virtually all African American novels that incorporate black soldiers' experiences overseas during World War I. The novels contrast French society and the U.S. Army as part of their thematic and tropological conjunction of the Civil War and World War I. They inscribe these wars both as specific events and as historical periods to emphasize temporal continuity in blacks' status as social liminals in American society. From this conjuncture emerges a narrative construct that projects history as a series of repetitious and contiguous formations that reveals the continuity and fusion of past and present. For example, the novels depict the primary function of black soldiers in World War I as supporting the military activities and to serve the personal needs of white soldiers much in the manner that the Confederacy used slaves in the early years of the Civil War.[11] For both the Confederate and Union Armies, blacks (including many of the Union's all-black combat units) functioned mainly as labor battalions. Approximately 380,000 of the 400,000 black men in the military during World War I played the same role.

Home to Harlem exemplifies the present-past and military-civilian parallels through a structural analogy between these two wartime periods. The novel's protagonist, Jake Brown, goes to France filled with dreams of how his active support of the United States' war efforts will bring him a better life at home. Jake's dreams are shattered, however, when he realizes that the U.S. Army is a microcosm of American society and has transported its racism across the Atlantic. Though "he had enlisted to fight," he is assigned to carry the "boards, planks, posts, [and] rafters" to build hundreds of huts to house the white American soldiers (4).

The novel's "happy chocolate company" (4), Jake's unit, is a fictional replication of one of the all-black combat units the War Department sent overseas. Even though these units had black officers, white officers normally commanded both the combat units (which were attached to the French army) and the all-black labor battalions. The War Department often chose southern whites to command black units, rationalizing that given the history of southern race relations, southern whites more easily could control blacks.[12]

Home to Harlem and other novels portray these white officers as incarnations of antebellum white overseers, commanding a group of blacks servicing the white power structure. Black officers in these units, like black antebellum slave drivers, occupy a medial position between the white officers and the black soldiers. Jake's "combat" unit performs common labor duties. Whether called service battalions, engineer regiments, depot brigades, development battalions, pioneer infantry regiments, or services of supply (General John J. Pershing's euphemism), virtually all black soldiers worked in what was sometimes likened to a new form of slavery.[13]

For Jake and other black enlistees deployed overseas, the transatlantic crossing is metaphorically a journey back in time. It is an inverted and ironic recapitulation of the Middle Passage, for at the journey's end blacks in effect become new slaves in the Old World. Shortly after Jake arrives in France, this realization forces him to discard his optimism about what World War I will mean for him and for the masses of blacks stateside. The narrative formation also draws into thematic focus the metaphorical civil war between American blacks and whites, now being fought on foreign soil.

To be sure, *Home to Harlem* is not about blacks' combat experiences during the war. It is, however, to a large extent a novel about a black ex-soldier's quest for Eden in the context of the war experience. As such, it is a representative example of an African American novel that does not use World War I as a focal theme but as context and trope to treat black-white relations during and after the war. By introducing Jake's story line with the civilian-military analogy that foregrounds racial discrimination and exclusion, McKay centrally situates the Eden trope to establish a foundation for the novel's thematic structure. Jake's experiences as an enlisted man lead him to conclude that following the war America will renege on its promises to blacks. Consequently, he deserts the army, a symbolic action that signals his total rejection of the myth and the reality of America. He decides to remain in Europe.

Having lost much of his naïveté by this point, he begins a series of migrations that evolves into his spiritual quest for Eden. As a modern-day black Adam, Jake's physical journeys through different cultures and subcultures are his attempts to gain Eden. McKay organizes the novel, then, with a series of episodes that are structurally and thematically variations of one another. These discursive formations are centered on places to and from which Jake migrates—from Petersburg, Virginia, to Harlem, to France, to London, and back to Harlem. His encounters with racism in each place structure his development from innocence toward experience, a process that is incomplete at the novel's end. McKay emphasizes that Eden is more readily found in a person than in a place.

The author builds each of these formations on a symbolic action or a symbolic character, each of which allows Jake to pierce surface appearances and reach a fuller understanding of his social environment and thus of himself. Deserting the army and rejecting France as a potential Eden, Jake migrates to London. There, the discursive formation that reveals England as a false Eden centers on Jake's relationship to his white girlfriend and the racial violence that erupts when the armistice brings "many more black men to the East End of London" (7). His London experience teaches him that he has been seduced by appearances (symbolized by his white girlfriend), that under the veneer of British humanity lies hard-core racism. In rejecting his white girlfriend, he rejects both the symbol and the substance of the white world. Considering any white community, whether in Europe or America, as Eden after the Fall, he henceforth directs his quest home to Harlem.

Through his travels Jake develops and grows spiritually, yet he never fully understands that "home," given the meaning of the term in African American culture, is much more an internal value system than a social space or physical place. Without spiritual values, even the black community of Harlem is not home. At this point in Jake's odyssey, *home* becomes a synonym for *Eden*. Though Jake is a black, he cannot shake off the influence of Anglo-American culture on shaping his mind. For example, he cannot rid himself of the belief that the mythic utopia is attainable through migration from place to place. At the novel's end, the Americanness of his character is revealed through his decision to take the symbolic journey to the West (Chicago). Like several of his fictional counterparts, Jake's experience in France sets in motion his quest for the true Eden. The form of this journey in *Home to Harlem* differs from its form in the other novels discussed in this chapter.

In some novels, as in Willard Savoy's *Alien Land* (1949), the soldier-subject is more a witness to than a victim of the U.S. Army's most brutal and dehumanizing treatment of black soldiers. In such cases the subject usually is an officer (such as *Alien Land*'s Charles Roberts or *The Fire in the*

Flint's Kenneth Harper) whose relatively privileged civilian life has shielded him from the harshest aspects of stateside racism. As a black officer he suffers racial discrimination but remains exempt from the extreme degree of dehumanization inflicted on the masses of black troops. Yet his witnessing of these unspeakable things (which usually remain unspoken in the novels) effects a partial metamorphosis in his subjectivity. The overseas ordeal does not strip the officer of his innocence about American race relations, but it does embolden him to pursue the American Dream more aggressively. As it does for the enlisted man (such as Jake), the ordeal decolonizes him. Officers such as Roberts, Harper, and Aaron George (*River George*) cling to their belief that life for blacks in the States will markedly improve following the war, and they return fortified for a messianic mission to effect this change.

Regarding France as an earthly paradise, many black soldiers chose to remain there following World War I. For the most part, however, such is not the case for fictional black soldiers or civilians. Though expatriate black characters in Jessie Fauset's *There Is Confusion* retain their image of France as an Edenic ideal and choose to spend the rest of their lives there, in most other novels black soldiers and expatriates return to the United States. Like Tom Brinley, the protagonist in Sarah Lee Brown Fleming's *Hope's Highway* (1918), they return because their ties to home outweigh the greater personal and social freedom they enjoy in France and in other parts of Europe. Or, like Jake Brown, they return because they discover that France (or Europe in general) is not the Eden they at first thought it was. Or, like Aaron George, they return because they believe they can reform American society.

Harlem: Black Garden, White Snake

Aaron George and Kenneth Harper typify those ex-soldier protagonists whose metaphorical quest for Eden is aligned with their spatial journeys and with certain narrative formations that had become conventions in the genre by the 1920s. One of these conventions is migration as a thematic structuring device. Several pre–World War I novels employ a linear or bipartite structure commensurate with the centered subject's travels from the South to the North or occasionally vice versa. In a few of these novels a subject's spatial movement is circular or tripartite in that he or she returns to the regional point of origin. In post–World War I novels, however, this circular migration becomes a standard feature and an integral formation in novels that employ the Eden trope.

Novels that incorporate World War I as theme or as trope typically follow the genre's conventional depiction of Harlem as a debilitating social and psychological space. This picture contradicts the idyllic image of Harlem (and of the North generally) that prevailed in southern black society. In the novels, this counterimage is linked directly to a soldier-subject's formation. Novels published between 1900 and 1920 reflect major changes in culture formation that resulted from southern blacks' migration to urban centers outside the South. To some degree, the majority of African American novels published between 1917 and 1960 dramatize how the austerity of life for southern blacks during the war years gave renewed impetus to the Great Black Migration, which began a generation before the war's end. In this migration's fictional representation, black characters in effect search for Eden in the Promised Land of the urban North. Following World War I, therefore, the mythic North as symbol and subject helps reconfigure form and content in the genre's portrayal of African Americans' visions and versions of the New Eden.

The symbolic function of the North is particularized when Paul Laurence Dunbar (*The Sport of the Gods*) and James Weldon Johnson (*The Autobiography of an Ex-Coloured Man*) inscribe this mythic Promised Land as New York's Harlem. These two authors use the social environment of Harlem's nightclubs and cabarets (Dunbar's "Banner Club" and Johnson's "the Club") to bespeak the city's social landscape, which drains the spiritual life from its black inhabitants. "The city is cruel and cold and unfeeling"; it "will bewilder and entice" the innocent "provincial" when he first comes into contact with it, Dunbar writes in *Sport* (70–71). He dramatizes this idea in the story line that centers the son and daughter of his novel's protagonist. In feminizing and personifying New York, both Dunbar and Johnson treat the black migrant's sojourn in New York metaphorically in terms of the biblical narrative of Man's Fall. For ex-coloured man,

> New York City is the most fatally fascinating thing in America. She sits like a great witch at the gate of the country, showing her alluring white face and hiding her crooked hands and feet under the folds of her wide garments— constantly enticing thousands from far within, and tempting those who come

from across the seas to go no farther. And all these become the victims of her caprice. Some she at once crushes beneath her cruel feet; others she condemns to a fate like that of galley-slaves; a few she favours and fondles, riding them high on the bubbles of fortune; then with a sudden breath she blows the bubbles out and laughs mockingly as she watches them fall. (89)

In essence, New York, particularly Harlem, is an Eve-like social landscape that tempts and seduces the southern black migrant and precipitates his spiritual and often his physical death. In their portraits of provincials and southern black male migrants, Dunbar and Johnson sketch the outlines of a prototype that becomes a stock character in novels through the 1950s and beyond.

Beginning with *Sport* and *Ex-Coloured Man*, African American novels present this quest for Eden through a tripartite thematic structure. Thematically and structurally, it is the protagonist's or a main character's (or characters') attempt to escape space in order to alter his or her place within the American social hierarchy, as in *Sport*, W. E. B. Du Bois's *The Quest of the Silver Fleece* (1911), Waters Turpin's *O Canaan!* (1939), William Attaway's *Blood on the Forge* (1941), and several other novels. Most often this journey-become-quest is intricately connected with the theme of identity (personal, spiritual, and racial) in the novel, which in various ways interfaces with the theme of miscegenation, as in *Ex-Coloured Man*, Jean Toomer's *Cane* (1923), and Nella Larsen's *Quicksand* (1928), among others. But whether the specific setting is Harlem, Chicago, Pittsburgh, or some other urban center in the North, African American novels of this period uniformly demonstrate that the proverbial Promised Land of the North (which is synonymous with the metaphorical New Eden) is little more than a social space filled with empty promises.

Creating the ex-soldier as a subject representative of the race allows the novelists to depict the various forms of the African American quest for Eden in postwar America. In most instances, the novelists invert the Eden trope to chronicle their protagonists' circular journey-quests from the South to the North to Europe to Harlem and finally back to the South. Couched in the context of the war experience, this series of migrations thematically structures the novel, as it does in *Home to Harlem* and *River George*.

As a premonition of what awaits the optimistic Aaron George and his fellow soldiers on their return from France to the United States, Lee describes their entry into New York harbor as a slave ship arriving in the Americas to "discharge" its "cargo" (203). Lee's narrative formation constitutes a revision of a historical formation narrativized in antebellum slave narratives (*The Life of Olaudah Equiano*), installed and further revised in early African American novels (*Clotel*), and further revised in early twentieth-century novels (*Ex-Coloured Man*). The initial installation and subsequent revisions speak to the marginalization of black subjects—indeed, the deformation of subjects to objects—in the American Eden. Johnson's analogy in *Ex-Coloured Man* depicts the arrival of southern black migrants in the mythic and seductive New York City. Lee's analogy makes the migrants also veterans of World War I.

The initial impression for Jake and for Aaron George when they return from the war is that Harlem is the African American new Eden. To them, Harlem is "home" (given the spiritual connotations of the term in black folk life), for they believe it to be an ideal social landscape. Yet for both protagonists this Edenic ideal is shattered when they realize whites' pernicious influence on black Harlem life. As part of their inversion of the Eden trope, McKay, Lee, and other novelists portray whites as the tropological snake in blacks' Edenic Harlem.

In the mid-1920s many whites flocked to Harlem in an attempt to escape the decadence of Anglo-American life. To these sojourners, Harlem served as a space for social and spiritual refuge where they could embrace (if only superficially) the meaning of an idyllic and exotic lifestyle and thus rejuvenate themselves from a spiritually fallen state.[14] But as McKay, Lee, Schuyler, and other novelists demonstrate, the influence of whites sucked the marrow of life from Harlem and from other black sections of northern cities. Characteristically, the novels portray these whites as interlopers who contaminate the Harlem garden with their "social diseases" (one of which is racism), and the many blacks who migrate there find that Harlem is not the spiritual wellspring of life they expected.

Jake comes to this realization before the end of *Home to Harlem*. The novel's narrative voice contends that the urban environment does not completely "rob Negroes of their native color and laughter" (191) and that the indigenous spirituality of many southern black migrants thrives in Harlem. But through Jake's experiences McKay shows that this spirituality is like a flower in a crannied wall. The black world in which Jake moves is at its core a reflection of the white world he has rejected. Intraracial and interracial prejudice, conflict, and violence walk hand in hand. What Jake finds is true of Harlem he applies to other urban centers in the North.

In *River George*, on first entering Harlem, George thinks that people such as James Weldon Johnson, Rosamond Johnson, Countee Cullen, George Schuyler, W. E. B. Du Bois, and Walter White spearhead a spiritual movement that includes most blacks in Harlem. George soon discovers that the artists and thinkers identified with the Harlem Renaissance are the exception rather than the rule. Spiritually diseased whites have contaminated the black masses, who are in a spiritually fallen state. When compared to life in the South or to life in the American military overseas, the small degree of overt physical conflict between the races in Harlem might lead to the conclusion that Harlem is indeed the new Eden. But the integrated groups George sees in Harlem do not indicate social equality between the races. Instead, they are the barometer by which one can measure a pernicious white influence in Harlem. As a companion tells him, "This isn't Harlem at all—this is Broadway moved uptown"—for the pleasure and profit of whites (215).

George discovers a Harlem that, like Broadway, is spellbinding and mind-bending. Lee portrays Harlem as a seductress who lures innocent blacks to their ritualized spiritual destruction. Whether these rituals are secular (acted out in the nightclubs and cabarets) or quasi-sacred (in the missions and storefront churches), they emanate from a spiritually destructive economic power structure that whites dictate and control. While secular Harlem dwellers worship a god of sexual wantonness and materialism that whites have imported into the black mecca, those in the sacred vein are caught in the stranglehold of any "one of Harlem's many black pseudo-messiahs" (216). In "a blind religious ecstasy," they sing "spontaneous songs of adoration, not to God, but to their human leader who seemed divine to them" (216). This deified human leader is a creation of a white-controlled society, and the god of whiteness reigns in Harlem. Indeed, the "ecstasies of Harlem love and those of Harlem religion" are "woven from the same cloth" (216). Witnessing this phenomenon makes George even more dedicated to his messianic mission and helps clarify in his mind his vision of the millennium.

Using sexual wantonness as the preeminent metaphor for Harlem's fallen state, Lee suggests that the urban black migrants who "had broken away from the limiting South" to seek Eden in Harlem have been lured away from the spiritual life of their slave grandparents and from the spirituality of their southern black experience. Instead of using the opportunities available to them to advance educationally, culturally, and in other ways, these southern black migrants use "their new freedom to parade their bodies before white men and pander to their desire for vulgarity" (219).

African American novels that inscribe Harlem as an Edenic social landscape often invert Negrophobes' vision of an all-white Eden in which a black presence is considered the potential source of contamination and in which sexuality serves as the metaphor for the society's impending moral and cultural dissolution. Such is the case in *Home to Harlem* and *River George*. Finding that what they envisioned as an all-black Eden has been polluted by a white presence, Jake, George, and other soldier-subjects in the genre reject and flee from Harlem to seek their vision of Eden elsewhere.

Concluding that it would not be "from this group of people [Harlem's black artists and intellectuals] that the spiritual emancipation of his race would arise" (219), George, like his former orderly, Popeye, decides to seek Eden in the South. Popeye's insights are much keener than George's, and on arriving from Europe Popeye proceeds immediately to Georgia, where he plans to immerse himself in the black folk community. The black South will be his Eden, and, he says, he will leave it to God to "change de white folks" (210). George, however, will attempt to become a part of the white South's Eden by reforming the white power structure.

Southern Edens and the "Spoils" of War

Northern black city-dwellers' utopian image of their region was severely tarnished immediately after the war. Black veterans and civilians realized that for them the war had not made (and would not make) America or any other Western nation a safe place for democracy. They began, therefore, to look outside the white Western world for their New Eden. They directed their quest toward the distant past, seeking Eden in Africa. Spearheaded by Marcus Garvey's back-to-Africa movement, many blacks began to regard Africa as their ideal promised land. Though the Garvey movement in the 1920s was concentrated in the Northeast, its influence extended to several parts of the nation and the world, and it was particularly attractive to the masses of African Americans who were under economic and social stress.[15] Primarily a sociopolitical movement, it also gained a foothold in African American literary, visual, and performing arts.

In embracing the African past as part of the period's artistic movement in primitivism, African American artists in essence sought to effect or to recapture an Edenic ideal, which existed more in their imaginations than in reality. To them, Africa represented a simpler, idyllic life, void of racism and other dehumanizing conflicts. The movement produced few novels that were set in Africa or that positively explored any part of the continent from the perspective of an idyllic existence or an ideal state, although short fiction, poetry, and other artistic forms did. When Garvey's movement faltered, its literary parallel quickly diminished.

One of the most significant African American novels published between 1917 and 1960 to explore the theme (through inversion) of an African utopia is George S. Schuyler's *Slaves Today: A Story of Liberia* (1931). Schuyler adopts U.S. history as a metaphorical framework to scathingly ridicule the descendants of those freed American slaves who founded the republic of Liberia a century earlier. The nation's name and that of its capital city (Monrovia) are just two of several instances in which Schuyler draws from historical reality to trope on America's Eden trope. In chastising the ruling class for its corruption and exploitation of the country's masses, the narrator in effect summarizes Schuyler's ideological stance toward his subject matter: "Everywhere in this vast tropical territory, as large as the American state of Virginia, the word of the grandsons of Negro freedmen was law. Their forefathers had come here to this expanse of jungle to found a haven for the oppressed of the black race but their descendants were now guilty of the same cruelties from which they had fled. The Americo-Liberians were to rule; the natives to obey" (100–101). The narrator's statement in effect summarizes the novel. By applying America's Eden trope thematically, inversely, and ironically to his treatment of an African American presence in Africa, Schuyler indicates that the emigrants' construction of their social utopia turns into a dystopia for the native inhabitants. Schuyler comes close to suggesting the possible consequences if black Americans had been able to found a post–World War I republic in Africa, as Garvey envisioned.

Blacks' disillusionment with the North as the Promised Land and their failure (for various reasons) to realize the Edenic ideal in Africa in large part caused them to direct their Edenic quest toward the more recent past, the black South. During the 1917–60 period, this formation prevailed more in literature and other arts than in life. This image of the black South as an Eden privileged a cultural condition over a physical place. It rivalled but never superseded the northern Promised Land ideal. The literary shift in interest from the northern Promised Land to the symbolic black South paralleled and in part was induced by a shift in emphasis from physical to spiritual emancipation.

Spiritual emancipation (to use Lee's term) rather than or as a precursor to physical emancipation is a key to African American novelists' projection of the black South as Eden. Many blacks who had come to the North during the war years began to see their dreams shattered as economic prosperity began its decline after the armistice. The unceasing influx of southern black migrants exacerbated conditions and problems attendant to this decline. As a result, northern blacks and incoming black migrants competed with each other for the decreasing opportunities in employment and housing. Nevertheless, the race's historical trek northward continued until the 1970s, until the southern white power elite had lost much of its stranglehold on black life, at which point for the first time in history more blacks willingly migrated from the North to the South than vice versa.[16]

In looking to the southern black cultural past for artistic inspiration, African American novelists of the 1920s do not uniformly portray the region as an Edenic ideal. In most such novels, the South as setting and symbol occupies a secondary and often negative position. But following the path that Toomer's *Cane* charted (the novel credited with having launched the Harlem Renaissance), several African American novels published between the mid-1920s and the late 1930s minimize attention to racial strife in the South and instead focus on the intraracial rhythms and beauty of southern black culture. In the genre during this period there are in essence two Souths, a black one of beauty and a white one of pain. The Eden myth is novelists' principal trope for inscribing both permutations, and it is not unusual for both to appear in the same novel. The postwar experience is most operative in those novels that have a contemporary setting and story lines and emplotments that foreground the pain of living black in the South. Novels that center an ex-soldier as subject devote far less discursive space to projecting the black South as Eden than to exposing the deformative impact of the Edenic white South on black (especially male) subjectivity.

With few exceptions, African American novels that use World War I as a historical context give less attention to the periods preceding and during the war than they do to how the war experience shapes the responses of black veterans to racial stratification in the United States. Narrating ex-soldiers' reentry into American society allows the novelists to give broad coverage to the general ordeal of blacks in postwar America. White's *Fire* and Lee's *River George* illustrate this phenomenon. These two novels and similar ones share a common set of narrative formations: the naive pro-tagonist voluntarily leaves or is ejected from the white South; he enlists in the army as an ostensible rite of passage into the Adamic family; he dis-covers that Europe and the North (including Harlem) are false Edens; he becomes a self-declared messianic figure intent on improving the condi-tions under which blacks live in the South; southern whites consider him a diseased subhuman whose potential infectious nature portends the de-struction of white civilization; he is accused of desecrating white person-hood, which mandates his death by lynching and which provides closure for his narrative.

Plot structure in the postwar sections of both *Fire* and *River George*, which are the final and most extensive sections of the novels, hinges on a conflict between the (ex)soldier-subject and (white) society at large. The discourse is predicated on a layering and interfacing of three principal tropes— Eden, disease, and war. For much of their story lines, both novels draw directly from historical reality.

White and Lee are among several African American novelists who use infectious disease as a trope, which derives primarily from the long-held belief among whites that blacks were genetically deficient (diseased ani-mals). Racist theorists of the World War I period produced "scientific" data to assert that blacks were a diseased race. The Wilson administration used this data as partial justification for its segregationist policies in federal employment. The federal government's example set back the clock for im-proved race relations, particularly in the South.

In fact, several Southerners were instrumental in formulating the Wil-son administration's Jim Crow policies, especially social science professor Howard Odum of the University of North Carolina and politicians James K. Vardaman of Mississippi and Benjamin R. Tillman of South Carolina.[17] Negrophobes of this era believed that including blacks in the American democratic fold would endanger (literally and metaphorically) the health and safety of American whites. Thus, several novels that treat postwar race relations in the United States use an infectious social disease as the nexus between black soldiers' military experience and the black population's plight in American society. These novels tropologically equate social disease and social dis-ease. In exploring this nexus, African American novelists appropriate and reflex the conflation of the biological and the ideological that white America used for its social construction of black (particularly male) subjectivity. In this way, these novelists maintain continuity with their literary predecessors by emphasizing the psychosexual underpinnings of strained race relations in the United States.

As a structuring device in the novels, the social disease / social dis-ease analogy links the periods preceding, during, and following the war and functions as narrative scaffolding for the construction of the ex-soldier's subjectivity, as in *River George* and *Fire*. The history of the war period reveals that many whites accused black men of harboring venereal diseases and asserted that such physical and moral disease would weaken the U.S. military effort. Many other whites feared arming such a large number of black men, and supporters of this stance argued that an armed black male population would be decolonized and consequently would petition more threateningly for fuller inclusion in American democracy. In the Negrophobic mind, therefore, the progression from the biological to the ideological, from social disease to social dis-ease, was quite logical. Racial tensions in the United States following the war were predicated on and often affirmed this reasoning.

Aaron George (*River George*) and Kenneth Harper (*Fire*) are black soldiers like those the War Department considered physically and morally the "choicest" of the race's men, the ones least likely to be agents of social disease and social dis-ease. Yet each protagonist grows ideologically as a consequence of his experience in France, and each then becomes an agent of a social dis-ease that is (potentially) contagious. In the postwar South, both George and Harper initiate actions that threaten white hegemony. In each novel, whites' fear of the protagonist's growing influence among (i.e., infection of) the black masses undergirds emplotment in the southern section.

African American novels reflect social and historical reality when they show that to southern whites a black male wearing an American military uniform signifies, among other things, that he raped white French women, is a potential rapist of white American women, and thus is an agent of a contagious social dis-ease that puts the dominance of white civilization in peril. A scene in *River George* based on an actual incident illustrates what many black veterans actually faced.[18] When George arrives in Vicksburg, Mississippi, in his army uniform, he thinks that whites will consider his uniform as certification of his loyalty to and sacrifice for the nation and that they will treat him with respect. To a group of white bystanders whom he encounters on his arrival, some of them also veterans of the war, the uniform signifies that George is a diseased interloper. He barely escapes lynching on the spot. The scene is standard in the genre and represents the immediate postwar period. The discursive formation also repeats events of the Civil War era, when disgruntled whites, North and South, brutalized and even lynched black soldiers because to them a black in a Union uniform signified the undermining of white civilization.

During World War I stories circulated in the United States that black soldiers stationed overseas, especially in France, were engaging freely in sexual relations with European white women. White soldiers stationed in France were the source of many of these stories, which at best were exaggerated and at worst fabricated. Near the end of the war there were widespread reports in the States that black "soldiers were attacking and criminally assaulting French women in large numbers."[19] Disregarding the findings of a federal team that investigated and refuted these allegations, many American whites (particularly Southerners) chose to accept them as truth. The stories increased southern whites' fears that black veterans returning from Europe would attempt to establish sexual liaisons with or rape American white women and that other black men would imitate their action. Several southern white leaders exploited this phobia among the masses. For instance, Vardaman urged that "the bravest and best white men" in every Mississippi community "should pick out these suspicious characters—those military, French-women-ruined negro Soldiers"—and make an example of them.[20]

River George and *Fire* are among the novels that dramatize this escalation of postwar violence. Each novel's emplotment makes it clear that though the federal government reneged on its prewar promises to the black population (the South never made such promises), black veterans and black civilians nevertheless demanded greater participation in American democracy following the war. Like a contagious disease, this demand infected large segments of the nation's black communities. When petitions for better treatment were rebuffed, an angry black population responded with violence, and the white citizenry countered with violence. The race riots that erupted during this era—some of the bloodiest of them in the North—repeated historical episodes from the Civil War period. "White citizens, in and out of the Klan, poured out a wrath upon the Negro population shortly after the war that could hardly be viewed as fit punishment even for traitors. More than seventy Negroes were lynched during the first year of the postwar period," and black veterans were special targets.[21] Lee and White situate their protagonists against this psychosocial background.

Like Daly in *Not Only War*, Lee uses the war as trope to explore affinities between interpersonal and interracial, interracial and interregional, and interregional and international conflicts. For George, an interpersonal relationship precipitates an interracial conflict. He attempts to extricate himself from an interracial conflict by joining an international one. Despite being a victim of the American military's racism in France, he returns to the United States believing that his dreams and hopes will become a reality. He comes full circle, for on his return he faces the intermingling of interregional and interracial conflicts that eventually bring about his death at the hands of a lynch mob.

In the first third of *River George*, set in rural Alabama, Lee uses the prewar years to develop a story line about racial conflict. Aaron George, a sharecropper, reluctantly becomes the leader of a group of local black farmers that intends to challenge the white economic power structure. Though he has a college education, George does not understand how deep-seated is the racism against blacks in this area of Alabama and the consequences for a black who engages in activities antithetical to the white power structure. Consequently, he commits one of the white South's unpardonable sins (striking and being accused of killing a white man), is forced to flee his home, and finds refuge in Memphis's black belt. George's attempts to elude his white pursuers resemble Adam's attempts to hide from God in the Garden of Eden (in some versions of the story). In the novel's fictive world, whiteness is omnipotent and omnipresent, so George's pursuers find him in his Memphis sanctuary. Eluding them and fleeing the South, he enlists in the army and considers his military service as the initial phase of his entrance into white America's Eden. In developing the story, Lee places at strategic points in the novel blues lyrics and blues characters as well as sacred lyrics and spiritual personae that help structure the novel's content by interpreting and foreshadowing its actions. One such lyric, which he places at the division between the novel's second and final thirds (shortly after the opening of chapter 19), comments on the metaphorical meaning of actions and foreshadows events that will occur later in the novel. With the themes of miscegenation, the sacredness of white personhood, and George's naïveté having formed the primary context for the actions that precipitate his flight from the South and then from America, the lyric (a fusion of blues and spiritual) therefore characterizes his predicament metaphorically as that of the Fall of Man (187).

George believes that a demonstration of his patriotism will help atone for the "sins" he has been accused of committing against the white power structure in his native Alabama or will prompt white America to treat him and other black veterans "like men" rather than like inferior creatures (199). This optimism sustains him through the harrowing experiences of the war in France and the degradation to which the U.S. Army subjects him, bolsters the messianic role he assumes on his return to the South, and organizes the thematic progression of the novel's last third, which is built on the conflict between black male subjectivity and southern white society. The resolution to this conflict is fatal for George.

In this and similar novels, the conflict between subject and society is narrativized tropologically as a civil war. The title of Daly's *Not Only War* is a précis of the explicit analogy between war and black life in the United States. The full statement of this analogy constitutes the novel's preface, and the war trope overarches the story's narrative action. Willard Savoy reiterates this war trope in *Alien Land*. In these and other novels that use World War I as social context and war as a trope, the authors make the analogy dramatically explicit by situating black soldier-subjects in contrasting social landscapes, specifically France (Eden) and the American South (hell), and by narrativizing the ongoing civil war between American blacks and whites.

Such is the case with Charles Roberts in *Alien Land*. Roberts's experiences in France teach him that there is "a parallel between the Negro and the soldier in combat. Just as soldiers in war who are subjected to shelling hour after hour become 'shell shocked,' so too is the Negro 'shocked.' He is shelled with abuse, ridicule, denial, in one form or another, every day he lives. I wonder if there is in this whole nation one Negro, just one, who is 'normal'—who has lived through this 'shelling' without damage to his heart or mind or soul. Just one—!" (258–59).

Returning from France as a decolonized black, Roberts becomes a combat soldier in the metaphorical civil war between the nation's blacks and whites. The American South—an "alien land"—is his battleground and the nation's legal system (he is an attorney) is his primary weapon. Roberts is not the protagonist in *Alien Land*, but his story line—which hinges on his metamorphosis into a decolonized black—is consistent with the structural pattern of those novels in which white Europeans' humane treatment of black soldiers and the U.S. Army's inhumane treatment of them link the pre- and postwar sections of the novels.

Like Roberts, George and Harper also are combat soldiers on a New South battleground, and they are dedicated to making the South safe for democracy. *George* and *Fire* are similar in emplotment, in the formation of the ex-soldier as subject, in using World War I contextually and the Civil War tropologically, in adhering to established conventions in the genre, and in installing the lynching bee as closure.

The war as context logically provides for the escalating conflict between the protagonists and the local white power structure in the region of the South where each novel is set. An idealistic veteran with a messianic mission, each subject returns to his southern home following the war and attempts to bring social reform to the area. They believe that the nation's reaffirmation of its democratic ideals during the war has softened southern whites' resistance to allowing blacks equal access to the privileges of the society. Both men reason that a leader is needed to create the utopian society of the American Dream, and each believes that his character, moderate views on race relations, military experience, formal education, and other personal and professional qualities suit him to the task. This belief in large part guides him, and the conflict between his actions and the social reality of the time and place—the clash between black male subjectivity and southern white society—helps configure each novel.

By concentrating thematically on economics as a primary index to racial tensions in the South, each author intends his novel's southern setting to typify the state of affairs in the postwar South. Economics is the social force that both binds and separates the two races as well as defines class structure within each race. The system of sharecropping or tenant farming, the mainstay of the region's economy, constitutes the economic nexus between the white exploiters and the blacks they exploit. While blacks and poor whites suffer under the system, those whites who control the social order's commercial and professional institutions thrive economically. The dissolution of this system most likely would mean a better life for blacks as well as for underclass whites but would dramatically alter the lifestyle of those whites whose prosperity depends on the continuation of this form of racist capitalism. With the ruling elite determining the region's discriminatory policies and with the Ku Klux Klan and similar groups enforcing the strictures of social relations between the races, life for blacks in the postwar South has not improved.

Against this psychosocial background White and Lee design plot structures in which economics regulates the social, educational, political, and other components of the region's social structure; one in which black men's alleged violation of white personhood is an excuse rather than a reason for white-on-black violence; and one in which the protagonist's naïveté about race relations in the South and his blind faith in the rhetoric of the American Dream cause him to behave in ways that are disastrous for others and fatal for him. In his somewhat curious formation of Harper as a flawed subject, White suggests that Harper is not only a snake in the white South's Garden but also a negative, even evil, intrusion into the internal order of his family's and other blacks' lives.

The war trope as Savoy specifies it in *Alien Land* is particularly applicable to White's narrative about the Harper family and the blacks with whom they interact. On this postwar social landscape blacks are continuously "shelled" with racist "abuse, ridicule, [and] denial, in one form or another." As a result, the Harper men and some other black men become casualties of this war of the races, and the Harpers and other black women who survive do so with their hearts, minds, and souls severely and permanently damaged. Whites murder the Harper brothers as well as brutally rape their sister, Mamie. They murder Bud Ware and sexually, physically, and psychologically abuse his wife, Nancy. Both Mamie and Nancy are left impaired for life. Rachel Harper, the family matriarch, and Jane Phillips, Kenneth's fiancée, are damaged beyond repair. Though most of these characters are direct victims of whites' abuse, all (except Bud Ware) are indirect victims of Kenneth Harper's naive actions and attitudes, for they are scapegoats through whom whites vent their antagonism toward Harper for his efforts to reconfigure the region's sociopolitical and socioeconomic landscapes.

Among its predecessors, *Fire* most resembles Chesnutt's *The Marrow of Tradition*. In fact, *Fire* can be read as a revision of *Marrow* that updates it to include the context of post–World War I race relations and to reflect the development of formalist and thematic conventions in the genre. Each novel has a young doctor as protagonist who as a "black leader" so misapprehends the intricacies of the South's social system that whatever actions he takes to change it to benefit blacks are at best ineffective. As a revisionist text, White's *Fire* engages in an intertextual dialogue with Chesnutt's *Marrow* that in some instances corroborates and in other instances repudiates stances that *Marrow* advances. In effect, *Fire* dramatizes how the plot of *Marrow* would play out after World War I.

Both novels present options—the moderate and the militant—that blacks might adopt to achieve social reform. Each novel counters its protagonist's moderate stance with the militant views and actions of another black male character, but neither novel definitively advocates one position over the other. Chesnutt presents this social ideology through a contrast of sociogenic brothers (William Miller and Josh Green); White uses biological brothers (Kenneth and Bob Harper). Through these contrasts both novels suggest that to unify sociogenic and biological brothers within the race to topple the white power structure is a more realistic goal than to create a coalition of blacks and poor whites to reform the system of political (*Marrow*) and economic (*Fire*) oppression.

Through his characterization of Bob Harper, White shows the militant resistance to white oppression—economic and social. Unlike his accommodationist father and his older brother, Bob understands that there is no compromise with a system designed to deny blacks the rights and privileges of society. Bob's subjectivity closely resembles Chesnutt's construction of Josh Green in *Marrow*. Bob's attitudes are laudable. As the narrative progresses, his impulsive nature seems to subside in favor of more strategic means of fighting the system, until his brother's actions and the chain of events they precipitate cause Bob to act without considering the consequences.

To avenge his sister's honor, he attacks the whites who brutally raped her, just as Josh Green gains revenge for the racist McBane's brutalization of Josh's mother and father. But in a system that whites dominate so oppressively, Bob's hasty actions are futile, and the narrator therefore condemns them in favor of more thoughtful ways of resisting and striking back at the oppressor. Through Bob (as Chesnutt does through his portrait of Josh Green), White calls for an active resistance to systemic racism, oppression, and racist violence, but not at any or all costs. Haste is, as both Chesnutt and White show, dangerous, self-defeating, and suicidal. Bob's precipitous actions make him a victim of the lynching bee. In that Kenneth Harper's naive actions set in motion a chain of events that leads to his brother's reactions, Kenneth indirectly is responsible for his brother's death.

Through *Fire*'s focus on the protagonist, its form and meaning coalesce and it can be read more fully as an intertextual revision of *The Marrow of Tradition*. The lynching of a black man for allegedly violating the sanctity of white womanhood is the principal theme that controls structure and other aspects of form in *Fire*, just as the intended lynching bee is the structural core of *Marrow*. The basic difference is that in *Fire* the protagonist is a victim of the lynching bee. Through actions and incidents centered on Kenneth Harper (the novel's voice of moderation), lynching as a symbol of volatile black-white relations emerges. Having grown up in the North and having served in the military overseas, Harper in effect is both a non-colonized and a decolonized black in the South and therefore an affront to the Southern Way of Life. He is able to escape the lynch mob for a time because, despite his many merits, he is ignorant about the depth of white racism in the South. The more he rids himself of this naïveté, the closer he moves to becoming a victim of the lynch mob; the more experienced he becomes in racial matters, the more his life is threatened.

White constructs the plot in a manner that makes it obvious that those whites who consider Harper a threat to the ruling class's economic prosperity feel it necessary to justify his destruction by means that will receive widespread approval from local whites as well as temper any national outrage over the lynching. As part of the story line, White places Harper in the position of saving the life of a young white girl who belongs to one of the town's prominent families, which for a short time places him alone with two white women. His white antagonists report to the general citizenry only those aspects of the situation that will incite the passions of a lynch mob—principally, that a black man was alone with a white woman in her bedroom. The situation provides easy justification for lynching Harper. Newspaper accounts of the lynching bee portray Harper as merely another black male rapist who received just punishment for his crime against southern white womanhood.

As a revision of *Marrow*, *Fire* ends pessimistically. The ending of *Marrow* lends itself to different and opposing interpretations. One is that the black middle class, of which Dr. Miller is the chief representative character, might be able to reform society by negotiating with the white power structure. Another interpretation is that social reform will come only when the militant forces in the black community, which Josh Green represents, mobilize to topple the white power structure. Most interpretations of *Marrow*'s ending cite evidence from the text that there is at least some glimmer of hope that the racial situation will improve. White's *Fire* offers little if any evidence that the situation will improve. By the novel's end the white power structure has destroyed both the militant and the moderate forms of blacks' resistance. In fact, the newspaper clipping that is the novel's closure reports that Kenneth Harper has been lynched for "attempted criminal assault on a white woman," that Bob Harper has been lynched for the "murder" of "two young white men," and that whites have restored a lasting order in the city (300). The novel's closure suggests that in the South's racial civil war blacks do not have any chance of winning major battles or the war. The social context of World War I has exacerbated rather than ameliorated the violent oppression of blacks.

Under the Eden trope as rubric, discursive formations characteristic of these "war" novels also are standard in other novels of the period. Migration is a conventional device for structuring blacks' pursuit (often thwarted) of the American Dream. Otis M. Shackleford's *Lillian Simmons, or the Conflict of Sections* (1915), Wallace Thurman's *The Blacker the Berry* (1929), and Waters Turpin's *O Canaan!* are examples of the wide variety of ways migration functions in novels published during the period. The title of Turpin's novel bespeaks one of several ways a novel's inversion of the Anglo-American Eden trope helps reconfigure the genre's traditional perspectives on the South and the North as symbolic spaces. The novels typically emphasize the southern landscape's spiritual sustenance and the northern environment's spiritual debilitation. Between the wars the genre shifted away from foregrounding the physical violence of race relations toward an exploration of a black community's internal order. (The "war" novels are the most obvious exception.) Whether the black community is situated on a southern landscape, as in Zora Neale Hurston's *Their Eyes Were Watching God* (1937), George Wylie Henderson's *Ollie Miss* (1935), and

Arna Bontemps's *Black Thunder* (1936), or on a northern landscape, as in Jessie Fauset's *There Is Confusion* (1924), Nella Larsen's *Passing* (1929), and Countee Cullen's *One Way to Heaven* (1932), the novelists typically incorporate some facet of the Eden trope, though they differ in how they employ it.

Novelists of the period prefer males over females as centered subjects representative of the race's experiences and aspirations. Several novelists concentrate on the subject's naïveté as a character flaw. When the subject is male, this character flaw often is fatal. When the subject is female, the flaw often leads to her psychological destruction. Whatever the setting and theme, novels of the period give more attention than their predecessors to a conflict between the centered subject's internal and external impulses. One manifestation of this phenomenon is the dramatization of a psychological war that ensues between black and white males, with women (often white ones) as a pawn.

Larsen's *Quicksand* is one of the best examples of an African American novel from the period that does not use World War I as a framing construct but does share most of the formalist and thematic features indicative of the war novels. A series of migrations structures the protagonist's journey-quest for the metaphorical Eden in an odyssey whose closure disavows the black South as an Edenic ideal. Larsen's thematic closure duplicates the thematic closure of *Home to Harlem, River George*, and other novels that emphasize the theme of identity as a conflict within the protagonist and that project Eden as more a state of mind than a geographical place. This does not mean that post–World War I novelists fail to use the specificity of physical space to convey Edenic qualities and to connote the converse of these qualities. For instance, it is not unusual for African American novelists (and other writers and artists) of this century to use Georgia metaphorically as a utopian landscape (social and physical) in the black South, just as they use Mississippi (and sometimes Alabama) as a dystopian social and physical landscape that embodies the pain of living black in a southern society that whites oppressively dominate.

Novelists after the 1930s continued to create black male protagonists whose innocence is one of their most obvious characteristics and faults. Many of these protagonists become involved with or are accused of being involved sexually with white women. Innocence and interracial sexuality converge as part of the novels' thematic structures to give new figurations to the genre's tropological use of the Bible's Eden story. In fact, characters such as Jake Brown, Montgomery Jason, Aaron George, and Kenneth Harper are precursors of the black Adamic character type that would develop more fully as part of a novel's thematics and schematics during and after the 1940s. The skeletal outline inscribed in these soldier-subjects is given flesh in Richard Wright's *Native Son* (1940), the novel that signals a major transition from the genre's tropological utilization of the Bible's narrative of Eden to a more specific exploration of the biblical narrative that centers Adam.

Black Adams

Subjectivity and the Adamic Paradigm

AS EARLY AS the 1880s African American writers explicitly invoked the relation between Adam and Eve in the Garden of Eden as an analogy for a sexual union between a black man and a white woman to suggest what such a union symbolized in the American social structure. Two works from this decade, Frederick Douglass's poem "What Am I to You" (which he probably wrote in 1883) and Charles Waddell Chesnutt's tale "The Fall of Adam" (1886), are illustrative.[1] Douglass, the speaker, addresses the poem to Helen Pitts, the white woman who later became his second wife, and he characterizes his relationship with and prospective marriage to her as a transgression against social decorum that whites of his day will view as comparable to the transgression of Adam and Eve in the Garden.

In using the Adamic story as a trope to narrate his relationship with Helen Pitts, Douglass acknowledges that he is reinscribing "that same old story" told anew by each "new generation" to fit its contemporary context.[2] Metaphorically and symbolically for Douglass, Helen is the "precious gem of Eden." Peter Walker states that by marrying Helen, Douglass "at last entered his father's garden."[3] While this might be true in the poem's world, in the real world Douglass remained an acknowledged black and therefore remained a liminal in the American Garden.

In his discussion of triangular desire, René Girard points out, "The mediator's prestige is imparted to the object of desire and confers upon it an illusory value."[4] In the African American novel and in social formations upon which it bases this form of triangular desire, the reverse is true. The object of desire confers upon the mediator an illusory value. Such is the case in Douglass's poem, which is not to say that Douglass does not love the mediator of his desire; it is to say, however, that the subject's ultimate object of desire ("his father's garden") dictates the value the subject attaches to the mediator. In Douglass's case, marriage to a white woman ostensibly legitimizes him as a son of Adam and makes him symbolically a legitimate heir to his generic white father's Eden.

For a black man, such as Douglass or the protagonists in several passing novels, a miscegenetic marriage is a rite of passage, a symbolic action signaling permission to enter the mainstream's major institutions. Particularly in post-1940 African American novels, a black man's sexual union with a white woman in or outside wedlock carries the same symbolic meaning. As mediator of the subject's desire, the woman functions either as a barrier or as a conduit between him and the object he desires. As most of the novels indicate, the miscegenetic union leads to the man's physical or psychological exclusion from (rather than inclusion in) the Adamic society. This ordeal makes him a black Adam—tempted, seduced, and destroyed.

Chesnutt's "The Fall of Adam" articulates another perspective on the topic that can be found in the twentieth-century African American novel. Chesnutt chooses the African American etiological folk tale as his narrative model, and he structures "The Fall of Adam" as a tale within a tale. The text's core story (the inner tale) is actually an African American folk sermon that attempts to account for two things—Adam's Fall (literal and metaphorical) and the origin of the black and white races. A black vernacular revision of the biblical story, the core story revolves around the theme of sexual relations between a black man (Adam) and a white woman (Eve). The text's frame story (its outer tale) is in a dialogic relationship with the core story. The narrator's commentary and the dialogue between the frame story's two central characters, Elder Gabriel Gainey and Brother Elijah Gadson, establish the sociopolitical and racial undergirdings of the text's dialogics.

The crux of the core story is an instance of triangular desire in that the mediator of desire, Satan, tempts Eve and through her Adam to violate God's prohibition. Eve is seduced by the belief that eating the forbidden fruit will make her more godlike. In turn, she seduces Adam. After Adam and Eve transgress in the Garden of Eden, Adam attempts to escape God's punishment. Fleeing the Garden with God in close pursuit, Adam eventually escapes into the universe. As he passes the sun, the heat from this star is so intense that it halts his flight and scorches his body "black as a crips" and curls "up his ha'r so he nevuh couldn'n't git it straight agin." According to Elder Gainey, who narrates the core story (sermon), another consequence of Adam's encounter with the sun is that he falls back to earth, where God catches him, "an' sich anuthuh whippin' de Lawd give Adam de worl' have nevuh hearn tell uv sence."

Elder Gainey uses the whipping scene, a familiar symbolic action from the antebellum period that characterized power relations between whites and blacks, to convey metaphorically the severity of Adam's punishment for his part in the transgression. As filtered through this ex-slave preacher's imagination, the competitive conflict between God and Adam resembles that between a white slaveholder and a black slave. In Chesnutt's version and in other interpretative revisions of the Bible's version of Adam's Fall, the conflict decidedly is between two males for power and control. Though Eve is most directly responsible for violating the taboo restriction that precipitates Adam's Fall, she is a secondary party in this male competition.

As Gainey indicates, the sun having scorched Adam's skin during his flight, he reenters Eden as a black man. Subsequently, his children by Eve are black, which, according to Elder Gainey, certifies that the black race is the progeny of the original parents. In the Elder's words, God made Adam and Eve; everybody else was born. Previous to Adam's Fall, the children born to the union between him and Eve were white, which the core story says accounts for the origin of the white race. But at the sermon's end a "brother over in the amen corner," Brother Isham, points out to the Elder that children born to a black Adam and a white Eve would be mulattoes, not blacks.

To avoid confronting the socially and politically charged (even life-threatening) issue of miscegenation, Elder Gainey quickly moves on to another portion of the service. The frame story's point is twofold: the preacher avoids the technical contradictions regarding racial identity to avoid being seen as something other than the erudite man he pretends to be; more important, given the author's ostensible purposes for the core story, Elder Gainey avoids comment on the taboo subject of sexual relations between a black man (Adam) and a white woman (Eve). The narrative is obviously designed to be simultaneously serious and comic, a standard feature of this type of folk tale. The frame story presents the serious concerns while the core story provides the ironic comedy. Thus, while Elder Gainey avoids commenting on the implications of this sensitive sociopolitical issue, Chesnutt, speaking through the tale's narrative persona, makes his points quite clearly.

Chesnutt's "The Fall of Adam" asserts that blacks and whites are progeny of the same original parents; at the same time, it adheres to the theory of two Adamic origins, in this case a white one and a black one. Among the myths of human origin the belief that at least two Adams populated the world (as well as a belief in the pre-Adamite theory) existed in Western thought as early as the fourteenth century, and even earlier in non-Western societies.[5] The myth of dual human origin was especially prominent during the Enlightenment but had declined by the time Chesnutt published "The Fall of Adam."[6] Nevertheless, Chesnutt's text is replete with ideas associated with the Enlightenment. Through the dialogic interaction between Elder Gainey and Brother Gadson, Chesnutt integrates several of the eighteenth century's concerns with theology, society, politics, and knowledge into a discursive frame in which he centers the biblical narrative of the Fall as a trope to discuss American society and black subjectivity. Elder Gainey and Brother Gadson tackle the empirical relations of theological and social questions in a black folk setting ('Possum Hollow).

The dialogic and dialectic relation between the frame story and the core story reveals the text's principal themes about American society and black subjectivity. One of the text's central messages is that the time has not yet arrived for blacks to use revolution to gain their rightful place as legitimate sons of Adam in the American Garden. But the seeds of rebellion are sown deeply among the congregation, and, the narrative suggests, the black church soon will assume an aggressive leadership role in effecting a sociopolitical revolution. The narrative contends that as far as race relations in the United States are concerned, there is not and has never been a separation of church and state. The authorial perspective on religion's role in society can be gleaned from Chesnutt's direct allusions to theological, philosophical, and political events, persons, and ideas from the eighteenth century. For instance, the text suggests that Chesnutt incorporates Jean-Jacques Rousseau's views on the interrelatedness of religion and politics in a civil society, as Rousseau states in *The Social Contract* (1762), particularly the chapter entitled "Civil Religion," and in *Discourse on the Origin and Foundation of Inequality among Mankind* (1755). The society that contains 'Possum Hollow embraces a black civil religion.

In their relation to the white (civil) godhead, blacks in 'Possum Hollow (not only Gainey and Gadson) are much like Chesnutt's depiction of Adam in his relation to God in the Garden. While these blacks acknowledge the superior position whites occupy in the power structure, they do not submit completely to whites' arbitrary authority. When the inevitable confrontation with the godhead arises, they, like Adam in the tale, meet it with a challenge, win or lose. These blacks are New Negroes; they are New Adams who are nonsubmissive, challenging, and defensively assertive. Like the black Adam in the core story, they will not accept their lot in life without question or without resistance. For them, duty and desire are directed toward social change.

Chesnutt's assertive black Adam in "The Fall of Adam" is an early progenitor of a character type who becomes particularly prominent in African American novels and short fiction after the late 1920s. In its characterization and uses of the Adamic myth to explore the more aggressive side of racial protest, Chesnutt's text in part foreshadows how the prevalence of male protagonists in post–World War I novels alters the genre's contours. But prior to 1940, the defiant black Adam is more fully delineated in short fiction than in the novel. Richard Wright's "Big Boy Leaves Home," the lead story from his collection *Uncle Tom's Children,* is one of the better examples. Wright draws specifically from the Bible's Eden myth to configure structure, setting, imagery, and theme. The story's fall-of-man analogy appears more aligned with Milton's version of the Fall in *Paradise Lost* than with the King James Bible's version.

The story's Adamic trope centers two (Big Boy and Bobo) of four young black men who violate Will Harvey's (a white's) restriction on blacks swimming in a pond he owns. Having finished their swim, the naked young men emerge from the pond at the same time that a young white woman, Bertha, wanders into the area. Seeing them naked, Bertha is startled and retreats to the tree where the young men have left their clothes. She interprets their advance toward the tree to retrieve their clothes as sexual aggression. Her startled screams summon her companion, Jim Harvey (Will Harvey's son), who summarily concludes that he is witnessing the young men's attempt to rape Bertha. During his encounter with them, Jim (a World War I soldier) kills Lester and Buck and in turn Big Boy accidentally kills him. Big Boy and Bobo, poignantly aware of what the incident means, escape from the scene. Their families and the black community arrange for them to flee the South to avoid being lynched. However, a white mob catches Bobo and lynches him. Big Boy manages to elude the mob and the story ends with him en route to Chicago.

Structurally, "Big Boy Leaves Home" is divided into five parts, a segmentation that adheres to a thematic pattern of the temptation, transgression, judgment, ejection (punishment), and state of man after the Fall, as derived from the Bible's narrative of Eden. Wright interfaces various features of the myth with a series of symbolic actions to form the story's thematic structure. In each of its five divisions at least one major symbolic action indicates the extent to which formal and informal codes of behavior in the South regulate social relations between blacks and whites.

The story's opening evokes Eden before the Fall. The setting and actions indicate that the four young men are at peace with themselves and in harmony with their natural surroundings, as Adam and Eve were in Eden before the Fall. The young men's nakedness and their age signify their innocence, and Wright uses an inverted formation to indicate that Bertha is the snake in the young men's garden. Two symbols, a pond and a tree, dominate the opening setting. The pond is a symbol of blacks' desire and whites' taboo restrictions. The four young men gratify their desire and therefore knowingly violate the taboo. From the perspective of southern white civil religion, they commit a sin.

From this point on, symbolic actions consistent with the South's social codes and with the Adamic myth accent the story's theme and advance its actions. Wright focuses on the tree, in part to show that attempts to undo the initial transgression only compound the original sin. When they first see Bertha, the young men instinctively cover their groins, an action that signifies not shame but guilt and fear. A black man naked before a white woman, an unpardonable sin in the South's Eden, is tantamount to rape, and Bertha's scream certifies the young men's guilt.

In defending himself, Big Boy accidentally kills Jim Harvey and thus commits the second most deadly sin a black can commit. Once soothing and harmonious, nature now becomes a hostile force that, like the whites, summarily passes judgment and condemns the young men for their transgressions. As the two attempt to escape the scene of their sins, "Vines and leaves switched their faces," the once babbling creek now bubbles, the once soothing sun is now "pitiless," and the corn stalks bruise their feet (31). Practically all forces natural and human react to condemn them, and their inevitable sentence to death is their ejection from the South's Eden.

Southern white civil religion is Wright's contextural scaffolding to construct the story's third (judgment) and fourth (punishment) sections. From this purview, for a black to rape (given the broadness of the term) a white woman or to kill a white person (regardless of the provocation) is for him to profane all of white society. Given the statutory and social laws of the time and place in which Wright sets this story, it matters little that none of the young men actually touched Bertha or which of them actually killed Jim Harvey: in this social system, guilt is collective and punishment is automatic. The story dramatizes this point when whites indiscriminately terrorize and brutalize the black community once they learn of the boys' transgressions. Through the theme of innate and collective guilt, Wright also merges the myth of Adam and that of Canaan, as does Chesnutt in "The Fall of Adam" and as do several writers who use biblical myths as analogies for black-white relations.

The story's fourth division, the punishment, hinges on the lynching bee, and Wright treats it conventionally. As a symbolic action, the lynching bee, of course, is a ritual of purification and decontamination consistent with the assertion that white personhood is sacred. Through images and allusions Wright portrays it as both a religious rite and a sexual orgy.

Bobo is a sacrificial victim, but Big Boy defies the mob's godlike power to take life. Attempting to elude the mob by hiding in a hole he and his friends dug the previous week, he discovers that a snake, a symbol of evil, has invaded this sanctuary and now threatens his life. He metaphorically wrestles with and literally kills the snake (evil, the devil), a symbolic action indicating his resistance to the Fall and his reprieve from the lynch mob.

Nevertheless, he must forsake his family and home and flee the South. In essence, he is ejected from Eden and suffers the fate of an eternal outcast. This constitutes the story's fifth division, which ends with Big Boy heading north, hoping to be renewed in Chicago's Promised Land, the North's New Eden. But readers familiar with the African American novel's treatment of the Great Black Migration know that Chicago for this southern black migrant will not be a New Eden (a paradise regained) but a version of Eden after the Fall. Big Boy, of course, is a progenitor of Bigger Thomas.

As African American writers develop the Adamic black character in the twentieth century, at least two major portraits emerge in post-1940 novels. One is based on Adam as a victim of Eve's wiles and as a person who suffers God's punishment for a transgression for which Eve is the principal culprit. In the discursive formations that center this portrait in the genre, a white Eve tempts, seduces, and precipitates a black Adam's destruction. The pre-1940 skeletal form of this Adamic character type is recognizable in Chesnutt's Sandy Campbell (*The Marrow of Tradition*), Walter White's Kenneth Harper (*The Fire in the Flint*), and Victor Daly's Montgomery Jason (*Not Only War*), among other variations. Though this black Adam might stoically suffer the white godhead's punishment (usually lynching) for his transgression, he nevertheless is a rather passive victim.

The other portrait of black Adam is of a character who is challenging and defiant. Initially tempted and seduced through a white woman's wiles, he defies the white godhead's omnipotence and resists the punishment the godhead inflicts on him. Though he may not be able to evade punishment (often his death), his challenge to the power structure affirms his sense of self. The skeletal form of this Adamic type is recognizable particularly in Chesnutt's Josh Green (*Marrow*), White's Bob Harper (*Fire*), George Washington Lee's Aaron George (*River George*), and Wright's Bigger Thomas.

In the pre-1940 skeletal forms of these two types, the character seldom is sexually involved with a white woman; the nexus is more symbolic than actual. In the genre after 1940, the Adamic character typically is in close contact (often sexual) with a white woman. Girard's *external mediation* and *internal mediation* are useful terms for discerning the differences between these two novelistic situations. Girard uses the terms to describe spatial and spiritual distance between the desiring subject and the mediator of his desire. He speaks of "*external mediation* when the distance is sufficient to eliminate any contact between the two spheres of *possibilities* of which the mediator and the subject occupy the respective centers." He speaks of "*internal mediation* when this same distance is sufficiently reduced to allow these two spheres to penetrate each other more or less profoundly" (9).

When slightly modified and adapted to explain discursive formations in the African American novel, *external mediation* refers to a situation in which there is a substantial spatial and psychosexual distance between the desiring subject and the mediator of desire. The subject may not have any physical and certainly no sexual or psychological contact with the mediator, and often the two are unknown to each other. This typically is the situation in the pre-1940 novel, in which the subject is accused of sexual relations with the mediator so that the white male power structure, functioning as a godhead, can justify destroying him. *Internal mediation* refers to a situation, prominent in post-1940 novels, in which there is close physical and often sexual and psychological contact between the subject and the mediator, a situation that violates ultimate taboo and mandates the subject's destruction. The wide variety of fictional examples include Wright's Bigger Thomas and Mary Dalton, Ann Petry's Lincoln Williams and Camilo Sheffield (*The Narrows*), and James Baldwin's Rufus Scott and Leona (*Another Country*).

The Cosmography of Native Son's Fictive World

To create *Native Son's* fictive world, Wright blends salient features of the social, psychological, historical, and religious life of Anglo-Americans and African Americans. Critics generally agree that *Native Son's* first two books certify Wright as a master craftsman. Some critics, however, find the communist ideology he uses in book 3 to explain Bigger Thomas and his "crimes" too intrusive and believe that book 3 is artistically the novel's weakest section.[7] But consistent with its ostensible function in the novel's overall thematic structure, book 3 advances the narrative to logical closure as well as explains the ideological and imaginative foundation (the Adamic paradigm) on which Wright builds the novel's first two books.

The scaffolding with which Wright constructs book 3—and the novel—is a compilation of creation and origin myths, most of them variations on or extensions of the biblical myths of cosmogony and origin. The novel's title capsulizes Wright's intent to explain Bigger Thomas's origins as an American native son, both the external formation of Bigger's false subjectivity by an oppressive environment and his formation of an authentic self from the power of internal impulses. Wright shapes the novel's fictive world and Bigger's subjectivity from various myths of origin as they have defined American society and its race relations from the colonial period to the novel's present. *Native Son* actually contains two separate worlds, a white one (the larger) and a black one (the smaller). But the novel's black world is little more than a deformed appendage to the white world. Both were created and are dominated by white power. From Bigger's perspective, in the black world, with its rigidly defined boundaries, physical, social, and psychological landscapes certify that its creator (the white man) is like God: in ruling over this black world he arbitrarily exercises power over its inhabitants to give or to take life—i.e., both to create and to destroy.

The dialectical relation between Bigger and the white world is one between creation and destruction, a conflict that in part focuses each of the novel's three books. By the time book 1 begins, whites already have "created" Bigger as a psychopathic monster who poses a threat to the white world. Near the end of book 2 they are convinced that the veneer of civilization that has held his monstrous nature in check has fallen away and unleashed the savage beast it concealed. Guilty of raping and murdering his girlfriend, Bessie Mears, Bigger becomes the concrete manifestation of the bestial black man in the white mind. To the white power elite, his rape and murder of Bessie offers sufficient proof that he raped and murdered Mary Dalton. Having created a rapist and a murderer first in their imagination and then in reality, whites prepare in book 3 to destroy the monster they created. At this point in the novel, Bigger, facing his imminent destruction, becomes the source of his own re-creation.

Shortly after book 3 opens, biblical images and allusions bring into sharp relief the Judeo-Christian myths of the world's cosmogony and of the origin and the Fall of man. The biblical imagery here is consistent with the imagery Wright uses earlier in the novel to explain Bigger's (and by extension most if not all blacks') relation to the omnipotent, godlike whites. By highlighting the cosmogonic and Adamic myths at this narrative juncture, Wright glosses and synthesizes the first two books' contents as well as prepares for a systematic conclusion to the novel's narrative and thematic structures. The biblical imagery that pervades book 3's opening and closing sections brings to a logical culmination the thematic and structural pattern of birth-death-rebirth, which corresponds to the novel's three books.

Reverend Hammond, a black victim and perpetrator of an oppressive

Christianity, is Wright's vehicle that enables Bigger to interpret the psychological and physical events in his life (the novel's first two books), which have brought him to a point in time where his physical destruction (execution) and spiritual self-creation are inevitable. Reverend Hammond's prayer for Bigger's salvation is an instance of dramatic irony and signals Bigger's spiritual transformation in book 3. While Bigger feels and senses Hammond's words, filtering them through his own consciousness, "There appeared before [Bigger] a vast black silent void" filled with "familiar images which his mother had given him when he was a child" and which had "given him a reason for living, had explained the world" (241).

These images of the cosmogonic myth now "sprawled before his eyes and seized his emotions in a spell of awe and wonder." He imagines "deep murmuring waters" from which comes a voice that says, "Let there be light," "Let there be a firmament," and "Let dry land appear." His vision advances forward in time from the cosmogony to the origin of man, and he hears a voice that says, "Let us make man in our own image." In his vision he sees sea and earth and vegetation, and in this "garden of earth" there appears man—Adam. And after Adam, "A woman rose up and loomed against the night and the moon"—Eve. Then "out of the clouds came a voice saying *eat not of the fruit of the tree in the midst of the garden, neither touch it, lest ye die*" (241–42). The creator referenced in this section of the novel (the "us" and the "our") is collectively the white man, whose mythopoeic versions of the world's creation and man's origin exclude rather than include Bigger in the Adamic progeny.

Bigger's vision breaks off at this point, but it is apparent from what immediately follows that Wright intends an analogy between Adam's origin and fall in the Garden of Eden and Bigger's origin and fall in the American Garden. In Wright's parodic reinscription of the Adamic myth, Mary Dalton, whites' most sacred icon, is the snake in Bigger's garden. For Bigger, an iconoclast, Mary is both symbol and substance, both abstract and concrete. When he "pressed a pillow of fear and hate over its face to smother it to death," Bigger killed both Mary and the picture of creation she represented (242).

Patterns of cosmogonic, etiological, and eschatological images in book 3 support the birth-death-rebirth and the sight-vision themes that function as structuring devices in books 1 and 2. For example, in book 3 Bigger's oppression is so overwhelming and thorough that, ironically, his greatest fear is self-knowledge, a fear of confronting the extent to which whites' picture of life controls his body and mind. His acquisition of self-knowledge (as is evident in book 2) releases him from white racism's stranglehold. Only after he kills Mary does he neutralize the system's power over his mind and move toward a reformation of self. Indeed, in preparing for the certainty of Bigger's physical death beyond the novel's end, book 1 and 2 pave the way for his spiritual self-creation.

As part of the narrative's creation-destruction dialectic and beginning with the present as center, Bigger in book 3 simultaneously moves forward and backward in time until he crosses the boundaries of the white world's concept of time and space. Once he is outside historical time, he negates the forces that created his inauthentic self. At the beginning of book 3 he psychologically begins his temporal movement forward toward the moment when the white ruling order will destroy his physical being: "There was no day for him now, and there was no night; there was but a long stretch of time . . . and then—the end" (233). But the beginning is in the end and the end is in the beginning.

Bigger's retrogression in time takes him to the point of the white world's genesis, to the source that falsely identifies him as a subhuman; it also takes him farther back in cosmic time to the origin of his true identity as a human. "With a supreme act of will springing from the essence of his being, he turned away from his life and the long train of disastrous consequences that had flowed from it and looked wistfully upon the dark face of ancient waters upon which some spirit had breathed and created him, the dark face of the waters from which he had been first made in the image of a man with a man's obscure need and urge; feeling that he wanted to sink back into those waters and rest eternally" (234; compare Gen. 1:2).

From a Judeo-Christian perspective, for Bigger to "rest eternally" is for him to surrender and to accept the white world's definition of him as authentic. He rejects this utter and complete defeat by a world designed to erase the essence of his being (to turn him from man to beast). So in "the grip of a deep physiological resolution," he devises "a new identification" for himself (233–34). With this resolution, "he sprang back into action, alive, contending" (236), and from this point his idea of an authentic self begins to take definite form. He has moved beyond the white world's genesis.

Ironically, Reverend Hammond's prayer is the catalyst for Bigger's temporal journey towards a re-creation of self. Hammond's prayer is a prayer of healing, and the scene is a healing ceremony. According to Mircea Eliade, myth plays a functional role in the healing process: "As he hears the cosmogonic myth and then the origin myths recited, . . . the patient is projected out of profane time into the fullness of primordial Time; he is carried 'back' to the origin of the World and is thus present at the cosmogony."[8] Hammond recites for Bigger the white world's version of the cosmogonic myth and the myth of human origin (241–42). As "the preacher's words [register] themselves in his consciousness" (241), Bigger is transported from profane time back to primordial time where he is a witness to and a participant in the cosmogony.

The preparation for Bigger's transportation and re-creation begins in book 1, when he inadvertently ruptures the dominant social order. Wright uses mechanical time to characterize this order. The jolting sound of an alarm clock opens book 1. Thereafter, watches and clocks, symbols of mechanical time/order, structure narrative action. Clock time is a symbol of ordered behavior among whites, which is especially obvious in the interpersonal relations within the Dalton household. Clock time regulates social relations between whites and blacks, as exemplified in the relations between the Daltons and the Thomases. And within the black community, clock time determines how one person relates to another, such as how Bigger relates to members of his family and to his friends. Book 1 establishes clock time as an external reality in opposition to Bigger's internal reality.

Bigger resists conforming his life patterns to a mechanized order, indicating that he recognizes, though does not fully understand, that his essence is outside the white-imposed concept of order. With the alarm clock heralding the beginning of his day, his internal impulses for the remainder of the day will conflict with the external impulses that are designed to dictate his behavior. His first conflict is with his family, which urges him to behave in concert with criteria the white power structure imposes.

He is late getting out of bed, an act that suggests he might be late meeting Mr. Dalton, even though his appointment with Dalton is not until 5:30 that afternoon. His mother and sister apprehensively view this initial act as a premonition that Bigger's actions for the rest of his day will violate the behavior that the ruling society demands and expects. Such a transgression will jeopardize the family's welfare, and its welfare depends on

Bigger negating his internal impulses and affirming those of the external white order. The opposition between his internal and external rhythms precipitates an explosion of verbal violence (Bigger against his mother and sister) and physical violence (Bigger against the rat) in the Thomas household.

Tensions within Bigger increase as he moves spatially and psychologically outside his family structure to the black community, where again his personal impulses conflict with his social environment. The central example is his and his friends' plan to rob Blum's store, a symbolic action that "would be a violation of ultimate taboo; it would be a trespassing into territory where the full wrath of an alien white world would be turned loose upon them; in short, it would be a symbolic challenge of the white world's rule over them; a challenge which they yearned to make, but were afraid to" (12). For the challenge (the robbery) to be successful, Bigger and his friends must perform every act according to the white world's concept of time/order. White people, Bigger asserts, "work like clocks" (31), and if blacks are successfully to negotiate the white world, they, too, must operate according to clock time.

This and other scenes in book 1 bring to the fore a fissure in Bigger's subjectivity: "He was divided and pulled against himself" (21), but "that was the way he lived; he passed his days trying to defeat or gratify powerful impulses in a world he feared" (36). Aggressive violence directed against his family (verbal) and his friends (physical) constitutes his attempt to mend the rift within him, to synchronize internal and external rhythms.

Bigger's first close encounter with the white world—with the source of his internal chaos—is with the Daltons. Wright employs a pattern of imagery anchored in mechanical time to define this "secret" white world and to convey Bigger's relationship to it. When Mary Dalton fails to behave prescriptively, she creates chaos in the Daltons' orderly household; it expands and eventually ruptures the entire white world's order. More important, her violation of the household's established order sets in motion a series of actions that leads directly to her death, which is simultaneously an act of destruction and of creation. By killing Mary, whom the white world regards as its "symbol of beauty" (140), Bigger commits what for him is "a supreme and meaningful act" (99). After destroying the dominant order's most potent symbol, he begins to mollify his internal chaos by placing his internal impulses above those of the external world. After the murder, his internal world gradually becomes more ordered as the external world correspondingly becomes more chaotic, an inverse relationship that operates until book 3.

The murder is the root of his new genesis, for by performing a symbolic act of destruction (killing Mary) and one of purification (burning her body), he begins to create a new world that comes to fruition in book 3. By the end of book 3 Bigger understands the meanings of his actions in book 1. Having moved outside the white world's sense of time and order, he now understands that his space and place in the world's cosmography is not that of a subhuman, as whites' picture of creation would have it, but that of a human, with the consequent needs and desires.

The murder is a symbolic act that inverts power relations. One of the material indicators of Bigger's empowerment is the ransom note, which temporarily disorients those who pursue Mary's killer. The note negates clock time as the principle of order, the metahistorical framework through which whites view human origin and development. Their propensity to view external reality through their psychosocial eyes prevents them from "seeing" the language in which the note is written. Their blindness signifies that whites have failed to construct present race relations as a duplicate of past race relations. They have failed to halt time and thus to arrest blacks' (specifically Bigger's) social evolution. An excerpt from the newspaper article in book 3 explains the situation: "All in all, [Bigger] seems a beast utterly untouched by the softening influences of modern [i.e., white] civilization. In speech and manner he lacks the charm of the average, harmless, genial, grinning southern darky so beloved by the American people" (238). As whites view the situation, Bigger has failed the civilizing process because he has failed to evolve into a human deformity.

Book 3 also explains Bigger's negation of spatial fixity. He begins the process unconsciously in book 1, where space is literal, concrete. In book 2, he more consciously exceeds spatial boundaries, and the meaning of space becomes more abstract. Shortly into book 3 he finds himself "falling swiftly through space" (236). At this juncture in his and the novel's development, space assumes yet another level of meaning; it is now metaphysical, abstract, transcendental. Racist violence forced the Thomas family to migrate from Mississippi to Chicago, but in the Promised Land whites assign them to a restricted space, in essence putting them in a position to be contained, not liberated. Their experience in this instance represents that of other

African Americans. In effect, they are assigned to an urban reservation, contained within but separated from the white American Garden. The term *reservation* implies that the space does not belong to those who occupy it; in this case, the white realtors, agents of the power structure, literally own the space and force others to occupy it. From the power structure's perspective, establishing ghettos or slums is an appropriate means of separating the subhuman family (blacks) from the Adamic family (whites); it is consistent with their version of the divine plan.

Whites' claim to ownership of the American Garden is a product of their appropriation and transformation of the biblical Eden myth to formulate their picture of the cosmogony, and in this picture there is a symbolic relation between physical space and social place. In *Native Son*, the physical space one is allowed or forced to occupy within the nation reflects one's social space. Neither Bigger nor any other black has the right to venture freely into a space outside the one the power structure has reserved for him, as is evident from Bigger's fear and uncertainty about walking in the white neighborhood where the Daltons live lest some white is unaware that he has permission to do so.

Cordoning off the black community effectively prohibits blacks' egression but condones whites' ingression. Mary Dalton and Jan Erlone are free to invade the territory assigned to the black community (such as their visit to Ernie's Kitchen Shack) because as whites they have a superior rank in the social hierarchy. Because whites do not suffer spatial circumscription, they are free to exercise all social, political, and economic rights and privileges. The rules governing egression and ingression are not limited to spatial movement. The symbolic relation between space and place in *Native Son* is readily evident from the several contrasts Wright draws between blacks and whites generally, between the Thomases and the Daltons particularly, and more specifically between Bigger and white males.

The ruling society bases its formal and informal codes of individual behavior and social interaction on the physical and social spaces one occupies. These codes dictate one's rights and privileges. For instance, because he is black, Bigger does not have the right to fly airplanes. In the mini-drama in which Bigger and his friends "play white," they act out the desire to be free and unconstrained. Killing Mary Dalton loosens some of the bonds that restrain Bigger by giving him choices. After the murder, he consciously (not instinctively as before the murder) manifests behavior congruent with whites' definition of his assigned space and place. By deliberately "acting the nigger," he consequently diminishes their power to control him while he increases his power to control (i.e., to define) them.

Bigger's conscious behavior early in book 2 indicates that he is redefining the temporal, spatial, social, and psychological limitations whites have placed on him. Using the literally and symbolically blind Mrs. Dalton as the point of reference to redefine his environment, Bigger moves outward from his family, friends, and the black community to the Daltons, to other whites associated with the Daltons, to the entire white society, and finally to a cosmos predicated on whiteness. He redefines all persons (except one) in the cosmographic social structure as metaphorically blind. Indeed, they all are psychologically blind, because they cannot understand that their definitions of Bigger are contrary to the facts.

His psychological growth in book 2 and 3 is gradual and concurrent with his understanding of how sharply the dominant society's cosmography centers whiteness. Near the novel's end, he repudiates this cosmography, for it is antithetical to his essence. In tracing ontologically Bigger's (re)creations of his authentic self, Wright utilizes the African American novel's concept of southern white civil religion. The concept's application to *Native Son*'s fictive design is one of the fullest to be found in the genre. Through characterization, language, imagery, symbolism, narrative action, and other fictional techniques, Wright constructs the novelistic world as a parodic reinscription of America's Judeo-Christian social order. In this cosmography whiteness is the godhead. It is, like the Judeo-Christian God, a cosmic force—abstract, omniscient, omnipresent, and omnipotent. Whiteness is responsible for order and harmony in the world, arbitrarily metes out favors and punishments to humans, and demands from them strict obedience to its dictates. In *Native Son* (and in several other African American novels) whiteness is indeed a religion. Like most religions, it originated from a social group's need and desire to codify its worldview and ethos—to establish order.

Images of white, embodied in persons, objects, actions, and ideas, are profuse in books 1 and 2. Within the novel's cosmographic hierarchy, white people rank second only to the white godhead. White men are his chief priests, and their primary functions in the social organization are to interpret, execute, and justify the godhead to man. For Bigger, the arbitrary power any or all whites can exert over blacks makes all whites "like God" (299), "a sort of great natural force" (97). White people's self-deification is at the heart of power relations between blacks and whites. They regulate the society's institutions—economic, political, religious, educational, and others—for the benefit of whites.

Bigger sees Mr. Dalton, who represents white male domination of the society's economic institution, as a secondary deity, as "a god" (148). Dalton ensures that blacks' economic life is sufficiently limited so that they will not threaten the society's hierarchical structure. A parasitic slumlord, he bleeds the economically deprived black community, protects his fellow white slumlords' economic interests, and helps contain the black population within prescribed physical and social spaces. The sharp contrast between the Daltons' economic prosperity and the Thomases' economic austerity reveals Henry Dalton's success in regulating the economics of whiteness.

State's Attorney Buckley represents the society's political institution, which controls the legal system, charged with formulating and enforcing rules to keep the social order intact. Thus, the economic and political institutions are mutually supportive. Buckley enforces the law of the land, the law of whiteness. His signboard, which with an all-seeing eye casts a threatening shadow over black Chicago's ghetto, spells it out "in tall red letters" for Bigger and for any other black who might contemplate violating the law of the land: "IF YOU BREAK THE LAW, YOU CAN'T WIN!" (11). Consistent with Wright's adaptation of the Judeo-Christian myth of human origin, the slogan is analogous to the first law the Creator issued to regulate life in the first human social community, as his close paraphrase of Genesis 3:3 indicates (42).

As an institution, the society's church religion subserves whiteness, its civil religion. That whiteness as a force is more powerful than the Judeo-Christian God is dramatized through Mrs. Thomas's prostration ritual; she "prays" to Mr. and Mrs. Dalton rather than to God to spare Bigger's life. As Bigger sees it, the nation's institutionalized church religion (Christianity) and its institutionalized racism (e.g., the Ku Klux Klan) share the same principal symbols and espouse a theology that privileges whites and denigrates blacks. Rejecting the color white and the cross as sacred symbols signifies Bigger's repudiation of a socioreligious philosophy that prescribes his passive suffering and sanctions his destruction. This repudiation culminates in his (and thus the novel's) construction of an inverted cosmography in which white is the force of evil and black is the force of good.

To Negrophobes, Bigger's murder of Mary proves that he is the snake in the American Garden, a manifestation of the devil, as the symbols the legal system uses in his identification code indicate. The first part of his indictment number is 666; this is the sign of the beast (see Rev. 13:18). According to Buckley, "Every decent white man in America ought to swoon with joy for the opportunity to crush with his heel the wooly head of this black lizard, to keep him from scuttling on his belly farther over the earth and spitting forth his venom of death" (341–42; compare Gen. 3:14–15).

As it concerns relations between blacks and whites, this is the cosmography of the world in which Bigger exists in book 1, book 2, and much of book 3. Structurally and thematically, then, the novel traces his progression from a state in which whiteness arbitrarily and rather completely controls his mind and body to one in which blackness is the preeminent principle that organizes and controls his being. Bigger redefines and thus inverts the white-imposed cosmographic order. Once his redefinition has been completed, he has moved, as book 3 indicates, beyond the white world's genesis/Genesis. From this vantage he can see himself more clearly and thus he continues his process of self-formation. Part of this process is his fascination with the printed word in book 2, which grows into an obsession in book 3. Newspaper accounts of his crimes in books 2 and 3 help clarify for him how the white world defines and therefore circumscribes him. The novelistic context demonstrates that whoever controls the word controls the power to define. In book 2, Bigger, by writing the ransom note, begins to control the word, wresting power from whites, and thus begins to garner the ability to define not only his external world but also himself.

In possessing the power of definition, Bigger is a new version of Adam. In the biblical Garden of Eden God gives Adam the power to define all creations, which presupposes the power to distinguish man from beast. And Bigger essentially does the same in his redefinition of the cosmographic hierarchy when he includes himself among Adam's progeny. His reinversion of the white power structure's inverted history takes him back in time and space beyond the human origin myth. Hearing Reverend Hammond recite the cosmogonic myth transports Bigger beyond whites' historical version of the cosmogony all the way back to the primal event itself.

At this juncture in the narrative, "the word" assumes connotative and denotative levels of meaning different from those previous in the novel.

Having exceeded the boundaries of historical time and space, Bigger enters cosmic time and space, where he merges with the source of his original creation, becomes one with God, and begins to re-create himself in his own image. The origin myth Wright uses to underlay Bigger's self-creation is not from the Old Testament's Genesis but from the New Testament's Gospel According to St. John (1:1–5): In the beginning was the Word, and the Word was with God, and the Word was God. The same was in the beginning with God. All things were made by him; and without him was not anything made that was made.[9]

This section of book 3 provides a gloss on the end of book 2, the capture scene in which Wright portrays Bigger as a Christlike figure in historical time, a victim of oppression and passive suffering. In this section, Bigger is Christ in cosmic rather than historical time, and the Christlike imagery therefore takes on greater significance in terms of Wright's use of origin myths. As is evident in the beginning of the Gospel According to St. John, "The *Word* . . . of God is more than speech; it is God in action, creating," as Genesis reveals.[10] The Word is also Christ, who was present at the first creation. Thus the biblical images and allusions establish Bigger as one with God, the Word, and Christ and place him at the cosmogony. In addition, Bigger is Adam, for he is not only the creator but also the object of his own creation.

As the narrator repeats at several points in the novel, Bigger had killed and thus had created a new world for himself. At the end of book 3 he tells his lawyer, Boris Max, "what I killed for, I *am*" (358). Bigger's statement is a verbal signification of his subjectivity that repeats, with a difference, God's statement to Moses in Exodus 3:14: "I AM WHO I AM." For Bigger, the act of destruction is the first step in the process of creation. In killing Mary Dalton, he committed "a supreme and meaningful act" of creation. Now, like the God of Genesis, he declares that that act "must have been good" (358). But while Max can admit that the murders Bigger committed were "an act of *creation*" (335), he cannot accept the totality of Bigger's new picture of creation. Because he identifies himself with whites as the only sons of Adam, to accept Bigger's version of life would be to reject the myth that accounts for his own being.

Jan Erlone is the only person who affirms Bigger's picture of creation. In a "declaration of friendship," Jan admits Bigger's humanity. Bigger, therefore, can affirm only Jan. "The word had become flesh. For the first time in his life a white man became a human being to him" (246), and for the first time in his life he became a human being to a white man. So despite Max's sympathy for him, Bigger must define Max as blind in the same manner that he finally defines all others in this society (except Jan). Wright's paraphrase of St. John 1:14 ("And the Word was made flesh") not only indicates the reciprocal declaration of Bigger's and Jan's humanity but also supports the theme of Bigger's self-creation and the novel's use of origin myths to develop the theme.

Book 3 brings the thematic structure of *Native Son* full circle. The novel's tripartite organization ("Fear," "Flight," "Fate") coincides with its philosophical undergirdings. Bigger develops spiritually through the novel's three books from an emphasis on the body to an emphasis on the soul to an emphasis on the ultimacy of being. His gradual movement outside historical time and space in the novel progresses from the debased sign of his identity in book 1 to the essence of his being in book 2 to the logocentrism of his identity in book 3—that is, from the signified to the signifier to the transcendental signified. In the new picture of creation he has effected, he is a son of God, a son of Adam, and therefore a member of the human family.

Configurations of Desire in The Street

Each African American novelist who appropriates the Bible's Adamic myth usually imprints it with his or her own artistic signature. Yet it is standard among the novelists to assign biblical characters race- and gender-specific identities when pairing them with fictional characters: God is a white man; Adam is a black man; Eve is a white woman. Typically, novelists use this paradigm to center a black male experience, as Ann Petry does in her novel *The Narrows*. But in an earlier novel, *The Street*, she deviates from the pattern in interesting ways. By making her black Adam a female, Petry essentially couches a black feminist text in the mode of black masculinist fictive discourse. She makes the Adamic paradigm central to her artistic vision, but she inverts some of its norms as well as modifies several other conventions that had become established in the genre by the 1940s. She also adapts and foregrounds conventions from other African American art forms in ways uncommon for novelists of the 1940s.

Since the Harlem Renaissance, geometric patterns, especially circles and triangles, have been conventional features of the aesthetics that governs African American visual and literary arts. For example, circles are integral to form, content, and meaning in several of Aaron Douglas's paintings of the 1920s and 1930s; triangles have prominent hermeneutic functions in Jacob Lawrence's paintings of the 1930s and the 1950s; and geometric patterns that emphasize elongation and angularization are earmarks of Eldzier Cortor's "poetic paintings" from the 1930s and 1940s.[11] One example from the Harlem Renaissance of the geometric component of black aesthetics is *God's Trombones: Seven Negro Sermons in Verse* (1927) in which James Weldon Johnson's poetic text and Aaron Douglas's visual text illuminate each other and constitute one text.

From the 1920s onward, most African American novels that narratologically incorporate geometric patterns privilege the circle. The tripartite structure in novels such as *Cane, Native Son,* and *Invisible Man* are instances in which the respective centered subject initially embarks on linear (spatial and psychological) paths toward an object of desire. During the course of the narrative the protagonist grows from innocence to experience and consequently his object of desire changes from a material and external one to a spiritual and internal one. The subject's experiential growth and the redefined object of desire cause the narrative lines that initially formed a triangle of desire (subject, mediator, object) to bend gradually into a circular shape, which signifies the fusion of subject and object into an authentic self. A principal function of these and several other novels' tripartite, circular structure is to coalesce form, content, and meaning.

In *The Street* Petry departs from the circular structure that by the 1940s had become a norm in the genre; she privileges the triangle over the circle in this novel's narrative pattern. As the plot progresses, Petry bends the narrative's triangular configuration into a straight line, which results in a plot structure that is bipartite and linear rather than tripartite and circular. Her protagonist, Lutie Johnson, never fully turns inward to affirm black culture and the black self, never merges self as subject with a redefined object of desire. *The Street's* theme and linear plot structure underscore the centered subject's failure to develop internally.

Desire is the dominant emotion that structures this novel's main plot, focuses narrative formations that supplement the main plot, defines and interfaces the novel's several patterns of imagery, and delineates its protagonist and supporting characterizations. Structurally and thematically, *The Street* is a narrative of triangular desire. Economic and sexual desire undergird subject formation, action, and theme. Though at times complementary, these two principal kinds of desire more often are competing, placing the protagonist in opposition to each of the supporting characters, creating rivalries between some of the supporting characters (for example, between Junto and Boots and between Jones and Junto), and occasionally becoming oppositional forces within a single character (Boots is one such case).

The Street's narrative design contains two dominant story lines whose discursive shapes resemble equilateral triangles. The first of these is predicated on economic desire and is a framing device that defines and controls the novel's thematic and structural symmetry. It is the novel's principal triangle of desire—Lutie Johnson is the desiring subject, her object of desire is the American Dream, and the mediator of her desire is a rich and powerful white man named Junto who frustrates rather than facilitates the conjunction of subject with object. His functions as a representational and as an individuated character are indistinguishable in most instances: he is simultaneously *the* white man and *a* white man who is the main obstacle to Lutie achieving her goal. That for much of the novel she is unaware of his attempts to thwart her pursuit intensifies dramatic action.

Representationally, Junto is "the man." His name invokes the power elite that controls the nation as well as access to the American Dream. His name also refers to a select group of Anglo-American males who historically and economically were (and still are) bound together by a common interest and a common desire—to make "more and more money" (43). In the novel, membership in this *junto* cuts across social class and includes the affluent Chandler men and their associates as well as Junto. Indeed, Junto is white, male, rich, and powerful. When viewed from the perspective of a person who is black, poor, and powerless, such as Lutie Johnson, one of his characteristics presupposes the others.

In some respects, however, Junto's individuated character differs from his representational one. Though he is a member of the power elite—the white male junto—his characterization does not conform to the African American novel's stock portraiture of the white male antagonist. For instance, economics not race dictates his relationships to the novel's characters. Race does not shape his commercial and later "romantic" attachment to Mrs. Hedges. Commerce defines his relationship with Boots, with blacks on 116th and other streets, and with whites in the larger society. And though the novel suggests that Junto prefers black women, he does not intend to exploit Lutie sexually because she is a black woman, poor and ostensibly vulnerable, but because her poverty and economic desire make her vulnerable to a man who must substitute money and power for sexual appeal.

As both an individuated and a representational character, Junto's name encodes his race and gender into his personal history, the narrative of which repeats the American self-made-man myth whose structural components can be found especially in pre-1900 Anglo-American literary fictions, in autobiographical and philosophical writings such as Benjamin Franklin's, and in popular fictions such as Horatio Alger's.

The novel's second dominant story line centers Junto. As the novel's chief antagonist, Junto obfuscates the principal triangle's vortexes (subject, object, mediator) and connecting lines (narrative actions) by creating an equilateral triangle of sexual desire that shadows and competes with the novel's framing triangle. Junto designates himself the subject vortex and Lutie the object vortex; Mrs. Hedges (willingly) and Boots Smith (unwillingly) function simultaneously as the mediator vortex. The narrative of Junto's desire in effect constitutes a counterplot (or antiplot) in which he is an antihero. His pursuit of Lutie defines most of the secondary characters' roles in the narrative actions of both the principal and the shadow triangles of desire.

The intersection between the two narratives helps spawn other (and smaller) narratives of triangular desire in which Mrs. Hedges, Boots Smith, and William Jones are the desiring subjects and Lutie is their object of sexual desire. The novel's architectonics, then, is a configuration of triangular narratives of lives and relationships that intersect to create thematic tension and to advance the novel's plot. With Lutie as the object vortex in common among them, these secondary characters and Junto compete one against the others to possess Lutie. Thus, the narrative of each character's pursuit interlocks with the others and all with the principal triangle. Individually and collectively, these competing desires alter the trajectory of narrative lines connecting the vortexes in the principal triangle in such a way that the temporal (and to some extent, spatial) distance between Lutie as desiring subject and her object of desire is increased.

The subject vortex in one of these secondary triangles is Mrs. Hedges, who desires Lutie on two levels, fetishistic (sexual) and economic: hair is a symbol that links these two levels. On the first level, her desire is mimetic or imitative. A masculine woman afflicted with a negative self-concept, Mrs. Hedges believes her lack of hair signifies her lack of feminine sensuality. What she lacks, she thinks Lutie and the young women whom she employs as prostitutes possess. She reads their hair as a sign of their sexual appeal to and thus their ability to attract men. She believes that even her money cannot buy her the direct object of her desire—a black husband or, at the least, a black male lover. Though Mrs. Hedges is resigned to living without ever being the object of a black man's erotic desire and refuses to accept a white man (Junto) as a substitute, her desire nevertheless is not diminished. In constructing the psychosexual dimensions of Mrs. Hedges's subjectivity, Petry encodes this spinster's most intense desire in her title of address—Mrs.

On the economic level, Mrs. Hedges desires Lutie for her capital-producing potential. In the business of selling black women's sex, she recognizes that Lutie's exchange value would be very high on a flesh market whose principal buyers are white men. The construct in the novel is an exchange nexus in which a black woman and a white man are vying to be the seller and buyer of a black woman's sexuality. It is a triangular formation in which the narrative lines that connect the three vortexes (Mrs. Hedges, Lutie, Junto) are race, sex, and economics, and it draws upon a historical formation of the black woman's plight that dates back to slavery.

In part through her updated version of this matrix of desire (race-sex-economics), Petry follows a convention in the genre that links the novel's present-day black experience to its antebellum roots. The slave woman was a commodity that could (re)produce other commodities (exchange value) and in the process provide sexual pleasure (use value). Petry repeats this exchange value—use value duality through Junto's desire for Lutie. His plan is that once he tires of her as a sexual toy, he will change his role in the triangular relationship from buyer to seller, from desiring subject to mediator, by placing her in one of the prostitution houses he owns. Mrs. Hedges will benefit economically by mediating Junto's plan.

In addition to Junto and Mrs. Hedges, Mr. Crosse and Boots Smith also consider a black woman's ability to (re)produce sexual pleasure, especially for white men, a valuable commodity, and both propose that Lutie turn her sexual appeal into capital. Crosse proposes an exchange of commodities—he giving her voice lessons (a commodity that she then can turn into capital) in exchange for her giving him sexual pleasure. Reflecting on her encounter with Crosse, Lutie herself draws the analogy between the commodification of her sexuality and that of her enslaved foremothers (322). (The basic elements of this formation appear in Harriet Jacobs's slave narrative, *Incidents in the Life of a Slave Girl.*)

As *The Street*'s plot unfolds, different characters (Junto, Mrs. Hedges, Mr. Crosse, and Boots Smith) alternately occupy the mediator vortex in the novel's principal triangle of economic desire. At a point in the narrative's progression when Lutie believes Boots will facilitate her acquisition of economic stability, incidents alter the plot's geometric structure in such a way that Boots is forced to realign his relationship with Lutie; he must become mediator of Junto's erotic desire in the shadow triangle. This realignment reveals the fuller dimensions of Boots's character, adds complexity to the plot, and provides an occasion for Petry to incorporate another of the genre's twentieth-century narrative conventions—the psychosexual war between black and white men in which the black is the aggressor. Consistent with conventional praxis in the genre, she uses a world war (in this instance, World War II) as a source for the war trope (257–77)

Mediating Junto's erotic desire for Lutie creates competition between Boots's desire to possess Lutie and his desire to continue his affluent lifestyle. When Junto designates Boots his procurer, it occasions the intersection between the secondary triangle, in which Boots is desiring subject, and the shadow triangle, in which he is mediator of another subject's desire. Using the two characters representationally, Petry dramatizes the psychosexual foundation of power relations (essentially socioeconomic ones) between the males of these two races.

In Petry's version of this formation, the black woman is both a pawn and a weapon situated between and used by the two male combatants in their ritualized attempts to assert their power and thus to validate their psychosocial manhood. The situation intensifies Boots's internal conflict between desires. His economic desire is the victor, which precipitates an externalized conflict between desiring subjects (Boots and Junto) that advances the plot toward closure.

The psychosexual battle between Boots and Junto replicates a similar battle from earlier in Boots's life in which "the man" was manifested as his wife's white male lover. Boots lost the battle, and his wife, Jubilee, inflicted a wound that was psychologically crippling and physically disfiguring, signified by his facial scar. In this current battle with the representational "man," Boots strategically errs in attempting to objectify Lutie fully and to use her as a weapon against Junto. Boots loses not only this last battle but also the war, and the direct instrument of his destruction is a black woman, Lutie.

This psychosexual race war develops further in the novel's narrative of Jones's desire. His renewed battle against "the man" is one of the links between his narrative of desire and the novel's principal and shadow triangles. Among those who desire Lutie sexually, Jones's desire is the most intense, the most sexually aberrant, the most psychologically and physically threatening, the most diabolical, and thus the most frightening to Lutie. His desire for her so consumes his being that it radiates from him (51), causes him to tremble (236), dominates his thought processes, and motivates practically all of his actions.

Afflicted with a monomania induced by sexual desire, Jones misreads Lutie's rejection of him as a sign that "she didn't like black men" (283) and "was in love with Junto, the white man" (282). The rejection opens psychic wounds inflicted earlier in his life when black women spurned him in favor of white men (282). Jones generalizes the current situation until in his mind Lutie becomes the embodiment of all the young women he has ever wanted and Junto becomes the embodiment of all the white men—indeed, of everyone and everything—who have denied him whomever and whatever he desired.

As she does for Boots, Petry uses this formation to help situate Jones's key position in the novel's plot structure. In the first triangular formation that situates Jones as desiring subject and Lutie as his object of desire, Bub, Lutie's son, is the mediator vortex. Bub occupies a similar mediating position in the triangular formation that foregrounds Jones's desire for revenge against Lutie. Jones's machinations to effect the latter desire deprive him and practically all of the others of their desired object. His vindictive actions are catalytic. When the secondary triangle in which he is the desiring subject interlocks with the principal, the shadow, and other secondary triangles, it shatters them all.

While *The Street*'s thematics are predicated on desire as the ruling passion that delineates character and motivates narrative action, the novel's formalist features incorporate certain tropes in conventional and unconventional ways to interface with and support the novel's thematics. Petry's tropological utilization of fairy lore is a case in point. Novelists of the protest era frequently appropriate "Beauty and the Beast" for their privileging of the black male as a representative protagonist, for their emphasis on racism's psychosexual foundation, and for their adaptation of the Adamic myth (rather than the more general Eden myth) as a novelistic paradigm. These are some of the defining characteristics of the era's masculinist discourse, which Petry tailors (through revisions and inversions) to fit a female centered subject. She appropriates, revises, combines, re-reads, and centers two fairy tales in this novel's discourse, "Beauty and the Beast" and "Little Red Riding Hood." The tales significantly shape the novel's plot development, subject formation, imagistic patterning, and language.

Elements from both tales help structure *The Street*'s emplotment as a triangular narrative of desire. Much of the plot reads like a fairy tale. A beautiful, poor, and naive young black woman (the desiring subject) sets out on a symbolic journey from Harlem's "jungle" (8) to America's Garden (the object of desire). Her first major attempt to reach the "enchanted garden" (41) takes her from her cramped tenement on 116th Street to "a large open space where there was a house," white, gracious, spacious, and beautiful, in the Connecticut "forest" (37). However, circumstances halt her journey toward the "enchanted garden" and force her return to Harlem. When she resumes her symbolic journey to the American Garden, her path is beset with various metaphorical wolves—males and a female, blacks and whites—most of whom are false helpmates (the mediators of desire) and all of whom seek to devour her. Though she escapes from the wolves and kills the most deceptive of them (Boots Smith), the murder is not a transformative act of sacred violence for the heroine. In the novel's denouement, the heroine is not reborn into a higher level of consciousness; she does not return "home" a much wiser and experienced person. The triangle of desire is not bent into a circle, as would be typical for thematic structure in the genre. Instead, it is bent into a straight line, and thus at the novel's end Lutie continues her linear journey (spatial and psychological) on a path darkened by her continued naïveté and false optimism.

Each of the wolves (Junto, Mrs. Hedges, Boots Smith, and William

Jones) Lutie encounters on her journey toward the American Dream is an untransformed beast who is drawn to her captivating beauty and driven by a rapacious hunger for her. Petry uses imagistic patterns associated with predatory animals to underlay each of these characters' physical and moral qualities. And Lutie, like Little Red Riding Hood in some versions of the tale, is an unconscious contributor to her predicament. The beast in her is attracted (even if unconsciously) to the bestial nature of some of the wolves she encounters.

Physical and moral abnormalities signify which of the novel's characters are wolves and often indicate the degree of their wolfishness. Junto is the thing itself. His disproportional body includes a "squat" frame, shoulders "too large for his body," and a "turtle's neck" that supports a head out of proportion with the rest of his body (245). The images of food and consumption Petry uses to portray Junto's desire for Lutie indicate that his congenital physical deformities reflect his innate moral aberrations. The color gray also makes Junto's exteriority and interiority reflexive: he has gray skin, gray hair, gray eyes, and gray clothes (245, 246, 275). He is a gray wolf, and as a representational white male character his wolfishness is inbred. For the major black antagonists, however, wolfishness is an acquired characteristic, a result of an internal or an external transformation. Through the personal history she provides for each of these characters, Petry indicates how the dominant social environment (i.e., the metaphorical street) has transformed each into a wolfish beast.

Petry appropriates corporeal and moral transformation to construct the black antagonists' subjectivity. Though Mrs. Hedges is the most physically deformed of the novel's wolves (largely the result of having been trapped in a fire), there is a gentleness about her that is manifest in her voice. Yet her "rich, pleasant," and "purring" voice exacerbates rather than mollifies her monstrous appearance. Her physical deformities and consequently her moral deformation result partly from her marginality as a black woman in a society controlled by white males and their values.

Boots is the most gentle of Lutie's animalistic antagonists. Though the narrative voice frequently compares him to a pussycat, it emphasizes in the comparison the cat's predatory instincts. A handsome man—broad shoulders, lean, taut body, seductive voice—Boots gracefully and charmingly stalks Lutie as sexual prey. When Junto's desire for her creates competition with Boots's desire for her, Boots modifies his technique, which precipitates his internal transformation into a snake. Petry monitors this transformation through imagistic language (150, 151) and metaphor.

One pattern of imagery and metaphor that Petry uses throughout the novel focuses on the antagonists' eyes, giving particular attention to their snakelike eyes as signification of their reptilian natures and thus linking one antagonist to the others. To be sure, eyes and mirrors (fairy tale motifs) in this novel have similar imagistic functions: to clarify rather than to distort, to reflect situational reality, and to reveal a character's inner nature.

Once Boots realizes fully that he will lose the competition with Junto for Lutie, he becomes a metaphorical wolf, more rapacious and deadly than a snake. Petry hinges Boots's metamorphosis from the feline to the canine on a stock fairy-tale motif that she inverts. Typically in fairy lore, the beast transforms into a handsome prince and he and the beauty live happily ever after. In *The Street*, the handsome Prince, Boots, transforms into a fiendish beast, and the incidents that ensue preclude any happy-ever-after union between him and Lutie.

Petry highlights physiological abnormalities to reflect the abnormal content of the supporting characters' personalities. But the least physiologically malformed of these antagonists is the most animalistic—building superintendent William Jones, whose ordinary name is "the exact opposite" of his "obviously unusual, extraordinary, abnormal" personality (25). Jones's internal impulses reveal his bestial nature, usually associating him with the canine family, especially the wolf. To Lutie, Jones not only resembles his wolfish dog, Buddy, but at one point his and his dog's desire (which also are competing) for Lutie are simultaneously so intensely threatening that she regards the two as one and the same beast (191).

Though she constructs Jones as a moral monstrosity, Petry nevertheless humanizes him, as she does all the principal antagonists. Jones not only resides in a black community severed from the social order's mainstream, but within his community he is a marginal person, signified by his long-time occupation of basement apartments. Psychologically deformed by rejection and loneliness, his social estrangement within the black community has pushed him literally and figuratively to the lowest depths and precipitated his devolution on the human social scale. To construct Jones's subjectivity and in part to humanize him, Petry interfaces physical, social, and psychic spaces. The subterranean physical space Jones occupies mirrors his debased social space and his devolved psychic space. This nexus explains rather than excuses Jones's bestiality, for the distinction between cause and effect is not clear-cut.

Eating, ingestion, and consumption constitute one imagistic pattern that reveals the antagonists' bestial natures. This pattern along with images of animals are especially profuse in the discursive formation of Jones. Like Boots Smith, he devolves from human to domesticated animal (dog) to snake to wolf. Fairy-tale motifs reveal Jones as the most venomous of the novel's snakes and the most rapacious of its wolves. As a predator, he has a gnawing, insatiable hunger for young women, his source of psychological sustenance and nourishment. Like the wolf in "Little Red Riding Hood," he will consume older women, but his dietary preference is for young ones. Of all the women on the street and in the apartment houses at whom he stares "hungry-eyed" (89) and who "whetted his appetite for a young woman" (93), he considers Lutie the most appetizing morsel; he wants her "worse than he had ever wanted anything in his life" (87).

Petry's process for constructing Jones's subjectivity, a technique she utilizes for the novel's other formalist aspects, is to overlay desire and fairy-tale motifs with trappings from the Adamic myth. She employs standard imagistic patterns from one mode of discourse (i.e., fairy lore) to clarify and explicate her unorthodox application of images and formations from other sources (i.e., biblical lore). Stacking and interfacing images and ideas drawn from different sources is integral to establishing Jones as a person externally ordinary but internally a monstrosity—thoroughly evil.

Making Jones the arch tempter, Petry molds him most fully from the Eden trope. His eyes are more snakelike than Mrs. Hedges's, and his attempt to seduce Lutie is more cunning and vicious than Boots's or Junto's. On first meeting Jones, Lutie imagines he has "horns sprouting" and "a cloven hoof" (20). With a "hell-hound" as his attendant and a genuine fear of any sign of the divinity (such as Min's cross), Jones is Satan only slightly disguised.

The abundance of animal imagery; the imagistic patterns that foreground eating, ingestion, and consumption; the human qualities assigned to animals; the bestial qualities assigned to humans—these and other patterns and motifs all become centrally focused on the "street," which in its broad metaphorical function is the most deadly beast Lutie faces in the novel. The street is literal and figurative, human and animal, black and white, creator and creation. Like Junto, it is abstract and concrete—

"formless, shapeless, a fluid moving mass" (418). It is general in that it is "any street. . . . Any place where there's slums and dirt and poverty" (391–92). In particular, it is 116th Street. It is a physical space (black Harlem) that signifies social place—"the method big cities used to keep Negroes in their place" (323). The street is androgynous, both "an evil father and a vicious mother" (407). In some ways it affirms life, for Lutie and other blacks feel more human when in their own sociocultural space (57). More frequently, however, the street negates life: "It sucked the humanity out of people—slowly, surely, inevitably" (229). It turned Lutie's father into an alcoholic and it killed her mother in the prime of life (56). In assuming many shapes and inducing many conditions, the street is a monster. For Lutie, it is all the individual and collective forces that frustrate her life, "a walled enclosure from which there was no escape" (430).

Both *Native Son* and *The Street* use an invisible wall as integral to an imagistic pattern that conveys their protagonists' forced separation from the American mainstream and black people's confinement to a space (the ghetto) that constricts their economic and social development. Lutie's desire is for "a safe, secure, clean world" (408) outside "the wall [that] had been built up brick by brick by eager white hands" (324). This desire/quest opens and closes the novel and helps structure action in its middle section.

In foregrounding the symbolic relation between physical space and social place, Petry draws the Eden myth into focus and keeps the novel situated in the protest vein. As a metonym, the street contrasts the black and white worlds and signifies on the American Garden trope. As did Douglass in his 1845 *Narrative*, Petry critiques the American Edenic ideal by offering opposing vistas from which to view it. When the narrative prism draws into focus 116th and similar streets, the primary factors that characterize the inhabitants' lives are economic deprivation, shattered dreams, hopelessness, and resignation.

When the novelistic angle of vision is from the white world, the picture is exactly the opposite. In stark contrast to 116th Street is the main street of Lyme, Connecticut (29), which represents the white world. It evokes for Lutie sharp social and ecological contrasts: between herself and Mrs. Chandler; between her husband, Jim, and Mr. Chandler; and between her son, Bub, and the Chandlers' son, Little Henry; between her cramped, shabby, and dark apartment and the Chandlers' spacious, luxurious, and light-filled house; and finally between the "jungle" world in which she lives and the "enchanted garden" world of the Chandlers.

Lutie is so mesmerized by her observation of the Chandlers living the American Dream that she misreads what many of the dream's signs signify. As a result, she imbibes the myth without critically and fully examining it. Choosing Benjamin Franklin as her role model and absorbing the Chandlers' socioeconomic philosophy, she equates the American Dream with money and money with happiness. By analogy, she must deal with the same problem that Franklin's Junto confronted ("Junto" was Franklin's name for a coterie of white males he organized in the 1770s): how to get ahead, do good, and keep one objective from corrupting the other and thus the person. In pursuing the dream she confuses the means (money) with the end (happiness), and this confusion leads her into the clutches of Junto (the novel's character). Lutie's problem is not only her failure to examine critically the American Dream but also her dogged independence and self-reliance in pursuing the dream. The masculinist stance she adopts in her pursuit is identified with the mythic white American male, the American Adam, which Franklin represents.

The novel begins with the centered subject's acute ability to read signs. She can pierce surface appearances to determine exactly what the "for rent" signs signify. As the novel progresses, her ability to decipher other kinds of signs steadily diminishes. In the novel's concluding sections, Lutie's failure (or inability) to read accurately signs and sign systems thwarts her quest and traps her in a maze so entangling she loses her husband, her job, her home, and her son. The narrative of her desire concludes with a situation in which her life, liberty, and happiness have been severely jeopardized. Though she recognizes her journey has been "a series of circles that flowed into each other" (435), that while her starting and ending points have been in different spaces she has ended up "in the same place" (407), she has not learned from her experiences. Petry's geometric structure critiques both Lutie and the dream she pursues.

SEVEN

Totems and Taboos

Configurations of a Southern Fictive World

WITH THE BEGINNING of this century, African American novelists began to respond differently than their predecessors to the charge from whites that blacks had not evolved socially to the point of becoming fully human. Through World War I the novelists centered in their works culturally refined and morally upright black subjects, compared them favorably to the most cultured whites, and used this characterization to argue for black humanness and humanity. As the century progressed, the novelists increasingly appropriated one of the Negrophobes' most potent discursive weapons (evolutionary theory) and used it dialogically and reflexively. Through their detailed delineation of white society's social and cultural mores and their formation of white (particularly male) subjects, the novelists argued that white Americans and white society manifest earmarks of man in a primitive state.

The threads of this counterdiscourse are particularly apparent in early-twentieth-century novels that thematize the lynching bee. In *The Marrow of Tradition*, for example, Charles Chesnutt debunks assertions of whites' biosocial superiority, mainly through his formation of white male characters. He presents these characters' values, beliefs, and behaviors as representative of their race during the late 1800s and the early 1900s. Employing dramatic and verbal irony and character contrasts (whites with blacks), he allows the whites to condemn themselves as uncivilized. The novel's title suggests that this condition in southern white society is not recent.

James Weldon Johnson's approach to the issue in *The Autobiography of an Ex-Coloured Man* is principally tractarian. The novel's protagonist-narrator states straightforwardly the heart of the issue: "The main difficulty of the race question does not lie so much in the actual condition of the blacks as it does in the *mental attitude* of the whites" (166). He summarizes the focal points that emerged in the disputation concerning blacks' evolutionary status and their social place in American society: "The battle was first waged over the right of the Negro to be classed as a human being with a soul; later, as to whether he had sufficient intellect to master even the rudiments of learning; and today it is being fought out over his social recognition" (75).

Using query 14 of Thomas Jefferson's *Notes* as a parodic intertext, Johnson dramatizes this "battle" as a verbal duel (chapter 10) between a Texan, who expresses "the sentiments of the South" (165), and a Northerner, who articulates a counterpoint consistent with an African American perspective on the topic. Unable to win the debate on an intellectual level, the Texan's final rejoinder is that any white man who contests the racial superiority of whites is advocating sexual unions between white women and black men and thus is advocating the destruction of white civilization. As the novel indicates elsewhere, the lynching bee is a socially sanctioned ritual to avert this threatened destruction.

By periodically staging this barbaric ritual of human sacrifice, whites "gratify the old, underlying animal instincts and passions" (189). Like Chesnutt (212), Johnson characterizes white Southerners as a more primitive and savage social group than blacks (189–90). Through this ritual murder one witnesses the "transformation of human beings into savage beasts" (186).

Like man in the primal horde, whites' social organization is inextricably bound to their religious orientation. Both Chesnutt and Johnson emphasize that by the turn of the century the sociopolitical realm of southern white society had assumed rigid religious contours. In the society they depict, rites, rituals, and social mores, as well as politics, economics, and social relations, are anchored in its civil religion. Many twentieth-century African American novelists adopted this template to configure the genre's fictive world. Certain narrative incidents, images and imagistic patterns, symbolic actions, aspects of characterization, allusions, elements of plot and story line, and other formalist and thematic features common among novels between 1900 and the 1950s may appear tangential or insignificant when viewed in isolation or in the context of a specific novel's or group of novels' centered concerns. However, when these features are considered collectively, a fictive world that overarches the genre and that includes novels of different types and from different periods comes into focus. Within this composite fictive world, the novels present a white society (primarily but not exclusively southern) whose civil religion is a form of totemism.

There is detailed correspondence between this novelistic world and the description of primitive societies Sigmund Freud provides in *Totem and Taboo* (1913). As its numerous citations indicate, Freud's book synthesizes several researchers' published studies on totemism, taboos, and primitive societies. African American novelists early in the century could have been familiar with the subject's basic premises before A. A. Brill's English translation of *Totem and Taboo* was published in 1918. Novelists later in the century drew directly from Freud's book to help configure their novelistic world. For instance, at times *Totem and Taboo* is a specific intertext that shapes a novelistic episode or a particular character (as in the Emerson Jr. episode in *Invisible Man*); at other times, it is a designated intertext used to inscribe white society and white subjectivity in an entire novel (as Wright does in *Savage Holiday* [1954]).

Freud begins the first chapter of *Totem and Taboo* with the following statement: "Prehistoric man, in the various stages of his development, is known to us through the inanimate monuments and implements which he has left behind, through the information about his art, his religion and his attitude towards life which has come to us either directly or by way of tradition handed down in legends, myths and fairy tales, and through the relics of his mode of thought which survive in our own manners and customs" (1). By analogy, the statement describes the principal sources from which African American novelists constructed the genre's portrait of the totemic white South: they observed firsthand southern whites' sociocultural forms, manners, customs, and modes of thought, and they extracted whites' mode of thought from the region's textualized history (its discourse on the Edenic ideal), which included literary, social, political, historical, and religious texts as well as monuments, art objects, and other forms of textualized history. In the novelistic discourse they formulated, African American novelists also focalized Anglo-Americans' legends, myths, and fairy tales to help shape the genre's formalist and thematic contours. Though the novelists encoded the genre's portrait of a totemic South principally from their firsthand knowledge of this society, *Totem and Taboo* is a useful reference point for decoding this portrait.

Freud considers tribes residing in Australia's interior the most primitive people in the South Pacific. He observes, "They set before them with the most scrupulous care and the most painful severity the aim of avoiding incestuous sexual relations. Indeed, their whole social organization seems to serve that purpose or to have been brought into relation with its attainment" (2). This principle of totemic exogamy, what Freud also calls the horror of incest, has an inverted parallel (totemic endogamy) in the African American novel's portrait of white society. The genre inscribes a southern white society whose "whole social organization" is obsessively focused on avoiding miscegenetic sexual relations (totemic endogamy).

There are a number of correlations between the African American fictive world and Freud's description of totemic societies: whites' dominance over blacks when the two races share the same or adjoining physical spaces; the belief in a race's descent from a common, primal ancestor (the Adamic myth); the sacredness of white personhood and the profanation of black personhood; white women's iconic status in the social structure; whites' image of black men as iconoclasts; a system of prohibitions that strictly regulates interaction between whites and blacks. According to Freud, "Totemism is a system which takes the place of a religion among certain primitive peoples [i.e., clans] . . . and provides the basis of their social organization" (100). When two or more of these clans (unilateral kinship groups) coexist in the same or in contiguous geographical space, one clan usually dominates and considers the other or others "forbidden." Typically, each clan is distinguished by its totem, which, "as a rule," is an animal (in rare instances a plant or a natural phenomenon) that "stands in a peculiar relation to the whole clan" (2). A clan considers its totem sacred and often believes it is "the common ancestor of the clan," its "guardian spirit and helper" (2).

In the African American novel, the 1850s to the 1960s encompass the heart of the white South's totemic age. In the genre's portrait of American (particularly southern) society, whites are the dominant (the chosen or exalted) race / clan and blacks are forbidden. The belief in common ancestral descent to distinguish whites from blacks and to regulate social interaction between them are aspects of this novelistic world that derive from the nation's history of black-white relations and that conventionally in the genre novelists inscribe under the Eden trope. Several twentieth-century novels that install the Eden trope particularize it as the Adamic paradigm, foreground the origin myth embedded in the Adamic story, and embellish it with totemic features, especially between the 1930s and the 1950s. During this era the genre is replete with images, allusions, character clues, motifs, themes, narrative paradigms, and other formalist features that derive from the novelists interfacing biblical (Adamic myth) and anthropological (totemic) models of society. One result is a tropological construct about subjectivity that harmonizes the biblical and the totemic beliefs in common ancestry—the primal father.

The genre's various configurations of this construct reflect how the Adamic myth of origin (with the contention that Adam was white) historically has been applied differently to and by blacks. Though some whites acknowledged that all humans originated from Adam, others, such as the apologists for slavery, appropriated, transformed, and merged stories from Genesis to formulate alternative myths of blacks' origin. One of these myths asserted that whites and blacks shared a common ancestor in Adam but that the black race was a result of a curse and mark placed on the sons of Cain and on the progeny of Canaan (Ham's son and Noah's grandson). Further, this variant asserted that while Adam was generic man's common ancestor, racial distinctions between whites and blacks were a result of divine intervention following the original human creation. In both instances, the assertion was that blacks and whites descended from different totems (a black one and a white one, respectively).

The Cain and Abel story, the story of Noah and his sons, and the Abrahamic story about the origin of God's chosen people, all of which have been appropriated to account for differences between blacks and whites, are standard in the African American folkloristic world and are the sources for numerous formalist features in its novelistic world. In some novels, one, two, or more of these biblical stories structurally and thematically constitute the principal intertext(s). For example, the story of Cain and

Abel is a major intertext in Jean Toomer's *Cane* (note the sketch "Blood-Burning Moon"); the biblical story also provides an interpretative gloss on the entire book, as Charles Scruggs aptly notes.[1] Centralizing the protagonist's subjectivity, James Baldwin's *Go Tell It on the Mountain* (1953), which is predicated on the Abrahamic paradigm, examplifies how ingeniously an African American novelist installs and integrates these and other biblical stories as whites historically appropriated them to explain blacks' origin.[2]

It often is the case in the African American novel and in African American folklore that blacks consider themselves descendants of an original white Adam, while implicitly (at times, explicitly) accepting the contention that their color is a consequence of events following the original creation. The point is handled variously in the genre: Chesnutt's *The House Behind the Cedars*, Johnson's *Ex-Coloured Man*, Toomer's *Cane*, Mercedes Gilbert's *Aunt Sara's Wooden God* (1938), Willard Savoy's *Alien Land*, Will Thomas's *God Is for White Folks*, and Ralph Ellison's *Invisible Man* are among the variations. In most such novels the central theme is the biracial protagonist's quest for identity. The principal biracial male characters in *The House Behind the Cedars*, *Ex-Coloured Man*, and *God Is for White Folks*, for instance, identify themselves with their white fathers as the legitimate descendants of Adam and thus intimate that their black mothers are descended from a non-Adamic creation or from a cursed group of Adam's progeny.

In treating racial subjectivity from the perspective of ancestral descent, both biblical and totemic, the African American novel generally adheres to the rules that stem from the slavocracy by identifying a biracial character more closely with his or her mother than with the character's father, especially if the mother is black. Nevertheless, there are several instances in which a biracial character in the genre undergoes a racial transformation (passes for white) regardless of whether the mother is white or black. In these novels, the defining criterion is the whiteness of one parent.

For instance, in *Cedars* John (Walden) Warwick's self-effected subject formation is predicated on his patrilineal (white) descent. But in Savoy's *Alien Land*, Kern Roberts, the protagonist, rejects his black father's ancestry and embraces his white matrilineal heritage. Changing his name from Kern Roberts to Kern Adams (his mother's maiden name) signals his identification with whites, whom he considers the direct descendants of the Bible's primal father. In these and in most of the other passing novels, the respective protagonist affirms the common ancestor he or she shares with whites and negates his ancestral ties with blacks. In many of the passing novels, including *Alien Land*, *Ex-Coloured Man*, and *God Is for White Folks*, this perspective on the myth of human origin overarches the novel's thematic structure and is vital to its centered subject's biopsychological formation.

A totemic perspective on ancestral descent informs narrative formations in several African American novels that foreground a male protagonist's desire for a healthy relationship with his biological father. When this desire is not fulfilled, the subject often seeks a relationship with a surrogate father, as in *Appointed*, *Ex-Coloured Man*, *Cane*, *God Is for White Folks*, *Invisible Man*, and *Go Tell It on the Mountain*, among others. Several novels include a cluster of allusions to the sociopolitical origin of the nation that bespeaks the concept of a common ancestor. Though often the genre casts Christopher Columbus, George Washington (the father of the country), or the collective entity known as the Founding Fathers in the role of the nation's common ancestor, most often it assigns Thomas Jefferson (the father of American democracy) this mythic, quasi-religious status. When the novelistic context is southern white civil religion, Jefferson as the nation's primal father embodies the principal characteristics of a totem. In such an instance, fictive reality mirrors social reality. The sacredness that whites in the nineteenth and twentieth centuries attached to Jefferson raised him to the status of a deity in southern white civil religion, and whites revered him as the original parent of their sociopolitical group, the primal parent who sired the white American "new men."

Invisible Man contains several skillfully rendered instances of a totemic perspective on the nation's origin myth in relation to black subjectivity. The Golden Day episode is one example. Sylvester, one of the veterans, firmly believes that Mr. Norton is Thomas Jefferson and, therefore, his grandfather. Another veteran confirms Sylvester's claim by pointing out that Sylvester has features that were cast from the "identical mold" as those of Norton-Jefferson and thus all are progeny of a race that re-created itself in God's image (or vice versa) (60). In this episode Ellison parodically installs a premise racial theorists such as Charles Carroll (for example, in *The Negro Not the Son of Ham* [1898] and *"The Negro, a Beast"* [1900]) advanced in their discourse on race. Citing the Scriptures as authority, such theorists asserted that it was impossible for blacks to be the descendants of Adam and Eve, who, the theorists maintained, were white. The protagonist espouses a similar premise when responding to Sylvester's claim.

While Sylvester identifies Norton with a common ancestor generated from political myth (Jefferson), others in the Golden Day elevate Norton's status to that of deity. This deification replicates what Freud identifies as a practice from certain primitive societies in which clansmen elevate the common ancestor to the status of a god or consider him a surrogate for the totemic godhead (2). Moreover, to invisible man and to several of the veterans at the Golden Day, Norton as the primal father is also at times synonymous with the Word: he is both God the Creator and Christ the Messiah (60–61), a point that further accents affinities between southern white civil religion and totemism. The fact that Norton is white and a Bostonian does not contradict Ellison's portrait of the South as a totemic society. As a white in the Golden Day (a microcosmic social organization), Norton is an outsider in the black clan. As a Northerner, he is an outsider in the southern white clan. But in a totemic system, as Freud points out, an outsider can become a god for the clan and, frequently, becomes synonymous with the clan's totem (147–51).

Ellison's depiction of Norton's relation to the black community certainly fits Freud's description of the totem as a clan's common ancestor, guardian spirit, and helper. Specifically in his relation to the black college and to invisible man, Norton masquerades his paternalism as fatherly concern and philanthropy, and he defines his social role as the "first-hand organizing of human life" (33). His mask of philanthropy is a mechanism for mediating his incestuous desire for his daughter, as is evident in the Trueblood episode. As Ellison inscribes it, Norton's horror of incest is as much totemic as it is Christian. Ellison thus uses incest thematically to contrast Norton with Trueblood and to debate whether whites or blacks have progressed farthest on the evolutionary scale.

In few instances is the African American novel's fictive world more closely aligned with social and historical reality than in the genre's inscription of the generic white woman as white society's totem, its guardian spirit. She embodies all that inheres in white people and white institutions. This entire society is organized around this totem's sacredness. An elaborate system of phobias, prohibitions, and taboos regulates interactions between blacks and whites. Black intrusion into any facet of white society is tantamount to violation of the white totem.

Numerous discursive formations in the African American novel's fictive world indicate that whites' belief in their own sacredness is supported by a system of social and legal prohibitions that regulates practically all forms of contact between blacks and whites. This system is analogous to what Freud defines broadly as the "touching phobia" in a totemic society: strict rules regulate the conditions under which a forbidden clansman is allowed physical and mental contact with an exalted clansman. In the historical South, this system generally was known as Jim Crow.

Freud states, "Touching is the first step towards obtaining any sort of control over, or attempting to make use of, a person or object" (33–34). In the African American novelistic and historical worlds, a Negrophobic white considers a black's freedom to touch a white person as an instance of social equality and as a signification of eventual black dominance. Chesnutt's narrator in *The Marrow of Tradition* succinctly states this totemic premise that governs power relations between blacks and whites in the South: "The person of a white man [is] *sacred* from the touch of a negro" (303; emphasis added). The narrator couches the prohibition within the Eden trope when he adds that a black who violates this prohibition commits "the unpardonable sin, admitting neither excuse, justification, nor extenuation" (303). According to Freud, the prohibition is not limited to "immediate physical contact but has an extent as wide as the metaphorical use of the phrase 'to come in contact with,'" which includes mental contact (27). In the African American novel and the social and historical reality it reflects, eye rape is a familiar instance of prohibited mental contact between black men and white women. The numerous examples of the touching phobia dramatized and thematized in the genre do not exaggerate historical reality. In fact, the genre does not reflect fully how pervasive this totemic feature was in the South or in the United States before 1960.

As craft in the African American novel became decidedly more sophisticated during the second half of the genre's first century, so, too, did its use of the touching phobia in configuring its fictive world. Ellison's *Invisible Man* is one of the best examples of this development. *Touching* has the same broad definition and application in *Invisible Man* that it has in Freud's discussion and in the life of the totemic South. The numerous instances of the touching phobia in *Invisible Man* are integral to the novel's thematic and formalist treatment of power relations between the races. Through them

Ellison illustrates that whites' touching phobia is not just a mere aesthetic aversion to blacks but is vital to the dominant society's sociopolitical and psychosocial fabric.

In *Invisible Man*'s battle royal episode, Ellison stages a ritual reenactment of the touching phobia and thus underscores how complex and inclusive this precept is in the South's totemic social system. He makes the phobia salient in the novel's thematic and structural design and in its formation of the protagonist's subjectivity. The scene explores the conflicting internal and external forces regarding whites' prohibition against physical and mental contact between black men and white women. The ten black boys hired to fight the battle royal suffer from what Freud terms "psychical fixation" (29), feeling at the same time attraction and repulsion for an object of taboo (the dancing white nude). It is a conflict between the social prohibition and the boys' natural instincts. In describing his reactions to the nude, the protagonist demonstrates quite clearly how this touching phobia shapes the southern (black and white) male psyche and undergirds power relations between the races. He exhibits signs of what Freud describes as "the subject's ambivalent attitude" toward the tabooed object, which the ruling order says he must never touch. Freud explains that the subject in such a situation "is constantly wishing to perform this act (the touching), and looks on it as his supreme enjoyment, but he must not perform it and detests it as well" (29).

The protagonist's reaction to the blonde nude exemplifies Freud's assessment of "psychical fixation." When invisible man looks at her, he is filled with "a wave of irrational guilt and fear," a consequence of racial and regional conditioning. Yet, he explains, "I was strongly attracted and looked in spite of myself." The external prohibition is unable to curb his instinctive reaction. "Had the price of looking been blindness," he admits, "I would have looked" (16). He feels a strong urge to commit the two most heinous acts (homicide and rape) a black male can commit against a white in the totemic South. His urge is to violate totally the white clan's totem, to touch her (which would be tantamount to rape) and to destroy her (an instance of homicide). In his words, he wants "at one and the same time . . . to feel the soft thighs, to caress her and destroy her, to love her and murder her" (16).

The protagonist's psychological ambivalence in this scene is not limited to his reaction to the nude. In fact, his ambivalence toward the nude reveals his ambivalence toward his own subjectivity at this stage in his experiential development. He believes, if only subconsciously, that he possesses the totemic character that inheres in whites, manifested more in his intellect and cultural affinities than in his biological makeup (he is neither a dark-complexioned black nor a bright or white mulatto). He considers himself superior to the nine other black boys in the battle royal (15). He chooses to identify less with them and more with the whites who organized the smoker in which the battle royal occurs and whom he considers some of the white community's most important men. Therefore, his reaction to being "clustered together" with the other boys so that their "bare upper bodies" touch is a reaction one would expect in a totemic society that prohibits physical contact between members of different clans.

Given how violently the totemic white South reacted to any form of physical or mental contact between black males and white females, the dancing nude scene in the battle royal episode might appear at first a contradiction in whites' behavior. But Freud's comments about "the contagious character of taboo" (72) help explain the white men's behavior. According to Freud, when a taboo has been violated, "a collective feeling arise[s] among savages that they are all threatened by the outrage" and therefore they act out of their "fear of an infectious example, of the temptation to imitate" (71–72). By staging the scene between the nude and the boys, the white organizers are attempting to prevent what Freud calls the "transmissibility of taboo," a situation in which the violator of a taboo moves "constantly along associative paths on to new objects" (34).

Motivated by their fear of losing their power and control in society, the whites at the battle royal use fear to condition the behavior of those (black males) who pose potentially the greatest threat to white supremacy. By simulating an instance of taboo, these pillars of the white society exemplify Freud's premise that totemic societies stage rituals intended to avoid "the risk of imitation, which would quickly lead to the dissolution of the community" (33). Southern white men feared the chain reaction of sexual contact (in its broad definition) between black men and white women, and in the battle royal scene they consider the "disease" as part of the antidote. The context of totemism in part explains their reaction to the protagonist when during his speech he commits a Freudian slip and says "social equality" instead of "social responsibility" (24–25).

On the whole, in the totemic South the touching prohibition excepted neither age nor gender as is certified in the genre and the social history from which it draws directly. According to Freud, "If a member of a clan is killed by someone outside it, the whole clan of the aggressor is responsible for the deed and the whole clan of the murdered man is at one in demanding satisfaction for the blood that has been shed" (105). The crime "is avenged in the most energetic fashion by the whole clan, as though it were a question of averting some danger that threatened the whole community or some guilt that was pressing upon it" (4).

Several novels that portray this phenomenon draw directly from historical reality. The Harvey Meeks episode in J. McHenry Jones's *Hearts of Gold* is an illustration early in the genre of how the prohibition applied to black children (see ch. 4 for a fuller discussion of this incident). Jones apparently bases this episode on an incident that occurred in Manatee County, Florida, in 1896.[3] Sutton Griggs's *The Hindered Hand* provides one of the African American novel's earliest and most brutally graphic accounts of a black woman who is ritualistically lynched for allegedly violating the touching prohibition (in this instance, murder). The historical source for this gruesome lynching bee appears to be that of a dual lynching of Luther Holbert and his wife in Doddsville, Mississippi, in 1904 for committing murder.[4]

An interpolated scene from Toomer's *Cane*, "the story of Mame Lamkins" (from the "Kabnis" section), is another example of how children (even unborn ones), women, and blacks in general are judged guilty and held accountable for an individual black's violation of the white South's broadly defined touching prohibition. Again, an actual incident appears to have inspired this episode.[5] The novel evokes and invokes the biblical story of the first murder (Cain and Abel), and other aspects of *Cane* (including its characterization of Father John) thematize Anglo-America's appropriation of the biblical Eden myth and its application to black-white relations.

Cane is one among numerous African American novels whose characters are situated in a fictive world in which biblical tenets and practices interface harmoniously with totemic ones: Adamic descent parallels descent from a totem; the idea of a chosen people as distinguished from an outcast people melds with the idea of exalted and forbidden clans; specific biblical commandments that specify man's interaction with other men and with God fuse with prohibitions that regulate interactions within and between clans and dictate one's relation to the exalted clan's totem; sins are similar to taboos; and the ritual atonement and expiation of sins resemble in purpose and sometimes in form totemic atonement rites and purificatory ceremonies.[6]

Totemic Character and Biracial Liminals

African American novelists often situate their biracial characters in a social environment that exhibits features of totemism, particularly when the biracial character is a male and has a white father and is the focal character in a novel set or published after Reconstruction and when the novel includes a significant number of motifs from the Eden trope. In such novels the society's totemic features are revealed through different kinds of narrative formations: a focal character's adherence to (or rejection of) a value system that privileges whiteness to the point of deification (the series of passing novels); the theme of whites' (and sometimes, blacks') belief that whites are God's chosen people and, therefore, are sacrosanct (an idea that is incorporated into practically all African American novels that employ the Eden trope and those that thematize racial conflict); narrative action that projects whiteness as a universal force and asserts that this sacred quality inheres in all people and institutions defined as white (most novels that incorporate the lynching bee or other forms of racist violence). Whether the authors, narrators, or characters affirm or negate them, the ideas bespeak a society whose principal organizational cornerposts are anchored in totemism.

Freud's statement that "the totemic character is inherent . . . in all the individuals of a given class" (2) is an appropriate gloss for those novels whose central subjects are biracial and whose plot structures trace these subjects' attempts to enter the white mainstream. In the African American novelistic world, "totemic character" equates with race. Certainly through the World War I period, one of the principal centered subjects (as character and as theme) dramatized and narrativized in the genre is the question of racial (i.e., totemic) identity. When the character is a white mulatto, the narrative rubric typically is the dominant society's one-drop rule, which in its most extreme form posits that the slightest degree of African ancestry pollutes and therefore negates one's totemic (white) character.[7]

As the genre shows, an allegation that a person has at least one black ancestor, however remote, is sufficient reason for him or her (regardless of physiological characteristics) to be assigned to the black race and subjected to the social and legal conditions under which whites force blacks to live. When this aspect of racial subjectivity is assessed from the purview of totemism, the crux of the problem is the dominant society's distinction between those who belong to the chosen (white) clan and those who belong to the forbidden (black) clan as determined by direct descent from the white totem father (Adam). Typically in the genre, the higher a mulatto's degree of white ancestry, the more severe are his or her problems with subjectivity.

Most pre-1960 African American novelists who treat the mulatto's plight in the context of the one-drop rule draw more from its social than from its legal strictures. Chesnutt's novels are notable exceptions. In *The House Behind the Cedars* Chesnutt focuses attention on the rule's social and legal ramifications. He uses the social definition of race according to the one-drop rule to construct Rena Walden and her story line; he utilizes the statutory definition to construct John (Walden) Warwick and his story line. As an attorney, Chesnutt certainly was familiar with legal cases regarding racial identity, and he incorporates an 1857 court case from South Carolina as a specific intertext in *Cedars.* He also apparently constructs the novel in part from a court case in Virginia in the 1830s. The details of this case, including the plaintiffs' family name (Warton), closely parallel details of the Walden family's general situation in *Cedars.*

In the 1830s fifty whites from Stafford County, Virginia, petitioned the state legislature on behalf of a family of mulattoes (the Wartons) in response to a state law that free blacks must leave the state. The white petitioners acknowledged the Warton family's biracial ancestry, for the petition points out that the Wartons "are remotely descended on one side from a colored person," but contends that "more than three-fourths of their blood is derived from white ancestors."

The petition contends that the Wartons are free, have acquired property, have exhibited excellent character, do not associate "with persons of colour," have on occasion intermarried with whites, possess "partialities" that "are decidedly for whites," have aided the slavocracy in suppressing blacks, and in other ways have shown "that no evil would result to the Commonwealth" by their continued presence. In this light, "These persons are neither free negroes nor mulattoes; they are white persons and as such are subject to none of those laws which relate to free negroes and mulattoes."[8]

When in the aftermath of World War I the genre moved its focus away from bright and white mulattoes who straddled the color line, racial identity from a totemic perspective took different turns. Several novelists between the two world wars concentrated on demystifying the totemic character (whiteness), often by treating tensions within the black community between dark-skinned blacks and a focal character who physiologically is more white than black and by treating internal (psychological) tensions that arise from a character's cultural affinity for blackness and his or her pursuit of white-oriented standards. A number of post-1920 novelists embellished their works with features of totemism, including Wallace Thurman's *The Blacker the Berry* (1929), Mercedes Gilbert's *Aunt Sara's Wooden God*, and Will Thomas's *God Is for White Folks*.

Among the few passing novels published between 1930 and 1960, *Wooden God* departs most fully from its predecessors' norms by demystifying the white totem and positing through plot structure that the totemic character (whiteness) that inheres in the novel's protagonist is profane rather than sacred. For the most part, in earlier novels this demystification of whiteness through black character portraiture is confined to secondary mulatto characters, such as Jeff Wain in Chesnutt's *Cedars*. Interestingly, character portraits such as Wain's tend to affirm turn-of-the-century Negrophobes' assertion that the most degenerate blacks are those with discernible mixed racial ancestry. Gilbert contends that the white ancestry is the pollutant.

In his foreword to Gilbert's novel, Langston Hughes states, "The wooden God of Miss Gilbert's novel is a mulatto country boy, worshipped by his mother, but [he is] unable to fulfill the faith and belief she has in him" (vii). Sara Lou Smith Carter, whose community service and age have earned her the endearing title Aunt Sara, is the fourth generation (at least) of a line of black women who, except for her mother, "had half white bastard chillum" (12). Aunt Sara worships the totemic whiteness that inheres in her biracial son, William. Her veneration of William is more than a mother's overindulgence of a child as compensation for the taunts he receives from his peers, who marginalize him in this rural black community. Partially because she treats him as a "wooden god" (rather literally, he is her totem), William early in life becomes a spiteful, self-centered, and dishonest person.

Gilbert's formation of her mulatto subject as victimizer more than victim is rare in the African American novel's portraiture of mulatto protagonists. Unlike most of those African American novelists whose exploration of the psychology of mulatto characters suggests that these blacks suffer from a special form of liminality in a racist society, Gilbert's portrayal of William Carter suggests that his diabolical and degenerate nature is congenital, inherited from his white bloodline rather than induced by his marginalized social status. In essence, she suggests the innate evil of whiteness itself, that it is profane rather than sacred and thus is unworthy of worship. Consistent with his personality, William Carter's deification of whiteness is centered on himself rather than on his biological white father, Franklyn Gordon. Like John (Walden) Warwick in Chesnutt's *Cedars*, William becomes his own totem, his own surrogate father–deity. That both Carter and Warwick lack relationships with their biological fathers accounts in part for the recentering of the totemic character onto self.

In *God Is for White Folks*, this recentering does not result from the protagonist's white father being dead or absent from his life. Thomas's novel provides yet another variation on the topic of the white-male-father totem. Valorizing the white part of his biological heritage to the point of deification, Beau Beauchamps, the protagonist, identifies his inherent totemic quality with his patrilineal (white) descent. He is one of the very few white mulatto liminals in the genre who undergoes a conversion ritual that effects his complete psychological and social transformation into a white person. In a somewhat literal sense, this novel is an autobiography of an ex-colored man; it combines principal conventions of the fictionalized slave narrative and the passing novel. Its title suggests its grounding in the biblical and totemic myths of origin and identity, and it brings chronological closure to the genre's innovations in treating white mulatto male protagonists within the purview of totemism.

Totemism and White Male Subject Formation

Would you want your sister to marry a nigger? This well-worn adage from nineteenth- and twentieth-century American society—a variant of which substitutes daughter for sister—appears frequently in the African American novel as an aphorism and occasionally as a literal question. In Webb's

The Garies and Their Friends the adage receives its fullest thematization and dramatization before 1900. The Bates men—father and brother—are horrified at what the endogamous (miscegenetic) relationship between Birdie Bates and Clarence Garie implies, and other white men in the novel who are not Birdie's biological kin voice similar outrage. To be sure, the adage's reference to marriage is not incidental, as *The Garies* and, later in the century, *Hearts of Gold* verify. The reference calls attention to whites' fear of the deleterious effect such a legal union will have on the overall social structure. The adage's literalization and attendant narrative formations constitute the core of plot structure and theme in Joshua Henry Jones's *By Sanction of Law* (1924), a didactic novel that does not significantly revise previous novelists' treatment of the issue.

Twentieth-century novels that intricately weave the adage into the text's form and meaning develop a construct that appropriately can be called the sister complex. The construct is integral to the genre's psychoanalytic profile of whites, particularly its psychosexual formation of white male subjects. The sister complex describes what the genre depicts as a white male's obsession with the sanctity of white womanhood. When his obsession involves his female blood relatives, it has connotations (at times, denotations) of incest. But the women who are the objects (or victims) of his excessive protectiveness include his biological as well as his sociogenic kin. Thus the term *sister* is generic.

The construct denotes a psychosocial kinship system among whites and is part of the genre's portrait of the South as a totemic system. This novelistic usage is consistent with Freud's view that, in a totemic society, those descended from the same totem form a family unit that includes those of the most distant degrees of kinship (6). Explaining the context in which some of the societies he studied use the terms *brother* and *sister*, Freud states that "the kinship terms . . . do not necessarily indicate any consanguinity, as ours would do: they represent *social* rather than *physical* relationships" (7; emphasis added).

In the African American novel's fictive world, the totemic South's kinship system determines and in turn is defined by social relations within and between races (clans). Any white woman is the sociogenic sister of any white man. Regardless of blood ties, however, a black woman is never the sociogenic sister of a white man. The genre derives the premise directly from the psychohistory of relations between white and black males.

Female-centered passing novels often dramatize this situation: when a black woman is passing successfully for white, white men pay her the utmost respect; when they discover she is black, for them she no longer embodies the totemic character and, consequently, they treat her as taboo. In Chesnutt's *The House Behind the Cedars*, Nella Larsen's *Passing*, Walter White's *Flight*, and some other female-centered passing novels, this stock situation is a seminal part of story line and emplotment.

The sister complex finds its fullest application in twentieth-century novels with males as centered subjects. Johnson's *Ex-Coloured Man* is one of the earliest examples. The author simulates the generic social context that gave birth to the adage (the debate between the Texan and the Northerner, discussed earlier in this chapter) as well as uses the adage imaginatively to dramatize his protagonist's attempts to pass as a white man. Part of this dramatization includes the protagonist's psychological vacillation in his racial identity. For instance, when in the mental state of being a white man, he considers white women his sociogenic sisters and (from a totemic perspective) regards black men as iconoclasts.

When Johnson literalizes the adage in one of the novel's axial scenes, he reveals an interesting parallel (and distinction) between the totemism of primitive societies and that of the United States, particularly the South. The scene is a brief one during which the protagonist-narrator has a sexual attraction for a young white woman whom he immediately concludes is his half-sister. The shock he experiences at this revelation causes such a rapid vacillation in his mind between emotions (moral choices) induced by his dual racial identity that the effect is just short of psychological devastation. His sexual attraction to the young woman is simultaneously in violation of two taboos: as a white man, his attraction is incestuous; as a black man, it is miscegenetic. As a black, incest is the greater moral dread. As a white in this totemic society, miscegenation is the greater horror.

A variety of perspectives on the sister complex merge in Johnson's formation of ex-coloured man's subjectivity. He is both black and white, both northern and southern. Through his subject's duality Johnson shows that southern and northern white males manifest this psychosexual aberration. Other novelists indicate the same. Wright, for instance, uses the sociogenic component of the sister complex in book 3 of *Native Son* to help frame the deputy coroner's attempts to incite whites' passions against Bigger and to discredit Jan Erlone and Boris Max. When questioning Erlone at the coroner's inquest, the deputy coroner phrases questions so that Erlone in essence admits that he would not object to his sister having sexual intercourse with or marrying a black man. To whites, Erlone's tacit approval of this form of miscegenation (even more than his ties to the communists) thoroughly discredits him and brands him a traitor to the white race; it makes him, like Bigger, a snake in the Anglo-American Garden.

The sister complex centers the male, not the female, psyche. In African American novels of the 1940s and the 1950s, this centering of a male character's mind-set reshapes some conventional formalist features as well as produces a few new novelistic formations. One of them is the feminized white male, an aspect of white male subject formation intended to deprecate subjectivity and, by extension, to castigate the nation's totemic social structure. Freud does not foreground homosexuality in *Totem and Taboo* as a specific feature of primitive societies; he emphasizes their "horror of incest." Yet when Ellison uses a Freudian rubric for "sexual deviancy," he emphasizes incest (Norton-Trueblood encounter) and homosexuality (Emerson Jr.–invisible man encounter). *Totem and Taboo* is a specific intertext in the Emerson Jr. episode, whose thematic and formalist features inscribe male homosexuality. In American totemism, both miscegenation and homosexuality threaten the social organization.

Among pre-1960 African American novels that incorporate either the Bible's Eden myth or its Adamic myth as a major part of the novel's form and content, *Invisible Man* is one of the most important in which a white male character is feminized for purposes other than stock characterization. Through setting, allusions, images, and descriptive actions, the author feminizes Emerson Jr. The setting that opens the scene in which Emerson Jr. first appears is "a large reception room decorated with cool tropical colors" (137). The room's predominant color scheme (green) connotes the white character's feminization and, thus, sexual perversion in general.[9]

Even more than color imagery and ambiguous language and gesture, the intertexts Ellison installs to construct this scene and its meaning bespeak his feminization of this character. The principal intertexts provide a gloss for each other, and all interface intricately with formalist features to provide one of the most artful instances of intertextual layering in the African American novel. Paul Laurence Dunbar's poem "Sympathy" as an intertext in this scene has multiple levels of meaning. On one level, it accents the protagonist's naïveté, his inability and unwillingness at this stage in his development to read the signs before him. For example, "A large bird [in the room's aviary] began a song," but the protagonist represses his impulse to understand what the song means (138). As other allusions in the scene to the caged birds and the Dunbar intertext make clear, a bird's "song," "cry," or "scream" is a lament for its lack of freedom. The Dunbar intertext, whose themes of incarceration and frustration speak analogically about blacks' alienation from the mainstream, conjoins with other intertexts in the scene's thematic configuration. One image of the caged birds (though not extracted from the Dunbar intertext) evokes the adage that birds of a feather flock together, which has been applied to homosexuals.

By placing an open copy of Freud's *Totem and Taboo* in the scene, Ellison intertextually situates the theme of deviant sexuality (taboo) within the genre's traditional perspectives on the Eden trope, particularly the American Dream. Another of the scene's intertexts, the Calamus section from Walt Whitman's *Leaves of Grass*, not only helps establish Emerson Jr. as a feminized male but also supports the thematic conjunction of sexuality and American democracy. The character's motives (which may be "impure"[141]) for inviting invisible man to the Club Calamus are ambiguous, but there is the suggestion that he is inviting him into a social circle for gay men, as the club's name implies. Critics and readers of Whitman (including some of his contemporaries) have disagreed over the symbolic meaning of *calamus* in the Calamus poems, and there is much ambiguity of meaning in this section of *Leaves of Grass*.[10] While some critics and readers have attached homoerotic meanings to the calamus as symbol, Whitman stated that he used it as a symbol "for the counterbalance and offset of our materialistic and vulgar American democracy, and for the spiritualization thereof."[11] Nevertheless, homosexuality, among other meanings, can be gleaned from the Calamus poems' emphasis on manly love.

Other evidence suggests that in his feminization of Emerson Jr., Ellison draws directly upon Whitman and the Calamus poems. For example, the novel clearly identifies works by Ralph Waldo Emerson in its intertextual dialogics. Given the literary relationship between Emerson and Whitman, Whitman indeed can be considered an Emerson junior. In *Leaves of Grass* Whitman expresses concretely and boldly several ideas that Emerson advances philosophically, abstractly, and implicitly in his works.[12] Much of the encounter between the protagonist and Emerson Jr. turns on tensions between the abstract and the concrete, between the implied and the stated. Finally, themes in this scene and throughout the novel are consistent with themes in the Calamus poems in particular and with those in *Leaves of Grass* in general, especially the themes of man's love for his fellow man and of humanitarian and democratic relationships among men (both generic and gender specific).

By inviting the protagonist to the Club Calamus, Emerson Jr. attempts to establish a feeling of comradeship with invisible man. He says that the club is "very well known. Many of my Harlem friends go there. It's a rendezvous for writers, artists, and all kinds of celebrities" (141), implying that some of them are white and that it is a gathering place for men of a certain ilk. According to LeRoi Jones, male writers, artists, and celebrities of this ilk epitomize the feminized white male; they can be called liberals because at least superficially they espouse the cause of black liberation. In addition, Jones sees the "artist" as the "concentrate" of "the society's tendencies—the extremist. And the most extreme form of alienation acknowledged within white society is homosexuality" (219). The novel implies that Emerson Jr. feels alienated from mainstream society because of his sexual orientation. Invisible man is alienated from the mainstream primarily because of his race. Thus, Emerson Jr., who uses the inclusive "us" and "we" in his dialogue with the protagonist, considers his sexual liminality equivalent to invisible man's racial liminality—to him, birds of a feather must flock together.

The idea that alienation and frustration are conditions that bind black and white social liminals also is imbedded in the scene's parodic incorporation of another major intertext, Mark Twain's *Adventures of Huckleberry Finn.* The relationship between Huck and Jim reverberates throughout this scene. Invisible man and Emerson Jr. each alternately exhibits characteristics of Huck and of Jim, both of whom are social pariahs. The overtones are simultaneously social, racial, cultural, and sexual. Critics who agree with Leslie Fiedler maintain that the relationship between Huck and Jim also implies homosexuality. More important, however, Ellison's use of *Huckleberry Finn* as an intertext provides a historical context for this scene, and the significance of this historical (or psychohistorical) context can be gleaned from Ellison's own comments on *Huckleberry Finn,* particularly in *Shadow and Act.*

Of Fiedler's designation of the "friendship" between Huck and Jim as "homosexual," Ellison states that Fiedler was so "profoundly disturbed" by the "ambiguity" of this relationship that he "yelled out his most terrifying name for chaos. Other things being equal, he might have called it 'rape,' 'incest,' 'parricide' or—'miscegenation'" (50–51). Ellison's comments are on the mark, for in the African American novel's psychoanalytic portrait of an American power structure dominated by white males, the major taboos are rape, incest, homicide, homosexuality, and miscegenation. That Ellison's phrasing gives special emphasis to miscegenation is consistent with the genre's creation of an American fictive world as a totemic society in which taboo restrictions against miscegenation resemble the horror of incest in the primitive societies Freud describes in *Totem and Taboo*. Moreover, if a sexual encounter between Emerson Jr. and invisible man were consummated, it would be an instance of homosexual miscegenation—the horror of horrors.

Discourse always has been a battlefield on which blacks and whites (especially males) have waged their metaphorical civil war. The feminized white male (with its attendant narrative formations) is an African American novelistic construct that escalates this discursive war at the middle of the twentieth century. The construct is integral to the novelists' new counteroffensive. In its reflexivity, it is largely a response to Negrophobic discourse that projected the black male as a sex-crazed brute monomaniacally driven to rape white women, to profane whites' most sacred totem. The construct's formalist and thematic contours reflect changes in the genre's configuration already underway in the 1950s and apparent in Willard Motley's *Knock on Any Door* (1947), *Invisible Man*, *Go Tell It on the Mountain*, *The Narrows*, and Waters Turpin's *The Rootless* (1957).

Historiographic Counterdiscourse: The Rootless

The Rootless exemplifies how a 1950s African American novelist uses psychosexuality and totemic precepts to frame a fictional treatment of historical materials. The author states his novelistic and ideological intents in two epigraphs (addressed to a black audience) that precede the novel's discursive text. The first is a dedication: "To This Generation in Its Struggles and Hopes for a Brighter Tomorrow." The second is a challenge to a contemporary black audience and also states Turpin's novelistic method and purpose: "IT IS HELPFUL TO CONTEMPLATE THE PAIN OF THE PAST IN ORDER TO MEET AND UNDERSTAND THE TRIALS OF THE PRESENT WHILE ENVISIONING THE HOPE FOR THE FUTURE." This statement voices the purpose of perhaps the majority of African American novels during the genre's first century.

The way Turpin conjoins and foregrounds violence and sexuality makes *The Rootless* a transitional novel between the example of Richard Wright in the 1940s (novels that privilege violence as the principal index to race relations) and the example of James Baldwin in the 1960s (novels that accent the sexual foundation of racial conflict). The novel's inscription of psychosexuality and totemism as narrative frameworks situates its author and characters as combatants in the psychological war between black and white males that escalated on a literary battlefield during the 1940s.

Two aspects in particular distinguish *The Rootless* from most other African American novels published between 1940 and 1960. First, according to standard definitions, it is an African American historical novel, more in the realistic mode of John M. Paynter's *Fugitives of the Pearl* (1930) and Arna Bontemps's *Black Thunder* (1936) than in the romantic mode of the costume novels Frank Yerby published prior to the 1960s. Second, the way Turpin uses psychosexuality to form the novel's major subjects, to shape structural symmetry, and to thematize race relations closely aligns *The Rootless* with contemporaneous African American novels set typically in the present.

The Rootless incorporates several novelistic conventions (thematic and formalist) that the genre had constructed from the Eden trope and the Adamic myth. Into the novel's textual fabric Turpin interweaves specific metadiscursive references to the colonial period of discovery and development, to the revolutionary and early national periods, to the antebellum period's plantation idyll, to the postbellum chivalric tradition, and to the twentieth-century's American Dream. The novel's principal setting is in the South during the American Revolution, which, along with the Haitian Revolution and to a lesser extent the French Revolution, forms a contextual backdrop for the thematic foregrounding of rebellion, freedom, and the affirmation and assertion of black personhood. Turpin's specificity in using texts, sociopolitical conditions, persons, and events from the West's revolutionary age to construct aspects of the novel's setting and characterization magnifies *The Rootless*'s aura of historical realism. As intertexts, documents of state from the American revolutionary period undergird and advance the novel's parodic plot structure, and they rhetorically sanction blacks' revolt against the slavocracy. Employing the mode of historical realism allows Turpin to reinscribe parodically the American Revolution as a textualized event without burlesquing it.

The novel's plot is a miniature version of the rise and portentous fall of the morally corrupt southern slavocracy. Its focal setting, Delafield and Shannon Landing, plantations in fictional Shrewsbury, Maryland, is a microcosm of slaveholding America. Within this novelistic world, Turpin centralizes three generations of the Delaney family, whose history provides narrative and structural cohesion for the plot. The family's saga in effect constitutes a generic text, one of whose principal functions in the novel is to refute through parody the generic text of received American history that chronicles the founding, settling, and development of the American South.

The novel begins by focusing on Hubert Delaney, and Turpin's formation of this subject debunks one of the white South's origin myths. In depicting Delaney's rise from a poor white social outcast to a plantation aristocrat, Turpin works within a historical perspective (fact and fantasy) on the South as a region initially colonized largely with social outcasts from Europe, many of whom were criminals banished to the colonies.[13] The details of Delaney's origins and personal life, therefore, make him representative of the majority of southern whites who populate the novel. His father was a murderer who "escaped the gallows by transportation" from England to the colonies, "made his New World fortune in spite of himself, and [took] to wife a daughter of the County's respectable Blaines" (18–19). Delaney's father, therefore, is the antithesis of Thomas Jefferson's natural aristocrat and William Wirt's new man, and the son is cast from the same mold that produced the father. As Turpin presents it, Hubert Delaney's family history parallels and critiques the historical rise of those southern whites whose aristocratic lifestyle was built on and sustained by a slave economy. Turpin constructs Delaney as a symbol of the region's history, as the embodiment of an inherently evil and antagonistic force against which blacks eventually must rebel.

In addition to the collective family history, the Delaney clan's individual and collective bodies also are intertexts in the narrative. In part to show the depth of Delaney's and his progeny's moral and ethical degeneration, the author afflicts them with diseases both physical and mental, the latter (insanity) a consequence of the former (syphilis). Each of the novel's tripartite divisions focuses on a Delaney dynast who contracts a venereal disease, becomes demented, and slowly decays physically through most of the novel—Hubert in the first third; Louisa, his daughter, in the second third; and Mariah, his granddaughter, in the final third. This generational and dynastic nexus contributes to the novel's portrait of the slavocracy (from the late colonial period through the early national period) as a totemic social organization. Turpin tropologically applies the hereditary and transmissible nature of disease to his portraiture of the Delaneys in a manner that recalls Freud's comments in chapter 2 of *Totem and Taboo* about the transmissible and infectious nature of taboo. The corporeal and moral diseases that inhere in the family over generations are intended to show that by the end of the American Revolution whites, particularly Southerners, contaminated the American Eden.

Through this interfacing of tropes (Eden myth, disease, body as text), Turpin calls pointed attention to the irony and paradox embedded in the American Eden's transition during the revolutionary age from politically oppressed colonies to a politically autonomous nation. The stench of death and decay that reeks from the Delaneys' bodies during most of the novel bespeaks the steady decay of America's democratic principles, which is precipitated by institutionalized evil (slavery). The Delaney clan's bodies as texts, therefore, signify and signify upon the body politic.

Writing from the vantage point of several generations hence and using disease tropologically, Turpin strategically situates references to George Washington and the Revolutionary War, to Thomas Jefferson and the Declaration of Independence, to the Constitution, and to other specific persons, events, and texts prominent in the received history of the nation's formation to emphasize his point that the American Edenic ideal was and remains rotten at its core.

As he expands the disease trope to configure the novel's major themes and plot structure, Turpin interfaces two constructs, social disease (syphilis) and social dis-ease (slave rebellion); narrative incident, characterization, and other formalist features radiate from the hereditary and contagious character of these two diseases. The patriarch Hubert Delaney is the chief agent who transmits the infectious venereal disease and the contagious social dis-ease. In the first instance, he is in effect (though not literally) the catalytic agent through which venereal disease infects his progeny and others within his biological and social kinship groups. Genetic transmission and depraved sexuality are, therefore, Turpin's narrative vehicles for conveying the slavocracy's debased nature and forecasting its eventual implosion.

In the novel's plot structure, the first major presage of the slavocracy's dissolution is the sociogenetic link Turpin establishes between Hubert Delaney and his only legitimate child, Louisa, the first heir to the Delaney dynasty. Before Louisa dies from ailments largely precipitated by syphilis, she transmits her perverse nature to two of her three children. She also is the originating agent (directly and indirectly) from which others in the society are infected with venereal and moral diseases. Turpin conveys the genetic and moral depravity that inheres in the Delaney clan and their cohorts through the various forms of sexual perversion that run rampant at the Delafield and Shannon plantations—promiscuity, masochism, sadism, and homosexuality among them.

Like her father before her and her daughter after her, Louisa perpetrates numerous atrocities against humanity, including arranging for her husband to be murdered. This intrafamilial homicide brings into sharper relief the theme of the system's self-destruction as a consequence of its internal degeneracy; it is the principal murder in a series that helps structure the novel's plot and move it logically to resolution. Working within the context of biological determinism, Turpin has all four generations of the Delaney clan (white and black but excepting James Shannon) commit some form of murder—patricide, fratricide, and homicide—and he suggests that this "criminal nature" has been transmitted genetically from the first New World Delaney.

The "murders" the heroic slaves commit as part of the novel's theme of divine retribution and the resolution to its plot are also biologically determined actions, but they are not manifestations of a criminal nature. To the contrary, the novel shows that they reflect innate pride, courage, and human will to be free. They symbolically affirm rather than negate humanity. In this contrast between what the novel intimates is the essence of white subjectivity (physical and moral inferiority) and the essence of black subjectivity (physical and moral superiority) Turpin inverts and reflexes onto slaveholding whites the assertions of an innately debased moral, physical, and mental devolution.

By no means, though, is the novel's scathing attack on the slavocracy limited to its portrayal of whites' corporeal and ethical constitutions. For instance, Delaney's mulatto son, Hosea ("Hosie"), is one of the principal transmitting agents through which Shannon Landing's slave community becomes contaminated. The disease Hosie contracts and transmits is both literal and metaphorical. Literally, he contracts syphilis from sexual (including incestuous) intercourse with syphilitic whites, and then over time he infects the slave community (as does his father) through his sexual exploitation of slave women. On the metaphorical level, Hosie inherits and transmits his father's moral degeneracy. His traitorous acts against the slave community imperil the most rebellious slaves and daunt other slaves' self-affirmation. His "unnatural hatred" for his mother "approached matricidal intensity which only the fear of consequences allayed" (174). He does, however, with Mariah's instigation, fatally poison Hubert Delaney. By the novel's latter half, the venereal disease from which Hosie suffers has wrecked his body. Eventually, he, like his white kin, succumbs to his own evil.

In using the Delaney clan representationally and sociogenically, one way Turpin indicates that the American ideal becomes increasingly profaned is through the story line about Hubert Delaney's son-in-law, Lanrick Shannon (from whom the plantation Shannon Landing gets its name). A complicitor in sustaining the slavocracy, Shannon contracts the slaveholders' disease (greed, deceit, and cruelty are among the symptoms) from his partnership with Delaney smuggling slaves. He attempts to escape his tainted past (his illegitimate birth to an indentured servant and his 'illegal' trafficking in human flesh) by acquiring material wealth and social respectability through his marriage into the planter class. This marriage to Louisa Delaney, however, actually compounds the infectious and hereditary nature of the disease (literal and metaphorical) and creates conditions for it to spread more widely among the slaveholding class: the marriage exposes him directly to syphilis; the children born to this union inherit both parents' worst traits.

Turpin's principal ideological point illustrated in Lanrick Shannon is that efforts to camouflage the evils of the historical past often give license to subsequent generations to perpetuate those same evils. Shannon's personal history replicates Hubert Delaney's: evil reproduces itself. This general point structures the novel's latter two-thirds, in which Turpin more fully melds the social disease and social dis-ease tropes, more successfully thematizes and theorizes history and historiography, and thus more forthrightly presents the novel's overarching themes of rebellion and divine retribution.

The two children of Lanrick and Louisa Shannon (Perry and Mariah) are even more diseased in character and in body than any of their forebears. (Louisa's third child, James, is not Lanrick's.) They are symbols of white oppressive authority, and, through his depiction of their excessively perverse sexuality, Turpin most caustically assails the South's perversion of America's democratic principles. He feminizes Perry and his white male compeers. Moreover, by making Perry a member of one of the prominent social, economic, and political circles of his day, Turpin launches a scathing attack on America's pretensions of being a democracy during the years of its early nationhood; he depicts this elite circle of white males as a group of homosexual Negrophobes. In the 1950s when he published this novel, homosexuality still was widely considered a "preventable disease," and to label a male a homosexual was considered a vicious mode of character assassination.

Turpin's depiction of this white male coterie recalls a similarly tight-knit group of socially and politically eminent southern white males of the antebellum period whose sexual proclivities included incest and homosexuality. Perhaps the best-known member of this group historically was the apologist for slavery James Henry Hammond, who served as governor of South Carolina and as a U.S. congressman and senator. His diaries unabashedly reveal incestuous liaisons with some of his teenage (white) relatives as well as repeated incest with his daughter by one of his slaves.[14] Published letters to him expose his reputation as a stud for and among a group of homosexual white males from the southern aristocracy, a group that included Thomas Jefferson Withers, who was the uncle (by marriage) of Mary Boykin Chesnut and at one time served as "a judge in the South Carolina Court of Appeals."[15]

Like several other African American novelists, Turpin aligns subject formation and nation formation. In *The Rootless* there is a reflexive relationship between character and culture, and the worst aspects of the slavocracy's (and the new nation's) cancerous inhumanity are lodged in Perry and Mariah Shannon. Turpin's iconoclastic formation of Mariah (and of Louisa) as subject demystifies the southern belle and thus caustically debunks the social system for which she is an icon (totem). Mariah's sexual and moral depravity exceeds Louisa's. Her masochistic proclivities are as evident in her relations with her slaves as in her relations with her lovers. She indulges her homicidal tendencies as much as she does her sexual proclivities. She engages in sodomy with her cruel overseer, Garrett, and she attempts to exploit sexually the novel's black hero, Prince. Debilitated from a venereal disease, her slow but steady physical decline monitors the continual moral decline of the system she symbolizes. Tensions (sexual and otherwise) between Mariah and Prince are central to the novel's final third, in which Turpin emphasizes through the disease trope the reflexive relation between subjectivity and society.

In the middle section of the novel, Turpin foregrounds contrasts between the plantation aristocrats Perry and Mariah and the slaves Prince and Cindy. Intensified conflicts between the two pairs focus emplotment in the novel's final third. The births of Mariah, Perry, Prince, and Cindy generally coincide with the beginnings of the American colonists' revolutionary activities, and these four reach young adulthood about the time the revolutionary spirit gives birth to the new nation. Parodic echoes from Lincoln's Gettysburg Address support this parallel. In monitoring these characters' maturation, Turpin uses them for a variety of foils and contrasts to undergird the novel's principal themes and the narrative strategies that convey these themes. As Mariah and Perry mature, Hubert Delaney (a patrifocal and negative force associated with America) nurtures their congenitally inhumane and diabolical natures. As Cindy and Prince mature, Sula (a matrifocal and positive force associated with Africa) nurtures their humanity and the sacredness of their personhood. When the two pairs reach adulthood, they clash, and Turpin portrays this conflict as one between earthly (profane) and cosmic (sacred) history.

Consistent with the novel's meanings for masculine and feminine, Turpin places Prince's robust masculinity in binary opposition to Perry's femininity to emphasize the spirit and meaning of the American Revolution, the Haitian Revolution, and the resistance to slavery among blacks at Shannon Landing. His denigration of the southern white male includes plantation aristocrats who were Perry's sociogenic forebears. The novel's broad castigation of the southern planter class asserts that these men at best were armchair patriots who did not fight in the American Revolution for the privileged lifestyle they subsequently enjoyed. Extending this criticism to those New World blacks who have become southernized, the author points out that, unlike the blacks of Haiti, the peasants of France, and the slaves of Coramantee origin, these American blacks are not willing to fight for freedom.

Turpin's strategy of using the body textually continues into the novel's final third. He writes the black body as a text that inscribes a counterdiscourse to the white body as text. In effect, he engages in his own mythmaking and thus proffers a black mythopoeic reality as a substitute for a white one. Prince is the focal subject, and Turpin constructs him from several cultural, historical, social, and ideological traditions in black America. Though Prince is born (but, significantly, not conceived) in the New World, the brutal system of slavery never subdues his self-esteem. The totemic nature that inheres in him derives from a royal line of African Coramantees.

The Coramantees were an ethnic group that lived in the Gold Coast region of Africa. Like the Ashanti and other ethnic groups from the Gold Coast, the Coramantees were well known to slavetraders and slaveowners for their warriorlike stature, pride, physical beauty, courage, fortitude, and violent and continuous resistance to any form of domination, including slavery in the Americas. Known generically as Akans, Africans from the Gold Coast region were an ever-present threat to the slavocracy's tranquillity in the Americas. Traders and owners feared them, and for the second half of the eighteenth century England sharply diminished the number of Coramantee slaves imported into British holdings on the North American continent.[16]

Other aspects of Prince's subjectivity incorporate various historical sources contemporary with the novel's setting. His rebellious and unconquerable spirit duplicates that of the legendary Toussaint L'Ouverture, leader of the Haitian Revolution. The novel's emplotment in its final third reveals concrete and ideological ties between Prince and the insurrectionists at San Domingo. Historically, there were expressed fears within the slaveholding society that the Haitian Revolution would inspire slave revolts in the United States, including the Chesapeake area where this novel is set.[17]

The novel's narrative progression monitors the formation of Prince's subjectivity (his development from childhood to manhood) by frequent references to America's most revered revolutionary patriots. As a narrative and ideological strategy, black subject formation situates this novel squarely within the context of Anglo-Americans' appropriation and transformation of the biblical Eden myth. The discursive parallel between black subject formation and white nation formation highlights the paradox between Anglo-Americans' cries for liberty and their refusal to include blacks in their vision of and possibilities for the New World. Prince espouses the same views about human freedom as did Patrick Henry, Thomas Paine, and Thomas Jefferson, and his heroic actions dramatize Henry's most famous statement, "Give me liberty or give me death."

Prince's fight to the death for his and others' freedom reaffirms the character traits of the Coramantee warrior, underscores the concept of natural rights embedded in the revolutions in Haiti and America, and accents the irony of a country (America) that fights against an oppressor but will not apply the same principles of liberty to those whom it oppresses. Through his uses of a variety of cultural, ideological, and historical themes, events, and persons, as well as different anthropological and psychological frameworks, Turpin portrays the African American Coramantees as blacks whose defiance of superimposed authority and power is inseparable from their nature.

The merging of resistance to oppression with sexuality forms a prominent pattern in the novel's thematic and structural design. By endowing his chief black characters with a healthy sexuality and afflicting his chief white characters with a diseased sexuality, Turpin inverts from social history the myth of the diseased black that had currency through Woodrow Wilson's presidency. His conjoining of sexuality with rebellion in an antebellum setting keeps the novel within a psychohistorical context.[18]

Through the novel's form and content, Turpin refutes a historicist (implying Anglo-American and Eurocentric) view of earthly history that posits that immutable laws rather than human agency determine history. At the same time, he affirms a historicist view (implying Coramantee and Afrocentric) of cosmic history by dramatizing that human agency can indeed alter the course of earthly history. His various uses of the American, French, and (particularly) Haitian Revolutions underscore the latter point. Dual perspectives on historicism, installed through a series of inverted formations, constitute the heart of the novel's utilization of American history. Through several black characters' symbolic actions and a series of inverted formations, Turpin refutes the contention that the New World African was a savage whose enslavement was benign in that it provided him the opportunity to become civilized, asserts that the peculiar institution caused human devolution rather than evolution in the New World, and contradicts the slavocracy's claim that the perpetual enslavement of blacks accords with so-called natural laws. With the authorial advantage of writing from the future, he responds dialogically to the plethora of eighteenth- and nineteenth-century social history texts that viewed slavery as a linear construct and in essence contended that because the debased status of slaves in the United States was a natural stage in the social continuum, slavery would continue in perpetuity.

Emplotment in *The Rootless* proffers the conflict between blacks and whites as a conflict between the sacred and the profane. Perry and Mariah, the most vicious of the Delaney dynasts, are the quintessential personification of profane history in the United States, a history inextricably bound to slavery's institutionalized inhumanity. Prince and Cindy are the chief agents of sacred history, and through them this transcendent force asserts its supremacy. As the novel begins its dramatic conclusion, it focuses most sharply on Mariah, and its most prominent fictive construct is matrifocality, representing conceptions of both earthly and cosmic time (history). Despite the fact that the Delaney dynasty begins as a patriarchy, Turpin uses a matrifocal construct to resolve the novel's plot.

There comes a point in time, the novel demonstrates, when exponents of profane history stretch the limits of their inhumanity to the extent that they anger the transcendent force of cosmic history. At this point, what Turpin calls the "Moment," cosmic history reasserts its supremacy, and through its agents "dynasties tumble, empires waste and shrink and die as from disease, and cultures wilt back into the world loam from which they sprang, to feed in their turn the germination of other seedlings" (246). These agents are "born of forces and trends, of causes and effects, of multiplying energies generated from unseen sources" (246).

The transcendent "forces," "trends," and "energies" are innate in Sula, Cindy, Prince, Delilah, and the other Coramantees. All of them actively resist psychological and physical slavery and, like the Coramantees who helped precipitate the Haitian Revolution, remain outside the realm or "groove" (to borrow a term from *Invisible Man*) of the New World's profane history. While each generation of the Delaney family must contend with a Coramantee, the historical Moment occurs when the inhumane machinations of Mariah and Perry Shannon become so excessive that they offend and desecrate cosmic history. Casting Prince and Cindy as agents of the Moment, Turpin dramatizes the role of human agents in altering the course of earthly history.

Perry's extremely brutal treatment of Prince is the former's undoing. Prince leads a revolt on the slave ship taking him and other rebellious slaves south. His final insurrectionary act is to kill Perry Shannon during this slave mutiny. Other slaves kill other owners and traders on board. Those who manage to elude the avenging slaves perish when a raging storm wrecks the ship. Turpin portrays the scene as a symbolic action, one of purification by water in which Prince, an agent of cosmic history and aided by this transcendent force, precipitates actions that more clearly forecast the slavocracy's impending doom.

Mariah's excessively sadistic treatment of Cindy invokes the Moment. At the novel's end, Cindy scalps the diabolical Mariah and sets Shannon Landing ablaze. Evoking images of Sodom and Gomorrah, this destruction by fire is a symbolic act of purification. Prince and Cindy's actions signal the triumph of sacred time over profane time, of cosmic history over earthly history.

Turpin's apparent authorial fascination with the heroic slave characters he creates does not cause him to lose control of the novel's fictive vision. He exercises considerable artistic restraint in providing a resolution to the novel's plot and to the analogy he draws throughout between the Delaney dynasty and the United States. Thus, Cindy's physical destruction of the microcosmic Shannon Landing and its matriarch and Prince and his henchmen's destruction of Perry and the slavetraders do not portend the overthrow of the nation or the physical destruction of its power elite. Rather, these symbolic actions forecast the dissolution of the peculiar institution, thereby allowing the novel to remain outside the realm of historical romance and within the purview of historical realism.

The Rootless ends with the deaths of Prince and Cindy but with the birth of an abolitionist movement in the South. The two purificatory acts that constitute the plot's closure begin the new republic's decontamination and are harbingers of a new social order in which cosmic history will predominate. This new order portends principally in James Shannon, the last surviving heir to the Delaney patriarchy and the only Delaney not contaminated; in Delilah, a fugitive slave who joins James and others to initiate an active abolitionist movement in the South; and in the surviving child of Prince and Cindy, who inherits and, Turpin suggests, actively will perpetuate the Coramantee will to be free.

Having presented the distant slave past in the context of the American Revolution, the novel looks forward to the Civil War and its aftermath. But reading beyond the novel's ending, one knows that the Civil War failed to effect the New Eden's complete decontamination, that the social disease, to use Turpin's trope, only went into brief remission following the war and recurred periodically between the 1860s and the 1960s. One gleans this perspective from the novel's prefatory epigraphs in which Turpin highlights affinal relations between the historical past and the present. Looking to the future, the author calls for another kind of civil war, and he does not discount an armed struggle.

The Textualization of Blackness

Invisible Man

The Trope: "Here in This Eden"

WHEN THE PROTAGONIST in chapter 5 of *Invisible Man* recalls his college experience and muses about "those others . . . who had set me here in this Eden," he is using the Eden trope to speak on one level about the paternalistic relationship the college's self-deified white philanthropists have established with him and his fellow students. On another level, he is speaking generally of African Americans' historical relationship to Anglo-Americans. His story is simultaneously a personal narrative and an abbreviated history of African Americans. Within this novel's discursive praxis and consistent with the black novelistic tradition, *Eden* references geographical, historical, cultural, and textual spaces.

Columbus's "discovery" of the Americas in the 1490s and his claim to having found the original Garden of Eden were seminal events that helped shape the configuration of the identity that European immigrants in British North America contrived for themselves, the identity they assigned to diasporic Africans, and the identity these New World Africans forged for themselves. Invisible man's personal history (like those of other Americans), therefore, is inseparable from the country's actual and its mythic histories. In this novel, as in several other African American novels, the Eden myth is the trope that intertwines nation formation and subject formation.

Invisible Man thematizes African American subjectivity. It utilizes historical and linguistic structures to proffer an interiorized African American identity, which it places in opposition to those exteriorized identities that whites ("those others") constructed, largely from texts, and assigned to American blacks. From the early seventeenth century forward, through "words . . . violence and ridicule and condescension" they formulated and imposed upon African Americans "a treacherous and fluid knowledge of" black being. Even "their most innocent words were acts of violence" against blacks (87).

In its (re)inscription of African American subjectivity, *Invisible Man* installs numerous conventions from the African American novelistic tradition, many of them originating a century earlier. It takes several of these conventions to their most artistically sophisticated peak during the genre's first century. For example, miscegenation predominates in the genre. Installed in various discursive formats, it appears as theme, motif, symbol, or action in virtually every chapter of this novel. One particularly innovative installation frames the Sybil episode, in which Ellison inverts the beauty-and-the-beast trope by portraying the white female subject as Beast and the black male subject as Beauty.

Fairy-tale discourse is prominent in African American novels and especially in *Invisible Man.* The novel incorporates not only fairy tales such as "Beauty and the Beast" but also rhymes such as "Three Blind Mice" and "Humpty Dumpty," all of them viewed through an African American experiential lens and used to comment on society's "civilizing" and "socialization" processes. These processes encase Ellison's treatment of ante- and postbellum forms of slavery, as is apparent in the Trueblood episode, which also installs the genre's conventional portrait of white society as a totemic social organization and utilizes the Adamic myth to explore tropologically the prohibition against white female–black male sexual unions. The symbolic apple of temptation, which appears in a variety of forms in this novel, is a tin apple in this episode. *Invisible Man* shares numerous other general and specific thematic and formalist features with its African American predecessors.

The prologue is a key to this novel's form, content, and meaning. In the first line the narrator states a definition of his self—"I am an invisible man"—and then proceeds to refine and to clarify this definition by offering different perspectives on or aspects of it (which he dramatizes in the novel proper). One perspective on this self-definition derives from the narrative's indirect installation and modification of Plato's *The Timaeus*. In section 51, Plato uses the term/concept *receptacle* to mean "an invisible and formless being which receives all things, and in an incomprehensible manner partakes of the intelligible."[1] Ellison adapts this notion to his construction of *Invisible Man* the text and to invisible man the centered subject. Within the novel's eclectic mode of narration, the protagonist is indeed a modified version of Plato's invisible being.

By the time he narrates the prologue, invisible man has placed himself within "the great American tradition of . . . 'thinker-tinker[s]'"—those who reinvent reality and subjectivity (6). He has moved beyond Plato's invisible being without form (a state narrated in the novel proper), during which as a passive receptacle he imbibed others' definitions of him, to become an invisible being with form. In narrating this metamorphosis, however, he reveals the extent to which he has assimilated discourses and signifying practices from other cultural fields, particularly European, Anglo-American, African, and African American ones.

The discursive dismantling and consequent (re)formation of invisible man's individuated and representational being is a process that draws from those melting-pot cultures that historically were syncretized to form the nation and to form the African American. When this cultural syncretism is expressed through language structures in *Invisible Man*, it emerges as a matrix of intertextuality that installs, parodies, rereads, and interfaces texts of various kinds, from various disciplines, from different cultures, and from different historical periods.

American critics' appraisals of this novel generally have been based on the extent to which it reveals affinities with the Anglo-American literary tradition, which is characterized in large part by its tropological application of the Eden myth to American experiences. For instance, several studies cite the influences of Emerson, Melville, Whitman, Twain, and other prominent Anglo-American writers on *Invisible Man*. In the main, these studies concentrate on those aspects of the novel that critics find are directly aligned with conventions in mainstream American literature.[2] Conversely, several studies emphasize the novel's grounding in various African American cultural forms, and a few of these studies draw attention to literary techniques that *Invisible Man* shares with other African American novels.[3]

Other than literary historians, few commentators have written about the novel as part of a distinctly African American novelistic tradition. To be sure, *Invisible Man* straddles two literary traditions, Anglo-American and African American, and both of them are lodged in the literary representation of America as Eden. That both these literary traditions employ the Eden trope makes them distinctly American. What distinguishes them is that the African American literary tradition, particularly the novelistic tradition, debunks the myth. *Invisible Man* is a prime example.

By the time he narrates the prologue, invisible man has recognized and rejected the prefabricated identities (personal and generic) others have assigned to him. His rejection is signified by his ongoing "fight" (psychological warfare) with the Monopolated Light and Power Company, which on one hermeneutic level refers to whites' use of discourse to define and to control black subjectivity. On a symbolic level, the power company exemplifies the maxim that he who controls the word controls the power of definition. Having wrested control of the "word" from whites, he is garnering the power to define self, a by-product of which will be his power to define others (whites).

In the prologue, which narrates the end of his experience, the protagonist, "under the spell of the reefer" and "listening to music," has an out-of-body experience. Entering the music to which he is listening, he hears "not only in time, but in space as well," and in this fluid state of being he is transported from time and space in the present to times and spaces in the past. He enters a metaphorical underground that has several levels corresponding to different events in the African American historical experience. On one of these levels he observes a black vernacular preacher who is giving a sermon on and also bearing witness to the "Blackness of Blackness" (7).

The preacher's text, as discursive process and as subject matter, bespeaks salient features of this novel's form and function. The sermon parodically reinscribes and conjoins biblical and literary texts. It repeats and revises the Judeo-Christian myths of cosmogony and of human origin as well as installs and revises images from the Apocalypse. By juxtaposing the first book of the Old Testament with the last book of the New Testament, the sermonic text links the end (Revelation) with the beginning (Genesis), a narrative process that is replicated in *Invisible Man*'s thematic and formalist features. As part of its discursive formation the sermon installs a revised version of a sermonic formation from chapter 2 of Melville's *Moby-Dick*. This fusion of biblical and literary intertexts in *Invisible Man*'s sermon is an instance of intertextual layering; through thematic oppositions and inversions, it speaks to the transcendence of blackness as a creative force and the evil of whiteness as a destructive force, to the resurrection of good and the destruction of evil, and to blackness as sacred and whiteness as profane.

As subject matter, as language structure, as speech act, and as itself an intertext, the preacher's text provides a gloss on the meaning of invisible man's narrative as well as on Ellison's discursive process and his novel's textuality. The preacher's use of intertextual layering to shape his sermon's form and meaning is a discursive process that the protagonist replicates in the scene that contains the preacher's sermonic text, in the prologue, and in each of the twenty-five chapters of his narrative. The preacher, the protagonist-narrator, the author, and their respective texts exist in a microcosmic-macrocosmic relationship in that individually and collectively they foreground narrative techniques (particularly intertextuality and referentiality) that this novel posits in its form and overarching theme as earmarks of the text and the textualization of blackness. In large part, the intricate use of intertextual layering to construct the novel and its centered subject defines *Invisible Man* as a signifying American text of blackness par excellence.

The Subject: "Who Was I, How Had I Come to Be?"

Who am I? This often is a centered subject's voiced or unvoiced question in American novels through the mid–twentieth century, inclusive of the different racial, regional, ethnic, and gender perspectives on American reality an individual novel might privilege. The discursive posing and answering of this question varies among individual novelists and novels, among groups of novelists and kinds of novels, and across time. The concern with a subject's American identity is a characteristic the African American novel shares with the novels of other American groups, but the

African American novel is distinguished from other American groups by the fact that the overarching question about subjectivity is bipartite: Who am I, and how did I come to be? These questions form the core of *Invisible Man's* thematic and formalist configuration, and they situate this novel firmly within the African American novelistic tradition.

Though cast in a discursive format quite different from passing novels and some other subgroups in the African American genre, *Invisible Man* nevertheless expresses the same external and internal tensions that arise from a centered subject's dual identities as an American (an appellation often synonymous with white) and as a black. The novel's factory hospital episode is exemplary. Entrapped in a womblike machine, the protagonist imagines himself whirling about in his own mind as he ponders the question of his American identity and as, simultaneously, the doctors construct an identity for him. To his unvoiced question (Who am I?) the doctors, once their operation is complete, answer, "You're a new man" (186). Their definition is ironic on several levels. He is not a "new man" as the term has been used historically to define the American. His new personhood is not so new because the doctors have reconstructed him as a variant of his old, exteriorized self. He is merely a reformatted "walking personification of the Negative" (72), a subjectivity that whites manufacture for him at different junctures in the novel. Only after he verbalizes the bipartite question of his identity—"Who was I, how had I come to be?" (197)—does he take a significant step toward understanding and defining his own subjectivity.

By encoding and decoding a variety of dualities embedded in the subject's formation, *Invisible Man* adheres to novelistic conventions that typically though not exclusively are associated with African American novels that center males. In addressing the centered subject's formation—how he or she came to be—black masculinist texts in the genre posit that the subject cannot know fully (if at all) his authentic self until he has a more comprehensive understanding of how his inauthentic self (or selves) came into being. This knowledge of origin yields freedom (a term whose meaning varies among works in the genre). Invisible man's expression of this self-formation process is thus: "When I discover who I am, I'll be free" (185).

Few protagonists before the 1960s attain this knowledge and freedom. The freedom is internal rather than external, psychological rather than social, for blacks' external freedom in the society the novels depict remained severely restricted before the mid-1960s. Those pre-1960 protagonists who do achieve internal freedom as a consequence of self-knowledge are more often women than men, Iola Leroy (*Iola Leroy*), Regina Underwood (*Hearts of Gold*), Rena Walden (*The House Behind the Cedars*), and Janie Crawford (*Their Eyes Were Watching God*) among them. Nevertheless, groping toward knowledge and thus toward freedom is a standard narrative process that organizes the internal and external journeys toward self in many black masculinist novels.

This narrative palimpsest can be traced back to the conjunction of theme and structure in the male-centered slave narrative. In his 1845 *Narrative* Frederick Douglass inscribes thematically and structurally his false and then his true self. First, he refutes the false definition of his being that the slavocracy has constructed and imposed on him. Then through discourse (the power of the word) he constructs an authentic definition of self. His statement about the process of his deformation and his subsequent self-transformation (from slave to man) is one of the *Narrative*'s principal discursive guideposts (107). In the twentieth-century novel, this two-part statement bespeaks the binary relationship of the black subject's false (externally imposed) and true (internally generated) selves, and as a narrative paradigm it gives discursive shape to key male-centered novels in the genre such as *The Autobiography of an Ex-Coloured Man, Cane, Native Son, Go Tell It on the Mountain,* and *Invisible Man,* all of which through their form, content, and meaning address their protagonists' subjectivity by exploring the origins of their being.[4]

To develop *Invisible Man*'s subject matter and to construct its centered subject, Ellison builds upon several black novelistic conventions. He thematizes history and historiography, installs the revolutionary period's permutation of the Adamic (origin) myth, dialogically incorporates the nation's founding documents, and intertextually revises (through both refutation and affirmation) white-authored texts, particularly those that seek to define black identity. Ellison most clearly stamps this last convention with his artistic signature.

For instance, Ellison installs and revises Chesnutt's narrative formation in *The House Behind the Cedars.* To transform himself from John Walden (black) to John Warwick (white), Chesnutt's character constructs his new identity (as well as his sister's) from a collection of white-authored eighteenth-century texts. Ellison greatly expands this formation in *Invisible Man.* The novel's discursivity emphasizes the extent to which black subjects (male and female) in the United States have been formed and deformed by discourse and counterdiscourse, by specific narratives and counternarratives. Individual texts and groups of texts often dialogically revise each other, resulting in a highly sophisticated rendering of intertextual layering and dialogism. Ellison intends to illustrate how the protagonist, in his individuated and representational roles, is largely a creation of white texts and discourses and to repudiate his externally created subjectivity.

From this purview, *Invisible Man* is the quintessential work in the genre, for no other novel before (or since) so pervasively interweaves the historical textualization of African American subjectivity into its themes and formalist features. In black literature prior to the 1960s, as in black life, the typical answer to a black subject's bifold question about his or her American identity within the national aggregate is, simply put: a being constructed and periodically reconstructed from myriad white texts and discourses. Though the answer is a false definition of the black subject's essential self, it nevertheless applies to any black who lives within what Ellison calls the American "groove" of history. As Bledsoe points out to invisible man, "White folk have newspapers, magazines, radios, spokesmen to get their ideas across. If they want to tell the world a lie, they can tell it so well that it becomes the truth" (110). Whites control the word, the texts, and the discourses. They are the definers within the American groove, and definitions belong to the definers, not to the defined. Only those blacks who live "outside the realm of history" (333) can define authentic black subjectivity.

To inscribe his contention about the textual construction of black subjectivity through aspects of the novel's form, Ellison inserts a plethora of intertexts—written, oral, visual, literary (serious and popular), musical, historical, scientific, political, psychological, philosophical, sociological, and folkloristic, among others. He uses this conglomeration of texts to form subjects, to configure language, to structure narrative action, to establish clusters of images and metaphors, and to configure scenes and episodes. His interfacing of sociopolitical and literary texts exemplifies the novel's intertextual template.

Like many of his predecessors, Ellison anchors black subjectivity in the nation's founding documents. Through direct references (paraphrase and quotation) and other linguistic structures, through representational and symbolic characterizations, through symbolic settings and actions, and through other formalist features the African American novel through the 1950s typically incorporates these documents of state as explicit intertexts. The nation's founding documents generated a system of laws and statutes that through the mid–twentieth century legally sanctioned blacks' forced marginalization and played an integral part in whites' imposition of a variety of false identities on blacks—natural slave, perpetual child, subhuman beast, congenital criminal (rapist, murderer, thief), and incarnation of the devil. In his journey toward self-formation, invisible man imbibes, like Plato's receptacle, several of the definitions historically assigned to blacks, as he indicates in the opening of the novel. Such definitions range from accommodationist to revolutionary, pacifist to anarchist, homosexual to stud and brute rapist.

In *Going to the Territory*, Ellison says he hesitates "to trace too closely a connection between documents of state and literature" but adds that for his "own working orientation that connection exists in the United States beyond all questions of cultural chauvinism" (248). Though there are a few direct references in this novel to the Constitution, the Declaration of Independence, and other documents of state, Ellison most often installs these documents implicitly. He places his text in dialogic relationship to Anglo-American (particularly literary) texts, which themselves inscribe positively or negatively the founding documents' credo. He identifies "moral imperatives" as the discursive juncture between these documents and "classic novels" in the nineteenth century by writers such as "Hawthorne, Melville, James, and Twain" (248). Works by such writers are specific intertexts in *Invisible Man.*

Literary texts (predominantly written but also oral) constitute the largest group of texts and discourses Ellison uses to construct and to establish an inextricable bond between the novel's subject matter and its centered subject. The four major categories within this group of literary texts are canonical Anglo-American, classic European, canonical African American, and classic African (basically in this order of preponderance in the novel). Texts from the four categories are both individuated (specified by title, author, character, or some other identifying feature) and generic. At least one text from each group has a centralized place as a parodic intertext in either the novel's overall structure or its thematics. For instance, Whitman's *Leaves of Grass* (installed inversely) from the Anglo-American canon, Homer's *The Odyssey* from the classic European, Wright's "The Man Who Lived Underground" from the African American canon, and the transformed and revised tale of the hare (i.e., Brer Rabbit in his African Americanized form) from the African oral tradition offer a different perspective on a subject's attempts to return home. All of these texts (and the discourses they represent) share common thematic and structural ground with each other and with aspects of *Invisible Man.*

As the African American novel developed from the 1850s, its generic norms followed the path of the nation's social changes (or lack thereof) affecting blacks. The contours of these changes (and consequently the genre's generic norms) were anchored in the American Edenic ideal as the concept was expressed in the nation's documents of state. What Ellison says about the Anglo-American novel and its relation to social flux and to the making of a more perfect union applies also to the African American novel: "It thrives on change and social turbulence" (*Going to the Territory,* 245). Much of this change and social turbulence (wars, economic recessions and depressions, political and educational reforms) eventually raised moral questions about blacks' rightful place in the American Eden. Either directly or indirectly, through voicedness or through silence, the question of the black presence in America is tied to the moral imperatives that Ellison maintains configure classic Anglo-American novels and several canonical twentieth-century novels ignore (*Shadow and Act,* 25, 35, 38).

Ellison installs three primary kinds of Anglo-American literary texts to comment on the black experience: texts whose portraits of blacks affirm their humanity; texts that deny black humanity by presenting deformed black portraits; and texts that attempt to make black humanity invisible by erasing the black presence from the nation's sociocultural landscape. At times in *Invisible Man,* a specific text from one of the groups dialogically revises a specific text or texts from the other groups.

The first of the novel's two epigraphs, from Melville's *Benito Cereno,* affirms black humanity. In addition, it provides a contextural gloss on other Anglo-American literary intertexts that have deformed black being or excluded it from portraits of American life. The protagonist's reference to Edgar Allan Poe, which Ellison aptly places as the first direct allusion to an Anglo-American writer in the novel's narration (the prologue), is a case in point.

The reference reminds one of Poe's "The Gold-Bug," a story whose distorted portraiture of black character fits the image and interest of the antebellum South's Edenic design. "The Gold-Bug" also is one of the rare instances of a black presence in Poe's canon. In Ellison's scheme, Poe belongs to that group of Anglo-American writers who erase the black presence from the nation's cultural and literary landscapes. Nevertheless, as Ellison's heteroglossic language suggests, Poe's canon reveals that he is "haunted" by those invisible "spooks" whom he deforms in or erases from his fictive worlds.[5]

While from this novel's purview works by Poe and by some other canonical Anglo-American writers are flawed by moral evasion, Melville's and Twain's writings are among those distinguished by moral vision. Indeed, a major variation on deformative black portraiture that is dialogically opposed to Poe's is contained in *Invisible Man*'s inclusion of *Adventures of Huckleberry Finn* as a specific intertext.[6] Ellison's comments on *Huck Finn* and other Anglo-American literary texts that deal seriously and directly with the nation's "moral predicament" (*Going to the Territory*, 250) clarify part of his reason for including *Huck Finn* as a parodic intertext in the novel's Emerson Jr. episode (ch. 9). In the case of *Huck Finn*, the issue is slavery's contradiction to the American Edenic ideal (what Ellison calls the "American experiment" in democracy) within Twain's novel and the moral dilemma of late-nineteenth-century readers when assessing blacks' oppressed status within the structure of the nation's social organization. Well within the twentieth century, when readers were removed from the actual historical event of slavery, they could, if they wished, more easily ignore blacks' historical and contemporary plights. At this point, they as adults could approach *Huck Finn* without dealing directly with the moral issues it raised and the issues' relevance to contemporary society. In Ellison's words, readers "approach serious novels with distrust until the moment comes when the passage of time makes it possible for us to ignore their moral cutting edge" (*Going to the Territory*, 253). The way he positions these "serious novels" and other canonical white texts within his narrative's thematic texture highlights their moral cutting edge. He rereads (assesses from a perspective different from the norm) these standard texts and invites the readers of *Invisible Man* to do the same.

In addition to its direct reference to Poe, the prologue's opening paragraph also contains an indirect reference to a generic visual text and thus calls attention to other kinds of Anglo-American artistic texts that have engaged in black-image deformation. This indirect reference calls to mind D. W. Griffith's seminal film, *The Birth of a Nation*, a visual narrative that is a historically significant exemplar of black-image distortion. If one places Griffith within the category of what Ellison refers to later in the prologue as the Anglo-American tinker-thinkers, his film represents the extent to which American technology distorts and controls the black image. As Ellison puts it, "*The Birth of a Nation* . . . as with every other technical advance since the oceanic sailing ship, . . . became a further instrument in the dehumanization of the Negro" (*Shadow and Act*, 275). In the twentieth century, the nation's technological advances, as with its literary development in the nineteenth century, became more sophisticated in their ability to endow image with the illusion of life (a premise Ellison thematizes and dramatizes in the factory hospital episode). *Invisible Man's* reference to Hollywood as an industry of image makers and image controllers bespeaks this institution's central place in the nation's "institutionalized dehumanization" (*Shadow and Act*, 29) of blacks.

As a representative black, the protagonist's image in the white mind results from the white power structure's attempt to make the discursive construction of black being a reality (*Shadow and Act*, 25, 123). In the prologue's time frame, the protagonist has progressed beyond that stage in his life when he accepted externally imposed definitions of himself as authentic. He is now in the process of re-forming, reconstituting his self through language (through counterdiscourse). The second sentence in the prologue states this re-formation process as a rebellious speech act, as an oppositional discourse that refutes the white-imposed and exteriorized definition of his being: "I am not. . . ." What follows is a preponderance of references to canonical Anglo-American artistic texts (literature, film, music) that the narrator's text usually dialogically opposes.

Influence anxiety is not the primary reason Ellison gives more concentrated attention to the works of what he calls his literary ancestors (white authors) than to his literary relatives (black authors). Privileging his ancestors is integral to the novel's thematic and formalist exploration of black subjectivity. Having engaged in a self-conscious process of writing the self, the protagonist (and certainly Ellison) addresses his narrative primarily to a black audience (*Shadow and Act*, 267). The narrative process infuses formalist features largely from white texts and thematic contours largely from conventions in the African American novel, including white mulatto male protagonists who are identified (and who identify themselves) more fully with their white fathers than with their black mothers; the gradual darkening of complexion among protagonists who are intended to represent the race or a large segment of it; and the adaptation of Freudian models and premises to story lines, plot structures, and subject formations. These novelistic conventions converge and are manifested in altered form in *Invisible Man* as part of the protagonist's desire for a Great White Father. From Bledsoe to Norton to Brother Jack, invisible man embraces various white fathers and their surrogates during his development in the novel. In narrativizing this maturation process, he reveals an Oedipalized affinity for the same literary ancestors that his creator, Ellison, privileges.

Kaja Silverman's comments on how and why "the male subject 'dissolves' his Oedipal desires" as he matures readily apply to invisible man. Writing about Oedipalization, subjectivity, and the Freudian model, Silverman observes,

> If everything goes according to cultural plan, he identifies with his father by internalizing the latter's authority or "voice." This operation is in essence an assimilation of cultural prohibition, and it forms the superego. The male child will henceforth measure and define himself in relation to this repressive paternal representation, and thus to his society's dominant values. As a consequence of his successful Oedipalization, he will find himself "at home" in those discourses and institutions which define the current symbolic order in the West, and will derive validation and support from them at a psychic if not at an economic or social level. In other words, he will "recognize" himself within the mirror of the reigning ideology, even if his race and economic status place him in contradiction to it.[7]

In the novel's thematics, invisible man ultimately rejects the white fathers and their surrogates. In the novel's form, he affirms the white ancestors by measuring and defining himself "in relation to this repressive paternal representation, and thus to [white] society's dominant values." The Anglo-American intertexts that help configure his autonarrative are "discourses and institutions" in which he finds himself "at home." An adaptation of Houston Baker's concept of the mastery of form and the deformation of mastery seems apt.[8] Ellison as author masters the form and deforms mastery, while invisible man as narrator masters the form without fully deforming mastery. As a manifestation of Plato's receptacle, the protagonist's assimilation of white "discourses and institutions" too thoroughly defines his being. At the narrative's chronological end (which is its beginning), he has not broken free completely from being a "receptacle for [whites'] own self-disgust, . . . infantile rebellion, . . . fear of, and retreats from, reality" (*Shadow and Act*, 124).

Collectively, the nation's founding documents are analogous to what Mikhail Bakhtin calls "authoritative discourse": they constitute a sacred text that over the generations has inspired myriad other texts and discourses, fictional and nonfictional, that "interpret it, praise it, [and] apply it in various ways."[9] Novelistic discourse is one of the principal forms in which Americans have interpreted, praised, and applied this authoritative discourse as well as profaned, ignored, refuted, and revised it. Bakhtin refers to authoritative discourse also as the "authoritative word," as "the word of the fathers." "Its authority was already *acknowledged* in the past. It is a *prior* discourse . . . [with] a special (as it were, hieratic) language" (342).

Bakhtin's discussion of authoritative discourse provides a useful rubric for illuminating the African American novel's—particularly *Invisible Man's*—relations to discourse on the American Edenic ideal, both the primary text (the collective documents) and the Anglo-American novels this seminal discourse inspired. America's authoritative discourse is, to be sure, its authoritative word / Word, for it has been endowed with the powers of creation and creativity. As a sacred text, it is the word / Word of the Founding Fathers that inspired the self-reinvention of the American new man of the revolutionary era and subsequent periods. Invisible man intuits this same word / Word when in the factory hospital he is "whirling about in [his own] mind" (184), and he invokes it in this autonarrative to write his own subjectivity.

Subject formation in the African American novel from the 1850s through the 1950s is ensconced in the principles of America's authoritative discourse, in the American Word. Thus, subject formation in canonical African American novels—as in classic Anglo-American novels—has been immersed in sociopolitical and cultural ideology. "The ideological becoming of a human being . . . is the process of selectively assimilating the words of others."[10] For no other American group's novelistic genre is this truer than for the African American novel, in which the narratological process of the subject's coming to be is securely anchored in the word / Word (what invisible man calls the "principle") of the Founding Fathers and in the various permutations of this word / Word that have extended from this (collective) sacred text.

As invisible man writes his subjectivity, he simultaneously is being written (by Ellison). This dual process further underscores a premise in the novel that the black protagonist in his individuated and representational roles is a product of historical and cultural forces, that he—his false selves and his true self—exists within, not outside, discourse. Quite literally, of course, as an individual entity he does not exist independently of the novel that contains him. As a representative character, he embodies and reflects blacks' subjectivity outside of this specific novel. But those whom he represents are themselves products of discourse, having been constructed largely from generic and specific white texts. The protagonist's similarity to real-life African Americans notwithstanding, invisible man exists only within a fiction, only within language, and thus his being is textualized.

In his comments on the zoot-suiters whom he observes in Harlem, invisible man affirms the postulate that the true black man ("truth" and "man") exists outside history. Yet because history exists as text and textualized remainder, the novel never quite settles the question of this generic trueblood's subjectivity existing outside discourse. Even the character Trueblood, perhaps the most "authentic" black male in the novel—the true(st) blood—is textually imprisoned. Though in contemplating his "sin" Trueblood partially redefines himself by rejecting and moving outside social interpretations of the Bible's definitions of human subjectivity, the dominant white society attempts to retextualize him by reconstructing him within sociological and anthropological discourse. After learning of Trueblood's sin, even "big white folks" came "from the big school way cross the State" to hear his life's story, and they "wrote it all down in a book" (41). These recorders, quite likely sociologists and anthropologists, mediate his story, textualize his history and thus his being.

The philosophy that underlies the novel's dramatization of subject formation is contained in the prologue's first two paragraphs. Within the chronology of his experiences that coincides with the prologue's time frame, the protagonist has mounted a valiant effort to break free from textual prisons. He has not been completely successful, as signified by the incompleted lighting of his basement room, the liminal psychical and physical space he now inhabits. Though he proclaims his invisibility (meaning, in this instance, his freedom from white discourse and a white-constructed self), he has not arrived at a point in his process of self-construction where he is certain that he exists outside of a white-controlled discursive reality. He proclaims that his essence transcends his epidermalized being (the "bio-chemical accident to [his] epidermis") and his textualized being (a literary "spook" or one of the "Hollywood-movie ectoplasms"), but he is not quite convinced or convincing (3). Indeed, he is invisible because he still is limited by and functions within white-controlled signifying practices.

Having declared that he is an invisible man, he proceeds to state the nature and cause of his invisibility: "That invisibility to which I refer occurs because of a peculiar disposition of the eyes of those with whom I come in contact. A matter of the construction of their *inner* eyes, those eyes with which they look through their physical eyes upon reality." They, however, do not merely look upon reality; through a racialized phenomenology they construct it. The fact that whites manufacture reality explains the protagonist's frustration at being unable to convince them to recognize him outside the reality they have constructed (3).

Invisible Man's form and meaning coalesce especially in the discursive process Ellison uses to form his centered subject and the novel's subject matter. In a hidden polemic that dialogically and ironically responds to Crèvecoeur's seminal question—"What then is the American, this new man?"—this novel asserts that quintessentially he is an African American.[11] Forged from the biocultural syncretism of New World Africans, Europeans, and Native Americans, the African American (strong biological and cultural links to sub-Saharan Africa notwithstanding) is a racial and cultural being who emerged during approximately the same epoch as the Anglo-American new man. Ellison's mythoform refutes the Anglo-American one that defines "the American" only as white and male.

Formatted in the New World, the African American was woven from a variety of strands spun primarily from races, cultures, and ethnic groups situated in Europe, Africa, and precolonial America. Traces of these strands are manifest in the African American's language, physiology, worldview, and other features of his biocultural self, and they have been syncretized in a way that makes the African American distinct from any other group of blacks in the world, regardless of close biological, cultural, and historical affinities American blacks might have with blacks elsewhere.

Through the novel's intertextuality Ellison merges subject formation with discursive process. It is the doctrine of *e pluribus unum* narrativized and

applied tropologically to the protagonist's individuated and representational subjectivity. The process of his identity formation duplicates the
ideological process through which the nation was formed as a cultural,
political, and historical entity. Both the African American and the nation
were constructed out of chaos (a term whose meaning is broad in Ellison's
thought), and Ellison's attempt to "give pattern to the chaos," as he expresses in the epilogue, "goes for societies as well as for individuals" (438).
To be sure, in terms of subjectivity, the protagonist and the nation are
mutually reflective.

In writing their versions of the nation's mythic genesis, several writers,
cultural critics, and social historians have inscribed and reinscribed—positively or negatively—the ideology of the nation's identity formation.
Among these writers is one of Ellison's most revered literary ancestors,
Melville, whose texts Ellison places in dialogic refutation of Crèvecoeur's
Letters from an American Farmer. In *Redburn* Melville declares, "We are the heirs
of all time, and with all nations we divide our inheritance. On this Western
Hemisphere all tribes and people are forming into one federated whole;
and there is a future which shall see the estranged children of Adam re-
stored as to the old hearthstone in Eden" (163).

Ellison echoes this premise in *Invisible Man,* but he gives it an ironic twist,
a clearer sense of reality. "America is woven of many strands" (435)—
racial, cultural, ethnic, classist, and others—and diversity is the essence
of the nation's subjectivity. In addition to repeating Melville's proclamation from *Redburn* of what the nation should become, Ellison also echoes
Melville's assessment in *Mardi* of what the nation actually is, particularly in
regards to blacks: "In-this-re-publi-can-land-all-men-are-born-free-and-
equal"—"Except-the-tribe-of-Hamo" (423–24). Ellison uses a version of
this exception to the creed in the impressionistic Liberty Paints episode to
signify on the distinction between the nation's principles and its practices.
In writing black subjectivity, the black novelistic tradition revises received
American history by inscribing the history of blacks in America.

The Society: "The Patterns of Men's Lives"

According to invisible man, "History records the patterns of men's lives."
The recorders of America's received history, however, write down "only

those events the recorder regards as important." America's received history, therefore, is a compilation of "those lies" the "keepers" of the American Garden "keep their power by" (332). The protagonist's perspective on American history and historiography coincides with Ellison's.

"I don't think that history is Truth," Ellison said when speaking as a panelist at the Southern Historical Association's annual meeting in 1968. According to Ellison, most recorders of America's "official" history altered, suppressed, and in some instances erased "that which was given" to "justify racial attitudes and practices" of the past and of the present. Consequently, "so much of American history has turned upon the racial situation in this country" that with few exceptions the historians' record of the past is a mythopoeic text, a product of the recorders' attempts to reinvent the nation as well as its centered (white) and marginalized (nonwhite) inhabitants. Received American history is, therefore, "artificial"; like a novel, it is a fabulated account of reality.[12]

Form more than content generally distinguishes history from fiction, and the recorder's perspective on reality determines a text's degree of historical truth. Ellison regards the novel's form as more conducive to a truthful record of the past than the documentary model in which official American history typically is cast.[13] He admits, however, that truth is not solely contingent upon a particular discursive form. While "there have been a few [Anglo-American] novelists who decided to tell the 'truth'" about America's past, most have told a story in concert with those official historians who "altered" the record of the past "to justify racial attitudes and practices" (63, 69).

According to Ellison, among American historiographic writings, the highest degree of truth about blacks' (and thus the nation's) past can be found in the African American novel. One of the genre's principal functions is to commit to writing blacks' oral history, which contains the truth about the past. Dominick LaCapra writes, "The past arrives in the form of texts and textualized remainders—memories, reports, published writings, archives, monuments, and so forth."[14] These are among the forms of history Ellison and his protagonist use to extract and reconstruct the black past. Ellison and invisible man share one narrative voice because their discursive practices are the same. In relating his personal history and his personal view of his race's history, the protagonist is reconstructing those histories largely from memory and witness, filtering events through his own consciousness. By the time he is narrating, he has defied Bledsoe, Norton, Jack, Ras, and the many others who attempted (often successfully) to dictate the consciousness through which he should view past and present reality. He has arrived at a point where he privileges his perception of reality over others'. The process of reaching this point is integral to the novel's subject matter.

In narrativizing his immediate and his race's remote past, the narrator incorporates several artifacts as indicative of the past's textualized remains. For instance, there is the polished "leg shackle from slavery" that Bledsoe "proudly" displays in his office as "a symbol of our progress" since slavery (108). In actuality, the ornament signifies the extent to which the slave past's textualization has been sweetened to make the slaveholding class appear more favorable. In opposition to Bledsoe's ornament, Tarp's leg shackle inscribes a counterdiscourse. This crude and unpolished relic of the new slavery has "a heap of signifying wrapped up in it" (293). Its text contains a more accurate truth about blacks' historical experience and about the continuity of racial oppression across historical eras than Bledsoe's artifactual text. At the time invisible man sees each relic, he is unable to decipher the truth either embodies.

The college's museum displays "a few cracked relics from slavery times" (138) that collectively constitute a sign system, an artifactual text. To decipher the slave past that these artifacts individually and collectively contain, one must be able and willing to read them outside the obfuscating frame (the museum specifically and whiteness generally) in which they are situated. The protagonist (as well as other students at the college) is unable and unwilling to construct a truthful narrative history from them: unable because he willfully has been blinded by the ideological approach to historical reality (a whitewash of the past) the college promotes; unwilling because he wishes to avoid anything he regards as "unpleasant" about the slave past, about blackness itself.

The museum's slave relics are framed by the ideology of whiteness, which (con)textualizes both them and invisible man, skewing the angle of vision for both the seen (the relics) and the seer (the protagonist). The campus buildings annually are whitewashed with the same or similar Liberty paint manufactured for and used by the government (152–53). Thus, the college's stance toward history replicates the nation's institutionalized erasure of certain events from the slave past, the privileging of certain "facts" constructed from events, and the muting of certain truths about the past.

The protagonist's experiential development during the course of the novel reveals his increasing capacity and willingness to read the text inscribed by artifacts of the black experience. His first major application of this capacity is when he witnesses a group of whites evict Sister and Brother Provo from their "rented home" (their very thin veneer of the American Dream) and pile all their worldly possessions in the dirty snow on the sidewalk. These objects are signs in the Provos' "dream book" text (212), and collectively they contain a narrativized history of the couple's thwarted American Dream. Viewing these objects gives invisible man insight into their owners' lives. Though whiteness (the literal snow) contextualizes the signs in the Provos' artifactual text, invisible man apprehends the objects outside their framed context and sees "far beyond their intrinsic meaning as objects" to the deeper and fuller truths they individually and collectively signify (207). Consequently, he bears witness to the Provos' dispossession.

The clutter of objects (204–6) includes a few positive signs of the couple's attachment to African American culture, to family, and to the African past. Overshadowing these positive signs, however, are ones that signify misplaced values and beliefs, frustrated hopes and desires, false promises, and negative images of the black self externally and internally generated. Inherent in this collectivity of signs is a narrative of two lives that (as their "three lapsed life insurance policies" signify) have been stamped void. For the Provos, it is not that the dream has been deferred but that custom and law have rendered it null and void. The foremost object in this sign system of lapsed lives provides the syntactic order for and elucidates the underlying meaning of all the other objects: the Bible (ostensibly the King James version) is Mrs. Provo's most valued possession.

The King James version of the Bible, like Mr. Provo's "FREE PAPERS," is a white-authored text, and these texts have been ineffectual in facilitating the couple's access to the American Eden. Both have been duped; their being has been textualized by the Master's and the master's texts, respectively. As such, the Bible spawned numerous shadow texts—collectively, "The Great Constitutional Dream Book"—that erased the Provos from the narrative of America's Eden; the "pages" that contained the couple "went blank" (212). The couple's lives are representative, for the memories their relics evoke tell the generic story of many black lives dispossessed of the dream.

Objects are images that effect memory, and in turn memory produces knowledge. Memory is knowledge of the past (immediate or remote), and therefore, like witness, it is a form of textualized history. In *Invisible Man*, relics of the past (inanimate ones such as those in the college's museum and human ones such as Susie Gresham) and objects in the present (such as the Provos' "junk") constitute images that trigger the protagonist's recall of associated ideas, events, and experiences. Through their power to induce memory, images mediate between past and present; they link the protagonist's personal past to that of his race.

As Ellison demonstrates through the construction of his protagonist, one can have knowledge of the past without having existed in and personally witnessed it. This knowledge is a form of group (i.e., racial) memory, and it is akin to what Mary Warnock calls a subject's "genetically inherited past." [15] In his *Essay on the Intellectual Powers of Man*, Thomas Reid posits, "We are so constituted as to have an intuitive knowledge of many things past." [16] In this regard, one might say that invisible man has been "constituted" socially, culturally, racially, and historically in a way that he intuitively knows parts of the black past that are outside his personal experience. Within the novel, this process becomes readily apparent by the time he encounters the Provo couple, at which point immediate images (objects) elicit memories of his personal and his race's history.

Witnessing the Provos' dispossession, the protagonist begins to have "strange memories awakening" (25) in him. As he explains, these memories are "not so much of [his] own memory"—his definitive acts and thoughts—"as of remembered words, of linked verbal echoes, images, heard even when not listening at home" (27). The sight of the Provos' "junk" evokes in him images / memories of the immediate past, particularly of his mother. These visions threaten to reveal the larger historical pattern into which his mother fits and to cause memories (and therefore intuited knowledge) of his racial past to emerge in his consciousness. Though his discomfort with the images makes him continue to repress intuitive race memories, that he is able to recall them becomes apparent later in the chronology. In the prologue, for example, his rejuvenated, unrestrained powers of memory transport him back to an era situated between slavery and emancipation where he interacts with a slave mother/mistress.

The Provo episode marks a juncture in invisible man's psychological development, a point where he gains knowledge but not full understanding. To borrow his phrasing from the epilogue, he now recognizes the "plan of living" black in the United States into which the life experiences of Mrs. Provo, his mother, and the generic slave mother fit, but he does not fully understand at this point "the chaos against which that pattern was conceived" (438). Having been schooled in and having accepted received American history, he understands the relationship between law and order but not the connection between chaos and order. That understanding will come only after he fully has lighted his psychical space (symbolically, his basement apartment), at which point knowledge will confer power.

After one has witnessed an event and recorded it in the mind (a form of knowledge), it can be suppressed indefinitely from consciousness, but it cannot be completely erased. Acting on the belief that memory/knowledge indeed can be erased or at least permanently repressed, the "doctors" (clinical historians) in Liberty Paints' factory hospital perform an operation on invisible man to "clear" his memory of experiential and intuitive knowledge and to reconstruct his mind so that he no longer will threaten the white power structure. Confident that the operation is a success after the patient shows no symptoms of his malady, the doctors declare him cured. That the operation failed is readily evident in the Provo episode, but its failure is not fully certified until near the novel's end.

Though memory is knowledge, it does not automatically follow that knowledge is truth. Like witness, memory can be so textualized that it produces a distorted account of the past, particularly when the process of remembering is guided by the same principles that shape official history. Reality can be so mediated by a power structure (that inner eye the protagonist mentions in the prologue) that a witness's recollection of an event is actually a false memory. A case in point is Homer Barbee, who through memory bears witness to the Founder's dream. But his memory rings false, for it has been mediated by the guardians of the white power structure (i.e., Bledsoe and Norton) who have become the "Seeing Eye" (212) for the literally and metaphorically blind Barbee.

To be sure, *Invisible Man* is a novel of memory, a written recollection of past events narrated in the present. Infused with elements from Ellison's personal experiences and thoughts, the novel is cast in the autobiographical mode. One need turn only to *Shadow and Act* for verification. In this collection of essays on literature and culture Ellison interweaves data about his life and inserts his thinking, manifested as "symbolic action" in his writing of *Invisible Man*. As he explains, the "basic significance" of his essays is "autobiographical" (xviii–xix); and so is his novel. In an interview published as "The Art of Fiction," Ellison states emphatically that *Invisible Man* "is not an autobiographical work" (*Shadow and Act*, 167). This is true in the sense that invisible man is not Ralph Ellison. Yet Ellison's novel is autobiographical in the same sense that his essays are. A reading of his two collections of essays, *Shadow and Act* and *Going to the Territory*, will reveal the numerous personal experiences Ellison incorporates into the novel. As he puts it, *Invisible Man* is his novel and his protagonist's memoir (*Shadow and Act*, 57). With the novel narrated by and focused on the experiences and thoughts of its centered subject, *Invisible Man* also is the protagonist's autobiography. It is an instance of a particular life made general.

In constructing meaning from the protagonist's experiences, Ellison universalizes the particular and particularizes the universal, as is evident not only in the nexus between invisible man's personal life and his race's American history—the individuated made representative—but also between the historical condition of American blacks and what Ellison calls the human condition (*Shadow and Act*, 57, 104). Ellison achieves much of this universality through the signifying practices he employs, the numerous multicultural intertexts he parodically installs, and the autobiographical mode in which he frames the novel. As Warnock states, "The memory of an individual, encapsulated in autobiography, or in the autobiographical novel, has a general and universal meaning." [17]

"The act of writing," Ellison explains, "requires a constant plunging back into the shadow of the past" (*Shadow and Act*, xix). The shadow precedes the act. And what is true for Ellison also holds true for his novelistic persona. Memory is the vehicle that facilitates this plunging into history. What emerges in *Invisible Man*'s narrative process of reconstructing the past is the juxtaposition of a principal text (the protagonist's autonarrative) and a shadow text (his race's historical biography) that are mutually reflective and mutually reflexive. What invisible man experiences, witnesses, and bears witness to in the novel form new memories that give him a fuller knowledge of his subjectivity. His autobiographical act exemplifies in several ways how the created subject mirrors his creator. For Ellison, writing "fiction became the agency of my efforts to answer the questions: Who am I, what am I, how did I come to be?" (*Shadow and Act*, xxii).

Artifacts, monuments, witness, memory, and documents are indeed forms of history. But the standard and most accessible form in which the past arrives is, of course, published writings, particularly texts of history and literature. Writing history and writing historiographic fiction are attempts to reconstruct past reality. The difference between these two modes of discourse typically intimates a distinction between what is true and what is false. In its thematics and its formalist features, *Invisible Man* questions the validity of this distinction. For instance, when the protagonist muses, "Perhaps the truth was always a lie" (376), he affirms Ellison's assertion that the historiographic black novel is a much more truthful version of the black experience than is the text of official history or any historiographic novel that conforms to the official version of the past.

One is reminded that many Anglo-American texts that inscribe the nation's cosmogonic and origin myths are transdisciplinary ones, read both as history and as literature, including the colonial "histories" by William Bradford, Captain John Smith, and Robert Beverley, and the documents of state such as the Declaration of Independence and the Gettysburg Address. Texts such as these, the historical romances by William Gilmore Simms, James Fenimore Cooper, and by a long list of postbellum southern writers, and the texts of professional historians all have contributed to the textualization of the black American's identity. And it is whites' "Prefabricated Negroes" (*Shadow and Act*, 123), whom they inserted into these texts, that the black novelistic tradition revises.

In a statement that speaks specifically to the role of recorders of history (regardless of the discursive frame) as arbiters and chroniclers of truth and more generally to the relations between power and discourse (particularly discourse's power to manufacture reality), the protagonist asserts that blacks "write no novels, histories or other books" (332). Though the unqualified statement is false (after all, he is writing / has written a book that is both a novel and history), it is true for the novel's time frame that the academy privileges only those historiographic texts whose perspectives on reality whites sanction. When Ellison published *Invisible Man* in 1952, blacks remained marginalized and therefore locked out of the academy. There were few signs in 1952 that blacks' liminal position in the social structure would be altered. Invisible man aptly assesses the situation: since the beginning of blacks' American presence they have been kept "too distant from the centers of historical decision to sign or even to applaud the signers of historical documents" (332).

The protagonist makes these comments in the section where he vows to become the truthful recorder of Tod Clifton's death. As the narrative moves toward closure (its end and its beginning), invisible man also reveals that he is a self-conscious recorder not only of Clifton's and his own personal history but also of the history of his race in the United States. Having assumed the role customarily reserved for an official historian, he records what *he* regards as important (432). "So why do I write, torturing myself to put it down?" he asks rhetorically (437). His answer: to produce a text that writes himself and his race into authentic being, an act of textual production that is both subversive and carthartic (see also 438). This purpose and process help situate this novel squarely within the black novelistic tradition.

On one of its thematic and structural levels, *Invisible Man* is a historiographic novel. As Ellison writes his subject's being, he simultaneously inscribes salient features of blacks' history in the United States. The dual narratives form a microcosmic-macrocosmic relation between the particular and the general histories, as the novel's title, its historicized structure, its overarching theme, and other features of its textuality suggest. Like Toomer, Larsen, George Washington Lee, Hurston, Richard Wright, and other twentieth-century black novelists, Ellison uses his personal experiences to shape his centered subject and the figuration of incidents and ideologies in the novel. Following a convention that slave narrators established and nineteenth-century black novelists such as William Wells Brown, J. McHenry Jones, Frances E. W. Harper, and others continued, Ellison incorporates incidents and characters that allow him to survey typical experiences and conditions.

By intertwining the microcosmic and macrocosmic "histories" in the novel's signifying practices, Ellison thematizes history and historiography. Within a temporal sequencing of major episodes, events, and scenes, the novel's formalist features draw attention to the different sociocultural and sociopolitical programs from slavery to the novel's present that ostensibly were designed to move the race from the nation's margins to its democratic center. Concurrent with (re)writing the race's social history, the novel echoes and recapitulates black novelistic history, for its narrative structure reflects centered subject matter (blacks' desires and attempts to become a part of the Edenic aggregate) and builds upon the genre's earlier thematic and formalist conventions and traditions.

The novel's periodized structure highlights slavery, emancipation, Reconstruction, education, World War I, labor, migration, communism, and black nationalism as specific eras in black American social history.[18] Each of these eras corresponds to a major episode, segment, or chapter in the novel. Either the protagonist's experience replicates or is a variation on the group's historical experience during a particular period, or a character, incident, major allusion, or combination of formalist features highlights the period and the race's thwarted attempts to be included in the mainstream.

Rejecting the professional historian's documentary model for historiography, this novel narrativizes the race's history by centralizing the human agency within historical events and conditions and by privileging historical truths over historical facts. As the microcosmic-macrocosmic mirror texts unfold on parallel thematic and structural lines, the novel traces blacks' transition from objects in history to prospective agents of history. In doing so, it anticipates what Waters Turpin in *The Rootless* refers to as the "Moment," a point in time when assertive actions by blacks will change lived and recorded history.

Ellison anchors the macrocosmic / shadow text (the race's history) in the African American oral tradition. He configures the novel's periodized pattern by using a secondary character's story (witness and memory) to focalize the failed attempt to mainstream the black populace during any given era. He often uses two additional characters' situations to provide other perspectives on or to corroborate the point. The story of one of the additional characters in the triad provides transition to and continuity with the next period, and frequently this character's situation becomes central in the subsequent period. At times, the protagonist's situation provides the link between two sequential periods by analogy to past historical formations. The periods are not sharply divided; the story of one period flows into the story of the next.

The periodized narrative pattern begins in the prologue. The drugs, alcohol, and music activate the protagonist-narrator's memory so that it transports him spatially and temporally into the distant racial past. Here he encounters a slave mother–mistress and her mulatto sons. The woman recounts to him a brief personal narrative about the ambivalence of freedom and of the tensions between love and hate. Her narrative repeats a generic story that can be found as interpolation in slave narratives and in some nineteenth- and early-twentieth-century novels. As repeated in *Invisible Man*'s prologue, it is a story about the failure of miscegenation and mulattoism to effect black emancipation or freedom.

Narrative formations in *Invisible Man* repeatedly emphasize that there is a distinction between emancipation and freedom. With emancipation, blacks' dreams of becoming a part of the New Eden's aggregate seemed an imminent reality. But Homer Barbee's narrative of the Founder's life exemplifies that the race, though many or most lived under improved material conditions following slavery, remained marginalized following emancipation, and freedom receded into the distance. In effect, the imminence of freedom died with the Great Emancipator, a point that Ellison's parodic installation of Whitman's elegy for Lincoln ("When Lilacs Last in the Dooryard Bloom'd") underscores in the Founder's section.

The protagonist's grandfather's story about his life during Reconstruction and Trueblood's story about his economic predicament in the post-Reconstruction period bespeak the failure of emancipation to effect freedom for blacks after the Civil War. Like the Founder, the grandfather put his faith in external forces and programs directed and controlled by white people: "I give up my gun back in the Reconstruction" (13); thereafter, he suffered the consequences. Trueblood's socioeconomic situation illustrates one of the consequences for blacks when whites in the South reassumed power in the 1880s. The freedmen Trueblood represents in this instance received neither forty acres nor a mule. The attempt to make freedmen full participants in the nation's political economy failed. Trueblood's physical location as a sharecropper replicates the symbolic spaces and places blacks were assigned in the antebellum period. The central symbol of this new form of slavery is the Truebloods' cabin, a physical structure erected during slavery that signifies the family's fixed place in the postbellum social structure. Several late-nineteenth- and early-twentieth-century novels use this symbolic nexus between physical space and social place to treat blacks' plight.

Several institutions to educate the newly freed slaves were established to effect social (broadly defined) aggregation. After post-Reconstruction, education as the major "social program" designed to mainstream blacks and to make them self-sufficient moved to the fore, and Booker T. Washington and the Tuskegee Institute became the national exemplars. Ellison's treatment of the Negro college, its administrators and benefactors, and its students and alumni suggests the extent to which this program was controlled by whites and their ideology. He uses data from Washington's life and career to help construct the characters of the Founder and of Bledsoe, and through their delineation the narrative argues how ineffectively the system of black education attempted to create self-reliant blacks.

Though the Founder's "presence" frames the portion of the novel set in the South, he never appears in the novel's narrative action. A former "slave and a son of slaves" (92), shortly after emancipation the Founder began his program to uplift the race through education. But his dream now has been perverted, and he has been rendered nameless, voiceless, and invisible. His story is mediated through three voices—Ellison's (writing), invisible man's (memory), and Homer Barbee's (witness). The Founder's life story is so intertwined with the history of the race, as Barbee points out, that the two histories are reflexive. The narrative architectonics Barbee (and by extension invisible man and Ellison) uses to reconstruct the Founder's story conflate images, allusions, and references taken from the Bible, literature, and history. These architectonics echo African, European, Anglo-American, and African American cultural forms, particularly texts and discourses. This layered textualization of his life story exemplifies the novel's thematization of history and historiography. The reader, therefore, must pierce the textual veneers to see the truth and meaning of this invisible man's life. His story is an oral inner text whose discursive intertextuality encapsulates the entire novel's signifying practices.

Privileging a narrativized over a documentary form of historiography, Ellison uses the Founder's story to link the eras of slavery, emancipation, Reconstruction, and education. Burnside functions in a similar manner to conjoin education to the next sequence of eras and their respective social programs—World War I and migration. Paradoxically, those blacks, like Burnside and some of the other veterans in the Golden Day, who achieved the principles for which the educational program supposedly was designed were pushed to the nation's extreme social margins. In spite of the college's repressive educational program, the vets and others like them achieved the Founder's dream by becoming highly educated, an accomplishment that the white power structure regards as a threat. The paradox is glaring: their academic and intellectual accomplishments do not uplift them but instead mark them as targets for repression harsher than the race in general suffers, as their severely restricted space and place in the social structure signifies. The veterans' "Golden Day" is an ironic comment on the principle of social Darwinism, and Ellison foregrounds their predicament to corroborate the inefficacy of black education as a progressive social formation when it is controlled financially and thus ideologically by whites.

Burnside's personal narrative provides continuity, and he becomes the focus in the next national scheme to include the black race in America's Eden. As a veteran of World War I, his experiences at home and abroad typify how the white power structure tightened rather than loosened proscriptive reins on the black race during and after the conflict. Ellison's perspective on the issue is consistent with those of the novelists who preceded him.

Burnside's failure to be fully contained in his severely restricted space and place brands him a subversive, and he is forced to emigrate from the locale. This incident provides the principal thematic link to migration, the next era in the novel's periodized history and a narrativized social formation in which invisible man's experiences form a nucleus around which other characters' stories revolve. Invisible man's migration from the South to the North with dreams of becoming a full-fledged American exemplifies black civilians' plight during and after the war, when tens of thousands of black Southerners moved to the urban North. But as numerous African American novels from the first half of the twentieth century indicate, this change in geographical space did not effect many blacks' anticipated change in social place. As Burnside insightfully comments, the North is a dream, a mere symbol of freedom rather than freedom itself.

Migration as a narrative formation in the genre has its antecedent in the slave narrative. Invisible man's trek of approximately one thousand miles from Alabama to New York recalls fugitive slaves William and Ellen Craft's "run" from Georgia to Boston as recounted in their narrative *Running a Thousand Miles for Freedom* (1860). The Crafts discovered that they had to keep running to find freedom. As recounted in his autonarrative(s), Frederick Douglass learned essentially the same lesson when he escaped to the North in search of freedom. Douglass's presence looms large in this novel, haunting invisible man in much the manner as his grandfather's presence. The protagonist misapprehends Douglass's account of the relation between physical space and freedom, between migration and social transformation, just as he fails to understand his grandfather's story about the biblical Saul's transformation into Paul (288). That this formation is nationally sanctioned and continues is revealed through the protagonist's dream about his grandfather and a message contained in "an official envelope stamped with the state seal" and placed in the protagonist's briefcase: "Keep This Nigger-Boy Running" (26).

Migration was not the social panacea many blacks thought it would be, and its negative effects are corroborated in the stories of Mary Rambo and Rinehart, among others in the novel. But the extent to which the dream turned into a nightmare for many southern black migrants is best portrayed in the plight of the Provos, whose spatial movement metaphorically was "out of the fire into the melting pot" (117). This episode is situated near the novel's middle, and at this point invisible man becomes the principal character whose experiences conjoin migration with the remaining periodized social formations—labor, communism, and black nationalism.

The highly symbolic Liberty Paints episode (ch. 10) treats most fully the power structure's failure to mainstream blacks via equal access to the labor force. A manufacturer of "optic white" paints, the factory (a microcosm of America) creates optical illusions of reality. It is mere illusion that southern black migrants occupy a position in the industrialized North's labor structure dramatically different from the position they occupied in the agrarian South. In reality, the racial composition of labor forces in the United States have remained rather fixed across time and space, a point this episode conveys principally through characterization, image clusters, and thematized space.

The characters are representative. The white captain of this industry, Mr. Sparland, is the company's owner and its principal financial beneficiary. Whites (McDuffy and Kimbro) occupy the factory's managerial and supervisory positions and are charged with assuring the factory's uninterrupted productivity. The plant's black laborers, in this instance Brockway and invisible man, occupy the lowest rung on the labor ladder. Within the factory's means of production, they are on par with the machines. In fact, Brockway boasts that they are "the machines inside the machine" (165).

The factory's labor matrix is an instance of history repeating itself. In the slave economy, slaves in effect were human tools used for the production of human and nonhuman commodities. Epithets such as "Colonel," "slave driver," "northern redneck," and "Yankee cracker" (150, 151, 152) that are applied to the plant's white management signify the repetition of southern labor formations. Plantation owner, overseer, field boss, and black sharecropper (neoslave) formed a hierarchical labor matrix in the postbellum South that essentially replicated the labor formation consisting of plantation owner, overseer, slave driver, and slave in the antebellum South. The formation duplicates itself in the Liberty Paints factory, and blacks' marginality within the industrialized North's labor force is indicated by the subterranean space they occupy. The explosion invisible man inadvertently causes in the plant's basement threatens to disrupt the established order and to undermine the plant's productivity. This act and his tampering with the paint make him an inadvertent saboteur, a defective cog within the machine.

Occasionally in the novel, Ellison parodically installs the historically recurrent image of a rebellious black as a defective, diseased being. He foregrounds this disease / dis-ease trope in the factory hospital episode's clinical perspective on history. In the novel's recapitulation of blacks' historical presence in the American Eden, the "Negro problem," as the doctors in the factory hospital indicate in their "discussion of history," "has been developing some three hundred years" (180). The various "cures" for the patient's hereditary disease were ineffective. That is, whites tried different programmatic schemes to effect a "complete change of personality" in the black subject, while leaving "the patient . . . both physically and neurally whole" and assuring that the "dominant society will suffer no traumata on his account" (180). Each curative measure was a response to a central question that Thomas Jefferson succinctly poses in *Notes on the State of Virginia*—"What further is to be done with them"? (139)—a question asked repeatedly since the first generation of New World Africans in North America. But even after "the subject [has been] submitted to the anatomical knife, to optical glasses, to analysis by fire or by solvents" (*Notes*, 138), and to "every . . . technical advance since the oceanic sailing ship" (*Shadow and Act*, 275), the subject's disease has not been cured. Each attempt to erase the subject's humanity and to have him acquiesce in this deletion has been incomplete. So what further is to be done?

Answers to the question include not only efforts to exclude blacks from the American Edenic ideal but also blueprints to make them part of the national mainstream. Ellison parodically installs the oppositional responses to the question as both generic and specific intertexts in *Invisible Man*'s dialogics. In the first instance, "What is to be done?" is text as subject matter that frames the entire novel's periodized treatment of blacks' historical dilemma in the United States. In the second instance, the question is incorporated parodically as specific texts that contextualize and focus the novel's second half, the expansive Brotherhood episode. Principal among these specific intertexts are Jefferson's *Notes* (query 14) and Vladimir Lenin's 1906 discourse on the socialist-democratic system he proposes for Russia, entitled *What Is to Be Done*. Within the historical time frame that encompasses the Brotherhood episode, the answers to this question shape the two principal secondary characters (Jack and Ras) and their competing social ideologies (communism and black nationalism). In large measure, there is an inverse nexus between the two characterizations and these two intertexts. Jack ostensibly espouses a Leninist-like program that will move blacks from the nation's margins to its social and democratic center. Ras, on the other hand, promotes a separatist program that is akin to the colonization scheme Jefferson proposes in *Notes*. In its Garveyesque form, Ras's program will remove blacks spatially from the American Eden. Certainly from the eighteenth century forward, aggregation and colonization were competing ideologies advanced as solutions to the nation's "Negro problem." As the Brotherhood episode indicates, neither solution was efficacious.

Some critics have identified the novel's Brotherhood organization with the American Communist Party and this episode with communist activities in Harlem during the 1920s and 1930s.[19] Some have cited Ellison's short-lived involvement with the party as one source for this episode, relying in part on Ellison's statement that his brief association with communists in New York during the 1930s informs this section of the novel. There are certainly affinal relations between the American Communist Party's activities in Harlem between the two world wars and the novel's portrayal of the Brotherhood organization. But the organization's name is not a fictional title for the American Communist Party, nor is the novel's portrayal of the organization a fictive version per se of the party's activities. Rather, as organization and as episode, the Brotherhood is Ellison's conflation of several socialist (to use the term's broad meaning) organizations, leaders, and programs that competed for influence over the Harlem community from the end of World War I to the end of the depression. Such a conflation of historical forces and figures into fictive form meshes with Ellison's method and message in *Invisible Man*.

In the 1920s and 1930s, several socialist organizations, including the American Communist Party, A. Philip Randolph's Brotherhood of Sleeping Car Porters, and Cyril Briggs's African Blood Brotherhood, were rivals and allies in Harlem. All at some point embraced versions of Marxist social theory, and some of them intermingled their ideologies and memberships. One brief marriage of organizations and ideologies occurred between the African Blood Brotherhood and the American Communist Party. Ellison uses a union such as this one to construct the Brotherhood episode. Like the novel's Brotherhood, the membership of the American Communist Party in New York during this time included blacks and whites who, at least for a brief period, shared ideological approaches to alleviating American blacks' plight. Gradually, though, many black members became disillusioned with the party because of what they considered its racist ideology, a historical formation fictionalized as the Tod Clifton episode and with biohistorical sources in the lives of Ellison and Richard Wright.

To be sure, Jack and Ras, respectively the socialist and the black nationalist, are ideologically both oppositional and complementary. Ellison strategically and imagistically foregrounds both aspects of this relationship. In the novel's periodized history, Ras and Jack are the latest in a long line of social theorists whose proposed solutions to the "Negro problem" merely presented additional problems for blacks to confront in their quest for aggregation. It is their posing of the historical question and the answers they give that discursively place Ras and Jack in the "tradition" of Jefferson, Lincoln, Booker T. Washington, and other prominent historical figures who sought to dictate black reality. These two fictive social activists' link to actual social theorists is embedded in their respective variation on the question "What is to be done?" As Exhorter, Ras asks of his competitive antagonists (the Brotherhood), "What are you doing?" (362). When he does not receive a satisfactory answer, he decides what is to be done. Jack posits that the present is a period of crisis, a time of "indecision when all the old answers [to the historical question] are proven false," a time when "the people look back to the dead to give them a clue" (232). The present is a time of crisis when "all the old heroes are being called back to life—Jefferson . . . Booker T. Washington . . . Abraham Lincoln," and others. But the dead cannot "give the full answer to the new questions posed for the living by history" (233). Jack believes that he has the full answers to the new questions. Ironically, though, the questions are not new, nor are the answers Ras or Jack proffer.

As characters who are "often in contradiction and even self-contradictory" (13), Ras and Jack indeed follow the tradition of the "old heroes" mentioned in the novel. These two characters are living manifestations of principles without practice, form without substance, words without action. In constructing them as ideology personified, Ellison invokes the myth of the nation's origin as a political entity and a democratic society. In *Shadow and Act* he expresses his inscription of the origin myth thus: "In the beginning was not only the word but the contradiction of the word" (243). And as he states in *Invisible Man* and dramatizes through the novel's historicized structure, "The end is in the beginning" (5); the present is but an extension of the past. In the nation's beginning Jefferson articulated the word but was himself a living contradiction to it: he proposed emancipation and simultaneously advocated colonization; he espoused man's inalienable right to be free and simultaneously held blacks in bondage. Lincoln declared emancipation but did not deliver freedom; his emancipation of the slaves was motivated by political expediency rather than humanitarianism. Booker T. Washington, in his famous hand-fingers analogy, simultaneously espoused black aggregation and racial separation, a contradiction signified by the statue that Ellison incorporates as a monument of textualized history in the college episode. Norton advances the doctrine of self-reliance at the same time that he seeks to control black life. Bledsoe's principles are black self-sufficiency and upward mobility, while his practice is to tighten restraints on black advancement. Jack preaches to the dispossessed masses the doctrine of economic parity while he and his cohorts live in affluence. Ras the Destroyer promotes blackness while he himself is enshrouded by symbols of whiteness. Each of these social leaders and theorists, historical and fictional, is simultaneously "the word and the contradiction to the word." Each is a manifestation of repeated history.

As the Exhorter, Ras in some respects is a diametric opposite of Jack. But in his desire to control blacks and dictate their reality, he is, as Ras the Destroyer, also Jack's complement. He becomes obsessed with wresting power over the black community from Jack, with having, as Bledsoe and

Norton desire, power to organize black life firsthand. In his form as Destroyer, Ras has assimilated whiteness, which Ellison conveys through an imagistic melding of mythic and symbolic Africanisms with Anglo-Americanisms (such as Ras's leopard skin, spear, cowboy boots, and spurs). As Ras the Destroyer, he is chaos manifest. He and Jack, in all their contradictions, are allegorized portraits of history as a madman (333).

As the Exhorter and the Destroyer, Ras's characterization is a composite that encodes several principles of black nationalism that Marcus Garvey, Cyril Briggs, and others preached. That Ellison makes Ras a West Indian is quite appropriate for his treatment of black nationalism for this time period. West Indians in Harlem dominated the black nationalist movements, and they often linked black American liberation with the liberation of blacks in the Caribbean and in Africa. None of the black nationalist groups measurably improved blacks' material existence in the United States or effected a mass exodus from the United States.

So after so many failed programs, what is to be done? According to this novel, one should adopt the form and function of invisibility. Invisibility is a state of black being in which the subject recognizes clearly his or her historical space and place in American history and in American historiography. Several subjects in the genre arrive at this state of being. Their routes vary, as do the consequences of their arrival. For invisible man, the route is the same one Frederick Douglass took—to write the black self into authentic being.

Sutton Griggs (*Imperium in Imperio*), Martin Delany (*The Condition, Elevation, Emigration and Destiny of the Colored People of the United States*), and other nineteenth-century black writers and social critics viewed the black populace in the United States as a nation within a nation.[20] Though there were differences in the novelists' perspectives on this concept and in how they inscribed it in their novels, all acknowledged a nexus between the novel as form and the idea and ideal of America, between black personhood and nationhood.

This nexus is one of the characteristics of the black novelistic tradition. In the twentieth century, novelists such as Wright, Petry, Ellison, and Turpin, who used the novel as a discursive medium in which to (re)inscribe black subjectivity, dramatized the subject formation—nation formation alignment. *Native Son*, *The Street*, *Invisible Man*, and *The Rootless* exemplify the variety of approaches within the genre's treatment of relations between society and black subjectivity in the 1940s and 1950s. All four novels use the American Revolution's permutation of the Eden myth as a touchstone to explore this personhood-nationhood affinity. Perhaps Ellison states the premise best when he says, "The novel is bound up with the notion of nationhood" (*Going to the Territory*, 242). By paralleling his centered subject's formation with that of the nation, he certainly dramatizes the premise as well as any novelist.

Conclusion

ITS FOREGROUNDING OF Eurocentric texts notwithstanding, salient aspects of *Invisible Man*'s thematic and formalist configurations are anchored in the African American novelistic tradition. *Invisible Man*'s art and truth have kept it among the foremost American novels for the past forty years. A group of two hundred leading authors, critics, and editors predicted this outcome in 1965, when they—using art, truthfulness, and likelihood to endure as criteria—judged *Invisible Man* "the most distinguished single work" of fiction published between 1945 and 1965.[1] The novel won the National Book Award for 1952 (awarded in 1953), and thereafter it became both an anxious and an admitted influence on several novelists' craft.

Since *Invisible Man*, African American writers have received an unprecedented (for any group) number of regional, national, and international prizes. The number also is unprecedented when the works are viewed as a group that centers a specific component of a regional experience, living black in the American South. Notably, the prizewinning novels overwhelmingly have either focused exclusively on the southern slave experience or narrativized slavery's legacy.

Toni Morrison, a non-Southerner with immediate ancestral and artistic roots in the South, was awarded the 1993 Nobel Prize for her literary productivity. Two novels among her distinguished canon, *Song of Solomon* and *Beloved*, are grounded in a southern black experience. *Song of Solomon*, winner of the National Book Critics' Circle Award for 1977, solidified her national reputation as a novelist. *Beloved*, a fictionalized slave narrative, won the Pulitzer Prize for 1988. Georgia-born Alice Walker won a 1983 Pulitzer Prize and a National Book Award for her novel *The Color Purple*, set in the twentieth century but using several discursive formations from the slave-narrative genre. Charles Johnson received the 1990 National Book Award for his novel *Middle Passage*, whose title alone suggests its form as a fictionalized slave narrative. Octavia Butler and Samuel R. Delany, who together constitute approximately half of the African American science-fiction novelists, have received Nebula Awards for science fiction. Both Butler and Delany incorporate the southern slave experience into some of their novels (such as Butler's *Kindred* [1979] and Delany's *Stars in My Pocket Like Grains of Sand* [1984]).

Tennessee-born Ishmael Reed and Georgia-born Clarence Major are in the forefront of experimental and postmodern novelists, have won prizes, and have centralized the southern black experience. Reed's *Flight to Canada* is one of the most interesting experimental adaptations to date of the slave-narrative genre. The novel's futuristic approach to the black past germinated from a seed George Schuyler planted in 1931 with the publication of *Black No More*. *Flight's* historiographic and metafictional contours anticipated more recent works in the genre, including Sherley Anne Williams's *Dessa Rose*. Reed and Major constitute one end and Butler and Delany the other of a black novelistic continuun whose temporal and spatial narrativity juxtaposes and counterposes the past, the present, and the future in ways that recall—yet significantly expand—Ellison's narrativization of time and space in *Invisible Man*. *Invisible Man*, with its "experimental attitude" (as Ellison describes it in *Shadow and Act* [102]) is a benchmark for the genre. To be sure, *Invisible Man* is the most immediate ancestor of the black masculinist postmodern novel.

Building (and building upon) the black novelistic tradition since the 1950s often has included direct intertextual connections to novels of earlier periods. A few examples will serve as illustrative. Walker's *Meridian* (1976) and Clarence Major's *Such Was the Season* (1987) install Jean Toomer's *Cane* as a key structural and hermeneutic intertext. Gloria Naylor's *The Women of Brewster Place* (1982) incorporates narrative formations from *Cane* as well as from Ann Petry's *The Street* and Richard Wright's *Native Son*. One figural link among these three novels is the proverbial and symbolic wall systematically built by whites to marginalize blacks in the American Eden. The symbol's concrete analogue can be found in Frederick Douglass's 1845 *Narrative*, in which as a literal structure it is intended to prevent blacks from entering the slavemaster's garden and as a metaphorical construct it signifies their exclusion from America's Garden.

In *The Street* Petry reinscribes the wall as a sign of liminality. She inserts it metonymically in an urban novel whose physical and social landscapes are similar to *Native Son's*, contextualizes it with the revolutionary era's permutation of the Eden myth, and revises its form from masculinist to feminist to fit a black woman's experience. When Naylor reinstalls the wall as an emblem of the black novelistic tradition, she retains Petry's feminist revisions of Wright, expands the psychological contours of both Wright's and Petry's urban landscape, and revises both novels' closure by concretizing the wall (Petry had metaphoricized it as a brick barrier) and having *Brewster Place's* women begin to dismantle it brick by brick.

In the mystery-detective subgenre, non-Southerner Walter Mosely adapts conventions of the passing novel to his first published novel, *Devil in a Blue Dress* (1990). He constructs the centered subject of *Devil* (and of his subsequent novels in this series) in large part from the same social, cultural, and historical fabrics Chester Himes used to construct the two black detectives in his series of detective novels.

In North Carolinian Randall Kenan's novel, *A Visitation of Spirits* (1989), and in his short fiction one hears echoes from the historical, cultural, and artistic spaces that helped forge Charles Chesnutt's fiction nearly a century earlier. The affinal fictive visions that connect some of Chesnutt's short fiction to his novels are similar to those that connect Kenan's novel to his stories. The title story from Kenan's *Let the Dead Bury Their Dead* (a finalist for the 1993 National Book Critics' Circle Award) exemplifies in its form, content, and meaning the metafictional, historiographic, and intertextual dimensions that have defined sharply the black fictional (especially the novelistic) tradition of writing the authentic black self into being.

Before the 1960s, there were clear parameters that determined whom and what the black novel could center as subject and as subject matter. These guidelines contracted and expanded with each generation of novelists and allowed for variety in thematic focus and discursive mode. Yet diversity within these boundaries was limited primarily to issues of color, class, and locale in writing black subjectivity. After the 1950s, however, the strictures gradually then rapidly loosened as individual novelists followed the tenets of Langston Hughes's 1926 literary manifesto, "The Negro Artist and the Racial Mountain," put into practice Ellison's credo that "diversity is the word," and applied the premise of *e pluribus unum* to writing black subjectivity. Concurrent with cultural, social, and political changes in the nation after the mid–twentieth century, black novelists began to express a greater degree of freedom within (rather than from) the black novelistic tradition's thematic and formalist norms. Currently, this freedom among novelists is redefining the tradition by appreciably expanding it. James Baldwin was among the first to exercise this artistic freedom when he included homosexuality as an integral feature of black subject formation.

Baldwin's *Another Country*, itself a benchmark in the genre's evolution, is as firmly and as explicitly anchored as any novel in the genre's appropriation and transformation of the biblical Eden myth. *Another Country* voices dimensions of black (particularly male) sexuality previously muted or silenced, brings greater diversity to the discourse on black subjectivity, and thus charts new directions. The feminist frameworks in which Naylor (*Brewster Place*) and Walker (*Color Purple*) write explicitly about black lesbianism (a muted topic in earlier black women's novels), and the masculinist framework in which Kenan (*Visitation*) and Melvin Dixon (*Vanishing Rooms* [1991]) inscribe male gayness are examples of expanded diversity in writing the black subject within conventional modes of discourse in the genre. Butler's and Delany's treatment of third-sex otherness in some of their futuristic fictions not only is informed by American slavery and the legacy of racial otherness but also follows the narrative paths of writing sexual otherness that Baldwin can be credited with releasing from the tradition's closet.

Not all African American novels during the genre's first century incorporate the Bible's narrative of Eden or Anglo-America's Eden trope into their signifying practices, but the majority of standard works do so. The degree to which the trope configures a novel's exploration of black subjectivity and American society varies. As the black novelistic tradition evolved from the 1850s through the 1950s, its thematic and formalist norms were configured from the anchored position the Eden trope occupied in America's social, political, historical, and discursive landscapes.

NOTES

BIBLIOGRAPHY

INDEX

Notes

Preface

1. The studies vary one from another in approach, emphasis, and inclusiveness. Bernard Bell's *The Afro-American Novel and Its Tradition* (1987), Robert Bone's *The Negro Novel in America* (1965), Addison Gayle's *The Way of the New World: The Black Novel in America* (1975), and Noel Schraufnagel's *From Apology to Protest: The Black American Novel* (1973) are among the studies usually considered histories of the African American novel.

Introduction

1. Davis and Schleifer, eds., *Contemporary Literary Criticism*, 369.

Chapter 1: Genesis

1. Marx, *Machine*, 39–40; Howard Mumford Jones, *O Strange New World*, 1–8, 9–34 passim; Stith, *History*, 1–3.

2. Houben, *Christopher Columbus*, 263; Helps, *Life of Columbus*, 186; de Hevesy, *Discoverer*, 200.

3. Jones, *O Strange New World*, 4.

4. Marx, *Machine*, 39–40.

5. Nash, *Wilderness* (1967, ed.), 8–22; see also Jones, *O Strange New World*, 35–70.

6. David Brion Davis, *Problem of Slavery in Western Culture*, 5.; There were, however, some exceptions among southern colonists; see, for example, Alsop, *Character*. Some consider Alsop's section on the Susquehannas (and Native Americans more generally), which follows ch. 4 of the "history," the work's most valuable section.

7. Nash, *Wilderness*, 34–40.

8. For a brief summary of the statutory status of the earliest New World Africans, see Higginbotham, *In the Matter of Color*, 21.

9. Greene, *Negro*, 286.

10. David Brion Davis, *Problem of Slavery in Western Culture*, 10; see Alsop, *Character*, ch. 3, for his praise of indentured servitude. Alsop was probably the only indentured servant in the South to write a promotional tract in the context of the American ideal. His section on indentured servitude, however, speaks more of how the system benefits the servants than of how it benefits the masters; he does not discuss black slaves in this section. See also Lefler's comments on Alsop in "Promotional Literature," 14.

11. David Brion Davis, *Problem of Slavery in Western Culture*, 10.

12. For slaves' insurrections and other forms of physical resistance to slavery, see Aptheker, *American Negro Slave Revolts*, esp. chs. 4–9; for an example of black legal petitions for freedom, see Aptheker, *Documentary History*, 1–12; for a discussion of New World Africans' freedom suits in colonial America, see Higginbotham, *In the Matter of Color*, and Greene, *Negro*, 182–84.

13. Southern texts include ones by Captain John Smith, Robert Beverley, William Byrd II, George Alsop, Samuel Davies, George Fox, and Charles Woodmason; northern ones include those by John Winthrop, William Bradford, Edward Johnson, Samuel Sewell, John Woolman, John Cotton, Roger Williams, Increase Mather, and Cotton Mather.

14. Eliade, *Myth and Reality*, 21.

15. Herbert Aptheker includes the texts of two of these seventeenth-century petitions in his *Documentary History*, 1–3.

16. Robinson, *Early Black American Prose*, 101. For biographical information on Solomon and a fuller text of his narrative, see Curtin, ed., *Africa Remembered*, 17–59.

17. Marx, *Machine*, 73.

18. Wills, *Inventing America*, xv.

19. Bontemps, ed., *Great Slave Narratives*, xiv.

20. While there generally is agreement that Jefferson freed a few of his slaves, there is some discrepancy about exactly how many; see Jordan, *White over Black*, 431; John Chester Miller, *Wolf*, 107.

21. For a summary of Jefferson's views on the topic, see John Chester Miller, *Wolf*, 74–78.

22. See Article 1 of the Constitution (original version).

23. For a brief description of this society, see Aptheker, ed., *Documentary History*, 378–80.

24. See Bedini, *Life*.

25. For the text of one of Banneker's major letters to Jefferson, see Aptheker, ed., *Documentary History*, 23–26; Bedini's *Life*, 152–56, contains texts of the letters slightly different from those in Aptheker.

26. John Chester Miller, *Wolf*, 76–78.

27. Aptheker, ed., *Documentary History*, 378–80.

28. Taylor, *Cavalier and Yankee*, 76.

29. Kennedy, *Memoirs*, 1:179.

30. Taylor, *Cavalier and Yankee*, 72, 76.

31. Ibid., 81–82.

32. Kennedy, *Memoirs*, 2:51.

33. On the literary origin of the plantation legend, see Francis Pendelton Gaines, *Southern Plantation*, 18–94; see also Taylor, *Cavalier and Yankee*, 178–88.

34. Taylor, *Cavalier and Yankee*, 67.

35. Francis Pendelton Gaines, *Southern Plantation*, 144.

36. For a discussion of how the miscegenation debate reached a climax in the presidential campaign of 1864, see Wood, *Black Scare*, 53–79.

37. Miller, *Wolf*, 1.

38. Farrison, *William Wells Brown*, 134–35; Brown first published the story in the *Liberator* for 12 January 1849, 7. In 1860 the Crafts published their own version of the story.

39. Delany's novel was serialized in part in the *Anglo-African Magazine* (January–July 1859) and in full in the *Weekly Anglo-African Magazine* (November 1861–May 1862); for the novel's publication history, see Floyd J. Miller's introduction.

Chapter 2: Belles and Beaux

1. See, for instance, Burroughs and Ehrenreich's introduction to *Reading the Social Body*, Polhemus's "Social Bodies," and Douglas's *Implicit Meanings*.

2. van Gennep, *Rites of Passage*, 11, 21; Victor Turner, *Ritual Process*, 94–130.

3. Victor Turner, *Ritual Process*, 95.

4. Ibid., 94.

5. I borrow this term from Terence Turner, "The Social Skin," 15.

6. In the main, I use the terms *reaggregation* and *reincorporation* when the fictional context implies that the character as a black belongs to the human family; I use the terms *aggregation* and *incorporation* when the fictional context suggests that human is a state the character acquires.

7. Victor Turner, *Ritual Process*, 94.

8. For a summary characterization of the white belle in southern literature prior to World War I, see Seidel, *Southern Belle*, 3–25.

9. See Jordan, *White over Black*, 355, 362.

10. For the antebellum education of women (black and white), see Vinovskis and Bernard, "Beyond Catherine Beecher," 856–69.

11. See, for instance, Seidel, *Southern Belle*, 10–17.

12. Richard Beale Davis, *Intellectual Life in the Colonial South*, 2:518, 545, 556; Richard Beale Davis, *Intellectual Life in Jefferson's Virginia*, 71–118.

13. For a summary definition of socioeconomic class, see Gatewood, "Aristocrats." Gatewood explores the topic more fully in his book, *Aristocrats*. In *Life and Times* Douglass uses "black aristocracy" to designate the upper echelon of blacks.

14. Herskovits, *American Negro*, 3–17; Cash, *Mind*, 84–85. For a chronological summary of miscegenation in the South to 1850, see Williamson, *New People*, 5–59.

15. Compare Mary Chesnut's comments on the issue in her *Diary* entries for March 14, 1862, and April 20, 1861. See also Cash, *Mind*, 84–87; Johnston, *Race Relations*, 238, 249.

16. Blassingame, *Black New Orleans*, 17; Williamson, *New People*, 68–70; Bancroft, *Slave Trading*, 131, 313–16, 317–38; Genovese, *Roll, Jordan, Roll*, 416.

17. For the characteristics of the young white cavalier, see Taylor, *Cavalier and Yankee*, chs. 4 and 5; Cash, *Mind*, 3–21.

18. For example, the Mississippi Constitutional Convention of 1868 initially rejected but later passed a penalty for concubinage; see Wharton, *Negro*, 150.

19. Wyatt-Brown, *Southern Honor*, 307.

20. Eaton, *Growth*, 319.

21. Martin, *Harvests*, 89.

22. Malone, *Centennial Edition*, 3:6.

23. For a cogent discussion of the Liberty Tree as symbol, see Albanese, *Sons*, 58–70.

24. Clinton, *Plantation Mistress*, 209, supports this conclusion.

25. Regardless of her other attributes, Rena's race disqualifies her as a southern belle in the context of the novel's white society; see Seidel, *Southern Belle*, 3–25.

Chapter 3: Beauties and Beasts

1. Zipes, *Fairy Tales*, 3.

2. See esp. Fanon, *Black Skin*, ch. 6.

3. For a discussion of betrothal and marriage rites, see van Gennep, *Rites*, 116–45.

4. Fanon, *Black Skin*, 147.

5. See, for instance, Jordan, *White over Black*, 32–39, 151–54.

6. Williamson, *New People*, 89–90; Blassingame, *Black New Orleans*, 201–10; Clinton, *Plantation Mistress*, 210.

7. A concise statement about laws governing miscegenation and racial designation can be found in Poe, "Negro: By Definition."

8. Hill, *Reports*, 613–17.

9. Taylor, *Cavalier and Yankee*, 25–33.

10. Ibid., 86.

11. An interesting and useful discussion of versions of the "Cinderella" tale is Barbara Herrnstein Smith, "Narrative Versions."

12. For samples of ex-slaves' religious conversion narratives, see Clifton H. Johnson, ed., *God Struck Me Dead*.

13. For a discussion of this and other formulaic devices in the slave narrative, see Stepto, *From Behind the Veil*, ch. 1.

14. Lüthi, *Fairytale*, 135–44.

15. Lacan's "The Mirror Stage as Formative of the Function of the I as Revealed in Psychoanalytic Experience" (1949) is a revision of his 1936 paper "The Looking-Glass Phase." Fanon's "The Negro and Psychopathology" is ch. 6 of his *Black Skin, White Masks*.

16. Bettelheim, *Uses*, 307–8.

17. Tatar, *Hard Facts*, 174.

18. Ibid., 171.

19. See Marx, *Machine*.

Chapter 4: New Slaves and Lynching Bees

1. Walter L. Fleming, ed., *Documentary History*, 2:327.

2. Ibid., 2:347; see also Stampp, *Era*, 200. There is some debate about whether the KKK was formed in 1865 or 1866; see Franklin, *Reconstruction*, 154; Stampp, *Era*, 199; and Wood, *Black Scare*, 77.

3. See Wood, *Black Scare*, 105; Fredrickson, *Black Image*, 184.

4. McPherson, *Ordeal*, 105–6.

5. Ibid., 512–15.

6. See Wood, *Black Scare*, 105–6; Fredrickson, *Black Image*, 184; Franklin, *Reconstruction*, 49–50.

7. Charles Waddell Chesnutt, "Peonage."

8. See, e.g., White, *Rope*, 251–69.

9. Ibid., 227.

10. Ibid., 19–39; Cash, *Mind*, 122.

11. Cash, *Mind*, 117–18.

12. Bellah, "Civil Religion," 3–5.

13. Herbert, "America's Civil Religion," 77, uses this phrase to describe the American Way of Life.

14. Helen Chesnutt, *Charles Waddell Chesnutt*, 181–82; Charles Chesnutt, "Post-bellum," 193–94.

15. At least two other novels of the period incorporate the Wilmington riot of 1898, Fulton, *Hanover*, and Dixon, *Leopard's Spots*.

16. See Le Conte, *Race Problem*, esp. 367–75.

17. For a discussion of these men within this context, see Friedman, *White Savage*.

18. King, "Punishment," 163, 164.

Chapter 5: The Wars for Eden

1. For a discussion (from a religious perspective) of this alignment during the World War I years, see Wilson, *Baptized*, 161–82.

2. Quoted in Franklin, *From Slavery to Freedom*, 334; see also Henri, *Black Migration*, 246; and Du Bois, *Dusk of Dawn*, 234.

3. See Barbeau and Henri, *Unknown Soldiers*, 7.

4. For a summary of the conditions at Camp Wadsworth in Spartanburg, see Little, *From Harlem to the Rhine*, 48–72.

5. Quoted in ibid., 49.

6. For a historical perspective on this point, see Wilson, *Baptized*, 161–82.

7. Scott, *Scott's Official History*, 442.

8. As Hughes put it, "I was in France. . . . A dream come true" (*Big Sea*, 144).

9. Franklin, *From Slavery to Freedom*, 347; see also Barbeau and Henri, *Unknown Soldiers*, 144–45; Williams, *Sidelights*, 74–77.

10. Williams, *Sidelights*, 72; "Documents of the War."

11. See Wiley, *Southern Negroes*, 134–45; see also 110–33 for a discussion of military laborers during the Civil War.

12. Williams, *Sidelights*, 28–29.

13. See Barbeau and Henri, *Unknown Soldiers*, 89–110; Williams, *Sidelights*, 138–55; Scott, *Scott's Official History*, 315–27; Sweeney, *History of the American Negro*, 239–45.

14. Lewis, *When Harlem Was in Vogue*, 164–65; Osofsky, *Harlem*, 179–87.

15. Cronon, *Black Moses*, 202–12. Estimates of the number of Garvey's followers are disputed.

16. Johnson and Campbell, *Black Migration*, 170; Long and Hansen, "Trends," 601–14.

17. See Friedman, *White Savage*, 122–25, 157–68.

18. Scott, *Scott's Official History*, 430–31.

19. Franklin, *From Slavery to Freedom*, 346–47.

20. *Vardaman's Weekly*, 15 May 1919, quoted in *Burning at Stake*, 8.

21. Franklin, *From Slavery to Freedom*, 356–57.

Chapter 6: Black Adams

1. Walker, *Moral Choices*, 260, concludes that Douglass probably composed this poem in 1883.

2. All quotations from Douglass, "What Am I to You," are from one of two hand-written versions in the Douglass Papers, Library of Congress.

3. Walker, *Moral Choices*, 261.

4. Girard, *Deceit*, 17.

5. For pre-Adamites, see Poliakov, *Aryan Myth*, 131–34.

6. See Ibid., 137–44.

7. For instance, John Reilly takes this position in the afterword to the Perennial Classics edition of the novel (1966).

8. Eliade, *Myth*, 26.

9. May and Metzger, eds., *Oxford Annotated Bible*, 1284n.

10. Ibid., 1284n.

11. Porter, *Modern Negro Art*, 132.

Chapter 7: Totems and Taboos

1. Scruggs, "Mark of Cain."

2. See Fabre, "Fathers and Sons."

3. See Ginzburg, *One Hundred Years of Lynching*, 10.

4. See ibid., 62–63.

5. *Thirty Years of Lynching*, 26–27.

6. For Freud's distinctions between atonement and purificatory ceremonies, see *Totem and Taboo*, 20–34.

7. The percentage of black ancestry used in statutory definitions of one's racial identity varied from state to state and from one era to another in southern social history. See, for example, Poe, "Negro."

8. Johnston, *Race Relations*, 296–98.

9. Green and red are often said to signify gay and lesbian lifestyles. See, e.g., Katz, *Gay American History*, 52–53, 421, 539, 661–62n.

10. A recent study that synthesizes issues relating to the Calamus poems and homosexuality in general in Whitman's poems is Fone, *Masculine Landscapes*.

11. Quoted in Blodgett and Bradley, eds., *Walt Whitman's "Leaves of Grass,"* 112n.

12. Matthiessen, *American Renaissance*, 20–24.

13. Abbot Emerson Smith, *Colonists*, esp. 106.

14. Bleser, ed., *Secret and Sacred*, 19. See Bleser's comments and Hammond's diary entries regarding the "Hampton scandal" and Hammond's slave mistresses Sally and Louisa Johnson. Hammond's letter to his son, Harry, for 19 February 1856 is especially revealing.

15. Duberman, "'Writhing Bedfellows.'"

16. Curtin, *Atlantic Slave Trade*, 161; Pope-Hennessy, *Sins*, 58–59.

17. Jordan, *White over Black*, 380–86; Aptheker, *American Negro Slave Revolts*, 42–44.

18. Jordan, *White over Black*, 151–54.

Chapter 8: *The Textualization of Blackness*

1. Plato, *Dialogues*, 3:649.

2. See, for example, Nadel, *Invisible Criticism.*

3. See Charles T. Davis, *Black*, 313–25; see also Inge, Duke, and Bryer, eds., *Black American Writers*, 2:47–71.

4. Though *Cane* foregrounds women, I include it in this group of novels not only because Kabnis is the centered subject in the book's third part, but also because I see Kabnis as the narrative voice of the other sections, as the poet who writes the poems and sketches in parts one and two.

5. One of the most forceful statements about the absence/presence of blacks in white American literature is Morrison, "Unspeakable Things."

6. Though in several of his essays Ellison expresses high praise for *Huck Finn*, he states that in his youth Twain's depiction of Jim "struck me as a white man's inadequate portrait of a slave" (*Shadow and Act*, 58).

7. Silverman, *Subject*, 141.

8. Baker, *Modernism*, 49–51, 85–87; see also Baker's "Caliban's Triple Play," 381–95.

9. Bakhtin, *Dialogic Imagination*, 343.

10. Ibid., 341.

11. Crèvecoeur, *Letters*, 54.

12. "Uses of History," 69, 63, 62. The panel discussion included Ellison, William Styron, and Robert Penn Warren and C. Vann Woodward as moderator.

13. When Ellison published *Invisible Man* and when he spoke on the 1968 Southern Historical Association panel, the chronological or documentary model predominated among historians. Since the 1970s, however, the profession has broadened the form and the content of its historiographic texts. For a cogent assessment of how historiographic writing has changed in the past two decades, see Kammen's introduction to *The Past before Us.*

14. LaCapra, *History and Criticism*, 128.

15. Warnock, *Memory*, 6.

16. Reid, *Works*, 1:342.

17. Warnock, *Memory*, viii.

18. Russell Fischer identifies specific historical persons and events in his discussion of three major "roles" the protagonist plays that align him with historical epochs in twentieth-century African American history—education, migration, and the Communist Party ("*Invisible Man*"). Susan Blake ("Ritual and Rationalization") and John Callahan ("Chaos, Complexity, and Possibility") note briefly the general parallel between the novel's structure and eras in African American social history.

19. Most critics who identify links between the Brotherhood and the Communist Party and between Ras and Marcus Garvey acknowledge Ellison's statements that the Brotherhood is not a fictional representation of the Communist Party and that Ras is not a fictionalized Marcus Garvey. Nevertheless, Russell Fischer exemplifies the general critical

stance in his discussion of the Brotherhood and the Communist Party and of Ras and Garvey ("*Invisible Man*," 358–66).

20. The concept is stated in the title of Griggs's *Imperium in Imperio*. Delany uses the phrase, for instance, in *The Condition*, 12, 209.

Conclusion

1. "American Fiction," 2.

Bibliography

A bibliographical listing of critical studies of African American novels published between 1853 and 1957 would be extensive. I have excluded such an extensive listing from this bibliography. The *MLA International Bibliography* in hardcover and its computerized counterpart (listings are current within a month), the bibliographies published periodically in *African American Review* (formerly *Black American Literature Forum* and *Negro American Literature Forum*), in the *College Language Association Journal* (*CLAJ*), and in *Callaloo* will give readers interested in critical studies of African American novels ready access to this information.

Albanese, Catherine L. *Sons of the Fathers: The Civil Religion of the American Revolution.* Philadelphia: Temple Univ. Press, 1976.

Alsop, George. *A Character of the Province of Mary-Land.* 1666. Rpt. Ed. with an intro. by Robert A. Bain. Bainbridge, N.Y.: York Mail-Print, 1972.

"American Fiction: The Postwar Years, 1945–1965." *Book Week,* 26 Sept. 1965.

Andrews, William L. *The Literary Career of Charles W. Chesnutt.* Baton Rouge: Louisiana State Univ. Press, 1980.

Aptheker, Herbert. *American Negro Slave Revolts.* 1943. Rpt. New York: International Publishers, 1974.

———, ed. *A Documentary History of the Negro People in the United States: From Colonial Times through the Civil War.* New York: Citadel Press, 1962.

———. *Nat Turner's Slave Rebellion.* New York: Grove Press, 1968.

Attaway, William. *Blood on the Forge.* 1941. Rpt. Chatham, N.J.: Chatham Bookseller, 1969.

Baker, Houston A., Jr. *Blues, Ideology, and Afro-American Literature: A Vernacular Theory.* Chicago: Univ. of Chicago Press, 1984.

———. "Caliban's Triple Play." In *"Race," Writing, and Difference,* ed. Henry Louis Gates. Chicago: Univ. of Chicago Press, 1987.

———. Introduction to *Narrative of the Life of Frederick Douglass, an American Slave. Written by Himself.* New York: Penguin Books, 1982.

———. *Modernism and the Harlem Renaissance.* Chicago: Univ. of Chicago Press, 1987.

Bakhtin, Mikhail M. *The Dialogic Imagination.* Trans. Michael Holquist. Austin: Univ. of Texas Press, 1981.

Baldwin, James. *Another Country.* New York: Dial Press, 1962.

———. *Go Tell It on the Mountain.* New York: Dial Press, 1953.

Bancroft, Frederic. *Slave Trading in the Old South.* New York: Frederick Ungar, 1931.

Barbeau, Arthur E., and Florette Henri. *The Unknown Soldiers: Black American Troops in World War I.* Philadelphia: Temple Univ. Press, 1974.

Baym, Nina. *Woman's Fiction: A Guide to Novels by and about Women in America, 1820–1870.* Ithaca: Cornell Univ. Press, 1978.

Bedini, Silvio A. *The Life of Benjamin Banneker.* New York: Scribners, 1972.

Bell, Bernard W. *The Afro-American Novel and Its Tradition.* Amherst: Univ. of Massachusetts Press, 1987.

Bellah, Robert N. "Civil Religion in America." *Daedalus* 96 (Winter 1967): 1–21.

Benston, Kimberly W., ed. *Speaking for You: The Vision of Ralph Ellison.* Washington, D.C.: Howard Univ. Press, 1987.

Bergman, Peter M., and Mort N. Bergman, comps. *The Chronological History of the Negro in America.* New York: Harper and Row, 1969.

Berlin, Ira. *Slaves without Masters: The Free Negro in the Antebellum South.* New York: Pantheon Books, 1974.

Bettelheim, Bruno. *The Uses of Enchantment: The Meaning and Importance of Fairy Tales.* New York: Vintage Books, 1989.

Beverley, Robert. *The History and Present State of Virginia.* Ed. with an intro. by Louis B. Wright. Chapel Hill: Univ. of North Carolina Press, 1947.

Blackmore, David L. "'That Unreasonable Restless Reeling': The Homosexual Subtexts of Nella Larsen's *Passing.*" *African American Review* 26 (Fall 1992): 475–84.

Blackson, Lorenzo Dow. *The Rise and Progress of the Kingdoms of Light and Darkness. Or, the Reign of Kings Alpha and Abadon.* 1867. Rpt. Upper Saddle River, N.J.: Gregg Press, 1968.

Blake, Susan. "Ritual and Rationalization: Black Folklore in the Works of Ralph Ellison. *PMLA* 94 (Jan. 1979): 121–36.

Blassingame, John. *Black New Orleans, 1860–1880.* Chicago: Univ. of Chicago Press, 1973.

Bleser, Carol, ed. *Secret and Sacred: The Diaries of James Henry Hammond, a Southern Slaveholder.* New York: Oxford Univ. Press, 1988.

Blodgett, Harold W., and Scully Bradley, eds. *Walt Whitman's "Leaves of Grass."* 1965. Rpt. New York: Norton, 1968.

Bone, Robert. *The Negro Novel in America.* Rev. ed. New Haven: Yale Univ. Press, 1965.

Bontemps, Arna. *Black Thunder.* 1936. Rpt. Boston: Beacon Press, 1968.

———, ed. *Great Slave Narratives.* Boston: Beacon Press, 1969.

Bradford, William. *Of Plymouth Plantation, 1620–1647.* Ed. Samuel Eliot Morison. New York: Modern Library, 1952.

Bremer, Francis J. *The Puritan Experiment: New England Society from Bradford to Edwards.* New York: St. Martin's Press, 1976.

Bremer, Fredericka. *The Homes of the New World: Impressions of America.* Trans. Mary Howitt. 3 vols. London: A Hall, Virtue and Company, 1853.

Brown, William Wells. *Clotel; or, The President's Daughter: A Narrative of Slave Life in the United States.* 1853. Rpt. New York: Collier Books, 1970.

Bruce, Dickson D., Jr. *Black American Writing from the Nadir: The Evolution of a Literary Tradition, 1877–1915.* Baton Rouge: Louisiana State Univ. Press, 1989.

Burning at Stake in the United States. 1919. Baltimore: Black Classic Press, 1986.

Burroughs, Catherine B., and Jeffrey David Ehrenreich, eds. *Reading the Social Body.* Iowa City: Univ. of Iowa Press, 1993.

Callahan, John F. "Chaos, Complexity, and Possibility: The Historical Frequencies of Ralph Waldo Ellison." In *Speaking for You: The Vision of Ralph Ellison,* ed. Kimberly W. Benston. Washington, D.C.: Howard Univ. Press, 1987.

Carroll, Charles. *"The Negro a Beast," or, "In the Image of God."* 1900. Rpt. New York: Books for Libraries Press, 1980.

————. *The Tempter of Eve—or—The Criminality of Man's Social, Political, and Religious Equality with the Negro, and the Amalgamation to Which These Crimes Inevitably Lead.* St. Louis: Adamic Publishing Company, 1902.

Cash, Wilbur J. *The Mind of the South.* New York: Knopf, 1941.

Chatman, Seymour. *Story and Discourse: Narrative Structure in Fiction and Film.* Ithaca: Cornell Univ. Press, 1988.

Chesnut, Mary Boykin. *A Diary from Dixie.* Ed. Ben Ames Williams. Boston: Houghton Mifflin, 1949.

Chesnutt, Charles Waddell. *The Colonel's Dream.* New York: Doubleday, Page, 1905.

————. "The Fall of Adam." In *The Short Fiction of Charles W. Chesnutt,* Ed. with an introduction by Sylvia Lyons Render. Washington, D.C.: Howard Univ. Press, 1981.

————. *The House Behind the Cedars.* Boston: Houghton, Mifflin, 1900.

————. *The Marrow of Tradition.* Boston: Houghton, Mifflin, 1901.

————. "Peonage, or the New Slavery." *The Voice of the Negro* 1 (September 1904): 394–97.

————. "Post-bellum, Pre-Harlem." *Colophon* 2 (1931): N.p. Rpt. *Crisis* 40 (June 1931): 193–94.

————. "What Is a White Man?" *New York Independent,* 30 May 1889, 5–6.

Chesnutt, Helen M. *Charles Waddell Chesnutt: Pioneer of the Color Line.* Chapel Hill: Univ. of North Carolina Press, 1952.

Christian, Barbara. *Black Women Novelists: The Development of a Tradition, 1892–1976.* Westport, Conn.: Greenwood Press, 1980.

Clifford, James, and George Marcus, eds. *Writing Culture: The Poetics and Politics of Ethnography.* Berkeley: Univ. of California Press, 1986.

Clinton, Catherine. *The Plantation Mistress: Woman's World in the Old South.* New York: Pantheon, 1982.

Crèvecoeur, J. Hector St. John. *Letters from an American Farmer.* 1782. Rpt. New York: Albert and Charles Boni, 1925.

Cronon, E. David. *Black Moses: The Story of Marcus Garvey and the Universal Negro Improvement Association.* Madison: Univ. of Wisconsin Press, 1969.

Cullen, Countee. *One Way to Heaven.* 1932. Rpt. New York: AMS Press, 1975.

Curtin, Philip D., ed. *Africa Remembered: Narratives by West Africans from the Era of the Slave Trade.* Madison: Univ. of Wisconsin Press, 1967.

————. *The Atlantic Slave Trade: A Census.* Madison: Univ. of Wisconsin Press, 1969.

Daly, Victor. *Not Only War: A Story of Two Great Conflicts.* 1932. Rpt. New York: AMS Press, 1970.

Daniel, Pete. *The Shadow of Slavery: Peonage in the South, 1901–1969.* Urbana: Univ. of Illinois Press, 1972.

Davis, Charles T. *Black Is the Color of the Cosmos: Essays on Afro-American Literature and Culture, 1942–1981.* New York: Garland, 1982.

Davis, David Brion. *The Problem of Slavery in the Age of Revolution, 1770–1823.* Ithaca: Cornell Univ. Press, 1975.

———. *The Problem of Slavery in Western Culture.* Ithaca: Cornell Univ. Press, 1966.

Davis, Richard Beale. *Intellectual Life in the Colonial South, 1585–1763.* 3 vols. Knoxville: Univ. of Tennessee Press, 1978.

———. *Intellectual Life in Jefferson's Virginia, 1790–1830.* Chapel Hill: Univ. of North Carolina Press, 1964.

Davis, Robert C., and Ronald Schleifer, eds. *Contemporary Literary Criticism: Literary and Cultural Studies.* 2d ed. New York: Longman, 1989.

Day, Caroline Bond. *A Study of Some Negro-White Families in the United States.* Harvard Africana Studies, vol. 10. Cambridge: Peabody Museum of Harvard Univ., 1932.

de Hevesy, Andre. *The Discoverer: A New Narrative of the Life and Hazardous Adventures of the Genoese Christopher Columbus.* Trans. Robert M. Coates. New York: Macaulay, 1928.

Delany, Martin R. *Blake; or, The Huts of America.* Ed. with an intro. by Floyd J. Miller. Boston: Beacon Press, 1970.

———. *The Condition, Elevation, Emigration and Destiny of the Colored People of the United States.* 1852. Rpt. New York: Arno Press, 1969.

Dixon, Thomas, Jr. *The Leopard's Spots: A Romance of the White Man's Burden—1865-1900.* 1902. Rpt. New York: A. Wessels, 1906.

"Documents of the War." *Crisis* 18 (May 1919): 16.

Doty, William G. *Mythography: The Study of Myths and Rituals.* Tuscaloosa: Univ. of Alabama Press, 1986.

Douglas, Mary. *Implicit Meanings: Essays in Anthropology.* London: Routledge and Kegan Paul, 1975.

Douglass, Frederick. *Life and Times of Frederick Douglass. Written by Himself.* 1845. Rpt. New York: Collier Books, 1962.

———. *Narrative of the Life of Frederick Douglass, an American Slave. Written by Himself.* 1845. Rpt. Ed. with an intro. by Houston A. Baker, Jr. New York: Penguin Books, 1982.

Downs, Robert B. *Books That Changed the World.* Rev. ed. New York: New American Library, 1983.

Downing, Henry F. *The American Cavalryman: A Liberian Romance.* 1917. Rpt. College Park, Md.: McGrath Publishing, 1969.

Dreer, Herman. *The Immediate Jewel of His Soul: A Romance.* 1919. Rpt. New York: AMS Press, 1975.

Duberman, Martin Bauml. "'Writhing Bedfellows': 1826 Two Young Men from Antebellum South Carolina's Ruling Elite Share 'Extravagant Delight.'" In *Historical Perspectives on Homosexuality,* ed. Salvatore J. Licata and Robert P. Petersen. New York: Haworth Press and Stein and Day Publishers, 1981.

Du Bois, W. E. B. *Dusk of Dawn: An Essay toward an Autobiography of a Race Concept.* 1940. Rpt. New York: Schocken Books, 1968.

———. *The Quest of the Silver Fleece.* 1911. Rpt. New York: Negro Univ. Press, 1969.

———. *The Souls of Black Folk: Essays and Sketches.* 1903. Rpt. 7th ed. Chicago: A. C. McClurg, 1907.

Dunbar, Paul Laurence. *The Sport of the Gods.* 1902. Rpt. New York: Collier Books, 1970.

Eaton, Clement. *The Growth of Southern Civilization, 1790–1860.* New York: Harper, 1961.

Elder, Arlene. *The "Hindered Hand": Cultural Implications of Early African American Fiction.* Westport, Conn.: Greenwood Press, 1978.

Eliade, Mircea. *Myth and Reality.* Trans. Willard R. Trask. New York: Harper and Row, 1963.

Elliott, E. N., ed. *Cotton Is King, and Pro-Slavery Arguments.* 3d ed. Augusta, Ga.: Pritchard, Abbott and Loomis, 1860.

Ellison, Ralph. *Going to the Territory.* New York: Random House, 1986.

———. *Invisible Man.* New York: Random House, 1952.

———. *Shadow and Act.* New York: Random House, 1964.

Equiano, Olaudah. *The Life of Olaudah Equiano, or Gustavus Vassa, the African, Written by Himself.* In *Great Slave Narratives*, ed. Arna Bontemps. Boston: Beacon Press, 1969.

Fabre, Michel. "Fathers and Sons in James Baldwin's *Go Tell It on the Mountain.*" Trans. Keneth Kinnamon. In *James Baldwin: A Collection of Critical Essays*, ed. Keneth Kinnamon. Englewood Cliffs, N.J.: Prentice-Hall, 1974.

———. *From Harlem to Paris: Black American Writers in France, 1840–1980.* Urbana: Univ. of Illinois Press, 1991.

Fanon, Frantz. *Black Skin, White Masks.* Trans. Charles Lam Markmann. New York: Grove Press, 1967.

———. *The Wretched of the Earth.* Trans. Constance Farrington. New York: Grove Press, 1963.

Farrison, W. Edward. "Clotel, Thomas Jefferson, and Sally Hemings." *CLA Journal* 17 (Dec. 1973): 147–74.

———. "The Origin of Brown's *Clotel.*" *Phylon* 15 (1954): 347–54.

———. *William Wells Brown: Author and Reformer.* Chicago: Univ. of Chicago Press, 1969.

Fauset, Jessie Redmon. *There Is Confusion.* 1924. Rpt. New York: AMS Press, 1974.

Faust, Drew Gilpin, ed. *The Ideology of Slavery: Proslavery Thought in the Antebellum South, 1830–1860.* Baton Rouge, Louisiana State Univ. Press, 1981.

Fiedler, Leslie. "Come Back to the Raft A'gin, Huck Honey." *Partisan Review* 25 (June 1948): 664–71.

Fischer, Russell G. "*Invisible Man* as History." *CLA Journal* 17 (July 1974): 338–67.

Fisher, Rudolph. *The Walls of Jericho.* 1928. Rpt. New York: Arno Press, 1969.

Fleming, Sarah Lee Brown. *Hope's Highway.* 1918. Rpt. New York: AMS Press, 1973.

Fleming, Walter L., ed. *Documentary History of Reconstruction: Political, Military, Social, Religious, Educational and Industrial, 1865–1906.* 2 vols. New York: McGraw-Hill, 1966.

Fone, Bryne R. S. *Masculine Landscapes: Walt Whitman and the Homoerotic Text.* Carbondale: Southern Illinois Univ. Press, 1992.

Franklin, John Hope. *From Slavery to Freedom: A History of Negro Americans*. 4th ed. New York: Knopf, 1974.

——. *Reconstruction: After the Civil War*. Chicago: Univ. of Chicago Press, 1961.

Fredrickson, George M. *The Black Image in the White Mind: The Debate on Afro-American Character and Destiny, 1817–1914*. New York: Harper and Row, 1971.

Freud, Sigmund. *Totem and Taboo: Some Points of Agreement between the Mental Lives of Savages and Neurotics*. Trans. James Strachey. New York: Norton, 1950.

Friedman, Lawrence J. *The White Savage: Racial Fantasies in the Postbellum South*. Englewood Cliffs, N.J.: Prentice-Hall, 1970.

Fulton, David B. [Jack Thorne]. *Hanover; or, The Persecution of the Lowly: A Story of the Wilmington Massacre*. N.p.: M. C. L. Hill, 1900.

Gaines, Ernest J. *The Autobiography of Miss Jane Pittman*. New York: Dial Press, 1971.

Gaines, Francis Pendelton. *The Southern Plantation: A Study in the Development and the Accuracy of a Tradition*. New York: Columbia Univ. Press, 1925.

Gates, Henry Louis, Jr., ed. *"Race," Writing, and Difference*. Chicago: Univ. of Chicago Press, 1986.

Gatewood, Willard B., Jr. *Aristocrats of Color: The Black Elite, 1880–1920*. Bloomington: Indiana Univ. Press, 1990.

——. "Aristocrats of Color: South and North, The Black Elite, 1880–1920." *Journal of Southern History* 54 (Feb. 1988): 5–20.

Gayle, Addison, Jr. *The Way of the New World: The Black Novel in America*. Garden City, N.Y.: Anchor Press, 1975.

Genovese, Eugene. *Roll, Jordan, Roll: The World the Slaves Made*. New York: Pantheon Books, 1974.

Gilbert, Mercedes. *Aunt Sara's Wooden God*. 1938. Rpt. College Park, Md: McGrath Publishing, 1969.

Gilmore, F. Grant. *"The Problem": A Military Novel*. 1915. Rpt. College Park, Md: McGrath Publishing, 1969.

Ginzburg, Ralph. *One Hundred Years of Lynching*. New York: Lancer Books, 1962.

Girard, René. *Deceit, Desire, and the Novel: Self and Other in Literary Structure*. Trans. Yvonne Freccero. Baltimore: Johns Hopkins Univ. Press, 1965.

Gloster, Hugh M. *Negro Voices in American Fiction*. 1948. Rpt. New York: Russell and Russell, 1965.

Gossett, Thomas F. *Race: The History of an Idea in America*. 1963. Rpt. New York: Schocken, 1965.

Granzotto, Gianni. *Christopher Columbus*. Trans. Stephen Sartarelli. Garden City, N.Y.: Doubleday, 1985.

Greene, Lorenzo Johnston. *The Negro in Colonial New England*. 1942. Rpt. New York: Anthenum, 1974.

Griggs, Sutton Elbert. *The Hindered Hand; or, The Reign of the Repressionist*. 3d ed. 1905. Rpt. New York: AMS Press, 1969.

——. *Imperium in Imperio*. 1899. Rpt. Miami, Fla.: Mnemosyne Publishing, 1969.

——. *Overshadowed*. 1901. Rpt. New York: AMS Press, 1973.

————. *Pointing the Way.* 1908. Rpt. New York: AMS Press, 1974.

————. *Unfettered.* 1902. Rpt. New York: AMS Press, 1971.

Gutman, Herbert. *The Black Family in Slavery and Freedom, 1750–1925.* New York: Pantheon Books, 1976.

Hammond, James Henry. *Secret and Sacred: The Diaries of James Henry Hammond, a Southern Slaveholder.* Ed. Carol Bleser. New York: Oxford Univ. Press, 1988.

Harper, Frances E. W. *Iola Leroy, or Shadows Uplifted.* 1893. Rpt. New York: AMS Press, 1971.

Helps, Arthur. *The Life of Columbus, the Discoverer of America.* London: Bell and Daldy, 1869.

Henderson, George Wylie. *Jule.* New York: Creative Age Press, 1946.

————. *Ollie Miss.* New York: Frederick A. Stokes, 1935.

Henri, Florette. *Bitter Victory: A History of Black Soldiers in World War I.* Garden City, N.Y.: Doubleday, Zenith Books, 1970.

————. *Black Migration: Movement North, 1900–1920.* Garden City, N.Y.: Anchor Books, 1975.

Herbert, Will. "America's Civil Religion: What It Is and Whence It Comes." In *American Civil Religion,* ed. Russell E. Richey and Donald G. Jones. New York: Harper and Row, 1974.

Herskovits, Melville J. *The American Negro: A Study in Racial Crossing.* Bloomington: Indiana Univ. Press, Midland Books, 1964.

Higginbotham, A. Leon, Jr. *In the Matter of Color: Race and the American Legal Process: The Colonial Period.* New York: Oxford Univ. Press, 1978.

Hill, W. R. *Reports of Cases Argued and Determined in the Supreme Court of South Carolina.* 1857. Bk. 9, vol. 2. Rpt. St. Paul: West Publishing Company, 1919.

Himes, Chester. *If He Hollers Let Him Go.* Garden City, N.Y.: Doubleday, Doran, 1945.

Hopkins, Pauline. *Contending Forces: A Romance Illustrative of Negro Life North and South.* 1900. Rpt. Carbondale: Southern Illinois Univ. Press, 1978.

Houben, H. H. *Christopher Columbus: The Tragedy of a Discoverer.* Trans. John Linton. New York: Dutton, 1936.

Hutcheon, Linda. *Narcissistic Narrative: The Metafictional Paradox.* 1980. Rpt. London: Routledge, 1991.

————. *A Poetics of Postmodernism: History, Theory, Fiction.* London: Routledge Paperbacks, 1991.

Howard, James H. W. *Bond and Free: A True Tale of Slave Times.* 1886. Rpt. College Park, Md.: McGrath Publishing, 1969.

Hughes, Carl Milton. *The Negro Novelist: A Discussion of the Writings of American Negro Novelists, 1940–1950.* 1953. Rpt. New York: Citadel Press, 1970.

Hughes, Langston. *The Big Sea.* New York: Knopf, 1940.

————. *Not without Laughter.* 1930. Rpt. New York: Knopf, 1951.

Hurston, Zora Neale. *Moses: Man of the Mountain.* 1939. Rpt. Urbana: Univ. of Illinois Press, 1984.

————. *Their Eyes Were Watching God.* 1937. Rpt. Urbana: Univ. of Illinois Press, 1978.

Inge, M. Thomas, Maurice Duke, and Jackson R. Bryer, eds. *Black American Writers: Bibliographical Essays.* 2 vols. New York: St. Martin's Press, 1978.

Jacobs, Harriet A. *Incidents in the Life of a Slave Girl. Written by Herself.* 1861. Rpt. Ed. with an intro. by Jean Fagan Yellin. Cambridge: Harvard Univ. Press, 1987.

Jefferson, Thomas. *Notes on the State of Virginia.* Ed. with an introduction by Thomas Perkins Abernethy. New York: Harper and Row, Harper Torchbooks, 1964.

Johnson, Amelia E. *Clarence and Corinne; or, God's Way.* 1890. Rpt. New York: Oxford Univ. Press, 1988.

————. *The Hazeley Family.* 1894. Rpt. New York: Oxford Univ. Press, 1988.

Johnson, Charles. *Being and Race: Black Writing since 1970.* Bloomington: Indiana Univ. Press, 1988.

Johnson, Clifton H., ed. *God Struck Me Dead: Religious Conversion Experiences and Autobiographies of Ex-Slaves.* Philadelphia: Pilgrim Press, 1969.

Johnson, Daniel M., and Rex R. Campbell. *Black Migration in America: A Social Demographic History.* Durham, N.C.: Duke Univ. Press, 1981.

Johnson, James Weldon. *Along This Way: The Autobiography of James Weldon Johnson.* New York: Viking Press, 1934.

————. *The Autobiography of an Ex-Coloured Man.* 1912. Rpt. Garden City, N.Y.: Garden City Publishing, 1927.

————. *God's Trombones: Seven Negro Sermons in Verse.* New York: Viking, 1927.

Johnston, James Hugo. *Race Relations in Virginia and Miscegenation in the South, 1776–1860.* Amherst: Univ. of Massachusetts Press, 1970.

Jones, Howard Mumford. *O Strange New World: American Culture, The Formative Years.* New York: Viking Press, 1964.

Jones, J. McHenry. *Hearts of Gold: A Novel.* 1896. Rpt. College Park, Md.: McGrath Publishing, 1969.

Jones, Joshua Henry, Jr. *By Sanction of Law.* 1924. Rpt. College Park, Md.: McGrath Publishing, 1969.

Jones, LeRoi. "American Sexual Reference: Black Male." In *Home: Social Essays.* New York: William Morrow, 1956.

Jordan, Winthrop. *White over Black: American Attitudes toward the Negro, 1550–1812.* Chapel Hill: Univ. of North Carolina Press, 1968.

Kalm, Pehr. *Travels in North America.* London, 1772.

Kammen, Michael, ed. *The Past before Us: Contemporary Historical Writing in the United States.* Ithaca: Cornell Univ. Press, 1980.

Katz, Jonathan Ned. *Gay American History: Lesbians and Gay Men in the U.S.A., a Documentary History.* Rev. ed. New York: Penguin Books, 1992.

Kennedy, John Pendelton. *Memoirs of the Life of William Wirt, Attorney-General of the United States.* Rev. ed. 2 vols. Philadelphia: Lea and Blanchard, 1850.

————. *Swallow Barn, or A Sojourn in the Old Dominion.* Ed. William Osborne. New York: Hafner Publishing Company, 1962.

King, Alex C. "The Punishment of Crimes against Women, Existing Legal Remedies and Their Sufficiency." In *Race Problems of the South: Report of . . . the Southern Society for the Promotion of the Study of Race Conditions and Problems in the South.* 1900. Rpt. New York: Negro Univ. Press, 1969.

Kinnamon, Keneth. "*Native Son:* The Personal, Social and Political Background." *Phylon* 30 (Spring 1969): 66–72.

Kinney, James. *Amalgamation! Race, Sex, and Rhetoric in the Nineteenth-Century American Novel.* Westport, Conn.: Greenwood Press, 1985.

Lacan, Jacques. *Écrits: A Selection.* Trans. Alan Sheridan. New York: Norton, 1977.

LaCapra, Dominick. *History and Criticism.* Ithaca: Cornell Univ. Press, 1985.

Larsen, Nella. *Passing.* New York: Knopf, 1929.

————. *Quicksand.* 1928. New York: Collier Books, 1971.

Le Conte, Joseph. *The Race Problem in the South.* 1892. Rpt. Miami, Fla.: Mnemosyne Publishing, 1969.

Lee, George W. *River George.* New York: Macaulay, 1937.

Lee, John M. *Counter Clockwise.* 1940. Rpt. New York: AMS Press, 1975.

Lefler, Hugh T. "Promotional Literature of the Southern Colonies." *Journal of Southern History* 33 (1967): 3–25.

Lewis, David Levering. *When Harlem Was in Vogue.* New York: Knopf, 1981.

Little, Arthur W. *From Harlem to the Rhine: The Story of New York's Colored Volunteers.* New York: Covici, Friede, 1936.

Long, Charles H. *Significations: Signs, Symbols, and Images in the Interpretation of Religion.* Philadelphia: Fortress Press, 1986.

Long, Larry H., and Kristin A. Hansen. "Trends in Return Migration to the South." *Demography* 12 (Nov. 1975): 601–14.

Lüthi, Max. *The Fairytale as Art Form and Portrait of Man.* Trans. Jon Erickson. 1984. Rpt. Bloomington: Indiana Univ. Press, Midland Books, 1987.

McDowell, Deborah. Introduction to *Quicksand* and *Passing,* by Nella Larsen. New Brunswick, N.J.: Rutgers Univ. Press, 1986.

McKay, Claude. *Banjo: A Story without a Plot.* New York: Harper, 1929.

————. *Home to Harlem.* New York: Harper, 1928.

McPherson, James M. *Ordeal by Fire: The Civil War and Reconstruction.* New York: Knopf, 1982.

Malone, Kemp, ed. *The Centennial Edition of the Works of Sidney Lanier.* 3 vols. Baltimore: Johns Hopkins Univ. Press, 1945.

Martin, Jay. *Harvests of Change: American Literature 1865–1914.* Englewood Cliffs, N.J.: Prentice-Hall, 1967.

Marx, Leo. *The Machine in the Garden: Technology and the Pastoral Ideal in America.* New York: Oxford Univ. Press, 1967.

Mason, Julian D., Jr., ed. *The Poems of Phillis Wheatley.* Rev. ed. Chapel Hill: Univ. of North Carolina Press, 1989.

Matthiessen, F. O. *American Renaissance: Art and Expression in the Age of Emerson and Whitman.* 1941. Rpt. New York: Oxford Univ. Press, 1972.

May, Herbert G., and Bruce M. Metzger, eds. *The Oxford Annotated Bible, Revised Standard Version.* New York: Oxford Univ. Press, 1962.

Mellard, James M. *Doing Tropology: Analysis of Narrative Discourse.* Urbana: Univ. of Illinois Press, 1987.

Melville, Herman. *Mardi: And a Voyage Thither*. 1849. Rpt. New York: New American Library, 1964.

──────. *Redburn, His First Voyage*. 1849. Rpt. Garden City, N.Y.: Anchor Books, 1957.

Micheaux, Oscar. *The Conquest: The Story of a Negro Pioneer*. 1913. Rpt. Miami, Fla.: Mnemosyne Publishing, 1969.

──────. *The Homesteader*. 1917. Rpt. College Park, Md.: McGrath Publishing, 1969.

Miller, Ezekiel Harry. *The Protestant*. Boston: Christopher Publishing, 1933.

Miller, John Chester. *The Wolf by the Ears: Thomas Jefferson and Slavery*. New York: Free Press, 1977.

Miller, Kelly. *As to the Leopard's Spots: An Open Letter to Thomas Dixon, Jr*. Washington, D.C.: Hayworth Publishing, 1905.

Morrison, Toni. "Unspeakable Things Unspoken: The Afro-American Presence in American Literature." *Michigan Quarterly Review* 28 (1989): 1–34.

Mullin, Gerald W. *Flight and Rebellion: Slave Resistance in Eighteenth-Century Virginia*. New York: Oxford Univ. Press, 1972.

Nadel, Alan. *Invisible Criticism: Ralph Ellison and the American Canon*. Iowa City: Univ. of Iowa Press, 1988.

Naison, Mark. *Communists in Harlem during the Depression*. Urbana: Univ. of Illinois Press, 1983.

Nash, Roderick. *Wilderness and the American Mind*. New Haven: Yale Univ. Press, 1967.

──────. *Wilderness and the American Mind*. 3d ed. New Haven: Yale Univ. Press, 1982.

Oates, Stephen B. *The Fires of Jubilee: Nat Turner's Fierce Rebellion*. New York: Harper and Row, 1975.

Osofsky, Gilbert. *Harlem: The Making of a Ghetto, Negro New York 1890–1930*. New York: Harper and Row, 1966.

Petry, Ann. *The Narrows*. Boston: Houghton Mifflin, 1953.

──────. *The Street*. Boston: Houghton Mifflin, 1946.

Plato. *The Dialogues of Plato*. 4 vols. 4th ed. Trans. B. Jowett. Rpt. New York: Oxford Univ. Press, 1968.

Poe, Richard. "Negro: by Definition." *Negro History Bulletin* 40 (Jan.–Feb. 1977): 668–70.

Poliakov, Léon. *The Aryan Myth: A History of Racist and Nationalist Ideas in Europe*. Trans. Edmund Howard. New York: Basic Books, 1974.

Polhemus, Ted. "Social Bodies." In *The Body as a Medium of Expression*, ed. Jonathan Benthall and Ted Polhemus. New York: Dutton.

Pope-Hennessy, James. *Sins of the Fathers: A Study of the Atlantic Slave Traders, 1441–1807*. New York: Knopf, 1968.

Porter, James A. *Modern Negro Art*. 1943. Rpt. New York: Arno Press, 1969.

Pryor, George Langhorne. *Neither Bond nor Free*. 1902. Rpt. New York: AMS Press, 1975.

Race Problems of the South: Report of . . . the Southern Society for the Promotion of the Study of Race Conditions and Problems in the South. 1900. Rpt. New York: Negro Univ. Press, 1969.

Record, Wilson. *The Negro and the Communist Party*. Chapel Hill: Univ. of North Carolina Press, 1951.

Reid, Thomas. *The Works of Thomas Reid, D.D.* Ed. Sir William Hamilton. 2 vols. 8th ed. Edinburgh: James Thin, 1985.

Reilly, John. Afterword to *Native Son*, by Richard Wright. 1940. Rpt. New York: Harper and Row, 1966.

Redding, J. Saunders. *Stranger and Alone.* 1950. Rpt. New York: Harper and Row, 1969.

Render, Sylvia Lyons. Introduction to *The Short Fiction of Charles W. Chesnutt.* Washington, D.C.: Howard Univ. Press, 1981.

Reuter, Edward Byron. *Race Mixture: Studies in Intermarriage and Miscegenation.* New York: McGraw-Hill, 1931.

Richey, Russell E., and Donald G. Jones, eds. *American Civil Religion.* New York: Harper and Row, 1974.

Robinson, William. *Early Black American Prose.* Dubuque, Iowa: William C. Brown Co., 1971.

Sanda [Walter H. Stowers and William H. Anderson]. *Appointed: An American Novel.* 1894. Rpt. New York: AMS Press, 1977.

Savoy, Willard. *Alien Land.* New York: Dutton, 1949.

Schraufnagel, Noel. *From Apology to Protest: The Black American Novel.* DeLand, Fla.: Everett/ Edwards, 1973.

Schuyler, George S. *Black No More: Being an Account of the Strange and Wonderful Workings of Science in the Land of the Free, A.D. 1933–1940.* College Park, Md.: McGrath Publishing, 1969.

————. *Slaves Today: A Story of Liberia.* New York: Brewer, Warren, and Putnam, 1931.

Scott, Emmett J. *Scott's Official History of the American Negro in the World War.* Chicago: Homewood Press, 1919.

Scruggs, Charles. "The Mark of Cain and the Redemption of Art: A Study of Theme and Structure of Jean Toomer's *Cane. American Literature* 44 (1972): 276–91.

"Secret Information Concerning Black American Troops." *Crisis* 18 (May 1919): 16–18.

Seidel, Katherine Lee. *The Southern Belle in the American Novel.* Tampa: Univ. of South Florida Press, 1985.

Shackelford, Otis M. *Lillian Simmons, or the Conflict of Sections.* Kansas City, Mo.: Burton Publishing, 1915.

Shaw, O'Wendell. *Greater Need Below.* 1932. Rpt. New York: AMS Press, 1976.

Silverman, Kaja. *The Subject of Semiotics.* New York: Oxford Univ. Press, 1983.

Smith, Abbot Emerson. *Colonists in Bondage: White Servitude and Convict Labor in America, 1607– 1776.* Chapel Hill: Univ. of North Carolina Press, 1947.

Smith, Barbara Herrnstein. "Narrative Versions, Narrative Theories." *Critical Inquiry* 7 (Autumn 1980): 213–36.

Smith, Henry Nash. *Virgin Land: The American West as Symbol and Myth.* New York: Vintage Books, 1957.

Stampp, Kenneth M. *The Era of Reconstruction, 1865–1877.* New York: Vintage Books, 1965.

Stepto, Robert B. *From Behind the Veil: A Study of Afro-American Narrative.* Urbana: Univ. of Illinois Press, 1979.

Stith, William. *The History of the First Discovery and Settlement of Virginia: Being an Essay towards a General History of this Colony.* 1747. Rpt. Spartanburg, S.C.: Reprint Company, 1965.

Sweeney, A. Allison. *History of the American Negro in the Great World War: His Splendid Record in the Battle Zones of Europe.* 1919. Rpt. New York: Negro Univ. Press, 1969.

Tatar, Maria. *The Hard Facts of the Grimms' Fairy Tales.* Princeton: Princeton Univ. Press, 1987.

Taylor, William R. *Cavalier and Yankee: The Old South and American National Character.* New York: George Braziller, 1961.

Thirty Years of Lynching in the United States, 1889–1918. New York: NAACP, 1919.

Thomas, Will. *God Is for White Folks.* New York: Creative Age Press, 1947.

Thurman, Wallace. *The Blacker the Berry.* 1929. Rpt. New York: Collier Books, 1970.

———. *Infants of the Spring.* 1932. Rpt. New York: AMS Press, 1975.

Tocqueville, Alexis de. *Democracy in America.* Trans. Henry Reeve, ed. Francis Bowen. New York: Knopf, 1945.

Toomer, Jean. *Cane.* New York: Boni and Liveright, 1923.

Tragle, Henry Irving. *The Southampton Slave Revolt of 1831: A Compilation of Source Material.* Amherst: Univ. of Massachusetts Press, 1971.

Turner, Terence S. "The Social Skin." In *Reading the Social Body,* ed. Catherine S. Burroughs and Jeffrey David Ehrenreich. Iowa City: Univ. of Iowa Press, 1993.

Turner, Victor W. *The Ritual Process: Structure and Anti-Structure.* Chicago: Aldine Publishing, 1969.

Turpin, Waters Edward. *O Canaan!* 1939. Rpt. New York: AMS Press, 1975.

———. *The Rootless.* New York: Vantage Press, 1957.

———. *These Low Grounds.* 1937. Rpt. New York: AMS Press, 1969.

"The Uses of History in Fiction." *Southern Literary Journal* 1 (Spring 1969): 57–90.

van Gennep, Arnold. *The Rites of Passage.* Trans. Monika B. Vizedom and Gabrielle L. Caffee. Chicago: Univ. of Chicago Press, Phoenix Books, 1960.

Vinovskis, Maris A., and Richard M. Bernard. "Beyond Catherine Beecher: Female Education in the Antebellum Period." *Signs: Journal of Women in Culture and Society* 3 (1978): 856–869.

Walker, Peter F. *Moral Choices: Memory, Desire, and Imagination in Nineteenth-Century American Abolition.* Baton Rouge: Louisiana State Univ. Press, 1978.

Warnock, Mary. *Memory.* London: Faber and Faber, 1989.

Washington, Booker T. *The Story of the Negro: The Rise of the Race from Slavery.* 2 vols. New York: Peter Smith, 1940.

Washington, Joseph, Jr. *Marriage in Black and White.* Boston: Beacon Press, 1970.

Webb, Frank J. *The Garies and Their Friends.* 1857. Rpt. New York: Arno Press, 1969.

Wharton, Vernon Lane. *The Negro in Mississippi, 1865–1890.* Chapel Hill: Univ. of North Carolina Press, 1947.

White, Walter F. *The Fire in the Flint.* New York: Knopf, 1924.

———. *Flight.* New York: Knopf, 1926.

———. *Rope and Faggot: A Biography of Judge Lynch.* 1929. Rpt. New York: Arno Press, 1969.

Whitman, Walt. *Walt Whitman's "Leaves of Grass,"* ed. Harold W. Blodgett and Scully Bradley. 1965. Rpt. New York: Norton, 1968.

Wiley, Bell Irvin. *Southern Negroes, 1861–1865.* 1938. Rpt. Baton Rouge: Louisiana State Univ. Press, 1974.

Williams, Charles H. *Sidelights on Negro Soldiers.* Boston: B. J. Brimmer, 1923.

Williamson, Joel. *After Slavery: The Negro in South Carolina during Reconstruction, 1861–1877.* Chapel Hill: Univ. of North Carolina Press, 1965.

————. *The Crucible of Race: Black-White Relations in the American South since Emancipation.* New York: Oxford Univ. Press, 1984.

————. *New People: Miscegenation and Mulattoes in the United States.* New York: Free Press, 1980.

Wills, Garry. *Inventing America: Jefferson's Declaration of Independence.* Garden City, N.Y.: Doubleday, 1978.

Wilson, Charles Reagan. *Baptized in Blood: The Religion of the Lost Cause, 1865–1920.* Athens: Univ. of Georgia Press, 1980.

Wilson, Harriet E. *Our Nig; or, Sketches from the Life of a Free Black, in a Two-Story White House, North. Showing That Slavery's Shadows Fall Even There.* Ed. with an intro. by Henry Louis Gates. New York: Random House, 1983.

Wood, Forrest G. *Black Scare: The Racist Response to Emancipation and Reconstruction.* Berkeley: Univ. of California Press, 1968.

Wright, Richard. "Big Boy Leaves Home." In *Uncle Tom's Children.* Cleveland, Ohio: World Publishing, 1938.

————. *Black Boy: A Record of Childhood and Youth.* New York: Harper, 1945.

————. *Native Son.* New York: Harper, 1940.

————. *The Outsider.* New York: Harper, 1953.

————. *Savage Holiday.* 1954. Rpt. Chatham, N.J.: Chatham Bookseller, 1975

Wyatt-Brown, Bertram. *Southern Honor: Ethics and Behavior in the Old South.* New York: Oxford Univ. Press, 1982.

Zipes, Jack. *Fairy Tales and the Art of Subversion: The Classical Genre for Children and the Process of Civilization.* New York: Methuen, 1988.

Index

Abraham (biblical story), 205; as discursive paradigm, 84–85, 206
Adamic myth as discursive paradigm, 9–10, 169–
78, 195, 205, 223; and black females, 188;
and black males, 141–42, 146, 159–60, 167,
186, 198; and totemism, 204–5, 214; as
trope, 168, 188, 236
Adamic paradigm, *see* Adamic myth
Adventures of Huckleberry Finn (Twain), 221–22, 245
Africa, 269; as Eden, 18, 153–54
African American novel (conventions), 195, 201–
4, 204–9, 223, 263, 271–74; and civil religion, 119–20, 184, 202–3; and Harlem Renaissance, 155; and *Invisible Man*, 235, 238,
242–44, 246–48, 252, 259; and lynching
bee, 104, 119–20; and migration, 148, 151,
175; and miscegenation, 96–97, 121, 139,
216–19, 236; and new slavery, 104–5, 107;
and totemism, 10, 11, 201–4, 212–15, 217–
18; and World War I, 137, 143–45, 149; development of, 5, 8, 9, 10, 155–58, 161; in
nineteenth century, 3, 7, 17, 24, 40–41, 44;
religious influences on, 2, 119–20; structure,
148; subject formation paired with nation
formation, 269–70; with black soldiers and
veterans, 144, 147, 151, 155–58, 161; with mulatto women protagonists, 48
African Americans as subhumans (images of), 10,
27, 38, 47, 93, 231; and American Garden
trope, 101, 122, 186; and rites of passage, 58–
59, 78; and the Constitution, 40, 50; during
World War I era, 138, 144, 156, 160; in *Native
Son*, 177, 179, 182, 183, 186
Africans, 2, 14, 15, 235, 265

Age of Reason (Paine), 86
Alabama, 157, 166
Alger, Horatio, 85, 191
Alien Land (Savoy), 81, 94, 147, 160–61, 162; and
totemism, 206–7
American Adam, 25, 26, 35, 83, 85, 200; as father of
a chosen people, 18; blacks as, 168–76, 178,
186, 188; *see also* American new man
American Adam (Lewis), 6
American Communist Party, *see* Communism
American Dream, 101, 190, 196, 200, 220, 223; and
World War I, 96; as permutation of Eden,
134; blacks' pursuit of, 148, 161–62, 165, 254;
material aspects of, 8, 97; southern version
of, 8–9; *see also* Eden trope
American Eden, 7, 12, 17, 19, 99, 101; African
American counterimage of, 13–15, 18–24,
28, 44, 99; colonial counterimage of (wil-
derness), 13, 14, 15, 23, 74, 99; *see also* Eden
trope
American new man, 25–26, 35, 37, 83, 224, 248; as
trope in *Invisible Man*, 240, 250; blacks as, 32,
35, 84–85, 86–87, 105; *see also* American
Adam
American Revolution, 28, 32, 35, 67, 269; in *The
Rootless*, 223, 229, 231, 233
American Way of Life, 141, 142
Another Country (Baldwin), 176
Antebellum South, *see* Plantation idyll
Appalachee Red (Andrews), 5
Appeal to the Coloured Citizens of the World (Walker),
28
Appointed (Sanda), 117, 121, 207
Appomattox, 123

"Art of Fiction, The" (Ellison), 257
Army, French, 144–48
Army, U.S., 143–48, 152, 159, 161; *see also* War Department, U.S.
Athenian democracy, 26, 37
Athens, 37
Atlanta, 97
Aunt Sara's Wooden God (Gilbert), 206, 215–16
Autobiography of an Ex-Coloured Man, The (Johnson), 5, 93–94, 106, 132, 150, 241; and neurosis, 90, 91; and picaresque fiction, 89, 91, 95; and sister complex, 218–19; and subject formation, 76, 105, 202; and the slave narrative, 81, 89, 91, 92, 95, 151; and totemism, 206–7; biblical stories in, 95–96; fairy tales in, 89–91, 92–93, 94, 95; incest in, 92
Autobiography of Miss Jane Pittman, The (Gaines), 3, 5

Baby Sweet's (Andrews), 5
Baker, Houston, 247
Baldwin, James, 223
Banneker, Bejamin, 33, 53
Baptized in Blood (Wilson), 122
Barlowe, Captain Arthur, 16
"Beauty and the Beast," 7, 75, 76, 79–80, 236; as novelistic paradigm, 77–78, 89–93, 195; as trope, 82, 88–89, 96, 236
Beloved (Morrison), 4, 5, 272
ben Solomon, Job, *see* Diallo, Ayuba Suleiman
Benito Cereno (Melville), 244
Bettelheim, Bruno, 92
Beverley, Robert, 20, 23, 258
Bible, King James, 16, 172, 254
"Big Boy Leaves Home" (Wright), 9, 172–75
Birth of a Nation, The (Griffith), 246
Black aristocracy, 55, 64–65, 108
Black Boy (Wright), 5
Black Codes, 109
Black men, *see* Body as text; Subject formation; Subjectivity
Black nationalism, 264, 269
Black No More (Schuyler), 8, 76, 97–100, 101–3, 272; and double-consciousness, 97–98; and Eden trope, 98–102; and fairy tales, 97, 99; and rites of passage, 97; and technology, 97, 98–102
Black soldier(s), 133, 263; *see also* World War I
Black Thunder (Bontemps), 5, 35–36, 166, 223
Black women, *see* Body as text; Subject formation; Subjectivity
Blacker the Berry, The (Thurman), 165, 215
Blackson, Lorenzo Dow, 25
Blake (Delany), 44
Blennerhassett, Harman, 36
Blood on the Forge (Attaway), 150
"Blood-Burning Moon" (Toomer), 206
Body as text, 49, 51, 75, 76, 92, 120; black men's,

79, 90–91, 92, 107, 113–14, 144, 230; black women's, 48, 73, 125; white men's, 114, 224–25; white women's, 107, 125, 224–25
Bond and Free (Howard), 5
Bontemps, Arena, 27
Boston, 263
Boston Tea Party, 35
Bradford, William, 13, 19, 23, 258
Briggs, Cyril, 267, 269
Brotherhood of Sleeping Car Porters, 267
Brownlow, William G., 123, 129
Burr, Aaron, 35, 36
Butler, Octavia, 272
By Sanction of Law (Jones), 217

Calhoun, John C., 123, 130
Canada, 24, 57
Cane (Toomer), 132, 150, 189, 206–7, 212, 241; and Harlem Renaissance, 155; as intertext, 272
Captain Blackman (Williams), 5
Carroll, Charles, 64, 75, 122, 123, 207
Cash, Wilbur J., 118
Charleston (S.C.), 68
Chesnut, Mary Boykin, 64, 228
Chicago, 147, 150, 173, 174, 182, 185
Chivalric tradition (southern) 8, 100, 105–8, 118–19, 121; as literary construct, 38, 52, 63, 100; as social construct, 45–46, 48–49, 52, 61–65, 75, 86–87
"Cinderella," 7, 82, 88
Civil religion, 120, 122, 172; and totemism, 202–3, 207, 208; southern white, 119–24, 125, 130–32, 173–74, 184–86
"Civil Religion in America" (Bellah), 120
Civil Rights Act (1866), 109
Civil utopia, 6, 7, 25, 28, 29, 110; *see also* Eden trope
Civil War, 32, 134–36, 140, 145, 234; and racist violence, 158, 159
Civil War trope, 135, 146, 160–61, 165; *see also* War as trope
Clansman, The (Dixon), 4, 122
Clotel (Brown), 4, 23–24, 25, 58–59, 121, 151; and black female subjectivity, 48–49, 51–54, 55–57; and the slave narrative, 41–43; and Thomas Jefferson, 29–30, 42, 48–49; and white male subjectivity, 60–61, 62
Colonel's Dream, The (Chesnutt), 101
Color Purple, The (Walker), 272
Columbus, Christopher, 12, 16, 34, 45, 207, 235
Communism, 219, 264, 266–67
Communitas, 83
Concubinage, 60
Condition . . . of the Colored People of the United States (Delany), 33, 269
Constitution, U.S., 25, 34, 40, 84, 225, 243; and

blacks, 32, 33, 50, 136; and Equiano's *Narrative*, 27–28
Cooper, James Fenimore, 37, 258
Coramantee(s), 230–31, 232, 233
Corregidora (Jones), 4
Cortor, Eldzier, 189
Cosmogonic myth, 45, 176–80, 183, 186, 187, 238; American, 16–17, 25, 26, 30, 83, 258
Craft, William and Ellen, 42, 263
Creation myth, 16, 25–26, 176–80, 186–87; *see also* Cosmogonic myth
Crèvecoeur, J. Hector St. John, 1, 13, 26, 35, 83, 250
Cullen, Countee, 143, 152
Cult of southern chivalry, 64, 69, 70; *see also* Eden trope

Darwinism, 263
Davis, Jefferson, 123
Declaration of Independence, 25, 26–28, 34, 225, 243, 258
Defoe, Daniel, 86
Delany, Martin R., 33; *see also Condition . . . of the Colored People of the United States; Blake*
Delany, Samuel, 272
Desire, 93–94, 98, 172, 173; triangular, 169–70, 175–76, 189–94; *see also Street, The*
Dessa Rose (Williams), 4, 272
Diallo, Ayuba Suleiman, 18, 19
Dialogism, 4, 10, 242
Dialogues (Plato), *see Timaeus, The*
Dickson, Moses, 33
Discourse, 241, 242, 246, 248–49, 253; black feminist, 5; black masculinist, 5, 10, 188, 222, 241; Negrophobic, 47–48, 76, 95, 115, 122–23, 222; on race, 75, 76, 85, 207; *see also* Fairy-tale discourse; Tractarian discourse
Discourse on the Lives and Characters of Thomas Jefferson and John Adams (Wirt), 37
Discourse on the Origin and Foundation of Inequality among Mankind (Rosseau), 172
Disease, 224, 228, 231, 232, 265; as trope, 138, 143, 144, 151, 156–59; in *The Rootless*, 225–27, 233, 265; venereal, 225–29
Dispossessed Garden (Simpson), 6
Dixon, Thomas, 4, 123
Don Quixote (Cervantes), 86
Double-consciousness, 78, 91, 93, 94–95, 97, 102; defined, 81–82
Douglas, Aaron, 189
Douglass, Frederick, 22, 89, 168–69, 263–64, 269
Du Bois, W. E. B., 78, 152

Earthly paradise (America as), 6, 7, 12, 18, 25; African Amercian counterimage of, 23, 99, 110; in *House Behind the Cedars*, 74; *see also* Eden trope
Economics, 161, 163, 185, 190–91, 192–93, 199

Eden trope, 5, 99, 108, 132, 146, 223; American Dream permutation, 6, 8, 9, 134–37; and Africa, 153–56, 185; and black migration, 149, 150, 165–67; and civil religion, 120–21; and Civil War trope, 135, 139; and discourse on race, 75; and Douglass's *Narrative*, 22; and fairy tales, 7, 75, 82, 198; and Harlem, 148–53; and history, 4; and lynching bee, 117–20, 124–26, 131–32, 136, 141–43; and northern cities, 147, 149–50; and southern industrialization, 101; and totemism, 213–14; biblical stories, 85, 95; civil utopia permutation, 6, 7, 25–29; defined, 2; earthly paradise permutation, 6, 7, 12–17, 23, 25, 74; modern chivalry permutation, 6, 45–46, 62–65; plantation idyll permutation, 6, 17, 35–38, 40–41, 245
Edenic paradigm, 40, 46, 104, 195; *see also* Eden trope
Education, 31, 32, 53–54, 85, 101, 262
Eliade, Mircea, 17, 180
Emancipation Proclamation, 44, 57, 105
Emerson, Ralph Waldo, 220
England, 147, 230
Enlightenment (the), 171
Equiano, Olaudah, 18–20, 22, 27
Essay on the Intellectual Powers of Man (Reid), 255
Exchange value, 127, 192–93
Exogamy, *see* Totemism

Fairy tales, 89–90, 91, 92–93, 95, 99, 203
Fairy lore, 7, 97, 195, 197
Fairy-tale discourse, 75, 108, 194–98, 236
"Fall of Adam, The" (Chesnutt), 9, 169–72
Fanon, Frantz, 77, 90
Fauset, Jessie, 35
Feminized white male, 219–22, 228, 229
Feudal South, *see* Plantation idyll
Fiedler, Leslie, 221–22
Fielding, Henry, 86
Fire in the Flint, The (White), 143, 147–48, 156–58, 161–65, 167, 175; and black subjectivity, 105, 135; and *Marrow of Tradition*, 163–65
Flight (White), 5, 218
Flight to Canada (Reed), 4, 272
Fort Sumter, 123
Founding Fathers, 24, 26, 28, 29, 30, 36; and discourse as trope, 248; as primal father, 207
France, 140, 142, 147, 150, 157, 229; as Eden, 139, 143–45, 147, 148, 158, 159–61
Franklin, Benjamin, 83, 85, 191, 200
French Revolution, 86, 223, 231
Freud, Sigmund, 247; *see also Totem and Taboo*
Fugitives of the Pearl (Paynter), 5, 223
Fusion politics, 126

Garden of Eden (biblical), 9, 168, 170, 178, 186, 235; and blacks, 14–15

Garden trope, 13, 15, 110—11, 142; in Douglass's
    Narrative, 21—23; in *Black No More*, 101—3
Garies and Their Friends, The (Webb), 5, 43—44, 93,
    121, 217; and black female subjectivity, 49,
    52, 53, 54, 57, 77—80; and black male subject
    formation, 97—98; and rites of passage, 59,
    60, 78—80; and totemism, 217; and white
    male subject formation, 76
Garvey, Marcus, 153—54, 266, 269
Georgia, 153, 166, 263
Germans, 139, 142, 143
Gettysburg Address, 45, 229, 258
Gil Blas (Le Sage), 86
Girard, René, 169, 175—76
Go Tell It on the Mountain (Baldwin), 4, 5, 206—7,
    241
God Is for White Folks (Thomas), 81, 94, 206, 207,
    215, 216
God's Trombones: Seven Negro Sermons in Verse (John-
    son), 189
Going to the Territory (Ellison), 243, 257
"Gold Bug, The" (Poe), 245
Great Black Migration, 5, 9, 149, 175

Haitian Revolution, 223, 229, 230, 231, 232
Hammond, James Henry, 228
Harlem, 147, 149—53, 156, 195, 198; in *Invisible Man*,
    266—67, 269
Harlem Renaissance, 98, 152, 189; novels of, 3, 105,
    133, 155
Harper, William (Judge), 86
Hawthorne, Nathaniel, 13, 243
Hearts of Gold (Jones), 64—65, 96, 107—12, 113, 117—
    18, 241; and totemism, 212, 217
Helper, Hinton R., 123
Hemings, Sally, 29
Henry, Patrick, 28, 31, 231
Hidden polemic, 3, 4, 31, 250
Hindered Hand, The (Griggs), 4, 5, 105, 123—24, 132;
    and totemism, 212
History and Present State of Virginia, The (Beverley),
    16—17, 20, 21—23
Hollywood, 246
Home to Harlem (McKay), 96, 145—48, 150, 151—52,
    166, 167; France in, 143; war trope in, 135,
    145—48
Homosexuality (male), 219—22, 226, 228; and in-
    cest, 219
Hope's Highway (Fleming), 148
House Behind the Cedars, The (Chesnutt), 7, 76, 81, 91,
    93, 94; and biblical Eden myth, 66—67, 72,
    84—85; and chivalric tradition, 68—74, 86,
    87; and fairy lore, 73, 82—83, 88—89; and
    garden trope, 65, 66—67, 68, 86; and *Invisible
    Man*, 241; and liminality, 65—66, 83—84, 85,
    86, 87—88; and rites of passage, 66, 69, 72—
    74, 83—86; and totemism, 206—7, 215, 217,

218; compared to *Marrow of Tradition*, 105—6,
    132; court cases in, 86, 213—14
Howells, William Dean, 108
Hughes, Langston, 143, 215
"Humpty Dumpty," 236

Imperium in imperio, 32, 33, 269
Imperium in Imperio (Griggs), 25, 30—35, 60, 106,
    118—19, 121; and black female subjectivity,
    49, 52, 54, 57; and black nationalism, 269
Incest, 222, 227, 228; and miscegenation, 92, 204,
    217, 222
Incidents in the Life of a Slave Girl (Jacobs), 61—62,
    193
Indians (American), *see* Native Americans
Industrialization, 99—101
*Interesting Narrative of the Life of Olaudah Equiano, see
    Life of Olaudah Equiano, The*
Intertextual layering, 219, 239, 242, 262
Intertextual revision, 4, 113, 163—65
Intertextuality, 4, 99, 121—22, 126, 130; in *Invisible
    Man*, 237, 238, 241—42, 262, 266
Invisible Man (Ellison), 5, 10, 189, 203, 271, 272; and
    black subjectivity, 239—51; and Eden trope,
    235—39; and totemism, 206—8, 209—11; ho-
    mosexuality in, 219—22; intertexts, in 219—
    22; on history and historiography, 232, 251—
    69; on memory, 255—59; periodized
    structure of, 260—69; *see also* Intertextuality
Iola Leroy (Harper), 49, 52, 54, 57, 60, 241
Ivanhoe (Scott), 63, 69, 70

Jackson, Rebecca, 89
James, Henry, 243
Jamestown (Va.), 23
Jefferson, Thomas, 2, 25, 26, 28—29, 48, 123; and
    Black Thunder, 36; and *House Behind the Cedars*,
    83, 86—88; and *Imperium in Imperio*, 30, 33;
    and *Invisible Man*, 265, 267—68; and Sally
    Hemings, 29; and *The Rootless*, 225, 231; as
    fictional character, 29—30, 42, 54, 58—59, 61;
    as primal father, 207—8; in African Ameri-
    can novelistic discourse, 3; library of, 54; on
    African American subjectivity, 2, 33, 49, 51,
    52—53, 75; on white American subjectivity,
    33, 49, 223
Jim Crow, 110, 118, 136—38, 156, 209
Johnson, Charles, 272
Johnson, James Weldon, 152
Johnson, Rosamond, 152

Kennedy, John Pendleton, 38—39
Kindred (Butler), 4, 272
King, Alex C., 130
Knights of Nordica, 98
Knock on Any Door (Motley), 222
Ku Klux Klan, 107, 129, 162, 185

Lacan, Jacques, 90
Lanier, Sidney, 63
Larsen, Nella, 259
Last of the Barons (Lytton), 70
Lawrence, Jacob, 189
Leaves of Grass (Whitman), 220–21, 243–44
Lee, George Washington, 151, 259
Lee, Jarena, 89
Lee, Robert E., 123
Leopard's Spots, The (Dixon), 4, 100, 122, 123
Letters from an American Farmer (Crèvecoeur), 35, 251
Letters of the British Spy, The (Wirt), 37
Liberty Tree, 67
Life and Times of Fredrick Douglass (Douglass), 20–23
Life of Olaudah Equiano, The, 18–20, 151
Lillian Simmons (Shackleford), 165
Liminality (of blacks), 106, 196–97; female mulattoes, 49–51, 58–60, 108; in nation's social structure, 6, 40, 102, 151, 169, 243, 251, 265; male mulattoes, 94, 215, 216
Lincoln, Abraham, 45, 267–68
"Little Red Riding Hood," 195, 196, 198
London, 147
L'Ouverture, Toussaint, 36, 230
Lüthi, Max, 90
Lynching, 8, 128, 158–59, 173, 175; and chivalric tradition, 8; of black women, 116–17, 212; *see also* Lynching bee
Lynching bee, 9, 120, 161, 164, 174, 202; and civil religion, 121, 124–26, 129–32; and Eden trope, 104; and totemism, 213; in early novels, 115–19, *see also* Lynching

Machine in the Garden, The (Marx), 25
McKay, Claude, 143, 151
Major, Clarence, 272
"Man Who Lived Underground, The" (Wright), 244
Mardi (Melville), 251
Marginality, *see* Liminality
Marrow of Tradition, The (Chesnutt), 4, 5, 105–6, 121, 175; and civil religion, 122–24, 125–26, 130–32; and *Fire in the Flint*, 163–65; and lynching bee, 117, 122–24, 124–26, 128–32; and totemism, 201–2, 209
"Marse Chan" (Page), 63
Marx, Leo, 13, 25
Mather, Cotton, 13, 14
Mayflower, 13, 19, 23
Melville, Herman, 237, 243, 245, 251
Memphis (Tenn.), 159
Meridian (Walker), 272
Middle Passage, 19, 146
Middle Passage (Johnson), 4, 272
Miller, Kelly, 123
Miscegenation, 55, 97, 121, 132, 160, 175; and Eden trope, 132, 138, 142, 166–71, 236; and fairy

tales, 7; and homosexuality, 222; and incest, 218–19; and lynching, 116; and social equality, 117–18; and totemism, 217; and white men, 39, 55, 139, 191; and World War I, 158; as sin, 64, 125; as threat to white civilization, 41, 47, 49, 64, 80, 101–3, 138, 144, 202; Jefferson on, 49
Mississippi, 166, 182, 212
Moby-Dick, (Melville), 239
More Wonders of the Invisible World (Calef), 99
Morrison, Toni, 271–72
Mulattoism, 126, 261
Murder, 124, 162, 195, 226; and totemism, 202, 210; as unpardonable sin, 116, 165, 185, 210; in *Native Son*, 177, 182, 183
My Bondage and My Freedom (Douglass), 21

Narrative of the Life of Frederick Douglass (Douglass), 20–23, 89, 199, 241
Narrows, The (Petry), 96, 176, 188, 222
Natchez (Miss.), 42
Nation formation, 225; aligned with subject formation, 30, 228, 231, 236, 237, 250–51, 270
Nation within a nation, see *Imperium in imperio*
Native Americans, 13, 14, 15, 16, 250
Native Son (Wright), 5, 10, 167, 199, 241, 269; and civil religion, 184–86; and creation (cosmogonic) myth, 176–78, 180, 183, 186–87; and human origin myth, 176–78, 180, 182, 186–88; tripartite structure of, 189
"Negro a Beast, The" (Carroll), 64, 75, 85, 122, 207
Negro Not the Son of Ham, The (Carroll), 207
Neoslavery, 108; *see also* New slavery
New Adam, *see* American Adam
New Negro(es), 98, 101, 126–28, 131, 172; and human origin myth, 27, 32, 35
New slavery, 3, 110–15, 116, 129, 146, 253; and Black Codes, 109; *see also* New slaves
New slaves, 104, 105, 107, 113, 115, 146; *see also* New slavery
New South, 3, 66, 110–11, 129, 136, 161; and chivalric tradition, 68, 106, 107, 108, 119; and civil religion 122, 124, 125; and Eden trope, 8, 63; and technology, 100; economic system of, 112–14, 115; origin myth of, 45
Northrop, Solomon, 89
Not Only War (Daly), 143, 167, 175; French setting, 140–43; South Carolina setting, 136–40; war as trope in, 135–36, 160
Notes on the State of Virginia (Jefferson), 2, 25, 28, 32, 36, 52–53; as direct intertext, 202, 265–66
Nott, Josiah C., 123

O Canaan! (Turpin), 150, 165
Odum, Howard, 156
Odyssey, The (Homer), 244
Of Plymouth Plantation (Bradford), 13, 19

Old Dominion, 37, 39, 68
Old South, 66, 100, 111, 112, 136, 139; and chivalric
    tradition, 63, 106–7; and Eden trope, 64; as
    feudal system, 108; as plantation idyll, 37,
    40, 115, 125, 128
Ollie Miss (Henderson), 165
"On Being Brought From Africa to America"
    (Wheatley), 1, 18
One Way to Heaven (Cullen), 166
Origin myths, 17, 23–24, 176–80, 182, 186–87;
    about blacks, 40, 44–46, 51, 169–79, 206;
    about societies, 7, 9, 37, 203, 258, 268; about
    whites, 26–28, 30, 170–71, 206, 238, 241;
    and totemism, 205–8
Our Nig (Wilson), 44, 96, 97

Page, Thomas Nelson, 63, 123, 129
Paine, Thomas, 29, 83, 86, 231
Paradise Lost (Milton), 172
Passing (Larsen), 166, 218
Pennsylvania, 43–44
Pershing, John J., Gen., 146
Petersburg (Va.), 147
Picaresque fiction, 89, 95
Pilgrim's Progress (Bunyan), 86
Pitts, Helen, 168–69
Pittsburgh (Pa.), 150
Plantation idyll, 6, 35–41, 61, 100, 127, 128; and
    miscegenation, 64, 71; in postbellum litera-
    ture, 63, 64, 87; in slave narrative, 17, 42–
    43, 45; *see also* Eden trope
Plantation literature, 38, 45, 63, 113, 115
Plantation South, *see* Plantation idyll
Plymouth Rock, 23
Poe, Edgar Allan, 244–45
President's Daughter, The (Chase-Riboud), 29
"Problem, The" (Gilmore), 135
Prohibitions, *see* Taboo
Promised Land (North), 24, 87, 149, 154–55, 174,
    182; in early novels, 41, 44; in slave narra-
    tives, 44; in twentieth-century novels, 150
"Psalm of the West" (Lanier), 63
Puritans, 13, 14

Quakers, 44
Quest of the Silver Fleece, The (Du Bois), 101, 106, 150
Quicksand (Larsen), 5, 96, 150, 166

Race Problems of the South, 122
Raleigh, Sir Walter, 16, 37, 39
Randolph, A. Philip, 267
Rape, 116, 124, 162, 163, 173, 177; and black sol-
    diers, 144, 157–58; and totemism, 209, 210
Redburn (Melville), 251
Reed, Ishmael, 272
Revolutionary period, 25, 26, 29; *see also* Eden
    trope

Revolutionary War, 25, 134, 136, 140, 225
Richardson, Samuel, 86
Richmond (Va.), 42, 123
*Rise and Progress of the Kingdoms of Light and Darkness,
    The* (Blackson), 25
Rites of passage, 50, 97, 106; and black men, 81,
    83–88, 98, 156; and black women, 51–60,
    169; *see also* Subject formation
River George (Lee), 135, 148, 156–62, 166, 167, 175;
    Harlem in, 150–53
Roderick Random (Smollett), 86
Rootless, The (Turpin), 222, 260, 269; concept of
    history, 232–34; concepts of time and
    space, 233–34; disease as trope in, 226–29,
    231; uses of the revolutionary age, 223–25,
    229–31
Rosiebelle Lee Wildcat Tennessee (Andrews), 5
Rosseau, Jean-Jacques, 172
Ruffin, Edmund, 123
"Rules for the Society of Negroes" (Mather), 14
Running a Thousand Miles for Freedom (Craft), 263

Sally Hemings (Chase-Riboud), 5, 29
San Domingo, 230
Sancho, Ignatius, 53
Savage Holiday (Wright), 203
Schuyler, George S., 151, 152
Science fiction, 97
Scott, Sir Walter, 63
Scruggs, Charles, 206
"Secret Information Concerning Black American
    Troops," 144–45
Shadow and Act (Ellison), 221, 257, 268
Shakespeare and His Forerunners (Lanier), 64
Sharecropping, 8, 161–62; *see also* New slavery;
    New slaves
Sherman, William Tecumseh, 135–36
Simms, William Gilmore, 258
Sister complex, 217–19
Sketches of the Life and Character of Patrick Henry
    (Wirt), 37
Slave codes, 109
Slave narrative(s), 81, 151, 241; and early novels, 24,
    40, 41, 42, 44, 259; and Eden trope, 18, 23,
    27; and fairy tales, 89, 91, 92, 95
Slaves Today (Schuyler), 154
Smith, Capt. John, 16, 39, 258
"Snow White," 91
Social Contract, The (Rosseau), 172
Sodom and Gomorrah, 233
Sodomy, 228
Some Memoirs of the Life of Job (Diallo), 18
Song of Solomon (Morrison), 272
South (black) as Eden, 153, 154–55, 166; *see also*
    Eden trope
South Carolina, 43, 68–69, 136, 138, 139
Southern belle, 47–48, 53, 54, 91, 108, 121; black

women as, 53, 73, 91; demystification of, 121, 228

Southern Way of Life, 41, 109, 137, 138, 164; and civil religion, 120, 122; and miscegenation, 69, 101; and new slavery, 111, 117

Southerner, The (Page), 100

Spanish-American War, 135

Sport of the Gods, The (Dunbar), 105, 107, 112−15, 119−20, 150

Stars in My Pocket Like Grains of Sand (Delany), 272

State v. Vinson J. Cantey, 86

Stith, William, 39

Stowe, Harriet Beecher, 31

Street, The (Petry), 10, 269; as masculinist discourse, 188; economic desire in, 190−93, 200; fairy-tale discourse in, 194−98; geometric design of, 189−200; sexual desire, in, 190−94, 196; triangiular desire in, 189−94

Stringfellow, Thornton, 123

Subject formation, 44, 139, 192−93, 201, 236, 248; and the social body, 47−49; and war trope, 135−36; black female, 48−60; black male, 76−87, 89−90, 95−99, 115, 135, 137, 147−50, 176−77, 181, 193−94, 218; in New South, 121−22; of blacks, 30, 108−9, 230−31; of whites, 105−7; white female, 48−49, 98−99; white male, 60−65, 121, 129−30, 190−91, 196, 201−2, 217, 228; *see also* Nation formation; Southern belle; Subjectivity

Subjectivity, 102−3, 114−15, 137, 156−57, 214−16, 226, 230, 242; and society, 29, 60, 117, 124−32, 160−65, 236, 237; black female, 62, 192−93; black male, 70, 176−77, 181, 193−94; Jefferson on, 31, 52; of blacks, 40, 97, 170−71, 226, 238, 246; of whites, 97, 105−7; white female, 48−49, 98−99; white male, 201−3, 219−22, 226; *see also* Southern belle; Subject formation

Such Was the Season (Major), 272

Swallow Barn (Kennedy), 38−39

"Sympathy" (Dunbar), 219−20

Taboo, 126, 144, 170, 173, 181, 218; totemic, 204, 208, 210; infectious nature of, 211−212, 225

Tatar, Maria, 93

Taylor, William R., 38

Technology, 99−101

Tempter of Eve, The (Carroll), 64, 122

Their Eyes Were Watching God (Hurston), 165, 241

There Is Confusion (Fauset), 35, 96, 148, 166

Third Life of Grange Copeland, The (Walker), 5

Thomas, Bigger, 175, 176, 219; see also *Native Son*

"Three Blind Mice," 236

Tillman, Bejamin R., 156

Timaeus, The (Plato), 237, 243, 247

"To the University of Cambridge in New England" (Wheatley), 18

Totem, 204; *see also* Totemism

Totem and Taboo (Freud), 203−4, 208, 209−10, 212, 213, 217; and incest, 219, 222; as intertext, 203, 219, 220; in *The Rootless*, 225

Totemism, 10, 133, 203, 223; and black male subjectivity, 213−16, 218; and incest (exogamy), 204; and miscegenation, 210, 219; and novelistic conventions, 201−4, 205, 207, 208−13; and origin myths (biblical), 204−6, 208−9, 212−13; and southern society, 203−4, 205, 208−9, 236; and southern white civil religion, 203, 207, 208−9; and white female subjectivity, 216−19; and white male subjectivity, 216−22; as portrait of southern society, 201−5, 217, 209−13; defined, 204; in *Invisible Man*, 207−8, 209−11

Tractarian discourse, 32, 91, 108, 202

Tree of Knowledge, 67, 72, 85, 86

Tree of Life, 67

Trojan War, 140

Tuskegee Institute, 262

Twain, Mark, 237, 243, 245

Uncle Tom's Children (Wright), 172; *see also* "Big Boy Leaves Home"

Vardaman, James K., 156, 158

Vassa, Gustavus, see *Life of Olaudah Equiano, The*

Vicksburg (Miss.), 42

Violence, 104, 125, 129, 195, 202; and sexuality, 223; racial, 132, 158−59, 164, 165, 213; ritual, 105−6, 116−19, 121, 127, 130−31, 202; *see also* Lynching; Lynching bee

Virgin Land (Smith), 6

Virginia as Eden, 16, 20, 68, 42, 154, 214; as anti-Eden, 18, 20, 21

Walker, Alice, 272

War as trope, 10, 136, 142−43, 162; Civil War, 139−40, 145−46, 159−60; World War I, 9, 135, 145−46, 149, 156; World War II, 193−94

War Department, U.S., 144, 145, 157; *see also* Army, U.S.

Warnock, Mary, 255

Washington, Booker T., 262, 267−68

Washington, George, 28, 29, 34, 207, 225

Watterson, Henry, 123, 129

"What Am I to You" (Douglass), 9, 168−69

"What Is a White Man?" (Chesnutt), 84

What Is to Be Done (Lenin), 266

Wheatley, Phillis, 1, 2, 18, 19, 53

"When Lilacs Last in the Dooryard Bloom'd" (Whitman), 261

White, Walter, 152

White men, *see* Feminized white male; Subject formation; Subjectivity

White women, 10, 98−99, 100, 121, 132, 217; and

White women (*cont.*)
civil religion, 124, 125, 130; and fairy tales, 92; as icons, 48, 98–99, 101, 105, 178, 181; as totem, 204, 208, 228; body as text, 107, 125; French, 141–42
Whitman, Walt, 237; see also *Leaves of Grass*
Williamsburg (Va.), 68
Wilson, Woodrow, 136–37, 138, 156, 231
Wirt, William, 26, 35, 36–37, 83, 87, 224; and *Swallow Barn*, 38

Withers, Thomas Jefferson, 228
Wonder-Working Providence of Scion's Saviour in New England, The (Johnson), 99
World War I, 9, 134–35, 156, 158, 163, 165; and Civil War, 136–37, 145; as trope, 9, 135, 145–46, 149, 156, 160; in *Invisible Man*, 262
World War II, 193
Wright, Richard, 143, 223, 259; see also *Native Son*

Yerby, Fank, 223